THE BATTLE FOR FORTUNE

Studies of the Weatherhead East Asian Institute, Columbia University

The Studies of the Weatherhead East Asian Institute of Columbia University were inaugurated in 1962 to bring to a wider public the results of significant new research on modern and contemporary East Asia.

THE BATTLE
FOR FORTUNE

STATE-LED DEVELOPMENT, PERSONHOOD,
AND POWER AMONG TIBETANS IN CHINA

CHARLENE MAKLEY

CORNELL UNIVERSITY PRESS
Ithaca and London

First published 2018 by Cornell University Press

Printed in the United States of America

Library of Congress Cataloging-in-Publication Data

Names: Makley, Charlene E., 1964– author.
Title: The battle for fortune: state-led development, personhood, and power among Tibetans in China / Charlene Makley.
Description: Ithaca : Cornell University Press, 2018. | Series: Studies of the Weatherhead East Asian Institute, Columbia University | Includes bibliographical references and index.
Identifiers: LCCN 2017039231 (print) | LCCN 2017040967 (ebook) | ISBN 9781501719653 (pdf) | ISBN 9781501719660 (epub/mobi) | ISBN 9781501719646 (cloth : alk. paper) | ISBN 9781501719677 (pbk. : alk. paper)
Subjects: LCSH: Tibetans—China—Reb-gong Gser-mo-ljongs—Social conditions—21st century. | Tibetans—China—Reb-gong Gser-mo-ljongs—Economic conditions—21st century. | Reb-gong Gser-mo-ljongs (China)—Ethnic relations. | Reb-gong Gser-mo-ljongs (China)—Politics and government—21st century.
Classification: LCC DS797.82.R43 (ebook) | LCC DS797.82.R43 M34 2018 (print) | DDC 951/.5—dc23
LC record available at https://lccn.loc.gov/2017039231

For the Rebgong Tibetan community,
in the words of the song I heard often at the close of festive gatherings:

To the native lands of the great Tibetan people of this cool
snow mountain region,
And especially to Rebgong, the origin of wisdom,
May the auspiciousness of timely rain and excellent harvests come,
To all the snowland regions may the auspiciousness of
increase in wealth come,
May all have abundant prosperity and happiness!

And for Cain, my partner in all things

Contents

ILLUSTRATIONS

ACKNOWLEDGMENTS

This book is the culmination of some fifteen years of collaborative work both in and outside of the People's Republic of China. Ultimately, this work is my own synthesis of multimedia and multivocal sources on the cultural and linguistic politics of development for Tibetans in China. I take full responsibility for the stances I assume here and for any errors that may have escaped my notice. But the book is also fundamentally a collective product, the result of ongoing learning from multiple teachers and colleagues, which took me down a path far from where I had begun. I had never anticipated writing about protest and military crackdown among Tibetans, but the whirlwind events of China's "Olympic Year" (2008) overtook me like everyone else. It took several years for me to process those events and to figure out how I might ethically and credibly write about them. Through conversations with Tibetan and non-Tibetan colleagues, friends, and students, I came to reject the readily available roles (like media pundit or humanitarian "savior") held out to white foreigners who witness states of emergency. Paying attention to the multivocal ways Tibetans in and outside of China were responding to the events helped me understand how a more dialogic approach would be necessary, one in which I acknowledge my own complicities and confusions in the story.

State repression remains a reality of life in Tibetan regions of China. I thus have to extend my utmost gratitude to my Tibetan friends and colleagues there in the awkward and oblique terms of vague allusions and pseudonyms (see below). The courage and resilience of my Tibetan interlocutors across the Rebgong community in the face of capricious state repression continue to inspire me; they have been my teachers in ways that extend far beyond specifically Tibetan culture and language. I am particularly indebted to my Tibetan colleagues and teachers who worked closely with me on translating and comprehending Tibetan language materials: LG and Abho in the United States, but also Donyod Dongrup, SG, TP, TRB, PBT, LMT, GP, PMT, and DJT in Beijing, Xining, and Rebgong. Any depth of understanding I might have achieved about Tibetan culture and history stems largely from their teachings.

As always, family remains foundational to my ability to pursue such long-term research projects. My husband Cain's gentle yet firm partnership in and outside of China, and his unconditional support at home make all of my work possible. My curious and opinionated children, Noah, Anna, and Rosa, challenge any imperiousness in my views or attitudes. And my parents, John and Kathryn, continue to provide their indispensible emotional and financial support. I am particularly grateful to my sister, the independent documentary filmmaker Mary Makley, for all her help over the years with digital media and photography. While in Rebgong and Xining, my expat friends became key supporters during the state of emergency; I extend my heartfelt gratitude for their hospitality and recourse to KS, GR and EM, TV and SW, and to CJ. For their generous provision of that essential "room of my own" to write the final manuscript, I am deeply grateful to my friends, colleagues, and neighbors, Bill Ray and Kate Nicholson, and Brad and Liz Malsin.

I have been exceedingly fortunate to benefit from the constructive criticism and guidance of interdisciplinary colleagues as I have presented and debated my arguments about development and personhood in Rebgong. Emily Yeh, in particular, valiantly read the entire manuscript and gave me very helpful advice for a tighter and more accessible story. I thank as well my colleagues at Reed College for the inspiration of their incisive work, Betsey Brada, Robert Brightman, miishen Carpentier, Courtney Handman, China Scherz, Paul Silverstein, Rupert Stasch, and LaShandra Sullivan. Colleagues in anthropology, Chinese and Tibetan studies elsewhere have also been instrumental in honing my arguments: David Akin, Robert Barnett, James Benn, Anya Bernstein, Dominic Boyer, Katia Buffetrille, Jane Caple, Chris Coggins, Sienna Craig, Giovanni da Col, Donyod Dongrup, Yangdon Dhondup, Larry Epstein, Tom Felton, Allen Feldman, Magnus Fiskesjo, Frances Garrett, Jennifer Hubbert, Sarah Jacoby, Oren Kosansky, Robert Linrothe, Ralph Litzinger, Carole McGranahan, Dasa Mortensen, Françoise Robin, Geoffrey Samuel, Tsering Shakya, Andrew Shryock, Nicholas Sihlé, Antonio Terrone, Tim Thurston, Gray Tuttle, Benno Weiner, and Emily Yeh.

With the generous support of my mentors and recommenders, Jennifer Robertson, Webb Keane, and Eric Mueggler at the University of Michigan, this book project was funded by multiple national and international awards. I am grateful to the Fulbright Scholar Program, the Wenner-Gren Foundation, and the Chiang Ching-Kuo Foundation, without whose financial help and logistical support I could not have undertaken the complicated fieldwork on which this book is based. Reed College sabbatical funding supported both the fieldwork and the write-up stages of the project, and the Department of Anthropology's Harper-Ellis Fund supported multiple summer research trips as well as conference travel. Finally, the penultimate preparation of the manuscript was supported by a fellowship from the American Council of Learned Societies.

ABBREVIATIONS

CCP   Chinese Communist Party
CCTV   China Central Television
PAP   People's Armed Police
PLA   People's Liberation Army
PRC   People's Republic of China
TAR   Tibetan Autonomous Region
NSC   New Socialist Countryside campaign
KVUF   Kharnak Village Uplift Foundation

NOTE ON LANGUAGE

This book is based on ethnographic research conducted in both Chinese and a dialect of Amdo Tibetan that is pronounced quite differently from the more well-known dialects spoken in and around Lhasa. Therefore, I want to be very clear about how I rendered those languages in print. In the main text and endnotes, all first mentions of foreign language terms, except proper names, are italicized. In parenthetical glosses of words I rendered in English, I identify the language with an abbreviation before the word: "Tib." for Tibetan words, "Ch." for Chinese words, and "Skt." for the occasional Sanskrit word. For Chinese words, I used the standard pinyin transliteration system, minus tone markers for ease of printing.

At present, there is no commonly accepted system for writing Tibetan phonetically. Recent efforts to develop such a system have for the most part been based on the pronunciation of Lhasa dialects. I felt strongly though that I should represent, as clearly as possible, the Amdo dialect spoken in Rebgong. Yet I also wanted to preserve the etymological relationships of words spoken in Amdo Tibetan for readers unfamiliar with those dialects. Thus, I render Tibetan terms and important proper names in forms approximating their pronunciation in the lowland Rebgong Amdo dialect. But I also use the Wylie transliteration system in parenthetical notes to include the exact spellings of most Tibetan words I mention.

Since geographic nomenclature in this frontier region is notoriously complex, I include both Tibetan and Chinese names only for the most important sites and geographic features mentioned. For the sake of simplicity however, for the most part I use the name (rendered phonetically) that is most commonly used by Tibetan residents. In many cases the Chinese term, especially for administrative units newly demarcated with the establishment of the PRC, is the one both Tibetans and Chinese use most frequently. This is reflected on my maps and photos.

In order to protect the identities of my interlocutors living under intensifying state repression, I use pseudonyms for all persons' names except for main officials at the prefecture level and higher. In order to render them more generic, the pseudonyms I chose are all extremely common names among Tibetans in the region. Further, I do not give information about my interlocutors' work units, and I use pseudonyms for all the community and place names relevant to my main interlocutors (including lineage or "tribal" groupings) below the county level (e.g., township, village). Finally, I altered some of my principal interlocutors' main identifying characteristics.

All translations from Chinese language conversations and media are my own unless otherwise noted. All translations from Tibetan language conversations and media are the result of collaborative work between me and my Tibetan colleagues and teachers unless otherwise noted.

In any direct quotes from the original Tibetan or Chinese, I tried to keep diacritics to a bare minimum. Italicized words within such quotes designate oral emphasis in the original unless otherwise noted.

THE BATTLE FOR FORTUNE

Introduction

Olympic Time and Dilemmas of
Development in China's Tibet

On a hazy evening in September 2004, Olympic time officially began in the People's Republic of China (PRC), four years before the opening of the Beijing Summer Olympic Games. The forty-six-foot-high Olympic countdown clock was unveiled on the steps of the National Museum of China on Tiananmen Square. That was the same spot where, seven years earlier, the countdown clock for the return of Hong Kong to Chinese rule had marked that epic event. On the Olympic clock, the elegant, multicolored Beijing Olympics logo replaced the five national stars that had adorned the top of the Hong Kong turnover clock, and below, where on the Hong Kong clock a few Chinese corporate sponsors had been listed, a single logo had pride of place: Omega, Swiss maker of luxury watches, manufacturer of the countdown clock, and official timekeeper for the 2008 Olympics. The clock was beautifully backlit at night and featured red digital numbers, which, unlike the Hong Kong turnover clock that displayed only days and seconds, ticked off the days, hours, minutes and seconds until the auspicious date of August 8, 2008.

The Hong Kong countdown clock, brainchild of a Chinese corporate media official and entrepreneur in Beijing, had firmly established the countdown as a part of mass national culture in China. That first clock at Tiananmen had played maestro to a crescendo of countdown clock copies across the nation in anticipation of the return of Hong Kong, digitally performing

FIGURE 1. Olympics countdown clock, Tiananmen square, 1,161 days, 7 hours, 46 minutes, 20 seconds remaining until the Opening Ceremonies, Beijing, 2005. Author's photo.

the passage of a precise block of time that would finally end the humiliations of nineteenth-century European colonization.[1] At the turn of the twenty-first century, the Olympic countdown clock vastly expanded that quasi-millenarian culture of anticipation and national triumph in a narrative of China's global arrival as a political and economic superpower. The partnership with Omega, of Olympics and James Bond fame, added a luxurious and cosmopolitan gloss to China's Olympic time, beckoning to other high-end foreign investors to join the stream of progress—before they missed out.

Kicking off a four-year ceremonial period of preparation for the games, a delegation including the Chinese vice president of the Beijing Olympic Organizing Committee and the Swiss president of Omega started the countdown at precisely 6:00 p.m. From then on, in an era of digital cameras and the Internet, the Olympic countdown clock attracted people's participation in national linear time on a far grander scale than had the Hong Kong clock. Each digital milestone was marked with grand celebrations on Tiananmen, and Chinese families and foreign tourists frequently posed with the clock, posting their photos online. Copycat clocks and charts proliferated across China and abroad as the games drew near. As the one-year mark approached, foreign media watched amazed at the breakneck speed of Beijing's transformation into a premier global city and host to the world.

On August 8, 2007, fireworks above Tiananmen exploded at the exact moment the clock began the one-year countdown, and scenes from simultaneous celebrations across the city and country were projected on giant screens flanking the square. Echoing the national jubilation that had erupted when China won its bid for the Olympics in 2001, a massive celebration had been staged on the square for some ten thousand carefully arranged spectators in the final minutes before the one-year mark. The state-of-the-art stage, the central platform of which was also a giant LCD screen, was framed behind by the famous vista of the red Gate of Heavenly Peace, entrance to the erstwhile imperial palace, now adorned with Mao's portrait and backlit by radiating searchlights. As the Olympic Anthem played, national and International Olympic Committee flags were placed onstage, and Chinese Communist Party (CCP) Politburo member Wu Bangguo spoke: "It is a century-old dream of the Chinese people to stage an Olympic Games. By hosting the Olympic Games, we intend to further promote the Olympic spirit, world peace and development." Then, in the highly produced style of China's beloved song and dance pageants, a series of Olympic-themed performances unfolded, nationally broadcast on China Central Television (CCTV) and quickly uploaded to YouTube by fans abroad. Of those, the official theme song was "We Are Ready." As a digital clock in the upper right corner of the TV screen counted down the remaining minutes, singers from China, Taiwan, and Hong Kong lip-synched the rousing pop tune in Mandarin Chinese for global viewers:

Waiting year after year
We can finally see the future

Together with hard work and sweat, we've nurtured
The five Olympic colors

Waiting day after day
Our emotions surge even more
Building the world's largest stage
For this most heroic era

We are ready! [in English]
Uniting heart to heart
We are ready! [in English]
Uniting heaven and earth
We surpassed ourselves
and won a glorious victory
We use time to commemorate
the magic of our dream
We are ready! [in English]

Waiting each and every minute and second
The moment has finally arrived
Filling the sky, brilliant fireworks
proudly bloom.

It is a warm day in the third week of June 2008 in China's northwestern province of Qinghai. I am getting my breakfast in my little apartment in the old People's Congress building at the center of Longwu town in Qinghai's historically Tibetan region of Rebgong. I'm on edge listening to a BBC radio report online called "The Age of Terror," describing the horrific hijacking of a French plane by Algerian terrorists, an event said to have been a precursor to 9/11 in the United States. I'm thinking the story's tension and violence are too much for me, especially now, and I move to turn it off. My back is turned to the windows in my tiny kitchen when I catch a glimpse of a brilliant flash of light reflected in the metal cabinets and sink and then . . . BOOM. The roar of a massive explosion above sends me cowering for cover. I curse and run to the windows, searching the sky along with the women in the apartments facing me across the courtyard. I watch their alarmed faces as the smoke from the blast disperses above the town's main street, knowing that they know that this was no fireworks display. My first thought is that Tibetans had set off a bomb. My second is that the explosion came from the sports stadium in the middle of town, where Chinese troops had been garrisoned that spring. I realize finally that this is the troops' field artillery, firing blanks (I assume) from the stadium across the street. Over the next three days, such explosions go off at random intervals, enough to keep me and other town residents constantly anxious, but never surprised. The Olympic torch is on its way to Lhasa.

This book is a story of China's momentous Olympic year (2007–8), experienced from the nation-state's margins out west. That was the year I happened to be there pursuing anthropological research on what I was calling "dilemmas of development" among Tibetans in Qinghai Province. I had not anticipated, however, how the joyous countdown to the Olympics that year would set a collision course with Tibetans who felt excluded from the celebration. In the spring of 2008, as the Olympics shone a global spotlight on China, Tibetan Buddhist monks and laity airing a variety of grievances clashed with security forces in Lhasa and then attacked some Chinese businesses and shopkeepers. The scale and vehemence of the unrest that then spread across Tibetan regions in four western provinces took state officials and foreign observers alike by surprise.[2]

The subsequent military crackdown felt unprecedented for many; the Rebgong region where I lived had not seen such militarized state violence since the 1950s. By April 2008, there had been multiple street clashes between Tibetan residents and Tibetan and Chinese security forces in Longwu town. The town, along with many other rural Tibetan county seats, was then under de facto martial law, complete with military patrols, raids, detentions, and curfews. The silence that descended on the town's public spaces was stretched thin and tight as the goatskin drums that Tibetan village men use to fete the warlike mountain deities.

The Rebgong region's wide Guchu River valley (altitude around 8,200 feet) is about 850 miles southwest of Beijing and far off the radar of ordinary Beijingers. Long a center of Tibetan Buddhist heritage in the mountains that rise to the vast expanses of the Qinghai-Tibetan plateau, the region was relatively new to me. I had spent years focused on the Sangkok River valley (altitude 9,600 feet), another important Tibetan Buddhist center just a couple mountain passes to the southeast and not coincidentally a major hotspot in the 2008 unrest. These are lower Tibetan regions far east and north of the high Himalayan city of Lhasa (altitude 12,000 feet), erstwhile seat of the great medieval Tibetan kings and much later of the ascendant Dalai Lamas. Here, the mountains rise to the plateaus and peaks where Tibetan nomadic pastoralists have for centuries run their herds of yak and sheep, trading with lowland Tibetan, Han Chinese, and Muslim Chinese farming communities. These regions, which Tibetans refer to as Amdo, are not counted as part of Chinese-administered Tibet (Ch. Xizang, the Tibetan Autonomous

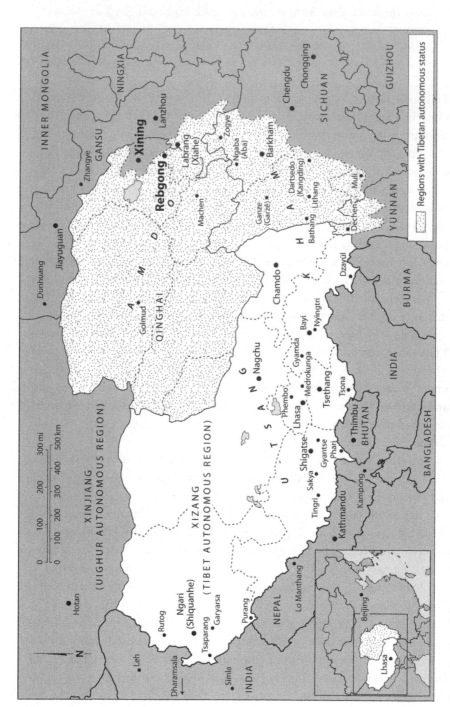

FIGURE 2. Map of Tibetan regions in the PRC. Based on a map by Atelier Golok.

Region, or TAR). They are instead designated as Tibetan Autonomous Prefectures under Gansu and Qinghai provinces. Those PRC administrative units only approximate the former realms of the Tibetan Buddhist polities under Rebgong's Rongbo Monastery and Sangkok's Labrang Monastery.

Rebgong has a uniquely complex history of state-local and interethnic relations that links it to Qinghai's capital city of Xining as well as to Lhasa in the TAR, and differentiates it from those cosmopolitan centers. According to the 2008 Qinghai Province Yearbook, the registered provincial population of 5.5 million was majority Han Chinese (almost 55 percent), most of whom lived in Xining. Meanwhile the percentage of registered Tibetans in the province had dipped from 27 percent in 1952 to 21 percent in 2007. Muslim Chinese (Hui) were 16 percent, and other minorities made up the rest.[3] The Rebgong region in the southeast however has long been home to a complex array of non-Chinese ethnic and linguistic groups.

Rebgong's Longwu town (after the Tibetan name of the monastery) is now the seat of both Huangnan Tibetan Autonomous Prefecture (population 231,000, established in 1953) and of the more rural Tongren County (population 80,000, established in 1928). Statistics from 2005 reported online claimed 91.4 percent of prefecture population to be non-Chinese minorities, including 65 percent registered as Tibetan, 13.6 percent as Mongolian, and 7.3 percent as Hui. There are also other smaller communities of residents such as those identifying as Mongour (Ch. Tuzu) and Salar. Meanwhile, Tongren County, which administers a wide range of highland Tibetan communities, reported 72 percent Tibetan residents in 2007, with the majority of non-Tibetans living either in Longwu town or in lowland agricultural villages. Most Tibetan residents speak dialects of both Tibetan and Chinese, and my Tibetan interlocutors tended to associate the Tibetan language with everyday domestic interactions and the work of the local state. Meanwhile they associated Chinese language with the more cosmopolitan contexts of higher-level state offices as well as the commercial pursuits of merchants and businesspeople.

I had come to Rebgong in the early 2000s to expand my understanding of the consequences for Tibetans of China's Great Open the West campaign (Ch. Xibu Da Kaifa). That was an effort launched by President Jiang Zemin in 2000 (as part of the tenth five-year plan) aimed at directing domestic and foreign investment to "developing" China's poorer western regions. Official rhetoric had it that the campaign was finally making good on former leader Deng Xiaoping's promise to allow the west to "catch up" with the wealthier central and eastern cities. Those metropolises were the powerhouses of China's rise that had benefited from preferential policies for capitalist economic growth since the 1980s reforms. The 2000 campaign drew unprecedented national and international attention to the marginalized western provinces where most of the country's ethnic minorities live, resulting in a "gold rush" mentality among would-be entrepreneurs and investors by the early 2000s.[4] Knowing about Rebgong's proud Buddhist heritage and Tibetan residents' robust support for Tibetan language secular education since the 1980s, I wanted to understand Tibetans' own forms of value and aspiration (development on Tibetan terms) as new sources of money and opportunity came to the valley.

During my visits in 2002 and 2005, my Tibetan friends and acquaintances in Rebgong expressed sentiments similar to those I and others have encountered among Tibetans throughout China: great optimism for the possibilities of post-Mao Tibetan cultural revival tinged with an intense ambivalence about their present situations and a dark anxiety about their futures as ethnic minorities left behind in China's rush to develop and "link up" with the rest of the world. Elders especially talked of their great relief at the improvement in standards of living since the traumatic Maoist years (1958–79) and the capacity to openly practice the rituals that were the very grounds of their communities. By the time I returned in summer 2007, however, Tibetans across the community were haunted by a deepening sense of cultural and economic crisis as they saw their children assimilating to Chineseness, lagging far behind their Chinese peers in school, and losing out to jobs taken by Chinese and Muslim Chinese residents and migrants.[5]

My roles in the valley that summer quickly became complex as I was pulled into supporting primary school renovation projects in highland Tibetan villages. In those restive regions, residents representing a wide variety of interests and jurisdictions urgently competed for foreigners' attention, and "projects" under the rubric of "development" (Ch. *fazhan*) were the safest, most sanctioned form of participation for visitors from abroad. Rebgong's proximity to the provincial capital Xining made the rural region a model site for developing, or "uplifting," Tibetan communities. As an increasing number of foreign NGOs and UN groups converged on the valley in the 2000s to pursue projects, mostly in Tibetan "cultural preservation" and education, Tibetan schools had became a crucible of translocal development politics in the valley.

But the spring 2008 unrest and subsequent martial law made it very clear that development and state violence were two sides of a coin in those parts. Reinvigorated "development," backed by military presence, was provincial and local state leaders' response to Tibetan unrest, both as an indictment and as a promise (see the epilogue).[6] When most foreigners were banned from Tibetan regions that March, I was only able to stay in my capacity as a school fundraiser. Yet the guns, riot gear, and surveillance vans of the Chinese troops sent to the valley enforced the clear message to all of us that development taken as Tibetan community-building was a threat— development should be on Chinese state terms, and that meant "peaceful" market participation.

In April 2008, Beijing authorities opened a major exhibition displaying the boons of development in Chinese-liberated Tibet, while another televised pageant marked the hundred-day countdown to the Olympics. Yet by then the ubiquitous Olympics media in Tibetan regions came across as the propaganda of another Maoist campaign. State-sponsored "Olympic Education" was intended in eastern cities to model to Chinese kids the cosmopolitan values of fair play, mutual respect, selfless service, and world peace.[7] In Tibetan regions however, the same slogans played as mandatory "Patriotic Education," an iron-fisted message to "protect social stability" above all. That fall, for example, the sports stadium in the center of Longwu town had been a site for local state workers' participation in Olympics-style contests sponsored by their offices. But after the unrest, the stadium served as a barracks for the troops sent to enforce such displays of proper citizenship and loyalty.

A Dialogic Ethnography

Why didn't I see it coming? I had been immersed in the ethnography and history of those regions for some twenty years. Still, China's Olympic Year was a turning point for me. The events of that year in Rebgong, I learned, were far from inconsequential conflicts at the periphery of the nation-state. They in fact encapsulated the nature and high stakes of China's meteoric rise as a key political and economic player in Asia and across the globe.[8] The happenstance of my presence there as a researcher meant that, similarly to how the anthropologist Frank Pieke (1995, 78) found himself conducting "accidental anthropology" amidst the 1989 protests on Beijing's Tiananmen Square, I faced the extreme liminality of a state of emergency that for many residents came to eclipse and reframe all past and present agendas and concerns.[9] As Antonius Robben and Carolyn Nordstrom and others point out, anthropological research on the front lines of conflict and violence raises profound questions about the nature and ethics of ethnography.[10] Ethnographers who first witness open violence, they say, can experience a sense of "existential shock." They describe that sensibility as a state of extreme disorientation and uncertainty about the boundaries of social order, life, and death that can dissolve the ethnographer's conceit of objective (and safe) distance from her interlocutors. In such circumstances, they remark, "there seems to be no higher ground from which to observe violence with relative detachment" (Robben and Nordstrom 1995, 13).

Of course my original ethnographic project for Rebgong, framed in compulsory social science terms for grant proposals, was always a conceit, especially for such politically sensitive Tibetan regions of China. Yet under the 2008 state of emergency there was absolutely no question of a simple comparative village study like the one I had outlined. And there was no possibility for the open collection of data through household surveys, interviews, and fly-on-the-wall participant observation. My primary concern under martial law, however, was not my own greatly curtailed access to information, but ensuring the safety of my interlocutors. My very presence as a Westerner with ties abroad was now dangerous in public spaces. Immediately after the unrest and crackdown in town my cell phone went silent as people retreated indoors. Just as observers of postprotest Lhasa have described it, life in Rebgong under martial law was not a relentless series of public clashes.[11] Instead, as everyone cleaved tightly to daily routines under the watchful eye of armed Chinese patrols, the deafening silence of public spaces spoke of thousands of private, furtive conversations. With a new unity of concern, Tibetans young and old, rural and urban, were grappling with the implications of this new era: How could they prosper in the new China if their very nature as Tibetans was so clearly a threat and a liability?

Just as Pieke found on Tiananmen Square, however, the state of emergency in Rebgong did not preclude anthropological understanding for me. The existential shock of state violence instead was an unprecedented challenge to my assumptions about development, culture, and the state, and about my own capacity to comprehend Tibetans' experiences of them: I needed to rethink my presence and project in Rebgong from the ground up. In the coming chapters, I tell the story of this process of rethinking as it played out in my own and my interlocutors' dawning awareness of the intertwined nature of development and state violence, our oftentimes awkward or uncertain mutual learning before and after the 2008 crackdown. I offer this book then as an effort in what I will call a "dialogic ethnography" of stateled development in Rebgong. Proponents of such an approach in anthropology have argued for decades that this is not about the ethnographer crafting narratives of harmonious "dialogues" with ethnic others, and thereby claiming an easy intimacy on equal grounds.[12] Dialogic ethnography pushes one instead to grapple with the everyday realities of unequal access to communication and voice. By that I mean the historical relations

of hierarchy and power that render some people disenfranchised and disproportionately vulnerable in this ever-connected world.

In the wake of Americans' shock and grief after the 9/11 terrorist attacks
on the United States, the philosopher Judith Butler wrote a trenchant book
called *Precarious Life: The Powers of Mourning and Violence.* In it, she reconsid-
ers the transnational roles and responsibilities of relatively privileged people
in the United States and Europe. She imagines as a new starting point for
global community and social action a common, human vulnerability and
interdependence as fundamentally social beings. Such an awareness, she
argues, would fly in the face of American fantasies of self-sufficiency and
mastery so ascendant during the George W. Bush years especially. "What
grief displays," she says, "is the thrall in which our relations with others hold
us, in ways that we cannot always recount or explain . . . in ways that challenge the very notion of ourselves as autonomous and in control" (2004, 23).
But she also wonders whose lives count in policy and practice as fully human
in that way? Who gets to feel confident, secure, indeed entrepreneurial?
When misfortune strikes, whose lives and what losses are publicly grievable?

A dialogic ethnography in the wake of state violence entails facing these
questions head on. But that is easier said than done. This kind of anthropological understanding, I found, moves at a pace outmoded by the frenetic
imperatives of market-driven goals.[13] The world China has worked so hard
to join (an effort epitomized in China's accession to the World Trade Organization in 2001) is now a tightening web of capitalist markets. "Economic
development" has created gleaming, high-tech infrastructures to quickly
move people (and financial speculation) through and away from the abject
margins (the poor rural, the urban slum, the shuttered factory). In the face
of time and political constraints, the best intentions to help the less fortunate
can find little purchase within recipient communities. But those constraints
can also serve conveniently as alibis for givers—to limit exposure to the vulnerability of the marginalized so as to maintain intact one's own sense of
security and recourse.

My goal in the writing here is thus not to dwell on the existential struggles
of my ethnographic self, nor is it to merely "give voice" to Tibetans as simply traumatized victims or heroic resisters. I seek instead to move beyond
the shock of moments of open violence to understand the larger cultural,
historical, and communicative conditions in Rebgong for people's vulnerability and complicity, as well as for their creative coping, resistance, and
survival. As Robben and Nordstrom put it, from an anthropological perspective, violence emerges not as an extraordinary "domain of death," but as a

fundamental dimension of everyday living (1995, 6). The specter of violence in everyday interactions, they argue, drawing on Foucault and others, can both shape and fragment the moral and historical grounds of recognized personhood and citizenship—the very boundaries of the social human. This is the ongoing process of mutual remembering, (mis)recognition, and evaluation of persons among Tibetans and their interlocutors that I came to call "the politics of presence."

Thus, for example, I found that for many Tibetans I met, the significance of the 2008 military crackdown could only be understood within a communal legacy of painful memory. The events of the late 1950s were world shattering for their elders. That was when Chinese troops under Mao Zedong finally put down Tibetan resistance to CCP-led collectivization and enforced the imprisonment of most Buddhist lamas, monks, and lay male leaders, the prohibition of most Buddhist and lay ritual, and the collectivization of all land and production. Since then, Tibetan communities in China have been rebuilt on searing, but silenced grief—the simultaneous loss of lives and social worlds coalesced for many elders especially in an anguished longing for the presence of the Dalai Lama, who escaped to exile in India in 1959.

Development, Culture, and the State

In chapter 1 I delve further into what a dialogic ethnography entails methodologically, and I unpack what I mean by the "politics of presence." Here I sketch out how the 2008 state of emergency compelled me to rethink the nature of development, culture, and the state in this light. My accounts in the five main chapters will then illustrate key aspects of this approach to state-led development as they became salient within a variety of encounters across multiple Tibetan communities in Rebgong.

In retrospect, I realize that I did not see the 2008 Tibetan unrest coming because I had not fully grasped what the anthropological critique of economic development agendas meant in practice. My previous work in Labrang, as well as my research proposals for the Rebgong project, took for granted the argument, most famously laid out by Arturo Escobar (1995), that cultural anthropology offers urgently needed qualitative methods to counter the standardizing quantitative approaches to development in economics and other social sciences. Such economistic approaches in the West, argued Escobar, came to the fore after World War II. Proponents at that time construed "economic development" and "modernization" for marginalized peoples as capitalist market integration. In the 1980s, capitalist frameworks for development were increasingly globalized in the agendas of international organizations like the World Bank and IMF. The methods and premises of economics thereby came to prominence among a variety of national elites as global standards for discovering and modeling objective truths and primary causes. Indeed Deng Xiaoping famously promoted his post-Mao market reforms in the PRC, especially after the crackdown on the 1989 Tiananmen protests, with the slogan "economic development is the first principle [lit., "the hard truth"]."[14]

The recent development push in Qinghai seems to have left my Tibetan friend Wanma with little time to dwell on ethnic tensions. She's in the public relations department of a prominent provincial government bureau in Xining, in charge of "entertaining" the many Chinese official visitors (all men) from the "interior." The summer months when I visit in the early 2000s are prime official tourism months and Wanma travels hundreds of kilometers a day picking up VIP guests of her bureau, accompanying them to tourist spots and sending them off again. She comes from an illustrious Tibetan family and she seems to know all well-placed and well-off Tibetans and Chinese in the city. Tonight, her round and jovial Chinese friend Little Wang hosts us for dinner at a sumptuous hotel, ostensibly to welcome me to Xining. He is the married son of a construction business boss, poised to take over his father's company. "He likes me too much," Wanma jokes, as Little Wang plies us with drinks and expensive delicacies and grabs her in hugs. He's the one she had tapped to pick me up at the airport in his dark blue Lincoln town car with the leather seats. Sealed inside that car, we had cruised by the dusty villages, defunct factories and massive billboards touting luxury cars and cell phones that now ring the city. Little Wang styles himself my ambassador to Qinghai, even though he says his father only came to Xining from Suzhou in the 1980s, and he himself only after college in 1995. As he teaches me Qinghai drinking etiquette with a bottle worth several times Wanma's weekly salary, he jokes that he is just one of the "ordinary folk." Wanma protests, matching his joking tone. "I am a member of the old aristocracy, you belong to the new aristocracy," she tells him, "now I'm just one of the ordinary folk!"

By the early 2000s in places like Rebgong's Longwu town, I found, the fundamental premises of market-based economics could be shared by a surprising array of competing agents. Many residents and officials had welcomed post-Mao decollectivization and celebrated the great promise of cultural, including Tibetan Buddhist, revival under market reforms. The Open the West campaign had reinvigorated market-based claims for a "new era"

(Ch. *xin shiqi*) of modernity and development. Thus many of my Tibetan and Chinese interlocutors spoke approvingly of universal, quantitative standards (e.g., relative prices or wages, income and debt levels, amounts of consumer goods purchased) for assessing the appropriate futures and values of persons and things, construed as exploitable "resources" for monetary profits. Like the English term *development*, the Chinese term *fazhan* (lit., "expand, spread out, evolve") in practice could conflate forms of capitalist market expansion with the supremely generous gift of money and infrastructure for post-Mao community uplift and modernizing advance. However, as Escobar and other anthropologists have argued, such standardization efforts under the sign of money can elide the actual sociocultural and political processes by which economic development projects, even under the best of intentions, can starkly marginalize the very populations they seek or claim to benefit.[15]

By contrast, cultural anthropologists' qualitative methods treat people as dynamic meaning-makers above all. Economics in this light is first and foremost an interpretive politics over the nature and sources of value, moral personhood, and proper exchange. Ethnographers must then use subtle analytic tools to understand the actually messy, unequal, and multivocal nature of development practices situated within specific sociohistorical and political contexts. Such work, theorists argued, counters older ethnographic methods that treated localities as isolated islands of culture and local residents as mere purveyors of collective beliefs and practices. This approach instead calls for historically grounded ethnographic research within a broader analytic horizon. "Local" processes are in fact seen to be inextricably linked to the translocal, and ordinary residents are treated as analytically commensurate agents with development industry elites, who are often operating with competing development premises and goals.[16]

However, when I began my research in the early 2000s, even though people in Rebgong, including prefecture police (PSB), knew me as a student and researcher of Tibetan culture and development, I found no easy way to stand apart and observe. Instead many of my Tibetan interlocutors recognized me primarily as another Western benefactor, there to offer development aid. In the ferment of twenty-first century Rebgong, fieldwork encounters were always also development encounters. Under the rubric of provincial western development agendas from the late 1990s on, for the first time in the history of the PRC large numbers of foreigners, as investors, donors, consultants, teachers, and tourists, were invited in to help "open" China's west (many Tibetan regions had been officially closed to foreign visitors until the mid-1990s). "Poverty alleviation," "cultural preservation," and secular education projects aimed at preparing Tibetans to participate in new job and agriculture markets attracted well-meaning Hong Kong Chinese, as well as foreigners (including exiled Tibetans and Taiwanese Chinese) from across the globe. In Rebgong alone, by the mid-2000s there were projects representing organizations from at least fifteen countries and several UN committees.

I now think that I was taken aback by the 2008 unrest and crackdown because, despite all my training to take a critical cultural perspective on development politics, in that context I was still at some level taking "culture" to be a depoliticized abstraction. And that in turn prevented me from truly grasping what was at stake for Tibetan communities in the PRC. As Emily Yeh and others have argued, the 2000s in Tibetan regions saw the rise (or return) of "development as spectacle" (2013, 236).[17] Ubiquitous state media touted dazzling urban lifestyles and urged citizens to style themselves as cosmopolitan consumers and self-sufficient, mobile entrepreneurs. In that context, depoliticized and commodifiable "ethnic minority" culture (e.g., as a set of exotic and photogenic beliefs, things, places, and performances) was the very substance of development work in Rebgong.

When I first arrived, in part due to political and linguistic constraints, and in part due to the assumptions and aspirations of Tibetan friends and colleagues, it could be very hard for foreigners to see beyond the guarded diplomacy and spectacular hospitality of development encounters, especially in the short time frames of quick fact-finding visits. Thus I was at first drawn, along with other outsiders, into thinking of development work in the valley as just a set of independent "projects" (Ch. *xiangmu*) aimed at supporting the revival of colorful Tibetan culture and ethnicity, all amidst the expanding personal freedoms of an open market. However, I remember being struck that many Westerners I met seemed to think of their development work as a way to access and support Tibetans and their culture directly, presuming that the Chinese state was relevant locally only in "Chinese" security forces. For them, Tibetan culture, ethnicity, and even agency were ideally abstracted from the goals and workings of the state.

The country runs on these kinds of events, I think, even here in Huangnan prefecture. This is how "relationships" [Ch. guanxi] are made and maintained. I'm at yet another party of elites in 2005, this time in Longwu town. My Tibetan friends Drolma and her husband Lobzang, a highly placed local official, have brought me along to the swankiest new hotel-restaurant in town, owned by their Chinese friends. Official cars, including a police jeep, pack the parking lot. Inside, the smell of high-test grain alcohol and the shouts of men's drinking games waft from the private rooms. We are ushered into the most elegant dining suite, complete with a karaoke system and wide-screen TV. Mr. Wei, another Chinese friend who runs a construction company here, is hosting a party to celebrate a pinnacle of family success: his eighteen-year-old daughter's admission to university back east. Drolma and Lobzang are the only Tibetans here. As they introduce me, they gush that Mr. Wei and his wife are their "very best friends." After we sit and the food and liquor start flowing, Drolma tells me in Tibetan that she doesn't know most of the guests here. They all know Lobzang though. Drolma's Chinese woman friend, wife of the commander of the prefecture army base, leans in to enthuse in Chinese about how much she loves Drolma, and how Lobzang's "open-minded" nature makes him "not like other Tibetans." Mr. Wei and his wife make me pose for photos with their daughter, urging her to speak English with me. She tells me the family moved to Rebgong only a decade earlier, but she and her brother were sent back east for middle school. She returned to take the college entrance exam here in Qinghai though, she explains, because "that way it's easier to compete."

As my understanding deepened into the spring and summer of 2008, the state of emergency in Rebgong finally brought home to me the real stakes of culture in development efforts there. Post-Mao Tibetan cultural revival was not simply a colorful ethnic "dress" laid on more fundamental (capitalist) economic interests and premises shared by all. Beyond the public spectacle, it was in fact a deeply embodied, and as Emily Yeh (2013) would put it, "territorialized" contest over the very terms and nature of sovereignty, the links people claimed between types of persons, authorities, exchange, and jurisdictions that legitimized forms of control over resources and livelihoods. That ongoing, often subtle contestation over sovereignties is in part what I mean by the "politics of presence." And to get at this we need much more nuanced analytic tools that will illuminate the hazardous, yet authorizing presence for Tibetans of both the state and of divine or invisible beings (lamas, Buddhas, deities, demons) in the face of development pressures.[18]

As observers have noted, the Open the West campaign in the 2000s merely intensified and spectacularized a much longer term process of the national incorporation of western frontier zones under central CCP development policies.[19] Campaign rhetoric in fact tapped the global charisma of market-based development to reinvigorate post-Mao Chinese state-building efforts out west: "market integration" now stands in for communist national incorporation. In Rebgong, twenty-first century development in this light was decidedly not just a set of discrete "projects." All such efforts were shaped by larger central and provincial state agendas that played out differently in China's wealthy east versus in poorer and minority communities out west. In the Maoist tradition of "mass mobilization" campaigns, such state-led development agendas were aimed at modernizing and administering whole populations or demographics, even as regional resources came under unprecedented state and corporate control. Now, however, to ensure citizens' participation the time pressures of monetary debt were supposed to substitute for the direct and indirect coercions of patriotic communal labor. In the coming chapters, we will see this cultural politics of persuasion and coercion play out for Rebgong Tibetans under official development rubrics such as "Compulsory Primary Education," "School Consolidation," creating a "New Socialist Countryside," grassroots "Party Building," urbanization, and the "resettlement" of highland pastoralist communities.

I found that, in ways unseen in those parts since the Maoist years, those state-led development agendas were challenging the very cultural grounds of post-Mao Tibetan sovereignties, threatening the fragmentation and even final dissolution of rebuilt Tibetan communities. I thus rethink post-Mao Tibetan cultural revival as constituted all along by Tibetans' partially unacknowledged efforts in regional counterdevelopment. By that I mean contested claims to the authority and techniques (whether "scientific" or "religious") for achieving fortunate futures on behalf of competing territories or jurisdictions. And such Tibetan counterdevelopment endeavors, I learned, drew on a variety of much older notions of landscape, jurisdiction, and sovereign fortune to envision hybrid, yet specifically Tibetan modernities. I refer to this contentious process throughout the book as the "battle for fortune" in Rebgong.

After all, the great optimism of Rebgong Tibetans in the early reform years (1980s) was for the return of the original promise offered them by Maoist PRC work teams in the early 1950s: the compromise between Maoist socialism and Tibetan regional polities that was called "Tibetan autonomous" governance (while CCP leaders would still be Chinese, implementation of policy would be the purview of majority Tibetan regional governments).[20] And Rebgong, as we will see, was a site of particularly strong and proudly ethnic Tibetan government, and therefore it was one of the most affluent and well-educated of Tibetan prefectures.[21] Even the Huangnan party secretary in the mid-2000s was said to be half-Tibetan (see the epilogue).

Yet, as forms of Tibetan autonomy seemed to dwindle under Open the West policies, spectacular performances of gratitude for the central state's gift of development were the very public condition of citizenship, pushing Tibetan counterdevelopment efforts further underground.[22] This trend of increasingly top-down development demands in Tibetan regions of the PRC is what I refer to across the book's chapters as the rise of "authoritarian capitalism." Tibetans' embrace of apolitical, abstract culture in those years was thus in part due to political expedience. Ultimately, I came to see the tumultuous events of the Olympic year in Rebgong as the culmination of a much longer politics of development out west. The Olympic spotlight during 2007–8 in fact apotheosized CCP-led capitalist development as global spectacle. And that in turn scaled up the stakes of development agendas in Tibetan regions under the millenarian time pressure of the countdown clock.

The State as Cultural Process

In the chapters to come, I tell the story of how these dilemmas of development played out for differently positioned Tibetans in Rebgong. In so doing, I rethink an anthropological approach to the state as itself an uncertain cultural process. From this perspective, the state is never separate from, but part and parcel of, the cultural politics of economic exchange and fortune. In practice "the state" encompasses much more than just a government. Theorists distinguish between, on one hand, the often contested realities of a state system, a network of institutions (political parties, schools, and services as well as congresses and parliaments) that works to uphold a government's sovereign claim to rule a specific territory and people; and on the other, the projected idea of a state, the media image of a government and its state apparatus as uniquely legitimate, unified, and authoritative.[23] This view of the state then compels us to look beyond the great theaters of the Chinese state during the Olympic year and grasp instead the everyday cultural intimacies and ironies of the state in practice, how it is narrated and embodied as much as it is resisted.

The state is so present here at the county level, I think as I chuckle at my Tibetan teacher friend Gendun's antics in his new apartment in Longwu town. It is fall 2007 and we're here, along with principal Tashi and county school district head Drakpa, to discuss the wall-building project for the primary school in their rural home village of Kharnak. Gendun points to a scroll painting of Sakyamuni Buddha in his otherwise empty home altar. He proudly shows me the Tibetan calligraphy on the scroll, which he swears is the Dalai Lama's signature, "this is a treasure," he says. I ask how he got it, and in an exaggeratedly conspiratorial tone, he points to the other two, "I can't tell you! Those two are CCP members!" Tashi's retort was quick, "I'm a party member, but when we looked at the painting together, I knew the names of the deities and Gendun didn't!" We sit down to plan, and the familiar push and pull of persuasion and sincerity takes on urgent tones. They are convinced Tibetan language secular education is the only path forward, yet few funds trickle down from higher-ups. "My job is to beseech the county for resources on behalf of schools," explains Drakpa in the even tones of the bureaucrat, "but they look down on rural regions and Tibetans can't compete." Tashi's voice in contrast comes across like a scream from the wilderness, "We are all Tibetans, and when we think about our identity, we get angry. Sometimes you don't know the road forward and you sigh in despair, but sometimes you know the way and you are just powerless to go there! It's getting worse and worse and worse for Tibetans, but we are powerless to do anything about it. In our hearts we all worry and worry. We think we are in dire straits."

These charged processes of everyday state presence are not unique to China. Instead we need to understand all states as ongoing cultural projects that present citizens with high-stakes dilemmas for moral participation. To get at these dynamics, anthropologists distinguish between people's shifting senses of affiliation and belonging (e.g., in forms of ethnicity and nationalism) and ruling groups' efforts to govern legitimately. All governments have faced similar issues in their efforts to feed and maintain order among their subjects. But with the rise of a new global order in the eighteenth and nineteenth centuries, the claim to lead a nation-state ("communist" or not) is a particular project to represent a government's efforts as "modern," and thus as uniquely efficient, delimited (to precise territorial boundaries), and representative of all citizens' interests. A modern state is supposed to be the sovereign legacy of a revolutionary national community, a "nation" ("the Americans," "the British," "the Chinese") that transcends all former regional and ethnic affiliation. Ironically, given China's much-touted Olympic slogan "One World, One Dream," the global importance of China's Olympic year was not that a "nondemocratic" or "non-Western" state hosted the games (versus the criticisms of protesters abroad), but that it demonstrated the continued relevance of a strongly sovereign nation-state despite claims and calls for global unity through capitalist integration ("globalization").

Yet Westerners have long treated both Tibet and China as global exceptions with regard to statehood and development. For many, they stand for profound hopes and fears about world peace, economic security, and human rights. Meanwhile Tibetans and Chinese themselves have often taken up those assumptions to various ends. In the 2000s especially, as the promise (or conceit) of U.S.- and European-led democracy and development seemed to be fading, Tibet and China have come to represent a kind of yin and yang of ideas about statehood in a new global order. Tibet, as epitomized in the Dalai Lama's Middle Way vision of Tibet as a "Zone of Peace," becomes a global nonstate (where peaceful Buddhists live autonomously within China), as well as a privileged site of antimarket development (environmental and cultural "conservation"). By contrast, China, as epitomized in Westerner's fears of the "rising dragon" or in the 2005 Chinese state white paper on China's "peaceful rise," becomes a global ultrastate.[24] It is on one hand a totalitarian threat, on the other, a model bureaucracy for ensuring stable (capitalist) development.

Thus foreign Tibet supporters in Rebgong or abroad could miss the intimate and deeply ambivalent ways in which Tibetans there live and embody the cultural premises of the Chinese state, as national citizens ("minority nationalities") and aspirants to modern futures, and as relatively well-paid state officials (including as police and military) charged with implementing the policies of their superiors. Meanwhile, like the ubiquitous images of Chinese imperial culture in Olympics media, Chinese citizens and their foreign supporters could traffic in deep assumptions about China defined first and foremost as a uniquely enduring state. "China" as a specific type of state order is after all what supposedly endured for millennia across the rise and fall of imperial dynasties.

In this, statehood and personal identity can be rolled into one so that when patriotic fervor peaks (like during the Olympic Year) the Chinese state seems to be inseparable from a profound sense of Chinese ethnic essence. Yet such moments of fervor belie Chinese citizens' growing uncertainties about the nature of the modern Chinese state (the People's Republic of China) under CCP rule. The focus on the state as Chinese ethnicity also flies in the face of rhetoric depicting the PRC state since its founding in 1949 as an ethnically neutral arbiter of a "multiethnic" nation, and it glosses over Mao Zedong's attempts to destroy that very imperial legacy in order to establish such a radically different, modern state. Finally, since post-Mao PRC leaders opened the doors to market forces, the central CCP, its unelected leaders still sole arbiters of policy while they and their family members are some of the wealthiest people in China, has increasingly struggled to retain its relevance as well as its moral legitimacy.

In the final days before the games in 2008, I watched every night in Rebgong as central state television (CCTV) news featured not only reports of exuberant preparations but also an endless series of ceremonial meetings as CCP leaders proudly hosted foreign heads of state arriving for the opening ceremonies. China's Olympic Games were just as much about the arrival of the CCP in a new global era as it was about the triumph of the Chinese people. Such triumphalism of course is conventional for national leaders hosting the games. But what was unique in the dilemmas facing Tibetan and Chinese citizens that year were the fundamentally cultural, even uncanny ways in which the Chinese state was rendered present, unitary, or morally legitimate for them, as against the reality of constant internal conflict and bureaucratic fragmentation. "The State," as we will see, was also a highly consequential, yet shifting figure or presence for people. During the Olympic year, the magic of the state worked on me, just as it did on Rebgong residents, not just through spectacular military force, but mostly through the psychological engineering of constant state media messages, quiet surveillance, and fearful rumor. Despite myself, I left in August with an unshakable sense of my own smallness in the face of what felt like the massive and monolithic presence of the Chinese state.

Yet the routinization of state terror and impunity in times of crisis only brings to light what is in fact an everyday cultural politics of the nation-state. In China, especially in the vast western provinces, the culture of the state is about grappling with the uncertain legacy of Mao. As heirs to Mao's Communist Party, reform-era CCP leaders had to both embrace and distance themselves from Mao's memory—the "socialist market economy" under Deng challenged anew the very nature of "socialism," especially in the wake of citizens' complaints in the late 1980s of rising income inequality and increasing official corruption.[25] Thus from the 1990s on, state media and education campaigns increasingly emphasized the idealized altruism of state officials working for "the People." And that even as leaders effectively reversed Mao's policies and advocated for versions of capitalist free market policies that offered a faster route to comfortable, even wealthy urban lifestyles (in 2002 president Jiang Zemin famously allowed businessmen to become CCP members). The promise to deliver that "comfortably well-off" (Ch. *xiaokang*) lifestyle was crucial to ongoing CCP legitimacy.

The events of China's Olympic year convinced me that the country's west has been a key component of that post-Mao state-citizen social contract. To really grasp the rising stakes for Tibetans of state-led development agendas, we have to see twenty-first century Sino-Tibetan relations less in the cosmopolitan and rarefied terms of "international human rights," and more in the prosaic terms of Chinese state officials' urgent interests in pushing capitalist markets west after twenty years of post-Mao reforms. Mao, just like current CCP leaders, drew on American and European ideas of modernization and development to claim for the PRC the fantasy (albeit a Marxist one) of rational mastery and efficiency that would lift citizens to a new life. That fantasy in part depended on the creation of its Other: the non-Chinese citizens of the new "multiethnic" state, most of whom lived in the sparsely populated western regions that the party claimed for the PRC. Those peoples (who in 2008 accounted for only about 8 percent of China's 1.3 billion citizens) made up the majority populations of what came to be the far western provinces of

Xizang (TAR), Xinjiang, Qinghai, and Inner Mongolia, as well as the western parts of Gansu, Sichuan and Yunnan. Non-Chinese peoples thus occupied 60 percent of the PRC's current landmass, in regions too high or too dry for agriculture but rich with "resources" like water, minerals, lumber, hydropower, natural gas, and oil.

In the Maoist stage theory of Chinese social scientists, non-Chinese citizens were classified as living in primitive or premodern stages of development (Tibetans' stage was called "feudal serfdom"). Meanwhile the Chinese majority (referred to as Han, after the imperial dynasty) were classified as occupying the most advanced stage. They were the ones with the technical knowledge and "brotherly" concern to help western minorities advance.[26] Like the "wild, wild west" in the United States, the western hinterlands like the Amdo Tibetan regions of Qinghai long figured in Chinese popular imaginations as a far-flung, uncivilized frontier, home to barbarian others, then (under Mao) as a space of exile for disgraced officials or unruly urban youth, and finally as a romantic tourism destination. But since the early twentieth century, Qinghai has been increasingly the object of development longing. Officials eyed and enumerated not only the products of pastoralism, but also the seeming abundance of arable land, minerals, lumber, and hydropower.[27]

It was not until the establishment of the PRC that Chinese officials were able to launch massive, centrally planned development projects in the region, from huge military installations, state-run farms, and mining operations with Han migrant labor in the province's west, to the rapid industrialization of the capital city of Xining in its east.[28] Half a century before the Open the West campaign, Qinghai saw centrally planned, rapidly implemented, and grand-scale development efforts that largely bypassed Tibetan residents and created a regional economy almost completely dependent on central subsidies. But the disastrous consequences of those Maoist projects, especially after the Great Leap Forward (1958), meant that post-Mao development efforts were construed by planners under Deng in opposition to the perceived irrationalities of such a socialist planned economy.

The new "socialist market economy" thus also meant shifting central priorities back to the east coast, where capital could be rapidly raised through export-oriented manufacturing. As Aihwa Ong (1999, 7) put it, post-Mao Chinese state leaders' answer to the ironies and tensions of combining Marxist and capitalist ideologies in order to advocate open markets has been to pursue "zoned" development and governance. Certain zones in the east (coastal special economic zones, and then certain urban districts) would be allowed to "open up" to private profit, foreign investment, and export manufacturing, while the western regions would wait until the time was ripe, all the while providing raw materials to fuel that growth. In other words, the

PRC's miraculous rise under the CCP was premised on a deliberate east-west divide, one that by the 2000s resulted in some of the starkest inequalities in income and opportunity in the world.

In Qinghai by the late 1980s, Han technocrats sought ways to overcome the province's seemingly intrinsic economic and cultural "backwardness" and its extreme dependence on central subsidies, and prioritized the pursuit of foreign investment and the encouragement of private entrepreneurship.[29] But frustrated planners found that the region could not compete with the preferred eastern provinces. Chinese and Tibetan elites alike began to look for causes in the low "quality" (Ch. *suzhi*) of Qinghai's relatively uneducated and politically restive ethnic minorities. By 1999 thirty-nine of the huge province's forty-six counties, the vast majority of which were rural components of Tibetan Autonomous prefectures, were officially designated as "poverty stricken." Rural Tibetans' living standards starkly contrasted with those of relatively affluent urbanites in and around Xining, where most of the province's majority Han live.[30]

As the Olympic countdown clock was set in motion, the great Olympic pageants in the east celebrated the wonderful new opportunities state-led capitalism had brought to Han urbanites, but the media events also reveled in the possibilities of China's recent westward turn. The Great Open the West campaign was launched just before Chinese leaders finally won their Olympic bid. And one of the ubiquitous cartoon mascots of the Beijing Olympics, the cute and friendly "good luck dolls," conceived with meticulous attention to national and Olympic symbolism, was Yingying, the cuddly Tibetan antelope (see chapter 5). Wearing a headdress designed to recall the ethnic dress of Tibetans and Xinjiang Muslims, Yingying was supposed to represent the newly enlightened state focus on protecting the environment and endangered species out west. By then, though, such public theater worked hard to obscure the impossible task facing central development planners: they needed to mollify increasingly resentful ethnic minorities in the west, all the while "sustainably" intensifying the exploitation of resources there to meet the insatiable demands of urbanites back east.

"We are lucky to have found a taxi," says Catherine, my ex-pat friend who teaches young Tibetans English in town. It is April 2008, just days after a bloody street clash between Tibetans and Chinese security forces, and we had hoped for momentary escape by hiking one of the main mountain peaks that rises from a historically prominent cluster of highland Tibetan villages. Ethnic tensions are now so high that no Han Chinese driver would dare to enter these

communities up here. Our Tibetan driver, speaking in Tibetan, tells us he hails from those villages. He proudly talks of his homeland's heritage, pointing out places where auspicious signs of Buddhist fortune had naturally occurred, and narrating the story of his community's guardian mountain deity. In the relatively safe space of his taxi, he shares some of his darkest concerns and fears. "We Tibetans are really bad off," he says, lamenting what he thought was unfair appropriation of Tibetan land and resources in recent years by state officials: "The State owns everything!" he sighs, "and now they say soldiers are coming up here at night to arrest Tibetan men."

Far from being incorrigible "ingrates" dismissing development aid lavished on them by the state (as online critics put it), Tibetan protesters in 2008 were in fact responding to recent changes that had increasingly marginalized them from the benefits of market-based development. As Andrew Fischer and others demonstrated, the Open the West campaign was not meant as a fundamental redirection of central development priorities to poor communities in the west. Instead, it was a relatively modest central investment in major infrastructure projects (highways, railroads, dams, mines) designed to consolidate central state control over western resources and bring about a grand vision of national market integration largely benefiting the east.[31] In Fischer's assessment (2009a, 52), the Open the West agenda was just a reinvigorated form of "boomerang aid" in Tibetan regions of the PRC, an intensification of the long-term norm of central state-led "subsidization" since the late Maoist years. That process in the 2000s, he argues, placed ownership rights in the hands of state and corporate entities located outside the region, effectively debilitating Tibetan regional economies and sending the lion's share of wages and profits back east.

Thus, even as development projects under Open the West auspices admonished Tibetans in Qinghai that secular education (and not Buddhist monasticism or mountain deity worship) was the ideal route to improving their "quality," state funding for education in the early 2000s was miniscule and cash-strapped prefecture governments devoted less than a quarter of their largely subsidized budgets to schools. In fact, as secular education was increasingly marketized and delinked from state promises of postgraduate jobs, illiteracy and drop-out rates among Tibetans (and other ethnic minorities) in Rebgong were many times higher than among the minority Han there.[32]

As I was pulled ever deeper into Tibetan rural school fundraising projects in Rebgong in 2008, I came to understand the actual cultural (and linguistic) stakes for Tibetans of state-led development. "Market integration" under

Open the West was in fact a multipronged assault on the sovereign grounds of Tibetan communities. Urbanization, education, and conservation as ultimate values were justifying state officials' efforts to a close off huge tracts of forest and grassland to Tibetan use, to appropriate rural lands for urban development, and to pressure Tibetan highlanders to move down from the mountains and settle in new lowland towns. Further, primary school construction, I discovered, was playing crucial roles in this process as both carrot and stick. At issue were the vital ritual worlds that authorized Tibetan communities' claims to lands and livelihoods, which they construed to be both their proud ancestral heritage and their hopes for future fortune and security.

China's Olympic time brought all this to a head; it precipitated a turning point in PRC history, not least because the spectacle of states of emergency that year for the first time publicly highlighted the east-west (ethnic and class) divide in China. By summer 2008, as Chinese citizens and supporters abroad rallied to CCP leaders' calls for revitalizing national pride, service, and unity, Tibetans in Rebgong under tightening military scrutiny quietly grappled with a building sense of collective inauspiciousness, moral ambiguity, and grief.

In chapter 1, I begin my story of that year by laying out the cultural and historical specificities of development encounters among Tibetans in Rebgong. I turn as well to explicating some of the main analytic tools I use to delve beyond the public spectacles of development and state violence. Fair warning: my voice in the writing will shift. As an attempt at a dialogic ethnography, the analyses in the five main chapters juxtapose and contrast multiple kinds of voices speaking of, to, and against each other. Thus throughout the book I include translated excerpts from a variety of Tibetan and Chinese language encounters, texts, and other media. I encourage intrepid readers not to just skip over them, but to read them aloud, listen to their cadences, and pay attention to their form and the figures they highlight: these are but a small sample of the contending voices at the front lines of the escalating battle for fortune in Tibetan regions of China.

As a contribution to the anthropology of development then, this book is my call for reinvigorating qualitative analysis against the great, global charisma of development stories that reduce—and quantify—all human aspiration as the mundane and utilitarian strivings of atomized individuals. The Tibetan characters you'll meet in this book are all based on multifaceted individuals, but they were never alone in their aspirations or in their pain. And even as the deepening state of emergency could pit individuals and communities against each other, Tibetans also met those challenges with reinvigorated ethnic solidarity, pride, and affection. Yet as we will see, the very nature of my interlocutors' own motives, fortunes, and misfortunes were not always clear to themselves or to others. Instead, in a reciprocal process that both set Rebgong Tibetans apart and linked them to other aspiring communities in and outside of the PRC, we all struggled to understand who our interlocutors were (including divine and invisible ones) and what fortunes they hoped for in particular encounters. As the stakes of personhood and power rose ever higher throughout China's Olympic year and beyond, those everyday battles for fortune were the very crucible of struggles over the meaning and efficacy of development in the Sino-Tibetan frontier zone.

CHAPTER 1

The Dangers of the Gift Master

The ferocious Warrior Queen, the divine Dharma Protector Palden Lhamo, had been sensing my presence all along, but I was oblivious. By early March 2008, nearly halfway through China's Olympic Year, I had been living in Rebgong's urbanizing Guchu River valley for some four months. But it was only when Palden Lhamo ejected me from the Tibetan village house where I was a guest into the twilight of a cold March day that I began to experience the awful implications of the Warrior Queen's jealous wrath. The precise nature of Palden Lhamo's active presence, form, or motives has never come clear to me. Yet over the past two decades of my research visits to the region, I had encountered her image in multiple contexts and media forms. In our household, she appeared in a five by seven, silver-framed print of her fierce, blue-black body, wreathed in cremation smoke, crowned by five skulls and riding her divine mule across seas of red blood. The colorful printed image, or *thangka*, stood amidst the offerings to the Buddhas in the glittering altar room adjacent to my guest bedroom, while the doors of the altar room offered constant prayers on behalf of the household in the form of posters carefully replaced every New Year:

tshe ring nad med skal bzang bde skyid 'phel

(May our life, health, good fortune, and happiness increase.)

FIGURE 3. Cover of inaugural issue of *Rebgong Culture* magazine featuring giant brocade image of the Warrior Queen Palden Lhamo, December 2007

As I try to make sense of that tumultuous year I spent in Rebgong, the presence of Palden Lhamo emerges only in murky fragments, expanding and contracting in scale as I come to realize how pervasive are the invocations of her among Tibetans in and outside of China. A highly ranked, enlightened Dharma Protector, Palden Lhamo in her Warrior Queen aspect (Tib. dmag zor rgyal mo) was the special guardian of the ascendant Dalai Lamas in Lhasa in the sixteenth and seventeenth centuries. Through her various media and protective actions in the face of crises of sovereignty, Palden Lhamo eventually rose to become a key link between an ideally united Tibet under the ancient kings and, after the Chinese Communist takeover in 1951, an imagined modern nation-state under the fourteenth Dalai Lama's exiled government in India (see figure 2 map).

But for my friend and hostess Drolma in this region far from those centers of power, the Warrior Queen was a protector much closer to home. Drolma had married Lobzang, the patriarch of the household, after her first husband had died young. For her, Palden Lhamo was most importantly the emplaced protector, or "support" (Tib. rten pa), of her own natal village across the river from us. Several years earlier Drolma had taken me to visit Palden Lhamo's temple back in her village, where her brother-in-law, a lay tantric Buddhist ritualist, presided over offerings laid before the deity's huge and snarling, shrouded statue. It was Drolma who had brought Palden Lhamo to her new household in Jima village when she remarried, placing her small printed image in the altar room of the brand new carved wood and adobe home that she and Lobzang had built in the early 2000s on his family's land.

Prayers invoking the Warrior Queen invariably describe her agency in terms of transcendence and pervasiveness, an all-seeing enlightened mind that can take any form it chooses and can carry out the four types of tantric action (pacification, increase, expanding power, subjugation) on behalf of all sentient beings. But the prayers also attempt to capture the Protector's attention for the goals of particular times and places. Supplicants seek guidance in identifying manifestations of her mysterious presence at key junctures (a vision in her famous Life-Lake, the sound of her voice, a dream apparition, the position of a divination stick, an unusual weather event, or the timely misfortune of an enemy army). For me in 2008, however, I was shocked to find that Palden Lhamo acted through Drolma, and I was the medium of potential enemies. And it all revolved around the most mundane and ubiquitous object that works to facilitate, indeed constitute, Tibetan social interactions and exchanges from the most routine to the most ceremonial: the silk offering scarf (Tib. kha btags).

Drolma and I had known each other for some twenty years, and I had watched her fortunes rise with her new marriage to Lobzang, who was ascending the ranks of an important local state bureaucracy and helped Drolma get a new, higher-status job in the same field. As residents of Longwu town, the new couple, it seemed, had greatly benefited from post-Mao market reforms.

Like other salaried officials, Drolma and Lobzang were enjoying the "comfortably well-off" middle-class lifestyle that had been touted anew under Open the West slogans. I had visited and stayed briefly in the blended households' beautiful new village home before. But when I returned to Rebgong in the fall of 2007, Drolma insisted for the first time that, because her household would move down to their heated apartment in town for the winter, my family and I should move into their village home. All went well until the New Year festival season in January, when women frenetically clean and ritually purify their homes in preparation for the lunar New Year and the obligatory hosting of friends and relatives. Drolma had told us indignant stories of the foreign woman Christian missionary to whom, following the lead of other Jima households in the early 2000s, Drolma had briefly rented the new house, only to unceremoniously evict her for being offensively "dirty" (Tib. *rtsog gi*). With that in mind, my husband Cain and I had made a show of helping with the New Year's cleaning, washing down the kitchen with microscopic care. But ultimately, as the village home became the ritual center of Lobzang and Drolma's hosting duties, we had to move to a hotel for the festival season, leaving our belongings in their guest room.

In early March, I had just seen my family off to the States and I was happy to stave off the loneliness back ensconced in Drolma's well-appointed guest room, returning to my rounds of visits to rural villages upriver as I was pulled ever deeper into acting as a donor or, to translate the Tibetan term more literally, a "gift master'" (Tib. *sbyin bdag*) in Tibetan primary school repair projects. Then, one evening after dinner Drolma told me as we sat next to the coal stove that she had something to talk to me about. She said that her dreams the night before had been disturbingly strange and bad. This had compelled her to take the highly unusual step of returning to her natal village to consult with her brother-in-law at the Palden Lhamo temple. To my astonishment, she said he immediately asked, "Has any offering cloth been brought into your house from other places?" That is when she remembered having seen stored in my guest room the great pile of scarves and brocade cloth that had been gifted to me by upriver village elders and school officials. Drolma said it was very bad for the household to have those scarves and cloth here, and I should remove them, wrap them up and store them at my foreign friend the English teacher's apartment: "That's why I had such a bad night," she concluded.

I was floored, and mystified. Drolma explained, as if to a child,

"You know villages have divine supporters, right? It's really bad to bring offering cloth from other villages and especially their deities' temples into a household. Palden Lhamo is really fierce [Tib. *btsan po*]. She's easily angered and offended by such things—especially if it came from a non-Buddhist [Bon] village like the one downriver! It's not good to have all those offering scarves from who knows where. They're not clean, and buying new ones only costs a few *yuan*. See how you have these right next to the wall where her image is [in the altar room]? She's easily angered! Take them to your foreign friend Dan's house, for him it won't be a problem."

"Why not?"

"Because he is not part of a village, he has no divine supporter and no faith in one."

I realized suddenly that she meant for me to do this right then and there, at dusk when streets had emptied and households had retired for the night. Lobzang approved as I shamefacedly packed up the cloth and made my way to the door: "Oh yes," he said knowingly, "you can't bring those things into the house, they would harm me. But if they came from Jima's own protector deity Shachong's temple, then that would be alright."

It is hard to convey in retrospect the depth of my bewilderment and sense of shame as I walked through the empty streets alone that night, the offending bundle under my arm. Outside the packed-earth and brick court-yard walls of village households, walking past the walls of Rongbo Gonpa, the Geluk sect Buddhist monastery and Rebgong's erstwhile ruling seat, I felt acutely my otherness as a Western foreigner, how easily recognizable that status was (tall, white woman dressed in jeans and parka). But now I felt marked off differently, like somehow the noxious influence of the alien scarves had permeated my very being. I wondered whether it was even okay to hand the scarves off to Dan. He was not home, it turned out, so I left the bundle on his doorstep with a note. He never did get them—someone stole them before he returned. Later that night, I wrote:

> How mortifying to bring pollution into a household. I had never been in that position before because I had always had my own apartment when I lived in Amdo. This has changed my whole view of offering scarves; my head is reeling from it—I had been treating them as inert objects, exchanged between humans as tokens of a certain relationship (or aspiration for one) at the time of the gift, and easily recycled for convenience. How many others had I unknowingly polluted? I always buy new from now on!

Of course, as an anthropologist I had long ago accepted the French sociologist Marcel Mauss's famous argument that objects of exchange are never inherently inert, but can carry with them the agencies and energies of their givers and places of origin, demanding unstated future returns.

The absolutely alienable and thus purely generous gift, Mauss claimed, is only a polite "social deceit" (1950, 3). But practical knowledge is another thing entirely. To really grasp the implications of this threatening vulnerability of the person to others' intentions, times, and spaces in twenty-first century Rebgong, I realized, I had to place the dangers of the gift master at the center of my account of the bewildering and traumatic events of that year.

The stakes could not have been higher. Just two weeks before Palden Lhamo ejected me from Drolma's house, during the lunar New Year festivities in February, Rebgong had seen the first of what would in subsequent weeks become the unprecedented series of Tibetan unrest and demonstrations that spread across the Tibetan regions of the PRC. But on the night of Drolma's bad dreams (March 3), that future of widespread unrest was still only an anxious prognostication. In fact, on the very morning after her bad night, just hours before Drolma brought up the problem of the scarves, she had told me in urgent tones that Lobzang had called from Qinghai's capital city of Xining where he was attending provincial government meetings. She said Lobzang had told her to warn me that the political situation was very tense because officials feared Tibetan unrest on March 10, the annual commemoration day among diaspora Tibetans of the Tibetan uprising against CCP rule in Lhasa in 1959 and the Dalai Lama's flight into exile in India.

Given the now-global profile of Tibet and the efforts in 2007–8 of Tibet activists abroad to organize demonstrations under the spotlight of the impending Olympics, officials in Tibetan regions especially were under pressure not to let any unrest besmirch the Chinese state and people's great coming-out party of the summer games. Indeed, in the annual Chinese-language New Year "appreciation letter" that the party committee of the Tongren County Public Security Bureau (PSB) circulated internally to its police, their collaborators, and families, the county PSB leaders put it this way:

> 2008 is the first year for implementing the spirit of the 17th National Party Congress, and it is also the year for celebrating and welcoming the Beijing Olympics. All police should make holding fast to scientific development and ensuring "a peaceful Olympics" your leading goals . . . and you should make every effort to protect state security and social stability while promoting social harmony and improving the people's livelihood. (January 30, 2008)

The very evening before Drolma relayed to me Lobzang's warnings, we had seen on prefecture news the first official speech addressing the February unrest in Rebgong. Immediately after that event, prefecture officials had downplayed it, adopting a conciliatory tone and quickly releasing all laymen and monks who had been detained that night. Now, as March 10 approached, the tone had changed. The grim-faced Tibetan prefecture deputy head, reading in slow, accented Chinese, assured viewers that those "criminal troublemakers" would be punished and urged all state bureaus and Rongbo Monastery to teach the law and strengthen discipline, intoning multiple times the central state's mantra, "protect social stability" (Ch. *baohu shehui wending*). Thus Lobzang warned me, using the same word for "fierce" (or "violent") in Tibetan that Drolma a few hours later would use to describe Palden Lhamo's protective action, that policy for now would be "fiercely implemented" (Tib. *btsan po byed rgyu red*). Drolma relayed his instructions:

> Since you registered with the prefecture branch of the National Security Bureau [Ch. Anquanju] in Rebgong, they will watch you carefully. Under such conditions, people will talk about you. Tibetans can have very black minds [Tib. *sems nag po*]. Unlike Chinese, they will talk bad about each other. If something happened, it would be very bad for both you and Lobzang. So temporarily, you should not invite anyone to the house, and you should not say you are living here. There are a lot of foreigners living in Jima village, but we are the only ones who are living *together*.

Those political hazards of my presence in the household could not but have been folded into the polluted offering scarves I had brought into the house, replete with the unknown motives of other givers. For Drolma, the wrath of Palden Lhamo, manifest in her ill-favored dreams, was a clarifying presence in the face of great anxiety and impending fear. But on those cold streets that March night, my own miserable confusion about my hosts' sense of proper exchange and fortune was in large part because I could not discern the relevant actions and scales of the persons and powers involved, especially as the unclear agency of the state seemed to increasingly impinge on the household. I was left with nothing but questions that ultimately reshaped my entire project: what processes create, configure, and valorize a person's presence and powers in particular situations? What kinds of beings are such quasi-invisible or partially absent entities as Palden Lhamo, or "the State" for that matter? As parties to consequential exchange, where, and *when*, are they located? How do human beings like me, Drolma, or

Lobzang perceive, mediate, or host the presence of powerful or dangerous others? With what goals and consequences? Who, in the end, gets to be the gift master?

Dialogic Ethnography and the Politics of Presence

I begin my story not with the usual arc of the ethnographic narrative, the arrival of the intrepid outsider and the establishment of rapport with a "local community." I begin instead with an account of my expulsion from Drolma's household and my re-othering as a potential threat to its fortunes. I do this not just to question older anthropological claims, like the dreams of many Western liberals, of an easy intimacy that enables one to understand and speak for or even as "the native." I also start with a focus on the shifting terms of my own otherness to highlight in this story the specificities of Tibetan notions of personhood and power in post-Mao Rebgong, as well as the particular stakes of that Olympic year. In fact, under the state of emergency in Rebgong, I spent the bulk of my time outside of Tibetan village houses, in what the French historian Michel Foucault would call the "other-spaces" (heterotopias) of urban apartments, hotels, state offices, and school grounds.[1]

Palden Lhamo was not the only superagent of my expulsion. So too was the state. Just five days after I removed the polluted offering scarves, army (PLA) and national guard (PAP) troops from outside the province arrived in the valley, took up residence in hotels and the town stadium, and began daily patrols. And just ten days later, after Drolma and I had sat aghast before CCTV footage of young Tibetans rioting on Lhasa streets ("but why are they attacking the Bank of China?" she asked. "It's China's, right?" I said. Soft gasp: "*No way,*" she breathed), I quietly left town and returned to Xining. Drolma told me later, with great relief, that it had been very good that I had left their house when I did. That very afternoon (March 16), I learned, young Rongbo Monastery monks, chafing under restrictions on assemblies and offering rituals in place since the New Year's unrest, held their own demonstration, an incense offering for the long life of the Dalai Lama on the mountainside behind the monastery, and then they marched toward the local state buildings in town. That move brought a swift military response and the monastery was surrounded by troops, police cars, and trucks. Checkpoints were set up on the new highway to stop all tourist traffic and all foreign visitors were told to leave.

When I finally returned to Rebgong, with some stealth, three weeks later, I never again stayed in Drolma's house. Instead, I rented an apartment in an old concrete-block state "work unit" building in town and worked from there as I concentrated on helping with several primary school renovation projects upriver, retreating inside when the political climate tightened so as not to be a liability to any of the Tibetans I worked with. In fact, I have not set foot in Drolma's house, or for that matter, in any Jima villagers' houses, since 2008. When I returned to Rebgong to visit in the summers of 2011 and 2013, the otherness of foreigners had been further complicated by the escalation of state-local tensions in a tragic (and unprecedented) series of self-immolation-by-fire protests by Tibetans in regions to the south (in 2011) and in Rebgong itself (at least 15 people in 2012). By 2016 a total of 146 Tibetans across the plateau had burned themselves in public (see the epilogue). In 2011 and 2013, development in Rebgong thus also meant the consolidation of a state surveillance media infrastructure in the valley, including new cameras on town buildings and in schools, sporadic campaigns to eliminate Tibetan residents' access to foreign media, and routine cell phone tapping of local state workers like Drolma. My meetings and meals with Drolma were thus very discreet, in restaurants as far from both state buildings and Jima village as she could manage. And yet, under such cover, Drolma would, as before, confide to me her darkest fears and anxieties in the face of this new situation—for her I had become the most hazardous of intimate others.

As I said in the introduction, such fraught self-other relationships under state repression highlight the ethical dilemmas inherent to ethnography. Here, I emphasize that a dialogic approach to ethnography can provide analytic tools for understanding the often subtle communicative conditions for mutual learning and (mis)understanding, even when political limits seem so stark. Proponents of dialogic ethnography see fieldwork as first and foremost a "negotiated intersubjective relationship between researchers and their interlocutors" (Nevins 2015, 72). That ongoing negotiation, they argue, can produce unpredictable (or "emergent") and hybrid forms of knowledge. And the complex give and take of such encounters challenges ethnographers' claims to either simple objective distance or pure subjective intimacy with their interlocutors. Theorists have located the methodological roots of this approach to ethnography in the anthropology of Franz Boas and his students in the early twentieth-century United States. The Boasians' focus on the historical dynamics and structural complexities of culture and language produced some of the earliest experiments with ethnographic writing (especially by women).[2]

But Eleanor Nevins and others point out that, even after the trenchant postcolonial and feminist critiques in the 1960s and 1970s of Western ethnographers' claims to scientific superiority, the full implications of a dialogic ethnography for anthropological knowledge-making were not widely taken up by scholars. That is, the messiness of relational ambivalence and hierarchy, and the partial and fragmented nature of mutual understanding, are often more evident in the fieldwork experience than in anthropologists' scholarly writings.[3] Just as Tedlock and Mannheim argued in their seminal volume on the "dialogic emergence of culture" (1995, 18), the conditions for objectivity and thus ethnographic authority still (increasingly?) pressure anthropologists to return "home" and present their findings as written monologues. In the writing, ethnographers must thereby minimize the voices of their interlocutors that might contend with their own, editing out the ways in which others' interests, theories, and objectifications frame and shape what was learned. If anthropologists are to avoid gross objectifications of interlocutors as distant or "primitive" others, we would have to ask, along with Johannes Fabian (1983), what does it really mean to "share time" with others in ethnographic practice?

As one kind of response to these conundrums, in the late 1990s and into the 2000s, anthropology saw a revived focus in some circles in the United States and Europe on the very fact of difference in human experience. Ironically, some argued that such an emphasis on absolute otherness among human groups is a way for researchers to circumvent the dominating influence of Western languages and ways of knowing, and thereby to achieve a more intimate (or even direct) knowledge of non-Western others. This was the argument, drawing on the influential work of the Brazilian anthropologist Eduardo Viveiros de Castro, that different peoples do not just inhabit the same natural or material world yet perceive it differently (through varying *epistemologies*, what older anthropologists used to call "culture"). Instead, they actually experience different ways of being (through varying *ontologies*) and thus inhabit and perceive different worlds entirely.[4]

I take this "multiple ontologies" approach to be a particularly provocative attempt to carry forward a decades-old alternative (or for some, post-) humanism in anthropology, a position that also grounds claims for the importance of dialogic ethnography: the critique of the universal, autonomous human subject or knower. Anthropology's critical humanism has long challenged modern Western presumptions about the foundational unity and rationality of both individual selves and nation-states.[5] In these most recent debates, proponents of "multiple ontologies" focus on communities' different, embodied ways of being, relating and perceiving (e.g., through multiple senses, not just speech or thought). That attention to embodied experience has pushed anthropologists to consider more carefully the materiality of bodies and things (versus thinking of culture or language as just a set of abstract ideas or beliefs). But the focus on distinct ways of being also challenged anthropologists to take seriously people's experiences of their mutually constituting relationships with nonhuman others (including animals and material objects, but also invisible and divine beings)—"dialogic" relations in this light would extend beyond just human interlocutors. As such, the multiple ontologies approach gels with wider efforts among anthropologists to rethink the nature of human kinship and personhood, not as fixed structures of geneological relations, but as open-ended processes of recognizing persons and negotiating different forms of relatedness.[6] Theorists in this line of thought also draw on certain anthropologists' arguments from the early 1990s about the potentially active influence of material things and environments on human experience, to locate persons not in bounded human "societies," but in complex "assemblages" of persons, bodies, things, institutions, and technologies.[7]

I take inspiration from these debates in this book, but rather than start from the ramparts of radically incommensurate "multiple worlds" to avoid objectifying others, my dialogic approach to ethnography derives from a different set of premises, drawn from the insights of linguistic anthropology. Linguistic anthropologists insist on the fundamentally reciprocal nature of intimacy and otherness, of subjectivity and objectivity, as the very grounds for all communication and copresence across cultural and linguistic differences.[8] Influenced by the work of the Russian literary theorist Mikhail Bakhtin, these theorists argue that multivoiced dialogue, and not the monologue of individual speakers or writers, is the primary form of all human discourse (Tedlock and Mannheim 1995, 1). "Dialogue" for Bakhtin and his circle was not just one-on-one conversation, but a variety of implied relationships among multiple social positions or voices that people invoke in specific interactions, even when they are talking to themselves (ibid., 7). As Tedlock and Mannheim put it, the methodological challenge of such a dialogic approach for ethnographers is to locate language and culture, their very conditions of existence, in neither individuals nor collectivities but in the "interstices between people" (ibid., 8). And that in turn would require more subtle tools for analyzing how communicative practice in fact produces human social relations, the ontological grounds—and politics—of social presence.

This dynamism of mutual interpretation and recognition among differently positioned persons entails a different starting point for ethnographers than more mainstream linguistic or anthropological approaches. Unlike some recent theorists then, I begin with the linguistic anthropological premise that language and other sign (or "semiotic") systems (e.g., gesture, music, image, dance) are not abstract symbolic structures that individual speakers or monolithic governments rigidly impose on the world. Instead, I take sign systems like language to be open-ended practices. This entails locating all communication not in the seemingly elegant certainties of codes, but in the messy vicissitudes of interactions. Humans' communicative practices in fact consist in simultaneously embodied and reflexive processes of interpretation. Interlocutors engage in those processes through a variety of media on multiple scales. They thereby, in a performative way, work to constitute and make real the very world that is represented.[9]

As Rupert Stasch put it, semiotic representation turns out to be a "deeply figurational process of making present" (2012, 11). That is, people can communicate with each other only by engaging in the reciprocal activity of invoking previously learned concepts or types (e.g., a concept of "Tibet") and manifesting them as particular instances or tokens through speech, gesture, or other media (e.g., a particular map of "Tibet" presented on a website). "A given form or act in human life," argues Stasch, "is not self-contained, self-same, or natural, but semiotic. The form or act is defined and supported by concepts, understandings, and other forms or acts in other layers of life, and it defines and supports them in turn" (ibid.). From this angle, humans can have no direct, unmediated access to objects or to others' worlds. Thus, especially in cross-cultural or cross-linguistic encounters, there is no escape from the complex patterns (and politics) of sign systems that mediate and figure our relationships with each other and with various nonhumans. The demeaning and dominating objectification of others does not derive from the semiotic nature of communication per se, but from the political, economic, and historical specificities of particular encounters (Keane 2003, 239).

A dialogic approach to ethnography thus highlights the profound methodological challenges of taking personhood as an unfolding politics of presence, a potentially contested process of mutual recognition in which the ethnographer is always already caught up. In other words, this perspective is a paradigm shift, one that has been articulated for more than a century but has remained marginal in the academy: we have to reorient ourselves to the empirical reality that all knowledge and experience, including of ourselves, is socially, or better, dialogically produced. Persons are materialized as figures or personas, that is, as types of presences (or absences) only contingently, as they are addressed or invoked in specific situations.[10] Thus the locus and nature of intention, agency, efficacy, and responsibility are emergent or empirically open, embedded and reshaped in times and spaces as interlocutors sense, confirm, or deny them over time. My analyses of the politics of presence among Tibetans in Rebgong in the coming chapters thus do not start from an abstract Tibetan "ontology" or "cosmology," but from embodied "scenes of encounter" (Keane 1997a), in which humans and nonhumans perceive, deny, or evaluate each others' personas and degrees of relatedness.

The inherent vulnerability or openness of persons to others' perspectives and interests helps explain why the implications of dialogic ethnography have not been fully taken up by anthropologists. To really "share time" with others in Fabian's sense, to treat them as fully commensurate (or "coeval") subjects, the ethnographer would have to portray herself as only a partial and learning persona, engaged in perhaps particularly fraught or awkward cross-cultural or cross-linguistic encounters. As Tedlock and Mannheim (1995, 15) put it, the ethnographer can be "drafted into a native hermeneutic that was already at work before [she] got there." In the chapters to come, I thus write my ethnographic self into the story, not to make my own struggles the primary object of inquiry, but to better portray and analyze the possibilities for understanding Rebgong Tibetans' experiences of state-led development agendas. "The very possibility of dealing squarely with the Other," argued the anthropologist Kevin Dwyer, "is tied to the capacity to put the self at stake" (1979, 205). Hence in my analyses of development encounters I try to grasp the specific ideologies or ethics of personhood, embodied presence, and authority that Tibetans across the valley invoked to communicate with and reframe interlocutors like me. Ordinary Tibetans, it turns out, reflect, evaluate, and theorize just as much as monks, state officials, or anthropologists, in both conscious and unconscious ways.

This of course is a very tall order. Such a dialogic approach to the subtle politics of communication and social presence in Rebgong was only possible for me after years learning to speak and read (Amdo dialect) Tibetan as well as Chinese. Further, linguistic anthropologists insist that dialogic ethnography is not about an exclusive focus on the microscale interactions of some constant here-and-now. Instead, they argue, all communication is necessarily replete with invocations of past and future contexts that extend far beyond moments of encounter (see below). Thus throughout the book I connect the various scenes of encounter I explore to broader-scale discourses and practices, drawing on my multisited fieldwork in Rebgong. During the Olympic year, I worked across local state (mostly county bureaus) and village contexts, and in my analyses, I drew on multimedia sources, such as Chinese and Tibetan-language state propaganda and policy in TV, radio, and printed forms, recorded interactions and performances, and built environments, as well as Tibetan language ritual texts, historiography, and videos produced in Rebgong.

Still, the utopic goals of a truly dialogic ethnography, which would include collaborative research and writing, and the open sharing of analyses with interlocutors, were impossible to achieve under martial law.[11] As Tedlock and Mannheim noted, dialogue in the Bakhtinian sense is "the universal object of suppression" by authoritarian elites (1995, 20). Indeed, Rebgong residents' experiences of disorienting and terrifying social fragmentation and public silence after the military crackdown were the direct result of state officials' efforts to suppress the inherent multivocality of citizens there, leaving room only for the monologic voice of the state. Thus here I can only claim a very partial knowledge of what was in many ways a highly opaque situation (and not just for me): As I mentioned in the introduction, after the military crackdown I had only limited access to people. I most regret that when my precarious political status in the valley narrowed my official roles to donor and collaborator in school repair projects (managed almost exclusively by Tibetan men), I spent relatively little time with Tibetan women. My account here thus does not pretend to be the comprehensive coverage of a single society in the manner of traditional ethnographies. Instead the development encounters I explore are presented as thematically linked episodes in multiple communities, reflecting the relative fragmentation and caprice of life under the pressures of state repression.

Furthermore, even as I became more familiar with the Rebgong region's Amdo Tibetan "farmer's dialect" (Tib. *rong skad*), I still often struggled to understand what was going on and who I was supposed to be to my interlocutors in situ. Though occasionally I was accompanied by Tibetan assistants or friends, I preferred to interact with Rebgong residents on my own (mostly in Amdo Tibetan, but Chinese loanwords and code switches were common). Sometimes I conducted formal, open-ended interviews and sometimes I just participated in encounters on my interlocutors' terms, recording many of those interactions with people's permission.[12] It proved particularly important for me to interact with Tibetans on my own after the military crackdown, since villagers especially would say they felt safer talking with me privately, and I did not want to jeopardize the political status of my Tibetan colleagues. My primary data in the book thus consist of verbatim discourse and performance, in the hundreds of hours of audio and video recording I did between 2005–13, backed up by the copious field notes I wrote and the media I collected. In the moment, however, my ethnographic self did not always grasp the dialogic nuances of our encounters. "Fieldwork" was thus not just confined to 2007–8, but the work unfolded for years afterward in a long-term process of collaborative reflection, translation, and mutual learning with Tibetan colleagues both in and outside of the PRC.[13]

Negotiating Time and Space in the Frontier Zone: Chronotopes and Personhood

In the chapters to follow, my own narrative voice joins and is shaped by those of Tibetans who have been narrating themselves for centuries as residents of fortunate communities in Rebgong. For example, in popular praise poems for homelands (Tib. *sa bstod*, lit., "place eulogy"), Rebgong is not a marginal frontier or a borderland but a powerful and auspicious Buddhist center and abode, an important part of a larger, mountainous Tibetan homeland that stretches up and across the high plateau to western Tibet. Consider this voice-over praise poem that opened a 2003 Tibetan-language video on Rebgong's Rongbo Monastery:

> This abode is located within the six mountain ranges of Kham and
>   Amdo, which is at the lowest reaches of the three great regions of
>   this snow mountain realm, along with the four districts of Central
>   Tibet in the middle reaches, and in the highest, the three districts
>   of Ngari [western Tibet].
>
> This homeland is the town of Amdo Rebgong from which springs all
>   knowledge.
> Here, in the heavens, the mandala of clouds, sun, and moon is
>   perfectly complete,
> and on the earth, the signs of fortune and the essence of vitality
>   gather and swirl together.
>
> From this town of Rebgong, the lands up- and downriver are filled
>   with the three kinds of ten-thousand-household communities,
>   making one hundred thousand large, middle and small households
>   of farmers and pastoralists.
>
> In this homeland, in the upper reaches, the peaks of the snow
>   mountains reach the sky,
> In the middle reaches, the turquoise leaves of the forests grow
>   densely together,
> In the lower reaches, grassy meadows offer up all kinds of fragrant
>   flowers, and
> golden threshing grounds are scattered around the land.
>
> The fields of excellent harvests of the six grains boundlessly fill the
>   land, thus this abode
> is called Rebgong the Golden Realm.

> The navel of this region, which possesses all ten of the good qualities,
>   is the foothills of the great rocky mountain abode of the divine
>   king Shachong.

> On the nearby bank of the blue Guchu River, which possesses
>   the eight qualities of good water as it gurgles down the
>   valley,
> Where at the waist of the valley which resembles a *vajra*,[14] the
>   great Dharma Protector Mahakala conquered enemies in all
>   directions,
> Rongbo Monastery, the great bliss of Rongbo, the Sanctuary of the
>   Dharma Wheel, was founded.

After the death of Mao and the beginning of the new CCP regime's "reform and opening up" policies, Tibetans' reverent praise for places as divinely favored homelands took on new and spectacular importance. In this, Rebgong and Rongbo Monastery were praised anew as privileged centers for the revival of Tibetan Buddhism. But Tibetans I knew also proudly placed the region at the heart of an unprecedented post-Mao movement to promote Tibetan-language secular education. By the early 2000s, Tibetan intellectuals and community

FIGURE 4.   Rongbo Monastery and Shartshang Palace (right), summer 2007. Author's photo.

leaders participated in a flourishing Tibetan-language regional history movement that plied the boundaries between Buddhist and secular interests in development. To me in the mid-2000s it seemed that every village, lineage group, and monastic or temple organization was competing to produce printed or filmed portrayals like the video for Rongbo Monastery above, praising both their historical origins and their contemporary conditions.

As I moved through communities as an ethnographer and fellow learner, my own persona, history, and future could not but be shaped and emplaced by those efforts. Far from being passive objects of my research, my Tibetan interlocutors attempted to draw me into their own projects, times, and places. I thus organized the chapters of the book to travel with me across multiple communities up the Guchu River valley. In chapter 2, I start from Jima, a wealthy, urbanizing village and key historical patron of Rongbo Monastery in what is now Longwu town, the lowland county and prefecture seat. In chapters 3 and 4, I move up to two rival villages in the so-called Upper Narrows of the Guchu Valley. Chapter 5 and the epilogue, in which I return to the lowland town to explore the politics of state-led development, death, and mourning after the crackdown, serve as a pivot to the widest scale implications of the 2008 unrest. As the state of emergency intensifies over the course of the book, I give readers a sense of how the terms of my own otherness shifted in a variety of development encounters. By that I mean the ambivalent ways in which Tibetans I knew addressed and figured me as, on one hand, a relatively close interlocutor (a welcome guest or friend with a Tibetan name, a proudly displayed quasi-daughter, a patron gift master) or, on the other hand, as a relatively estranged one: a nameless "non-Tibetan woman" (Tib. *rgya mo*), or the unspeakably hazardous magnet of misfortune and state scrutiny I became in Drolma's household.

To help shed further light on the dialogic approach to personhood that I'm drawing from linguistic anthropology, and to better focus on the narrative idioms and communicative strategies specific to development encounters in the twenty-first century Sino-Tibetan frontier zone, I look to Bakhtin's notion of the "chronotope" in his famous analysis of different genres of Russian novels (1981). Literally meaning "timespace," the single term *chronotope* reminds us that, far from being transcendent or abstract categories, people experience time and space as inseparably linked in the reciprocal dynamics of communication. Similarly to the way we say in English that someone's chosen word or phrase is "weighty," "loaded," or "carries baggage," chronotopes for Bakhtin are familiar idioms or figures that carry with them remembered times, spaces, and their associated values. Such idioms, when invoked in encounters, thereby work to shape and organize listeners' or readers' embodied experience of a narrative situation. To illustrate this, Jan Blommaert (2015, 111) uses the example of the common idiom "once upon a time," which invites listeners into a particular, magical relationship to past places. But key chronotopes can also be emblematic places, persons, things, or media forms that, through histories of usage, become ideologically "loaded" in this way. That is, like the post-9/11 era use of figures like "Wall Street," or "Main Street," or "W" (for George Bush Jr.) in U.S. popular discourse, chronotopes call to mind certain value positions on past (and future) times and places.

Blommaert glosses the term *chronotope* as "invokable tropic chunks of history" (112). In this book, I substitute for Bakhtin's awkward neologism the perhaps more familiar terminology of "historical idiom," or "historically loaded phrase (or object)." The point, according to Blommaert (112), is that the often immediate recognizability of such idioms brings the discourses of other times and places into present encounters and can thereby lend a sense of truth, importance, and relevance to a person's discourse. Bakhtin however emphasizes that invocations of historical idioms can bring to people's claims of realness a kind of palpable or embodied presence. When a narrator invokes a particularly loaded chronotope, says Bakhtin, "time . . . thickens, [it] takes on flesh, becomes artistically visible; likewise space becomes charged and responsive to the movements of time, plot and history" (Bakhtin 1981, 84). From this angle, we can appreciate how dialogic practice does not necessarily produce interactional chaos but often highly patterned or ritualized events. That is, people's invocations of historically recognizable idioms and objects work to organize the parameters and goals of encounters.

However, as the shifting terms of my own otherness in Rebgong illustrate, interlocutors do not always share the same timespace terms, not even during one encounter. I thus follow Blommaert in considering the dynamics of chronotopes in conjunction with a notion of "scale," or to use Anna Tsing's more dynamic phrase, "scale-making" (2000). I take scale-making to be a culturally specific process in which interlocutors work to situate communication, persons, and projects in time and space. Here, scale does not just mean relative size or extent. Instead, like a musical scale or a scale for weighing things, scale-making efforts can invoke graduated ranges of values, which in turn form interpretive systems for creating aesthetic experiences and measuring and evaluating persons and things. Thus, like the way development workers in Rebgong could assess the relative "quality" of persons and places in terms of perceived degrees of urbanity, the politics of presence take shape as interlocutors attempt to claim shared or varying timespace grounds and scopes for communication and exchange—what it means, where-when, to be a sane human, or a sentient interlocutor, or a generous patron, or a proper citizen.[15] The dynamics of chronotope use can thus demonstrate how interlocutors work to contextualize any present situation in wider scales of social relations, in potentially competing ways. For example, in my analyses, I do not treat Tibetan villages as fixed and bounded locales but as always partially shifting and translocal jurisdictions invoked by situated people.

Ultimately then, I analyze development encounters in Rebgong as particularly consequential and often awkward attempts at recruiting others into competing timespace scales; development projects are first and foremost scale-making efforts. From this angle, as observers of any encounter we could not just project onto it our own assumptions about the relevant times and spaces of the action. We could not just presume the historically loaded idioms of "local/primitive/static versus global/modern/progressive" so prevalent in international development circles. And we could not take for granted the modernist timespace scales of citizenship in the PRC: the state administrative hierarchy Chinese Communist Party leaders inherited from the Soviets that starts "up" at the urban center, Beijing, and moves "down" through province, prefecture, county, and township or town to the "grassroots" rural village. By contrast, my Tibetan interlocutors could attempt to recruit visitors to inhabit very different sensibilities of translocal landscapes and jurisdictions, which were linked to alternative communal histories.

This makes clearer why people's choices of genre and media in particular encounters are so significant: as chronotopes organizing participation, the formal features of genres of communication (histories of use, styles of delivery, material channels, forms of metricality, relative prestige, appropriate occasions and performers or users, reproducibility, transportability) all carry recognizable presumptions about the moral presence of both speaker/performers and addressees. Thus, for example, the praise poem for Rongbo Monastery I cited above was not presented in that written, English-language form at all. Instead, the male narrator's voice was layered with aural and visual cues linked to that genre and its associated timespaces: the serious, monkish tone, the high register of the Amdo Tibetan and common Buddhist-inflected tropes of the words, the soundless footage of the video beginning with the palace of the monastery's main incarnate lama, Shartshang, and layered under a soundtrack of monastic horns and the synthesized flute music that lent the whole an air of ethereal mystery. As such, the Tibetan language video, copied on the newly available, cheaply produced and widely disseminated VCD format, worked to scale up the monastery's relevance and value. It addressed a larger contemporary Tibetan public extending beyond Rebgong in the early 2000s, framing that public as potential lay devotees, and claiming the moral presence of Rongbo Monastery (versus, perhaps, other revived monasteries) as their unwavering "field of merit," the appropriate object of their faithful offerings.

Finally, to really grasp how interlocutors can experience idioms, performance genres, and objects as "loaded" with ideologically charged times and spaces, we need a few more semiotic tools. To get at these dynamics, we can't rely exclusively on the old Western notion of a "symbol," a sign or emblem that arbitrarily stands for some otherwise unrelated, abstract concept, thereby seeming to impose itself between a person and "reality." Instead, linguistic anthropologists draw on the philosopher Charles Sanders Peirce (1839–1914) to point out the different ways that signs can make aspects of worlds present, real, and palpable to people. They note that interlocutors do not just posit arbitrarily symbolic relations between emblems and their referents (like a cloth flag to represent a nation-state). But in practice, people also posit intimate relations of likeness ("iconicity") between emblems and referents (like the red and gold colors of the PRC flag making the leadership role of the CCP analogous to traditional Chinese colors for fortune and wealth). Further, and perhaps most importantly, people can experience emblems and referents not as separate things, but as inextricably touching or mutually causing each other ("indexicality"), as in the way a cloth flag can feel so loaded with the awesome or sacred weight of the nation-state that people can be moved to violence if the flag is seen to be defiled.

From this angle then, all media of communication are inherently indexical in practice. That is, people experience media as caused by or embedded in both present encounters and the distant timespaces through which they circulate. But the politics of presence unfold as the media of communication slip the grasp of their users, their formal features available for others' perceptions of their likenesses or causal efficacies—the meaning and efficacy of any media form is never fixed in stone.[16]

The Battle for Fortune: Tibetans and the Dangers of Hospitality

This then brings me back to the significance—and precarious slipperiness— of the Tibetan offering scarf, that ubiquitous medium of exchange and communication among Tibetans that I encountered in Drolma's house that tumultuous spring of 2008. Informed by this approach to communicative practice, I came to see the offering scarf as a particularly pivotal chronotope for Tibetans. It is a material medium loaded with the timespaces of a larger, indeed all-encompassing genre of exchange that has great implications for a politics of presence specific to post-Mao Rebgong, one that includes the active presence of invisible and divine others. As I discovered in Drolma's house, the offering scarf is a key component of a Tibetan ideology of materiality and ethical exchange. Hung around ordinary human recipients' necks at gatherings and celebrations, offered up to the hands of monks and lamas, lovingly placed on altars or around Buddha images, the "silk" scarf (usually white but also in the familiar primary colors that came to be icons of forms of tantric Buddhist action) has no widespread utilitarian function except as a medium of exchange among humans and their divine interlocutors—a gift, supposedly, of generous intention alone.

Indeed the Tibetan term *khatak* (*kha*, "mouth," but indexically, "speech," "face," or even "relational person"; and *btags*, "bind to," "put on [the body]," but iconically, "mark," "designate," "name") links the gift object to the pragmatics of its use. The offering scarf is a key aid or material means for publicly binding (or claiming to bind) the outward signs of speech or bodily affect to the inner sincerity of generous minds or hearts (Tib. *sems* or *khog*). As a chronotope then, the Tibetan offering scarf locates communication and exchange and the possibilities for past and future relationships in the embodied and situational stakes of hospitality encounters. That is, recalling the American sociologist Erving Goffman (1981), offering scarves are key "framing devices," across multiple contexts and scales, for publicly recognizing interlocutors as bound in relationships between gift masters or hosts and their recipients or guests. As the Amdo Tibetan scholar Dorje Tshering put it, "For Tibetans, offering scarves . . . are the indispensible practices of everyday life" (CGDJTR 2006, 83).

During the late 1990s to early 2000s, Tibetan scholars like Dorje Tshering, however, were debating anew the meaning and function of offering scarves among Tibetans both in and outside of the PRC.[17] Amidst the dilemmas of modernity in exile in India or of state-led capitalism in the PRC, those Tibetan scholars emphasized the iconic quality of offering scarves above all else, making the white scarf, with its analogies to unstained purity and the snow mountains of the plateau, an icon of both Buddhist compassion and the Tibetan people or nation writ large. Their Tibetan-language analyses were thus ultimately didactic; they addressed a larger contemporary Tibetan public and touted the offering scarf as a symbol or model (Tib. *mtshon pa*) of ideally altruistic reciprocity at the heart of Tibetan (Buddhist) social relations.

Ironically, just two days before my polluting scarves were ejected from Drolma's household in 2008, I watched on the Qinghai Tibetan-language TV channel as the young scholar Tsepten Dorje read his didactic paper on offering scarves. With great passion, he pointed out the ubiquity of Tibetan scarves in Qinghai with the "development of the market," (Tib. *tshong gi 'phel rgyas*) and their cheap, factory-made availability. And he decried their indiscriminate and excessive use, such that givers did not know the ancient traditions or value of them, making no distinctions between times, places, or appropriate recipients (men, women, young, or old). Alternating between an older term for all Tibetans (Tib. *ezo'i Bod*, we Tibetans) and the newer PRC term for ethnic groups or nationalities (Tib. *mi rigs*, Ch. *minzu*), he counseled Tibetans that such "extremely mixed up and confused" (Tib. *nyog drag song*) giving of scarves had led to the weakening of their value and of Tibetan culture in general. Voicing tradition by citing well-known proverbs, Tsepten Dorje ended by urging Tibetans to give scarves judiciously and correctly, thereby protecting and promoting Tibetan culture:

> Doing our best to preserve and respect all Tibetan traditions means that from today on, we *neeeever* stop "holding to, protecting and promoting" them. So the correct way to give scarves is as they say, to give "rarely and properly; with respect and affection." Then when we have a need to offer them to someone, no matter what the context, it will be done in the appropriate *place* and *time*.

Such urgent nostalgia in the face of a perceived cultural crisis invoked widespread narratives I heard from Tibetans across communities in the 2000s, in part voicing older Buddhist historical idioms of the inevitable degeneration of the Dharma (Buddhist teachings) in the world of humans. People of all stripes would lament to me Tibetans' rapid moral decline with their increasing integration into transregional markets and the rising threat of their assimilation to "Chinese" (Tib. *rgya*) ways. By 2007, it seemed, the great optimism and sense of collective purpose of the 1980s-1990s post-Mao cultural and Buddhist revival years had faded. Intellectuals and monks I spoke to tended instead to repurpose historically charged Maoist idioms of great "waves" or "floods" of inchoate collective forces impinging on them from the east and outside, in many cases evaluating fellow Tibetans' behavior in the process much more harshly than that of Chinese.

One of my most influential interlocutors was my teacher Lumoji, an erudite retired professor born in the 1950s. For her, reading regional Tibetan history was an occasion to school me on her moral critique of recent changes. Like Tsepten Dorje, she vehemently criticized Tibetans' indiscriminate and hedonistic interactions with others in what she saw as the corrupt government and business world of quasi-secret patronage and nepotism (Ch. *guanxi*), but she reserved special vitriol for monks' and incarnate lamas' frequent fundraising travels to Chinese regions. "Now it is the era of money," she said, "people's minds have been obscured and polluted by exposure to external influences!" For Lumoji, the rapid pace of market reform and the

rise of an increasingly wealthy urban middle class in town had made people
less human. Citing Buddhist doctrine in the high tones of written Tibetan,
she insisted that "'the definition of a human is one who can use speech
clearly and comprehend its meaning'! But these people who only care about
food, drink, and clothing are no better than dumb animals, like pigs!'"

Yet from the perspective on the politics of presence I am developing here,
we would have to consider the relevant times and spaces of all exchange and
communication as inherently contested. Confusion and mixing are not just
the consequences of post-Mao state-led capitalism. A focus on hospitality as
an overarching genre of moral encounter and exchange in the Sino-Tibetan
frontier zone allows us instead to hone in on the changing nature and stakes
of interlocutors' claims to be the gift master or host, and of the varying
temporal and spatial grounds of authority and agency they thereby evoke. In
this, I am inspired by a recent collection of essays (Candea and da Col 2012),
in which a group of anthropologists advocate rethinking Mauss's famous
arguments about the actually ambiguous and power-laden charge of gifts
through ethnographic accounts of the inherent risks of host-guest intimacy,
what Andrew Shryock referred to as "the existential danger at the heart of
social life" (2012, S21).

At stake is nothing less than competing scales of sovereignty or jurisdictions of authority over exchange, as hosts and guests, opaque to each others'
true motives and origins, assess their relative intimacy and estrangement and
attempt to control the terms and benefits of the hosts' generosity. Guests can
be menacing enemies as much as friends or relatives. The source of the ambiguity and threat, these theorists argue, is the "scalar slipperiness" of hospitality (Herzfeld 2012, S211)—just who is the host or gift master (and for what
jurisdiction, in what times and spaces) is not necessarily clear. Hospitality
relations are rarely between individual persons; instead they are often para-
digmatically about household units or residences, but in one particularly pervasive form of scale-making, the terms of ritualized hosting can be extended
to more macroscale collectivities instantiated in different types of historically
charged environments, like villages, deities' realms, and even nation-states
(as in China "hosting" the Olympic Games).

This is not just a spatial politics, of hosts embedded in static spaces defending preconstituted boundaries by controlling potentially menacing visitors.
Instead as we have seen, contested temporalities are crucially at issue. This
is particularly important in Tibetan communities. In recent decades Tibetan
studies in the West have seen a trend away from the abstract textualism of
Geluk scholasticism, the dominant mode of inquiry in Tibetan Buddhist
(monastic) thought.[18] Instead, scholars have noted Tibetans' widespread

adherence, across an eclectic array of Buddhist and non-Buddhist, lay or monastic communities, to what Bakhtin (1981, 94) would call "chance-time." This is the notion that human persons and collectivities, their actions and aspirations, are vulnerable to, indeed constituted by the uncontrollable interventions of nonhuman forces and beings. As we have seen with the Dharma Protector Palden Lhamo, Tibetans' ritual practices from the everyday to the elite address, indeed demand, the presence of divine and demonic beings as interlocutors, and their notions of materiality, efficacy, and power have been profoundly shaped by those efforts.[19]

My focus on the politics of presence in post-Mao Rebgong in the coming chapters thus requires me to take divine or invisible beings seriously as consequential interlocutors for Tibetans. This is particularly important because their presence has been at the heart of state-local tensions since especially the advent of the PRC in 1949, when the CCP's modernist timespace idioms of citizenship made atheism official. As Dipesh Chakrabarty put it (2000, 16), challenging the secular logic of such modernist notions of the political requires us to "take gods and spirits to be existentially coeval with the human." I thus reject the state's legal categories of (normal) "religion" (Ch. zongjiao) versus (folk) "superstition" (Ch. mixin), categories which are now, I found, often habitually evoked by Tibetan Buddhist monks and lamas to dismiss the practices of some laity. My approach instead allows us to consider all relations with invisible others as commensurate processes within a single analytic horizon.

Indeed, Tibetan themselves often place nonhuman beings in a shared universe of causes and effects. Most Tibetans identify as Buddhists, and thus presume all types of sentient beings (conventionally classified in a hierarchy of six types of "goers"; only humans can achieve Buddhist enlightenment) to be related in their common subjection to the moral-karmic forces of past deeds. All beings thus move through a potentially infinite time frame of pleasure and suffering (Skt. samsara) that extends beyond lifetimes and does not guarantee a future human rebirth (as a consequence of im/moral action, a person's status as type of goer can morph across, and even within lifetimes). Yet, as we saw in Lumoji's vehement critiques, types of sentient beings like humans, mundane deities, and animals do not necessarily share common forms of sentience, perception, and communication.

In practice, these human-nonhuman relations do not play out as a single cosmology or ontology. Instead, in Rebgong, shared presumptions about ritualized hospitality as risky events of encounter with others bring multiple, contested beings, times, and spaces into dialogue, across lay, monastic, sectarian, and even as we will see, state and secular development contexts.[20]

In this book then, I draw on the recent work of Giovanni da Col and others to place hospitality events at the core of what I am calling "battles for fortune" among Tibetans encountering state-led development projects in Rebgong. da Col argues that all Tibetan persons, vitalities, and fortunes must be understood within the event-time of *tendrel*, or "happenstance" (Tib. *rten 'brel*, lit., "depend-connect").[21] In part jibing with linguistic anthropological notions of the dialogic emergence of meaning and efficacy, the term *tendrel* was elaborated on in Tibetan Buddhist discourses as the abstract concept of "dependent arising," the notion that all aspects of social worlds are the reciprocal outcomes of physical-mental-ethical relations. In ordinary usage, however, it means the perceivable signs or omens (classic indexes) of an auspicious event, eruptions in the present of absent causes and intentions. da Col emphasizes that in Tibetan practices aimed at discerning the causes of misfortune and ensuring fortune and prosperity, ordinary humans are themselves contingent nexuses of both self and other "continua" (Tib. *rgyud*), including their karmic and geneological inheritances (self continua), but also their life forces (Tib. *bla*) and relations with forms of impersonal fortune and luck (other continua). The ground of all long-term human fortune and prosperity, however, is *yang* (Tib. *g'yang*), the very essence of vitality and productivity, which Tibetans conceptualize as a kind of naturally swirling force gathered to vitalize key social units (households, villages, monastic polities), like that mentioned in the praise poem for Rongbo Monastery above. However, the status of such a shifting nexus of forces and entities at any moment is always obscure to ordinary humans, and fortune, vitality, and luck can weaken, leak, or be captured by others.

The key historical idiom of emplacement for Tibetans then, one that links materiality with efficacious human and divine action, is the container (Tib. *snod*). As da Col (2012a, 2012b) points out, Tibetans take bodies and material objects, as well as important social groups and their associated territories and environments, to be different kinds of containers of fortune.[22] Notions of abiding, residing, and staying (e.g., Tib. *gnas pa, stod pa*) are thus the main acts of being emplaced (as in the terms for "abode," *gnas*, in the praise poem above). And notions of filling, completing, and increasing (e.g., Tib. *bkang ba, sgrub pa, rgyas pa, 'phel ba*) are the main acts of ensuring fortune (as in the praise poem's reference to Rongbo Monastery's territory as "filled" with patron households and fertile fields). As hosts for particular scales of containers, Tibetans must in a sense turn outward, seeking extrinsic sources of sovereign vitality and fortune through translocal (or transdimensional) reciprocal exchanges, thereby staving off the efforts of others (consciously or not) to steal or absorb them. Containing fortune in this light thus entails residents' ritualized work at constant extension and relocalization. Hospitality encounters, as battles for fortune, are, to paraphrase da Col, not about protecting a static inside, but they are efforts to capture or incorporate and control an always capricious and shifting outside (2012a, 77).

Just like human visitors, deities (such as regional mountain lords, or *zhidak*) and demons are potentially menacing strangers and guests. Their presence and forms of communication are difficult to discern, their motives and even loyalties obscure. As particularly important nonhuman persons (Tib. *mi ma yin*), mundane protector deities are themselves partible, their various emanations and emissaries distribute their agency across multiple contexts and supporting objects. Human hosts then use the hospitality of ritual feasts (both invoked verbally and materialized in offerings) to attempt to capture them or render them present as interlocutors and guests, obligating them to help fight for, shore up, or expand human fortunes on behalf of particular container-abodes. Mountain deities, for example, do not just protect land per se, but specific human-divine territories tamed by lamas and shaped by the topography of watersheds (see chapter 2). Crucially though, the pragmatics of hospitality in invocation rituals—offering feasts as media of communication and commensuration across human-divine divides—are the source of great ambivalence in Buddhist monastic discourses.

This was readily apparent in my conversations with monk friends in Rebgong. Akhu Tenzin, in our discussion about the relationship between offerings (Tib. *mchod pa*, with connotations of feasting) on one hand and on the other their targets, the material or embodied "supports" (Tib. *rten*) or containers of a Buddha's body, speech, or mind, laughed as he explained that offerings work to create a pleasant environment to make a Buddha or lama happy and contented. But he was quick to qualify that pleasure as in fact a gift *back* to the donor: "If I offer him something that pleases his mind, that in turn makes *me* happy!" Akhu Konchok, however, was less equivocal. When I suggested that basic Buddhist offering rituals echoed host-guest hospitality relations found in many lay rituals, he baldly denied any connection: "Unlike mountain deities," he insisted, "you don't *have* to give something to a Buddha for the Buddha to give back. You just need to have a sincere and pure mental intention!" In fact, in the Sino-Tibetan frontier zone, Buddhas, and their human representatives or incarnations, monk assemblies and lamas, are interlocutors positioned in the transcendent perspective of enlightenment. As persons apart, who altruistically mediate human-divine relations on behalf of sentient beings, they are supposed to be the ultimate gift masters. They are ideally "reference points," "targets," or "fields" for offerings, never mere recipients.

Yet recent theorists have pointed out the ambivalence of the Buddhist claim to the pure, and thus unreciprocated gift (Skt. *dana*), in that rewards for compassionate giving were traditionally touted as advancing even the Bodhisattva's progress on the path to enlightenment.[23] Buddhist monastics worked to resolve that ambivalence by inserting themselves into exchanges as essential purveyors of the highest value: the nebulous, time-delayed, and transferable reward of karmic merit. But the gift of merit also accrues more merit for the giver, and laity still expected worldly services in exchange for their offerings.

In Tibetan forms of tantric Buddhism, it is the charismatic figure of the trulku, or incarnate lama, who trumped the tensions of the gift. As incarnations of Buddhas and Bodhisattvas usually seated at monasteries, trulkus' intrinsic blessing power (Tib. *byin rlabs*), their capacity to pivot between mundane and absolute timespaces and automatically gather and enhance vital forces like *yang*, derives from their transcendent position in tantric rituals. In them, trulkus perceive and command the service of (lit., "tame"; Tib. *'dul ba*) legions of place-based protector deities on behalf of human patrons. In effect, such claims to timespace transcendence are efforts to appropriate and scale up the pragmatics of hospitality relations, resolving their inherent risks by permanently positioning the lama as the model gift master and protector (Tib. *skyabs mgon*), the compassionate host of particular "offering abodes" (Tib. *mchod gnas*) for human and divine patrons (Tib. *yon bdag*). These are the familiar "patron-preceptor" (Tib. *yon mchod*) or "lama-lay leader" (Tib. *bla ma dpon po*) relations through which Buddhism, in tantric battles for fortune that could pit competing sects and their lay or non-Tibetan military allies against each other, "tamed" the Tibetan-Mongolian plateau.[24]

Indeed, outsiders' histories of the settlement of Rebgong and the founding of Rongbo Monastery (in 1342) describe it as a centuries-long process of strategic political alliances among competing lay leaders of patron communities (the various *nangso*, or regional chiefs, and the *qianhu*, or thousand-household heads, holders of imperial seals), Buddhist lamas (founders of temples and monasteries and their ruling trulku lineages), and especially Mongol lords in the waning years of the Mongol Yuan dynasty (1279–1368) and beyond.[25] Such accounts, particularly those produced in the PRC, tend to depict Rebgong's Tibetan elites as primarily mediums and agents of imperial powers to the north and east. But regional Buddhist histories narrate Rebgong's origins as a gradual taming and purification process, through a series of arrivals of "sacred strangers" (da Col 2012b, 83) from the south and west.[26] Those are the tantric Buddhist yogins who, following in the footsteps of the great Indian lama Padmasambhava, traveled to Rebgong after the fall of the

Tibetan empire (ninth and tenth centuries). Able to perceive the subtle tantric landscapes inaccessible to ordinary humans, they opened the Rebgong region to human fortunes by taming indigenous deities "under their feet" and, eventually, gathering and containing *yang* in blessed "treasure vases" (Tib. *gter bum*) that they buried along with Buddhist texts in key locales to create empowered Buddhist abodes.[27]

That last is how Gendun Palzang, the Rongbo monk who wrote a popular Tibetan-language history of Rebgong (2007, 11), portrayed the tantric conquest of the region in the mid-thirteenth century by a Sakya sect yogin. According to legend, the yogin had been sent there by his own lama, who was in turn informed by divine foresight received in dreams, to claim it for their lineage. When Rongbo Monastery was founded by the Sakya yogin's grandson almost a century later, it was as a Sakya seat. Hence the praise poem for the monastery I cited above alludes to that battle for fortune in the work of a particular form of Mahakala (Gurgon), the Dharma Protector brought to Rebgong by the Sakya lamas. Gurgon remained Rongbo's main Dharma Protector, even after the monastery's jurisdiction expanded to claim eighteen branch monasteries and "18 outer and 12 inner districts or tribes" of Tibetans and non-Tibetans as lay patrons and Rebgong residents, and gradually shifted to Geluk sect leadership under the Shartshang trulkus in the seventeenth century.[28] To this day Gurgon resides in Rongbo's main protector deity temple, off limits to all but the initiated.

Gendun Palzang, however, ultimately narrates Rebgong's Buddhist history as a process of progressive, and then precipitous moral decline, one that follows the topography from the high and pure mountain hermitages first established by tantric yogins to the increasing adulteration, mixing and human intrigues, and violence of the settled valleys (see chapter 4). This was apparently already an issue by the seventeenth century: he cites a long letter from the first Shartshang lama's uncle and teacher, charging him with bringing Geluk-style discipline and meritorious exchange to his newly founded monastic college at Rongbo: "Some monks will study only a little and then go off to Lhasa to do business . . . or taking on the mantle of great lamas, they will run around like dogs providing ritual services in lowland Amdo villages! They'll gather up food offerings and horde them for themselves! . . . I urge you especially not to get involved in and defiled by the donated property of Rongbo's lay patrons" (2007, 48).[29] Reading this with my teacher Lumoji in 2008, it was clear that this historically loaded idiom of Buddhist decline resonated strongly with her experience of Rebgong under Chinese Communist rule. Indeed she organized her commentary around the same, world-shattering date as did Gendun Palzang in his book: 1958, the year CCP leaders brought in PLA troops to crack down on lay Tibetan resistance to collectivization efforts, and for the first time publicly attacked Buddhist institutions as exploitative, counterrevolutionary forces, imprisoning and defrocking monks and lamas, and implementing "Democratic Reforms" that subjected Tibetans to public class labeling and collectivized all farmers and pastoralists into massive communes.[30] For Rebgong Tibetans, just as throughout Amdo, 1958, not 1949, was the time when they were truly incorporated into the new PRC nation-state. Gendun Palzang (2007, 23) refers to that time, along with the violence and chaos of the Cultural Revolution (1966–76), in which most of the Buddhist monasteries and other temples left standing after 1958 were destroyed in Maoist antitradition campaigns, as an "end-of-an-eon, world-destroying tornado" (Tib. *dus mtha'i rlung 'tshab*).

Gendun Palzang's list of incarnate lama lineages with residences at Rongbo Monastery then prompted Lumoji to list how each lama had fared after 1958 (this one was imprisoned, that one died in a labor camp, and the worst: those who married and lived as laymen, or those whose incarnations, like the current eighth Shartshang at Rongbo, were discovered among former elites' or wealthy relatives' lineages).[31] As we saw above, for Lumoji, as for many of my Tibetan intellectual friends, the great rupture of the Maoist years had profound moral consequences for Tibetans, opening the way to the post-Mao capitalist allure of the individualistic or cunning pursuit of fame and money. In that context, if humans were becoming more like dumb animals, incarnate lamas were becoming more like ordinary people.

In her view, most incarnate lamas no longer commanded the tantric blessing power and moral authority to wage authentic battles for fortune: "I have such doubts!" she insisted one day. "I see those people who come to worship lamas and wonder if it's all just appearances. *I* go instead to the Dharma Protectors like Palden Lhamo—she is *real*; she has no need for such corrupt relationships [Ch. *guanxi*]!" Unlike today's corrupted lamas and, she was careful to add, in contrast to mundane, unenlightened deities like mountain gods, Palden Lhamo's omniscient presence could still penetrate mind and body: "When I go to make offerings, I close my eyes when I come to the Dharma Protectors, otherwise they will enter my dreams!" Indeed, Lumoji made much to me of her close relationship with Palden Lhamo, narrating multiple stories of Lhamo's divine aid that she herself had personally experienced and thus "could not *but* accept as fact!" (Ch. *bu de bu chengren*). And she took me with her to the temple for Lhamo that was dedicated to the protection of the monastery's main "college,"[32] the very one the first Shartshang had founded over three centuries ago, where the great fanged statue, carefully shrouded, towered above a large photograph of the current Dalai Lama.

That temple was in fact one of the most frequented by lay worshippers in the revived monastery, so much so that during the 2008 New Year, the courtyard was literally knee-deep in the refuse of offerings, and the monastic college's council, now pressured by state religion policy to move away from traditional "compulsory" alms collection in patron villages and to encourage "voluntary" offerings from individuals instead,[33] was moved to put up posters there advertising to pilgrims the services of its monk assembly for completing their confession and appeasement rituals for Palden Lhamo:

> Please come to the College's Lhamo temple and, with single-minded conviction and faithful, pure intention, offer riches for ritual services to our great and virtuous monk assembly.

Whenever I went there with her, Lumoji's offerings were not "riches," but they were among the most correct and complete of all. For her, only the highest-quality medicinal incense, barley flour and sweets would do for the burnt offering to Palden Lhamo in the temple's courtyard ovens, and, I noticed, she was one of the very few to regularly place a white silk scarf on top of the fragrant, smoking mound.

The Dilemmas of Post-Mao Development: Hopes Surge Like Summer Seas

> This abode is the fertile soil from which religious art flourishes and
>   expands.
> This homeland is the great treasure house where folk culture, like
>   butter, takes shape.
> This land is the heavenly realm in which political, economic, and
>   cultural hopes surge like summer seas.
>
> Rebgong!
>
> This golden country, which has surged forth, driven by dreams
>   on the mountains and plains of the high plateau,
> Is the ancestral land of culture.
>
> Rebgong!
>   —Praise poem for Rebgong, performed on Qinghai Tibetan radio, summer 2005

We are now in a better position to understand the mounting dangers of hospitality for Rebgong Tibetans amidst the great optimism of Tibetan cultural revival under post-Mao reforms (1980s–1990s) and then the Great Open the West campaign (2000–). In this light, the increasingly problematic scalar slipperiness of my polluting scarves in Drolma's household in 2008 comes clearer. I take Tibetan offering scarves in Rebgong to be primary media for invoking and attempting to bind gifts to hosts' generous intentions. As such, they exemplify the ongoing battle for fortune as an interpretive process in which interlocutors, recalling Peirce, must strive for indexicality. By that I mean, as in Lumoji's earnest insistence to me that her experience was indisputable empirical evidence of Palden Lhamo's presence, the ways people strive to naturalize the character and presence of certain media forms by sensing them as contiguous with—literally touched or caused by—nonhuman forces or beings, and thus as inextricably loaded with the values and intentions of particular past and future times and spaces.

We could see the offering scarf as the quintessential index for Tibetans in this light. In fact, the particular material and semiotic features of offering silk, what Keane (2014) would call its "affordances," are explicitly linked in Tibetan Buddhist ritual tradition to the physical compulsions of sensory desire. As a soft, silky, warmly encompassing object, the scarf is supposed to afford givers with a kind of captivating, mediated touch above all (another term for offering scarf, after all, is *lha reg*; lit., "deity-touch"). Indeed it is perhaps the most ubiquitously exchanged and displayed of the "five offerings of sensory enjoyment" (Tib. *'dod yon sna lnga*). Those are the five icons of the most compelling attractions to each of the five senses of higher beings, including deities and (peaceful) Buddhas (sight/mirror, sound/musical instrument, smell/incense, taste/fruit, touch/scarf). The emblematic scarf-mediated touches, however, the ones that establish the highest values and the highest quality of scarves, are those between devotees and lamas or Buddhas. Recalling the ambivalences of Buddhist hospitality, in those generic encounters, especially when the lama immediately returns the scarf to the donor, the scarf becomes imbued with (an index of) the lama's blessing-power.

Thus, as we saw in recent Tibetan scholars' portrayals of the scarf, the exchange value or captivating quality of all offering scarves derives from those baptismal moments of supposedly pure Buddhist faith and compassion. This dynamic is nicely illustrated in the proverb I heard used several times in Rebgong as a polite preamble for a humble yet well-intentioned gift:

dge btags chung rung lha rdzas yin.

(My [meritorious] scarf is small but it is a divine gift.)

In encounters between ordinary humans, scarf givers in this way attempt to imbue or empower their scarves with not only their own good intentions, but also with those of their avatars or protectors, deities, Buddhas, or lamas, thereby striving to guarantee that sincere or authentic quality will trump quantity in the exchange over time. As material media then, offering scarves are supposed to carry those sincere hopes (Tib. *re ba*) beyond the encounter and into the future, compelling recipients to act accordingly. In other words, capturing scarf recipients (emplacing them in specific timespaces or jurisdictions) as particular kinds of guests is about discovering and staging encounters as auspicious events (*rten 'brel*), which then reframe both the pasts and the futures of host-guest intimacy and obligation.

As media of exchange fixed with the giver's hopes, scarves are not supposed to be fungible, that is, quantifiable and thus interchangeable or transferable to other purposes. Recalling Tsepten Dorje's critique, ideally, scarves are not a currency, a form of "social capital"; instead they are in a way tokens of antimoney, attempts to claim and contain fortune for particular persons and timespaces alone. But as we've seen, like other material media in the frontier zone (including money), scarves circulate across precariously porous bodies, persons, habitats, and territories, and as such they materialize the inherent risks of communication and exchange—mixing on others' terms.

In the coming chapters, I argue that the stakes of these hospitality relations in post-Mao Rebgong were reconfigured and heightened in specific ways. And this process played out as the battle for fortune was pushed underground or offstage, under the state-sanctioned revival of Tibetan "culture" and "autonomous" governance, now touted as reaching for the glorious national futures of "market-based economic development" (Ch. *shichang jingji fazhan*). I thus refer to these new terms for hospitality relations as the post-Mao silent pact: an unspoken agreement between ordinary Tibetans and state officials not to publicly acknowledge the timespace grounds and political economic implications of specifically Tibetan sources of authority and fortune. And this even as programs to develop and commodify the region and its resources were pushed through under the auspices of distant Chinese CCP leaders.

Throughout my time in Rebgong, it became clear that for Tibetans, the embodiment and key chronotope of this fraught post-Mao revival period was the figure of the tenth Panchen Lama (1938–89). Second in stature only to the Dalai Lama, the tenth incarnation of the Panchen Lama had inherited centuries of tensions between them as pressures on Tibetans from the Manchu Qing and then Chinese nationalist regimes intensified into the twentieth century.[34] Across Rebgong in the early 2000s, his presence was still ubiquitous in secular as well as Buddhist contexts, in the form of material "supports" (*rten*): images, photos, body amulets, commemorative thrones and relics, sometimes appearing with the exiled fourteenth Dalai Lama, and sometimes, by proxy, marking his absence.[35] Born on the cusp of the CCP-led revolution, the tenth Panchen as a young adult was always a hybrid and somewhat problematic persona, exploring like his senior the Dalai Lama the promise of competing modernities for Tibetans' futures. But when the Dalai Lama fled to exile in 1959, he remained and eventually spoke out against "leftist" atrocities in Tibetan regions, ending up publicly beaten and humiliated, and then imprisoned for some fourteen years.[36] When he was finally released in 1978, he returned to lay life and married, taking on official appointments as deputy head of the TAR's People's Congress and as head of the National Buddhist Association.

But when he triumphantly returned to Amdo in the fall of 1980 and toured Rebgong, it was the tenth Panchen's transcendent status as an incarnate lama, his intrinsic blessing power to purify and recapture time and space as again auspicious, that for many residents grounded his authority to speak for Tibetans' modern futures. By the time of his visit, Rongbo Monastery's main assembly hall had already been cleared out, purified and reopened by returned lamas and monks and their lay patrons. But to this day, as intellectuals struggle with a mounting sense of moral decline, Rebgong Tibetans I knew credited the tenth Panchen above all, using the phrase he himself reportedly coined, with the era-changing "redissemination," (or the second historical restoration) of the Buddha Dharma in Tibet (Tib. *yang dar*).[37] Indeed, in 1980 party officials in Rebgong were taken aback when the Panchen Lama, dressed in the ceremonial robes of a layman, drew tens of thousands of worshippers straining to touch him, and if they couldn't do so directly, throwing the few offering scarves they had toward his body or the jeep in which he rode. The Rebgong Tibetan scholar Chong Thargyal described his arrival in the upriver Tibetan communities this way:

> On that auspicious day, the sky above Tsekok County was clear as a turquoise mirror, as if swept free of any layers of black clouds. As the fragrant clouds of offering smoke filled the air, soon they seemed to transform the sky into a natural manifestation of pale blue, dancing offering goddesses. On either side of the main road leading from Rebgong to Tsekok, multitudes of lay and monastic, men and women, Tibetan, Mongol and Hor faithful waited, straining their eyes eastward, hoping, like the starving for food or the thirsty for water, that the supreme Precious One would quickly arrive. [As soon as the Panchen Lama appeared] many of the faithful began to weep involuntarily, and clasping their hands together to their hearts in the shape of a lotus, holding fast to the wheel of the Dharma, they cried out prayers and requests for his protection. (1994, 107)[38]

In his subsequent series of meetings and lectures, the tenth Panchen emphasized his role as disseminator of the new CCP regime's enlightened nationality policies, assuring Rebgong residents that party leaders now recognized the violence and destruction of the 1950s and 1960s as "leftist mistakes," and advocating a return to Tibetan autonomous governance and cultural-linguistic revival in especially Tibetan-language secular schools. But, according to Chong Thargyal (1994, 110), he had particularly pointed words for lamas, monks, and lay tantric ritualists, urging them to stave off leftist critiques of "religion" and help laity discern the truth of Buddhist compassionate efficacy:

> Here I offer you my own hopes: In your practices, follow the teachings of the Buddha. If you do that, the Masses will have faith and the State will support you. That means it is not allowed to lie, to take enjoyments from the masses, to trick them by divining and telling them you see demons when you don't, that demons are coming to harm them when they aren't, and thereby prescribe ritual obligations for them. Nor is it allowed to look at the quantity of the masses' offerings and serve only those who offer a lot, while ignoring those who offer a little. We especially have to remember that all those Leftists say "Oh you religionists are boastful liars. You exploit the Masses!"

Importantly, the Panchen Lama's speech here reveals a voice and a persona in part at odds with the intrinsic blessing power his own devotees attributed to his body and presence. His final direct citation of "Leftists'" criticisms, and his use of historically loaded Maoist figures of personhood like "the Masses" (Tib. *mi dmangs*), reframe the whole passage as an indirect citation of the modernist skepticism of divine presence and of lamas' tantric prowess that was so violently performed in the 1960s' struggle sessions he himself had endured. As he and others had discovered, Maoist rituals of citizenship demanded a new politics of presence and exchange that denied the agency of divine beings and fetishized human collective labor as national liberation under the paternal figure of Mao: "We had to talk to Mao's portraits every day," said Lumoji, incredulously describing the 1960s Cultural Revolution era. "We had to tell him what work we would do that day, or else we would get in trouble."

Indeed, given the ongoing hegemony of CCP rule, and especially Chinese state control of land ownership (see chapters 2 and 4), the tenth Panchen's hopes for Tibetans' post-Mao future in Rebgong were not for a simple revival of the worldly battle for fortune that had placed Rongbo Monastery and its trulkus at the center of a tantric Buddhist polity.[39] Instead, he was advocating *yang dar* (Buddhist restoration) as a new era of Tibetan Buddhist counterdevelopment embedded in modern timespaces. Taking up older lay-monastic tensions over the indexical nature of invisible beings (e.g., as palpable presence versus as abstract symbols for philosophical principles), in this quote the tenth Panchen attempts to domesticate the battle for fortune by closing off (or narrowing) tantric practitioners' roles as mediators of human-nonhuman exchanges.[40] Thus, in line with post-Mao state religion policy that banned treating offerings as compulsory payments and confined monastic authority to monk assemblies alone, he implies that Buddhist officiants should more properly provide the relatively abstract and universalized compassion of the field of merit. In this way, he defers Buddhist efficacy to the accumulation of merit for patrons' future lives, clearing the way for their this-worldly participation in modernizing development on Tibetan terms.

The Panchen Lama's efforts here to achieve a hybrid vision for a Tibetan future illustrate that the politics of presence under post-Mao development pressures in Rebgong did not play out as the revival of a single, indigenous Tibetan ontology countering the equally discrete ontologies of powerful outsiders. In fact, recalling Bakhtin, the competing timespace terms of agency, efficacy, and responsibility were inherently dialogic and thus translocal as interlocutors invoked them in high-stakes hospitality encounters. Grounding my analyses in the dynamics of such encounters thus allows me to treat such seemingly modern phenomena as the nation-state and the capitalist market as inextricably caught up in the politics of presence in the Sino-Tibetan frontier zone. From this perspective, neither "state" nor "market" denotes a discrete, rational order. Instead those entities emerge in partial and contested ways in practice as people invoke them through figures of moralized, even sanctified persons, times, and spaces or, by contrast, in the form of powerfully pervasive abstractions or absences (see chapters 2 and 5). This is not then a story of Tibetans' recourse to a monolithic and reactionary "occult economy" as a way to cope with the pressures of state-led development. Rather, my analyses reveal multiple forms of occult exchange, where privileged access to prowess, networks, and knowledge benefit particular human (and nonhuman) agents.[41]

For example, after I was "captured" as a donor and fundraiser for Tibetan village primary school repair projects in Rebgong, I found in the communicative practices of my various interlocutors not multiple, discrete ontologies but dialogic engagements with others' historical idioms of fortune and development. And that ongoing dialogue played out more generally as layered intersections, implied contrasts, and partial compatibilities among three major historical idioms for translocal scales of moral (and amoral) exchange and fortune: (1) lama-lay leader alliances (Tib. *bla ma dpon po*) claimed within a morally refigured (either romanticized or vilified) battle for fortune that included invisible beings grounded in Tibetan ancestral homelands; (2) Maoist socialism (Ch. *shehuizhuyi*) evoked as ideally fair redistribution of resources among national citizens, presided over by the hierarchically administered modern state and the benevolent figure of Mao based in Beijing; and, especially since the 2000s Open the West campaign, (3) authoritarian capitalism (officially dubbed "New Socialism," Ch. *xin shehuizhuyi*) touted as the display of entrepreneurial prowess in new urban spaces, regulated by an abstract, technocratic state based in Beijing, but authorized by the natural (and thus amoral), cosmopolitan force of "the market" (Ch. *shichang*).

Importantly, up until 2008, these complex dialogues in post-Mao Rebgong were enabled by the shared performative premises of the silent pact: interlocutors' willingness to keep any major tensions and incompatibilities offstage. Consider for example the Qinghai radio praise poem for Rebgong at the beginning of this section, and contrast that with the video's praise poem for Rongbo Monastery in the previous section. Performed in 2005 by a pair of male and female announcers who alternated lines until they delivered the praiseful epithet "Rebgong!" together, the radio program's poem voices the peak optimism of the yang dar years, where political participation and economic development do not arrive from the outside but flow out and forward from an autonomous Tibetan homeland and culture. Like the poem for the monastery, this one avoids any direct reference to the state (not to mention Maoist violence). But unlike the other poem, this one also excises any mention of Buddhism or even of the monastery.

Yet both the state and Buddhism are there dialogically. The poem secularizes, localizes, and commodifies Tibetan "culture" as emanating from the "folk," echoing local state development rhetoric that, since 2000, has emphasized ethnic tourism and Buddhist art as Rebgong's primary export commodities. Meanwhile, note how the poem takes up familiar Tibetan Buddhist idioms of fortune and replaces divine agency with that of humans (here, "religious art," "folk culture" and "political, economic, and cultural hopes" stand in for the Dharma and its divine protectors). That substitution, along with the same aural tropes of breathy, echoey speech and mystical flute music, lend the palpable authenticity of otherworldly Buddhism to the poem's claims for a utopic, yet secular Tibetan Rebgong.

By 2005, as hundreds of NGO workers (both foreign and domestic) arrived promoting development "projects" in Rebgong, such artfully implied dialogue under the silent pact was facilitated in development encounters by the conceits of hospitality spectacles. Just as in Tibetan residents' first encounters with Chinese PLA and CCP officials, in such events, which were often recorded and displayed in print and television media, Tibetan offering scarves figured prominently as signs of mutual recognition and welcome. But post-Mao development encounters, where the origins, motives, and powers of givers and recipients were particularly opaque and unequal, provided quintessential occasions in which offering scarves could be interpreted in opposing ways. Most of the time, the indexical ambiguity remains unspoken, enabling the public diplomacy of photo ops even as the timespace terms of the hospitality are increasingly dictated by powerful others. Consider for example encounters in which CCP officials claimed to replace lamas as supreme gift masters, so that scarves presented to them were supposed to indicate Tibetan submission and nationalist gratitude; or when donors and development workers took scarves bestowed on them by rural Tibetans to simply indicate villagers' intentioned agreement to contracts they could not even read; or most egregiously in recent years, when scarf-holding Tibetans (most often women) are recruited to pose as backdrops to corporate contract signings in which they played no part.

This, finally, brings us back to the story of my expulsion from Drolma's household in 2008, and the shifting terms of my otherness as a foreigner, a donor, and a guest. I came to see that event as in fact emblematic of a

FIGURE 5. Foreign donors covered with offering scarves at Tibetan school opening, Rebgong 2005. Tongren County Education Bureau brochure.

watershed moment in the frontier zone battle for fortune: the end of the Decade of the Foreigner. As we saw in the introduction, through the first twenty-five years of post-Mao reforms, (the yang dar years in Rebgong), state-led economic development privileged opening markets and promoting consumer lifestyles back east in China. Thus, into the 1990s, as the moral authority of monks and lamas waned,[42] and local state budgets relied heavily on meager central subsidies, a wide variety of foreign donors (including Buddhist devotees and Christian missionaries) stepped into the role of powerful strangers bringing fortune to be captured and channeled in Amdo Tibetan communities. In those encounters, often bereft of a common language, Tibetans' public gifts of offering scarves could suggest to foreigners their felicitous encompassment, cultural participation, and aid to Tibetans in the face of Chinese domination or state violence and neglect.

But by 2008, the national spectacle of the Olympics loomed large in Rebgong, heightening for many the gap between rhetoric and reality—the yang dar years, it seems, were over. At such moments, the possibility for scarf-mediated diplomacy begins to break down, the indexical ambiguities become too much to bear. And for the first time since the 1950s, the silent pact threatened to dissolve. In early March 2008, my scarves (and myself as a guest) became polluting to Drolma's household, requiring divine intervention, at the unexpected, misfortunate clash of multiple historical idioms of exchange in which collective pasts and especially future fortunes were vitally at stake. And in that first week of March, all of them demanded Drolma and Lobzang's simultaneous loyalty and attention, pushing the precarious balance they had struck all along to a breaking point.

By then, the Olympic campaign had put on display the great wealth and luxurious lifestyles of those who had benefitted most from capitalist reforms, yet as prominent local state officials (Tib. *las byed pa*) Drolma and Lobzang also had to demonstrate their willingness to work hard and fairly for the masses (Tib. *dmangs tshogs*). In Rebgong, in fact, the old socialist state apparatus was still the only career for Tibetans trained in the Tibetan-medium education system that the tenth Panchen had so strongly advocated. And March was when the duties of the annual work calendar of the couple's bureaucracy peaked, to which was added new duties, after the February unrest, to disseminate national policies on "social stability." Finally, the impending peril of the March 10 Tibetan Uprising Day happened to coincide exactly with the imminent terror of the college entrance exams, for which their son was preparing. Now that jobs were no longer assigned to graduates, Tibetan students were finding it difficult to compete for scarce access to higher education and salaried careers—all urban households' futures in the valley now depended on that success.

In effect then, the happenstance of March 2008 brought the historically loaded idioms of the central state's Olympic campaign into direct confrontation with those of the exiled Tibetan government's National Uprising Day over the precarious future fortunes of Drolma and Lobzang's household: a tale of national victory and linear progress, "blooming" and arrival (as in the Olympic anthem "We are Ready") versus the commemoration of a terrible defeat and a repressed past, the culmination of moral degeneration and decline. The close juxtaposition of such collective moral claims under deepening state scrutiny in Rebgong threw into relief the submerged question of the motives and origins of competing gift masters—to which jurisdictions did they actually play host? As everyone sought hidden advantage in quantified terms (cash), were the qualitative reciprocities that enabled generosity—and, crucially, the generation and containment of vital fortune (*yang*)—even possible?

And I, the foreign donor and guest recipient of Drolma and Lobzang's hospitality, unwittingly exacerbated those questions in their household. In fact, in the optimistic early years of the 2000s, they had proudly displayed me to friends and colleagues as a kind of social capital, a link to the prestige of cosmopolitan connections and, perhaps, a future donor for their children. But by winter 2008, as Drolma confided to me, village neighbors had begun to gossip about me, wondering about why I was housed in their best guest room and whether or not this meant Lobzang was rich—benefitting, they implied, from hidden corrupt dealings in his state bureau work. Envy and alienation are perfect openings for draining *yang* from a household. I myself was drawn in to participating. By treating the scarves I received not as inextricably imbued with the givers' intentions and timespaces but as a form of social capital (e.g., like money, as more abstract symbols of completed past exchanges now transferrable to others), I had brought other, unknown hosts' competing efforts to capture fortune directly into the household. Whose fortune was I in fact enhancing?

As a young widow and now a married-in bride, Drolma was always already a polluting interloper there. It was her son from her previous marriage who was prepping his college exams, and as her friend from that earlier time, I inevitably brought the shadow of Drolma's previous catastrophic misfortune with me as a guest in her new home. Drolma was thus frantic to purify the household after discovering my scarves. In the subsequent days she sought multiple opportunities to turn her hospitality back to its proper timespaces: the divine supporters of her household and of both her natal and her new villages. The next day she moved me out of the guest room and into the common room, decking out the guest room as if to receive a lama, and closing the curtain to Palden Lhamo's altar room that was adjacent to the wall. She bought conspicuously expensive offerings to present at the annual propitiation dance at her village's Palden Lhamo temple, and in my former room, sponsored lay tantric specialists to chant the ritual hospitality of appeasement feasts for both Palden Lhamo and for Shachong, Rebgong's mountain deity king and special protector of Jima village.

In spring 2008 I was no longer primarily a friend or a fortuitous guest in Drolma and Lobzang's household, the powerful stranger potentially enhancing the vitality of its fortune. Instead, I was contributing to the dissolution of that container of fortune, its opening to the misfortune of the scrutiny and grasping desires of other unknown villagers and their divine protectors, as well as of the state. As it turned out, I left there none too soon. A month later, as PAP Special Forces troops camped in the town stadium and launched their daily patrols, I told Drolma while we again sat next to her stove that I had found an apartment in town. Drolma's relief was palpable. She lowered her voice to a bare whisper so that I had to lean forward to hear, "things are very tight in the village," she murmured, "our cell phones are tapped, and you know there are paid spies among villagers. People have been talking about the presence of foreigners here." And, with the utter conviction of repeating an empirical fact, she insisted, "They've put listening devices into village homes on wires strung through the stove holes." Drolma had always kept that stove meticulously clean, regularly purifying it with juniper incense. But now it seemed, for her even the stove (Tib. *thab*), that most inner of sanctums and the ground of Tibetan household hospitality, opened an uncontrollable channel to the desires of unwelcome guests.

CHAPTER 2

The Mountain Deity and the State

Voice, Deity Mediumship, and Land
Expropriation in Jima Village

To begin to get at the stakes and heightened
risks of hospitality relations for Rebgong Tibetans, we turn in this chapter to
considering a public dispute within Lobzang and Drolma's urbanizing village
of Jima. The dispute revolved around the problematic presence of mountain
deities and the state as competing agents of village development goals. I was
a guest in Lobzang and Drolma's home during those early years of the Open
the West campaign (2000–7), and in the summer of 2007, I was drawn into
exploring the nature of the village conflict along with various Jima residents
who had their own interests in the investigation. The story I tell here will set
the stage for understanding how the battle for fortune in Rebgong had shifted
in partially stealthy ways under new post-Mao development efforts in the
valley. Unbeknownst to me and my fellow investigators, the conflict over the
mountain deity and the state in Jima threatened to lay bare villagers' unspoken resentments and fears in the wake of state-led urbanization pressures.[1]

Here is the way to practice with accompanying music. Recite:

Padmasambhava, the essence of the Buddhas of the three times, sits at
the head of the assembled guests. In front of him, out of the center of
dense rainbow light, comes a rocky mountain peak that is the head of
the divine garuda bird. . . . On a lotus-sun throne sits the king of the

regional deities Shachong Garuda, with beak and claws of heavenly iron, brandishing his two horns of wisdom and means. The top of his head is adorned with a flaming wish-fulfillment jewel. The feathers of his open wings are like a thousand sharp weapons. . . . There resides the extremely wrathful Lord of the Skies.

—Opening invocation of Jima village prayer entreating
the mountain deity Shachong

In the summer of 2007, I was still happily ensconced as a guest in Drolma and Lobzang's household in Jima village.[2] That summer, after weeks of fervent preparation, we watched as Dorje, the village's principal mountain deity medium (Tib. *lha pa*), took center stage at the annual harvest festival. His ritual actions thereby kicked off the sixth lunar month festival season or, as Tibetans in the farming villages of the lower reaches of the Guchu River valley called it, the Great Month of the Gods. Dorje's body had been inhabited by the powerful mountain deity Amnye Shachong, Jima village's main protector or foundation lord (Tib. *gzhi bdag*). King of all mountain deities in Rebgong, Shachong resides in the highest peak (~15,500 feet) just southwest of Rongbo Monastery and Longwu town.

FIGURE 6.   Shachong wall painting, fierce garuda aspect, Jima temple, 2007. Author's photo.

Just like the many other deity mediums at other lowland villages' harvest festivals, Dorje's wild and unpredictable movements that summer were the center of attention for villagers and visitors alike, attracting a frantic scrum of Chinese and foreign photographers. Those photos in turn would serve to market the Rebgong region in China and abroad as a benign and colorfully ethnic tourist destination, a project explicitly promoted in prefecture party leaders' recent development plans for the region. With the new impetus of the Open the West campaign, prefecture planners took the Tibetan "culture industry" (Ch. *wenhua chanye*), with the "folk culture" (Ch. *minsu wenhua*) of Lurol as a cornerstone of the Rebgong tourism brand, to be the driving force for the region's modernizing and "civilizing" development.

By the first years of the new millennium, Jima village was one of the wealthiest, most central, and rapidly urbanizing Tibetan villages in the valley with more than two thousand residents and three hundred households. In the early yang dar years of the 1980s, Jima village in fact had led the way in reviving its three-day lay harvest festival, called Lurol (Tib. *klu rol*, lit. "entertainment for the Nagas"), to new splendor.[3] In 2007, the formal pageantry of Jima's Lurol festival, held in the courtyard of the village's beautifully renovated temple (the largest in the valley), seemed to exemplify unchanged village folk tradition. As before, Lurol was staged just before harvest season, when oil-seed and barley crops were supposed to be ripening in farmers' fields. It consisted of all-day sequences of dances, repeated three times in as many days, in which men and women were recruited to perform as ideal village subjects under the watchful eyes of Dorje and a committee of elders. The dances were framed throughout as offerings to the village's protector deities by the propitiation prayers of elder chant masters and the array of sumptuous altar gifts and burnt offerings directed by Dorje and the elders. This, then, was the annual culmination of post-Mao village-scale hospitality, a multisensory feast of epic proportions aimed at gathering and containing collective fortune and vitality on behalf of the village.

The finale of the 2007 Lurol seemed to nicely demonstrate the harmonious coexistence of Tibetan villagers' and state officials' interests in ensuring collective fortune. After the final communal offerings were completed, photographers turned their lenses back to the center and the assembled villagers faced the village temple dressed in their festival finery. Dorje, entranced as Shachong, then shared the temple veranda with Tshering, Jima's Communist Party secretary, who proudly wore a white offering scarf, redolent of welcome and legitimate presence, around his neck. Both made final comments praising the proceedings and calling for continued village unity and prosperity.

Yet from the perspective on the politics of presence I'm developing in this book, we would have to consider Tibetan deity mediums in Rebgong as particularly problematic objects of state-sponsored promotion. Official tourism portrayals of villagers' relationships with mountain deities in fact attempted to limit deity mediums' presence and thereby diminish and domesticate them because they were a fundamental threat to the post-Mao developmentalist state. They were a threat not just because their seemingly exotic practices flout the officially atheist CCP's laws against "superstition." More important, under Open the West policies prioritizing state-led capitalist development, Rebgong deity mediums gave flesh to a battle for fortune that, despite the best hopes of the Panchen Lama, had in fact been (partially) revived under the post-Mao silent pact. That is, village deity mediums publicly embodied (or literally, hosted) and voiced alternative divine authorities who were grounded in a legacy of fiercely guarded Tibetan autonomy.

As Dorje's writhing, puffing, and threatening gestures opened the 2007 Lurol season, the brute power and ferocity of Rebgong's mountain deities (and thus of ideal Tibetan communities and their male leaders) were clearly onstage. Further, by 2007 the semblance of state-local harmony as Dorje and Tshering shared the veranda at the climax of Jima's Lurol was a highly strained one, stretched thin over the increasingly problematic nature of both the presence of the deity and the presence of the state in the village as development pressures raised the stakes for all involved.

Deity Mediumship, Voice, and the Deferral of Author(ity)

Establishing Socialist Values: The 8 Honors and The 8 Shames
2) To serve the people is honorable;
   To depart from the people is shameful . . .
6) To be honest and trustworthy is honorable;
   To forget one's promises at first sight of profit is shameful . . .
8) To struggle arduously is honorable;
   To wallow in luxury and pleasure is shameful.
            —Excerpt from poster in Rebgong schools and state offices citing
                 President Hu Jintao's 2006 speech on socialist values

In this chapter, I unpack some of the consequences of this strained silence and state-local ambivalence around the status of Tibetan deity mediums and their village jurisdictions in post-Mao Rebgong. This in turn will help to flesh out what I mean when I conceptualize the politics of presence in the frontier zone as an ongoing battle for fortune embedded in risk-laden hospitality events. Here I use linguistic anthropological tools to take practices of deity mediumship seriously as consequential forms of communication and claims to regional dominion that posed acute interpretive dilemmas for villagers and state officials alike. In this, my approach is inspired by Bakhtin's perspective on the inherent dynamics of voice in a "contradictory and multi-languaged world" (1981, 275). Bakhtin famously insisted on the creative, even agonistic dialogism at the heart of any expression of authoritative personhood, a take he conceptualized, not coincidentally, under Soviet repression.

As we began to see in chapter 1, a dialogic perspective on personhood and power is a paradigm shift, one that requires us to discover the meaning and stakes of all self-other relations in intersubjective scenes of encounter. In this chapter, for example, Bakhtin's approach provides important analytic tools for rethinking modern states. We consider states not as uniquely unitary and rational administrative orders encompassing discrete local realms, but as, in practice, contested claims to particular forms of supreme authority or sovereignty that require constant embodiment and invocation by situated people. Starting there allows us from the outset to reject the powerfully influential, common sense idioms of statist modernity and development that relegate to the margins of sovereign and sane human order all that is wild, occult, or nonhuman. In this view then, margins are not just spatial peripheries. They emerge instead in the unacknowledged contestations and uncanny authorities at the heart of all practices of governance, what Veena Das and Arthur Kleinman have called "the secret life of the state" (2000, 6).[4] In other words, despite official rhetoric, the CCP-led Chinese state, like any other nation-state, is not radically secular or scientifically modern in practice.

From here we can also begin to understand how practices that stage communication between humans and invisible beings, which Western observers have traditionally labeled "possession," have been so enduringly elusive and even threatening to state officials and social scientists, because they are taken to be fundamentally antimodern.[5] That is, in the persistent claim to speak and act as a normally invisible being, practitioners bring otherness into the very core of the cohesive, conscious self that grounds modern notions of human meaning and agency as intentioned action. Indeed, the English language category "possession" points up the shockingly aberrant nature of such practices to modern Western (liberal) sensibilities: the hold over or ownership (like slavery?) of one sovereign self by another, as in the social anthropologist I. M. Lewis's hyperbolic terms, "the seizure of man by divinity" (1971, 15).[6]

By contrast, my Bakhtinian perspective allows me to conceptualize both Dorje and Tshering's efforts to voice authoritative discourses as fundamentally commensurate processes in a high-stakes politics of presence that erupted between 2005 and 2007 and deeply factionalized Jima village. At Jima's 2005 Lurol festival, villagers had been shocked when Dorje, entranced as Shachong, brutally evicted the group of prominent elders who had organized the festival that year without consulting the deity. Dorje's Shachong then appointed a group of Dorje's supporters instead. The evicted elders, along with Party Secretary Tshering, then publicly questioned Dorje's authenticity as a deity medium, thus raising doubts as to the legitimacy of his actions on behalf of the village. "What have we have done?!" an elder reportedly yelled at Dorje, "have we eaten [embezzled] the temple funds? Who are you!? A ghost!?" The elders' position was then strongly opposed by Dorje's supporters and Dorje refused to even show up the following year at the 2006 Lurol. The conflict came to a head in 2007 when the leading lama of Rongbo Monastery, the young eighth Shartshang, was invited to the village temple to authenticate Dorje in front of the assembled villagers. Only then, with Dorje back on his throne, did the 2007 Lurol resume its ideal appearance for tourists' cameras.

As my interlocutors and I tried to make sense of the conflict in Jima, I came to see the presence of the deity as the crux of an unacknowledged struggle over the very nature and future of Tibetan land ownership, collectivity, and political representation in the valley. Historically, the voice of the divine ruler Shachong, publicly staged and managed in Lurol since the festival's inception in the nineteenth century, was supposed to reauthor the landed grounds for Jima farmers' collective fortune and prosperity under male elders' guidance—development on Tibetan villagers' terms. Yet Jima's conflict over their deity medium in the 2000s came after a decades-long process of state-mandated urbanization that had annexed the vast majority of the village's valley floor farmlands to the burgeoning town of Longwu—by then, the agrarian festival was exceedingly anachronistic; no Jima household farmed anymore.

Further, the conflict erupted at precisely the same time as prefecture officials, in line with central government development campaigns to "Construct a New Socialist Countryside" (Ch. *jianshe shehuizhuyi xin nongcun*) while rebuilding CCP presence at the grassroots, formally restructured most of the valley floor's farming villages into landless urban neighborhoods or "communities" (Ch. *shequ*) supposedly under direct party control. That top-down

FIGURE 7. Longwu town and abandoned hillside fields. Rongbo Monastery on right, summer 2007. Author's photo.

imposition, I discovered, rested uneasily over decades of unspoken resentment and suspicion. Many Rebgong villagers, I learned, came to experience post-Mao urbanization as the culmination of Tibetan disenfranchisement under Chinese rule.

As I gradually learned more about the Jima conflict, participating in discreet conversations in village homes and ricocheting off walls of secrecy, I came to realize just how precarious were the terms of Tibetan hospitality under the silent pact. "We never talk about such things publicly," said one young man, a scion of an important Jima lineage, "that would destroy relationships." Talk itself, as village gossip (Tib. *mi kha*), was conceptualized as a threat in this regard. "In the end," joked a prominent village man and state official, who had eagerly shared his views with me about the conflict, "we will say the conflict was caused by the foreign woman [anthropologist] in our midst!" In this, the spate of scholarly accounts of revived Lurol and deity medium practices in Rebgong, produced in collaborations between Tibetan villagers (themselves often low-level state officials) and foreign scholars, worked to minimize that threat.[7] Those accounts in fact kept unspoken history at bay by depicting such post-Mao lay rituals as the simple revival of unchanged village tradition, an annual set of offerings that, as before, unproblematically function to please deities and thereby re-create a unified village as an abstract, indeed deterritorialized social order.

But the paradigm shift we're pursuing here pushes us, uncomfortably, to think beyond the terms of silent pact diplomacy. My approach instead rehistoricizes Lurol and deity mediumship by locating them within the exceedingly martial history of Rebgong Tibetan villages as first and foremost landholding units and arbiters (containers) of collective fortune and productivity. In line with anthropologists' efforts to rethink the roles of religion and place-making in state-local relations in post-Mao China,[8] my Bakhtinian focus on voice as contested presence turns our attention to the dynamics of human and divine subjectivity in ongoing battles for jurisdiction over land and resources. And such dynamics were playing out as the post-Mao rush to market-based development exacerbated long-simmering crises of authority in the valley. Crucially, public speech, politicized since the Maoist years as the most important sign of the authentic, nationalist grassroots subject,[9] held out particular risks for Tibetans as their loyalties came under increasing scrutiny into the 2000s. Deferral and avoidance, not public avowal, was the art of living in Rebgong.

Linguistic anthropologists, more than others, have looked to Bakhtin to operationalize his alternative approach to discourse as an embodied and dialogic social process in everyday life.[10] In Bakhtin's understanding of linguistic practice, "voice" is decidedly not the disembodied speech of a singular self. Instead, it is always manifest as a historically loaded figure or chronotope. Interlocutors create and coordinate various voices most powerfully by invoking hierarchically arranged speech genres. For example, recall the way the tenth Panchen Lama voiced the Maoist state in his 1980 speech to Rebgong Buddhist leaders by quoting "Leftist'" criticisms of Buddhism. Bakhtin's approach to voice is thus one way to get at the cultural politics of authority, not as the actions of intrinsically "charismatic" individuals,[11] but as an embodied dynamics of presence and absence. In other words, voicing practices are one way to explore the ways in which people dialogically recognize and contest the presence of visible and invisible authorities and their relations to various events and places.

From this angle, all linguistic forms that speakers invoke are linked to or dialogue with the competing timespaces and moral stances they carry from their histories of use by people situated in stratified societies (Bakhtin 1981, 271–72). Thus, in a fundamentally unequal and multivoiced world, the speaking subject in practice is never unitary but emerges as a variety of voices or "complexes of points of view" (Hill 1986, 94). That is, particular signs are embodied and recognized in a person's speech as linguistically constructed social personas struggling for dominance—even within a single utterance. This approach then would seem to jibe in part with Tibetans' own highly agonistic theories of self and other, which, as we saw in chapter 1, posit contingent, partible, and violable subjects and "life-forces" (Tib. *bla*) as extrinsic beings contained or hosted in people's bodies which must then be purified, protected and strengthened.

But a Bakhtinian approach provides us with ways to understand the specific processes through which certain personas can still be rendered provisionally coherent and authoritative, or deliberately ambiguous across contexts. In this light, presence is not primarily bodily coexistence but a posited or claimed interlocutor status (an invisible or disembodied being can be strongly present, while certain personas can rely on their absence to remain powerful). Thus, speakers attempt to use the stylistics of language choice, genre, register, intonation, and reported speech to position different voices and their sources relative to the current event, thereby attempting to render present certain moral personas for their interlocutors while keeping others absent. In Erving Goffman's terminology, all speakers, while addressing others, assess the stakes of being held accountable for their messages, and work to project certain participant roles as producers of utterances: "author," a speaker to be taken as the origin of the utterance, "animator," a speaker to be taken as merely relaying the words of others, and "principal," a speaker to be taken as responsible for the utterance's position (1981, 144–46). A speaker can, for example, attempt to merely report (animate) the words of another without claiming to be responsible (a principal) for the moral stance they carry.

Yet in the jostle of everyday interactions and interpretive politics, no speaker can guarantee which personas their interlocutors will sense and recognize. As Bakhtin put it, in particular situations, the boundaries between a speaker's voices can be highly ambiguous, even deliberately so (1981, 308). Even against the will of the speaker, the presence of other personas and moral stances can "leak through" into the interaction. Interlocutors thus often collaborate to clarify the boundaries between voices by drawing on local cultural and linguistic practices to mark the differences among social personas and their associated communicative events, appropriate behaviors, and scopes of authority and responsibility. From this angle, any discourse interpreted as clearly single-voiced ("monologic") or authoritative is the provisional outcome of much social, linguistic, and political work, oftentimes through state disciplinary practices.

Tibetan deity mediumship from this perspective is a genre of communication in which the human speaker, if successful, is nothing but a physical animator for a uniquely present other's voice. The normally invisible deity, like many other types of presence managed in interactions, becomes socially embodied as an author and principal of his communications and thus as an interlocutor for others (see figure 10). Just like other personas, deities' presence and intentions must be collaboratively interpreted by a culturally grounded "community of witnesses" (Irvine 1982, 248). Thus far from being radically exotic or occult, we could see Tibetan deity possession as in fact exemplifying and dramatizing the inherently dialogic nature of all human communication, in which, in Bakhtin's words, "no less than half [of uttered words] belong to someone else" (1981, 339).

From this angle, the persistence of Tibetan deity mediumship in Rebgong in the face of state-sponsored modernization is best understood not as the ultimately unmanageable resistance of a heteroglossic "folk," as Bakhtin, in his more romantic moments, would assert (1981, 273). Instead, among Tibetans the "performative breakthrough" to possession and especially to deity speech (Tib. *lha skad*), provides particularly compelling ways to transcend what the anthropologist Webb Keane called "the pragmatic present" (1997b, 66). That is, any authorities, in order to be taken as representing broader collective interests and therefore as legitimately conveying directives and moral evaluations, must in public settings defer to authoring voices that transcend the petty interests of their own present situation and local personas. Their behavior and speech styles at those junctures must be taken to be extraordinary and collectively representative even as their ordinary personas and interests threaten to leak through.

These dynamics have particular implications in Tibetan regions, where as I argued in chapter 1, the demand for the embodied presence of a wide range of invisible divine beings has grounded humans' claims to power, causation, and legitimacy. In this, recalling Lumoji's complaints about humans becoming "dumb animals," Tibetans historically valued the pragmatic power of speech (Tib. *skad*, voice or vocal sound) to both substantiate conscious personhood and cement collective agreements. Speech, often sealed with an offering scarf, constitutes a key public marker of a direct link between "mouth" (Tib. *kha*) and a body's "interior" (Tib. *khog*), the locus of life force. Sustained silence then could be read as a sign of absence and pollution, a life-threatening evacuation leaving a person catatonic or landscapes devoid of divine interlocutors.[12]

Importantly, then, after mountain deity mediums rose to the fore with the advent of Lurol in the nineteenth century, deity speech was the main causal sign (index) of authentic divine presence in mediums' bodies. As many villagers explained it to me, the normally invisible mountain deity "descends" (Tib. 'babs) into the medium's chest cavity, temporarily overpowering the medium's own life force and consciousness—this is not a "possession" per se, but a habitation ("my body is like a house for the deity," one medium told me).[13] Yet communication across the human-deity divide is extremely difficult, physically trying, and subject to interpretive doubt (see figure 10). A prospective medium was authenticated only when the deity inhabiting him spoke before a prominent Buddhist lama, using the versified speech genres encoding traditional wisdom, to declare his identity and loyalties. The lama's omniscience and transcendent power, it is said, precluded all but the proper deity from speaking out in his presence. Jima's deity Shachong, for example, was said to have been tamed, humanized, and made a virtuous god of the "white side" (Tib. dkar phyogs) by Rongbo Monastery's head lama Shartshang, when he converted the monastery to the Geluk sect in the early seventeenth century.

In this light, we should take public presence to be the capacity for an authoritative social persona to be voiced onstage unchallenged, and thereby to both claim a legitimate standing and embody the historically and morally charged idioms on which such a persona depends. In twenty-first century Rebgong, this was as applicable to Tshering, Jima's CCP secretary, as it was to Dorje, Jima's deity medium. Thus, for example, the legacy of the socialist state and the recent central government revival of socialist values propaganda (e.g., in the poster cited above) in the face of deepening popular anger at official "corruption," meant that all local officials had to draw on sanctioned state authors (like President Hu) to voice the ideal altruism of an official working first and foremost to "serve the people" (Ch. wei renmin fuwu). Given the particularly institutionalized nature of deity mediumship in the Rongbo valley,[14] we could then see both Tshering and Dorje in the mid-2000s as problematic mediums for competing sources of monologic speech.

But under the post-Mao silent pact, the recognition of their commensurate nature is precisely what Chinese state rhetoric and discipline worked to preclude. Indeed, the legitimacy of both state voices and those of Tibetan deity mediums hung by a thread amidst the divisive allure of new forms of state-sponsored wealth in the marketizing valley. As we will see, the great danger of state-sanctioned deity mediumship in this context was that, even against the will of the participants, the very forms and voices of the practice would publicly reveal the actually amoral and hierarchical nature of the Chinese state and state-local relations in Rebgong under market reforms.

The Voices of Tshering: Top-Down Urbanization and the Demise of the Dewa

Bring into Full Play the Party's Core Role;
Push Forward the Construction of the Jima Urban Community
The Longwu Town Street Party Organization is the leading core for all activities and organizations of the Jima Urban Community. The work of establishing the Party in the Jima urban community must . . . strictly revolve around the great goals of reform, development, and stability. . . . Officials must ceaselessly strengthen the capacity of the Jima Urban Community Party organizations to do battle, to consolidate, and to unite the broad masses of residents within the boundaries of the Party organizations.

—Poster in new Jima urban community office, summer 2007

Amidst this moral ferment, the conflict that erupted at Jima's 2005 Lurol threatened to unmask the increasingly absurd fiction of village unity and state-local harmony that buttressed the post-Mao silent pact in Rebgong. In this, Party Secretary Tshering was a lightning rod for villagers because he epitomized the crisis of Tibetan village elders' moral authority under CCP rule. As theorists of rural China have recently argued, grassroots officials like Tshering were increasingly situated at the crux of post-Mao politics.[15] I was able to interact with and interview many such officials in Rebgong. Here I draw on a method pioneered by Jane Hill (1995), in which she focused on the discourse of a particularly pivotal official to analyze the dialogic processes in which all were engaged. Further, the interview was a marked and familiar genre of interaction in Rebgong that required officials to take self-conscious stances vis-à-vis various outsiders. As such, I found, it was an important and increasingly fraught occasion for the delicate politics of presence and absence, of deferral and disavowal.

I finally got to interview Tshering in August 2007, after he had shared the veranda with Dorje at the capping moment of that year's fateful Lurol. Despite himself, Tshering had been construed by Dorje's supporters as the deity medium's moral foil and chief opponent, even though Tshering had not been one of the routed elders in 2005. As it turned out, Jima villagers' enthusiastic revival of Lurol since the 1980s reforms was not just the reiteration of quaint folk custom. Instead the festival was at the very center of ongoing battles for jurisdiction over fortune on Tibetan terms.

Since the early twentieth century, Chinese nationalist development planners have taken landscapes in the western frontier zone to be unruly, yet inanimate "nature" requiring heroic, scientific management (see chapter 4).[16] Consider for example the Chinese language street placard entitled "What Is 'Land?'" that was part of a 2007 Legal Education campaign in Rebgong just months after Jima's harvest festival that year:

> "Land" is a composite made up of such natural elements as air, plant life, hydrology, topography, landforms, soil and rocks as well as the outcomes of human social economic activities. The outcomes of human activities include such elements as all built environments created from humankind's past and present social economic activities as well as the manmade fertility of the land. Looking at it from the perspective of both land formation and natural elements on the one hand and humankind's social economic activities on the other,[we] must see it as an historical product, a natural-economic composite.

Here, presented to teach residents the conceptual premises of land management laws (and perhaps, to naturalize the emerging status of land as a commodity), "land" (versus "soil") is a definitively secular and material assemblage, encompassing all the added value of human action on nature. By contrast, Tibetan farmers in Rebgong historically experienced landscapes as profoundly emplaced and animated, caught up in the moving cosmos of nonhuman forces and beings impinging on human bodies and livelihoods. As farming communities settled in reciprocal relations with the expanding monastic complex, a community's principal mountain deity was figured as a sovereign of the basic unit—and container—of communal territory transcending households, the "dewa" (Tib. *sde ba*, translated here as "village").[17] All those born within it were his subjects. The principal deity is native villagers' "birth god" (Tib. *skyes lha*), thereby transcending any household-specific deities. In rites of passage and rituals marking the lunar year, villagers needed to host and recruit mountain deities as divine avatars, addressing them as "ancestors" (Tib. *a mnyes*) and military commanders. Well-feasted deities ideally worked to fight demonic forces and secure or contain *yang*, that all-important yet abstract force of vitality or fortune, on behalf of collectivities (households, villages). Such dewa-deity relations are centuries old among rural Tibetans, but I found evidence that Jima dewa's elaborate Lurol festival emerged relatively recently, as a response to heightened competition over land and jurisdiction in the late nineteenth century.[18] In that context, Jima's Lurol staged dynamic scenes of encounter among multiple interlocutors, highlighting above all the ideal dialogue between elders and the mountain deities inhabiting mediums' bodies. In the elders' prayers and the deity's speeches, the ultimate aim was to dramatize and substantiate the dewa, over

and above individual households, as the main landholding unit arbitrating
and containing collective fortune and productivity. In Lurol, the dewa for
Rebgong farmers was ideally a communal life-giving territory and ancestral
heritage (Tib. *pha gzhis*) under the joint rule of mountain deities and councils of village elders, a "fortunate and wealthy community" (Tib. *g'yang sde
phyug mo*).[19]

The container (Tib. *snod*), recalling chapter 1, is the key historical idiom
for emplacement among Tibetans, yet in practice it is not a static object but a
dynamic and risky process. Sovereignty as inviolable jurisdiction in Rebgong
was thus a fundamentally dialogic and translocal affair, constantly vulnerable
to the whims of voracious mountain deities and the vicissitudes of human
politics. In Lurol, a successful medium could voice the deity Shachong as the
originating author of ancient wisdom, thereby transcending the petty interests of households and networks. But under the close management of elders,
the deity's communications were ultimately supposed to voice the collective
dewa as the moral principal, with leading elders as the main interpreters—
secondary mediums—for villagers. After all, as a culminating villagewide
hospitality event, Lurol was supposed to prove elders' capacity to obligate
and command divine response to their collective prayers; elders were supposed to come out on top as gift masters and hosts:

> You mountain deities and your retinues, eat! Then destroy all adversity
> facing our people and our wealth and provide us with all positive condi-
> tions. Do everything you can to fulfill all our wishes the way we want!
> (Offering feast section of Jima village prayer to Shachong)

A successful festival thus demonstrated elders' battle victory in securing
divine presence as protectors of collective fortune for the dewa as a communal territory—over both demonic forces and the divisive multivocality of
intra- and interdewa politics.

As Jima's party secretary, however, Tshering had no such divine mandate.
He voiced instead an abstract persona, "the State," (Tib. *rgyal khab*, Ch. *guojia*) that villagers experienced as both distant (based in Beijing) and problematically intimate (embodied in community leaders and lifeways).[20] Yet recall
that, for many I spoke to, the Chinese state was established in Rebgong only
in 1958, through the world-shattering betrayal of militarily enforced collectivization. In Jima, the dewa and its leading elders were for the first time
overthrown in favor of the commune and its Chinese-led "activist" leaders,
an unprecedented valleywide unit based in what would become Longwu
town.[21] Jima elders' moral authority was militarily annulled—Lurol was
banned, Shachong's temple destroyed, all mediums and most elders sent to

labor camps, and households lost use rights over their ancestral fields. This for most villagers was a devastating moral and ethnic assault, but one that had to remain unacknowledged for decades against ubiquitous state rhetoric that portrayed socialist transformation, and the new impunity of local officials, as the will of the People.

Thus, as both a Jima elder and the State's principal medium during the conflict in the 2000s, Tshering's difficult task was similar to that facing Dorje: in voicing the State, he had to come across as merely an animator (e.g., just reporting policy), and not as an author or moral principal of his words. But unlike Dorje, whose authority turned on making the deity's presence in his body visible, Tshering's moral stature in the dewa depended on limiting or erasing traces of the State's presence, even as he was required to speak publicly. Thus, during our interview, I glimpsed the many contending voices Tshering struggled to manage and present. The dialogue was not only with me, but also with his absent dewa critics.

Even though I was explicitly interviewing him in his capacity as party secretary, and kept returning to that status in my questions, Tshering insisted on adopting the moral voice of the dewa by framing himself first and foremost as a simple dewa elder and farmer (his household, like most in Jima, hadn't farmed in years) (see figure 8). In this way, Tshering's voices staged an epic battle in the valley between the State, associated with the encroaching Chinese city (as the Chinese loanword *chengshi*) and the dewa as an endangered Tibetan farming community. Despite Tshering's best efforts, in the end I was not at all clear as to his ultimate moral status in the story; the presence of the State emerged in his speech as what Bakhtin called "internally persuasive discourse," a voice he could not fully suppress (1981, 347). Tshering after all spoke not as Jima village's party secretary, but as the recently promoted party head of the Jima Urban Community (Ch. *shequ*). Tshering the official thus presided over the new administrative unit that since 2005 officially erased Jima dewa entirely, merging it with two other villages to form an urban neighborhood of Longwu town, and thereby culminating the very urbanization processes that Tshering the farmer so decried.

I came to realize that in the Lurol conflict, Jima villagers were playing out the moral consequences of state-led urbanization processes that had been set in motion decades earlier. In the onstage violence of the deity medium and the offstage anger of villagers, I glimpsed villagers' profound rage and anguish at the loss of dewa jurisdiction over valley floor lands.[22] Indeed, my monk friend Akhu Tenzin told me stories about my Jima host Lobzang's own elderly aunt, a woman widely known to be mentally "unclear." He said she would frequently visit him to sob and lament that new wealthy households

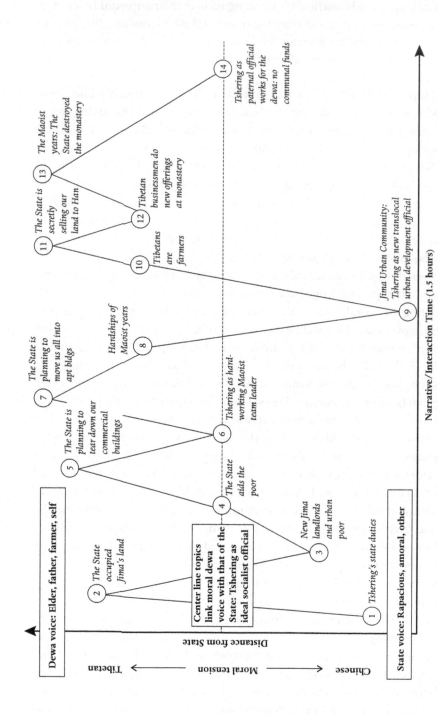

FIGURE 8. Tshering's voice shifts relative to topic change during interview

Content within the figure:

Dewa voice: Elder, father, farmer, self

State voice: Rapacious, amoral, other

Distance from State

Tibetan ← Moral tension → Chinese

Narrative/Interaction Time (1.5 hours)

1 Tshering's state duties

2 The State occupied Jima's land

3 New Jima landlords and urban poor

4 The State aids the poor

Center line topics link moral dewa voice with that of the State: Tshering as ideal socialist official

5 The State is planning to tear down our commercial buildings

6 Tshering as hard-working Maoist team leader

7 The State is planning to move us all into apt bldgs

8 Hardships of Maoist years

9 Jima Urban Community: Tshering as new translocal urban development official

10 Tibetans are farmers

11 The State is secretly selling our land to Han

12 Tibetan businessmen do new offerings at monastery

13 The State is secretly selling our land to Han

The Maoist years: The State destroyed the monastery

14 Tshering as paternal official works for the dewa: no communal funds

in town were occupying "our" (e.g., Jima dewas') land, and she still harbored bitter resentment at the loss of her own father's lands to the first Chinese settlers in the valley during the late nineteenth century. Post-Mao urbanization for such villagers was definitively not a natural process of socioeconomic development, but a top-down imposition that carried forward the disenfranchisement begun so brutally in 1958. Most elders knew that dewa unity was crucial for negotiating favorable terms in the development projects pushed by prefecture officials. However, after the initial land allocations of the post-Mao Household Responsibility System in the 1980s, Jima villagers had entered into a trade the terms of which they did not fully understand or control. That is, when all households were given official urban status (Ch. *hukou*) in the early 1990s, villagers were promised household autonomy and state-mediated cash income in exchange for the landed heritage that had grounded the dewa's autonomy as a collective entity.

Under China's uniquely complex and ambiguous property laws, all land designated "urban" comes under direct state ownership (residents merely enjoy "use rights"), while "rural" land can be owned by a variety of officially recognized collectives. In many ways, Jima villagers were subject to a process playing out across China in the 1990s. As Peter Ho put it, rapid urbanization was in practice a kind of stealthy scaling-up of property rights, in which villages' collective ownership rights were transferred to higher-level state units (2001, 417).[23] However, as Emily Yeh (2004) points out, the specifically ethnic nature of state-local tensions in Tibetan regions meant that rural Tibetans had even less recourse to legal resistance than their Chinese counterparts because any such moves were easily construed as antistate ethnic separatism. The eighty-year-old former Jima village head Gabzang put it this way in our interview:

> They said they needed the land [for government offices and enterprises] or else they would not be able to do the work of the State. We were forced to agree. If they saw us as forcibly stealing it back, the police would . . . they would say we were resisting and come here and arrest us. So we can't say anything. They won't call what they're doing "business!" They'll just say we are resisting the CCP.

As valley floor land was increasingly commodified into the 1990s, Jima Tibetans found that their main sources of secure income, social mobility, and benefits (both on and under the table) were careers in local state bureaus.[24] Beginning in the late 1980s, urban status for households whose land was expropriated for new state enterprises meant low monetary compensation and a few (menial) salaried positions in those units. By the 2000s, most households strove to place a least one member as entry-level bureaucrats in the very offices that now stood on the dewa's former fields.

In the mid-2000s, despite state rhetoric pushing socialist altruism as in the poster cited above, Jima Tibetans' private rumors and jokes cast doubt on the motives of any villager with a plum state position, evoking the Chinese loanword *fubai* (lit., "rotten") from state anticorruption campaigns to ironically voice the Chinese origins of such actions. Alternatively, the Tibetan phrase "eating money" (Tib. *sgormo za*) evoked the violation of dewa reciprocity by selfishly consuming communal funds. In this moral universe, I found, Buddhist notions of compassionate or sympathetic affect (Tib. *snying rje*) had merged with socialist notions of democratic fairness, and residents tended to place the "People" or "the Masses" (Tib. *dmangs tshogs*) as relative innocents at the bottom of the state bureaucratic hierarchy, in rural villages and remote pastoralist camps, while state officials (Tib. *las byed pa*) were associated with canny urbanity and higher levels in the administrative geography. Thus in the waning years of the yang dar period in Rebgong, I found that Tibetan speakers' references to the State (Tib. *rgyal khab*, lit. "king's palace" or "court") substantiated residents' profound moral ambivalence about the PRC nation-state. First used in Maoist work-team classes in the 1950s as a gloss for the Chinese term *guojia* (lit. "country household"), the Tibetan term took up the pretensions of PRC state builders to the uniquely abstract and thus transcendent sovereignty of the modern nation-state, even as they made claims to the intimate timespace idioms of household hospitality.[25] As illustrated in official awards to model citizens and party members in Rebgong, this was supposed to mean a nation-state, a national community in which the speaker claims objective membership. However, in my formal and informal conversations with Rebgong Tibetans across the valley, uses of the term *rgyal khab* as a neutral nation-space or community were very rare and marked. Instead, Tibetan speakers routinely framed the State as a narrative figure, a monolithic, abstract, and alien agent operating in and through rapidly shifting communities, as in Gabzang's description of the 1958 crackdown on Tibetan resistance:

"da *rgyal khab* gis bzung dang na, a khu lo lo bshad sa mi 'gro gi mo."

(If *the State* arrested you, there was no way to plead for mercy, you know.) [emphasis mine]

Yet in practice the abstractness and referential ambiguity of the Tibetan term for the State, as a gloss for any bureaucratic level higher than the speaker, allowed for convenient deferrals of responsibility (and thus moral claims to be closer to the People) up or down the ladder regionally, or up and out of Rebgong altogether, to Beijing and faceless Chinese authorities. Thus unlike for the figures of Mao and Deng (recall Lumoji on talking to Mao's portrait), few Tibetans I knew ever mentioned subsequent central CCP leaders by name. For Tibetan officials, the abstract persona of the State could be a convenient scapegoat. But as the Chinese language increasingly pushed Tibetan speech genres off public stages, Tibetan officials' unconscious use of Chinese loanwords and Tibetan neologisms voiced the figure of the State that they could never completely erase.[26] In this ferment, actual flows of land compensation funds in the 1990s were obscured under layers of secrecy and rumor and local officials were the safest targets of dewa ire. I learned that all Jima leaders, like Gabzang, who had helped negotiate the reform-era land transfers and compensation funds were suspected by villagers of having "eaten money" to benefit their own households and networks.

Villagers' most intense rage, however, was directed at Party Secretary Tshering. For many, he epitomized the venal, corrupt State from which they themselves sought moral distance. Tshering (b. 1947) had become a party member in 1967, and then a Jima production team leader under the elder Gabzang. Tshering's party status brought him a promotion over Gabzang as Jima's party secretary after reforms, but he rose to prominence and controversy only after he was urged by Longwu town officials to come out of retirement and take the post again in 1996. I was told that one night in the years just prior to the Lurol conflict a group of Jima village men, enraged at rumors that Tshering was using his position to "eat" dewa land compensation funds, painted a damning black mark on his household door. "Your reputation never recovers from that!" one man insisted to me, his wife gravely nodding.

Thus, as the Lurol conflict heated up in 2005, for Dorje's supporters, Tshering, who had close kin ties to several of the evicted elders, became the face of what one couple referred to as "the elders faction" (Ch. bangpai). Tshering's supposedly venal motives were then suspected of influencing otherwise good men, so that they themselves were rumored to have shared in eating dewa land funds. Now leading dewa elders, instead of protecting collective fortune on behalf of all, were suspected of handing over the dewa's ancestral heritage to benefit their own households.

Tshering's impossible task during our conversation was thus to limit the voice of the State even as he relied on its authority; he had to claim the dewa as his primary base even as he had no real mandate from the People or the deity (see figure 8). Over the course of the conversation, Tshering repeatedly deflected my direct questions about his status as an official in favor of narrating Jima's fate after reforms. Those were the moments when the voice of the dewa emerged most prominently and the State rose to the fore as the agent responsible for the forced and unfair expropriation of Jima's farmlands, a process Tshering depicted as beginning in 1958. This deferral of responsibility to the State was almost immediate in our conversation. After I opened by asking Tshering about his duties as Jima's party secretary, he offered some awkward and halting explications of his job as merely a mouthpiece relaying the State's policies "down" to the grassroots and then made an abrupt topic shift:[27]

> Those [officials] they . . . the State did. . . . In the beginning, Jima had many fields. . . . It had over 2200 mu, but the State occupied [Ch. *zhan*] them all and now there is nothing left.

However, as the Chinese word *zhan* ("to occupy," a legal term for land taken under state's rights) indicates, Tshering's unconscious use of Chinese loanwords work against his efforts to distance himself from the State at key junctures; they indicate his deep entanglements as the principal local implementer of state policies. As Nicolas Tournadre and Peter Brown (2003) note, the vast majority of Chinese loanwords in Tibetans' speech are substantive nouns referring to state apparatuses, while verbs and modifiers are much less frequent and syntactic changes are extremely rare. Thus in Tshering's Tibetan speech, the voice of the State is increasingly present as the number of loanwords increases and Chinese verbs and modifiers creep in.

When Tshering continued his narrative, the State haunted his efforts to depict the unexpected vicissitudes of reform-era land transfers as a breach of the socialist social contract:

> There were no more fields left. Then the State gave us bank accounts [Ch. *zhezi*, i.e., for compensation funds and subsidies] and we were changed to urban residents [Ch. *jumin*]. When we were changed to urban residents then all our fields were taken. So the State took care of us [Ch. *zhaogu*] by making some former farmers into salaried workers [Ch. *gongren*] [in new state firms]. But these days, as for that "care," now the state firms have gone bankrupt [Ch. *daobi*] and every one . . . all those workers have been laid off [Ch. *xiagang*] and hang out at home.

Tshering was referring to the mid-1990s, when central authorities withdrew subsidies and allowed local state enterprises to compete with burgeoning Han Chinese and Muslim Chinese (Hui)-dominated businesses in town or go under. His portrayal echoed Jima villagers' experience of such marketization processes as the State's socialist sleight of hand: the promised security in exchange for their land had evaporated as soon as market forces were given free rein.

This framing of the State and market forces as colluding against unsuspecting Jima villagers then allows Tshering to make perhaps his most important narrative move. In the mid-1990s, precisely the time that Tshering was reappointed as Jima's party secretary, the prefecture's marketization efforts actually privileged a group of Jima households whose initial land allocations were close to town roads. Encouraged with low-interest loans to build commercial buildings on their plots, by the late 1990s those households were bringing in substantial rental incomes, the majority of which were from new Han and Hui-owned businesses.[28]

Importantly, Tshering and most of the elders associated with him in the 2005 Lurol conflict, as commercial building owners, were members of that emergent class. In 1998, when Shachong, through Dorje, ordered the renovation and expansion of his temple, it was those landlord households who were the main dewa donors. Elders worked hard to complete the gorgeous temple by 2000, at the same time as the last of Jima households gave up farming altogether. Just as their donations and public voluntarism for the dewa moralized Jima landlords' newfound monetary wealth, in our conversation Tshering worked to distance himself from the moral implications of capitalist inequality by linking the voice of the dewa with that of himself as an ideally compassionate socialist official. These were the moments when Tshering allowed his voice to merge with that of the State because he appears as a loyal father figure working on behalf of the dewa (see figure 8, dotted midline). Thus he proudly described his work helping Jima's poor get welfare payments and proclaimed, "The State aids the poor [Ch. *fupin*], the State gives them help."

This moral stance then grounded Tshering's most adamant dewa voice when he turned to narrating the State's most egregious breach of socialist ideals from the mid-1990s on: the sale of Jima's former fields to outside investors and therein the planned demise of the dewa. Further, the vehemence of that critique worked to limit and morally neutralize the strongest and most problematic state voice that came across in our conversation: Tshering the party secretary of the new urban community, whose career rose as the dewa declined (see figure 8, topics 7–13).

Land for Tshering's dewa voice is essentially farm fields (Tib. *sa zhing*) as long term household capital and security. In this, he depicts the State after 1958 as a swindler all along, even though it was only in the 1990s that central land policies allowed state officials to openly sell urban land-use rights. The State for Tshering the farmer thus comes across as an enduringly corrupt agent who, unlike the early 1950s CCP practice of "buying" (Tib. *nyos dang*) land with silver dollars, used socialist ideals to "take" land (Tib. *blangs dang*) from villagers after 1958 and then sell it off for large profits after reforms. Thus for Tshering the farmer, the inexplicably rapid inflation of land prices mapped a covert shift from land as an inalienable territory to land as an impersonal commodity: the legalized land market is the final unveiling of the State's colonial endgame. For him, the State (unlike new Tibetan landlords, who seek to keep urban land within Jima households) acts as a super-landlord operating under translocal market principles, thereby reducing all Jima villagers, regardless of class, to servants of state-led urban development:

> Now there are no fields left. We elders will be okay, but our children . . . in the future our children won't be able to get by. Having done this, as for our land, our Jima, the State has made plans [Ch. *guihua*], it has made thorough plans. So in the future, gradually it will be hard for us to continue living in our *courtyard homes* [Tib. *khang pa*]. . . . We will be made to live in *apartment buildings* [Ch. *dalou*], that's it!! [Ch. *zai bu cheng*], it won't be long now! [emphasis mine]

Tshering's juxtaposition here of the Tibetan term for traditional courtyard homes (*khang pa*) with the Chinese loanword for apartment buildings (*dalou*) signals their status as historically charged idioms of (mis)fortunate living, in which courtyard homes entail larger territories of subsistence lands and longer time frames of lineage heritage. Indeed, he went on to ruefully remark, "We *need* courtyard homes! *People* will always die, but courtyard homes never die!" He thereby voiced a dewa view of urbanization as planned sinicization, and the high pitch and increasing speed of his words mirrored the speed of development in the valley—to which there are no longer any regional impediments. In his most adamant indictment of the State, Tshering the farmer depicted this process as a secret collusion between the State (as prefecture officials) and Chinese bosses, and portrayed himself at meetings vainly advocating for the dewa:

> When state firms are profitable, the land belongs to the State. When they aren't profitable, they sell it again and it becomes private! That's how the State is these days you know!! . . . It's mostly Chinese bosses [Ch. *laoban*] they sell it to. There's so much land that was bought cheap from us and then sold away for a lot of money. . . . [sighing] There's

nothing we can do. These days they say it's for Constructing a New Socialist Countryside, and if they want to force construction projects through they can.

Tshering's identification of the State with local urbanization officials in Rebgong reflects new realities in Tibetan regions since the Great Open the West campaign was launched in 2000. The campaign implemented in the west the same market-based development practices previously established in China's eastern cities, placing great pressure on provincial officials to compete for new central government and private investment funds. In this, officials in Tibetan regions have taken up and adapted the policy focus on urbanization as an ultimate good and engine of modernizing development, especially since the unprecedentedly wide-scale Construct a New Socialist Countryside (NSC) campaign, launched just months before my interview with Tshering.[29] As Carolyn Cartier and others have argued, China's post-Mao reforms did not mean a loss of state authority to market forces, but a rescaling of state authority to municipalities. Thus since the 2000s, urbanization policies in Tibetan regions have targeted rural communities as a (legal) way to overcome ethnic autonomy and ensure President Hu's harmony and social stability on terms amenable to outside investors. In Rebgong's Tongren County, with fewer natural resources on offer, the compulsory development drive ironically focused on constructing a Tibetanized modern tourist town, complete with high-end hotels, restaurants, and retail shops.

Thus in my interview with Tshering, the most tension-wrought moments came when I asked him about the new Jima Urban Community (see figure 8, topic 9). At that juncture, the voice of the State clearly overwhelmed Tshering's moral dewa voice. This is because, I argue, in addressing the topic with me, he had to embrace his status as a grassroots official whose local authority had expanded only as any vestige of rural dewa autonomy was definitively erased in favor of a new municipal system of governance. In striking contrast with the rest of the interaction, Tshering's neutral official voice lapsed into a proliferation of Chinese loanwords and Tibetan neologisms as he located Jima in the new urban valley. Jima dewa, he explained, was now only one neighborhood of the larger Jima Urban Community, which now included two other former farming dewa. Jima Urban Community in turn was one of three such units whose leaders were now directly appointed by Longwu town party officials:

Now the urban community [Ch. *shequ*] has been established. Now that it has been established, I am the party secretary [Ch. *shuji*] of the urban community. Now the Masses . . . now, except for me, all leaders are the State's officials.

In fact, in recently rural Tibetan valleys like Rebgong's Longwu town, the urban community, an administrative unit developed in selected eastern Chinese cities in the late 1990s, was a particular adaptation. In large Chinese cities, the urban community was supposed to replace the old socialist work unit (Ch. *danwei*). Most important, the new unit addressed the perception among central leaders that the CCP urgently needed to rebuild its relevancy at the grassroots, especially after the unsettling rise of the Falungong movement. The urban community then was supposed to be a key grassroots site for "constructing" (Ch. *jianshe*) the presence of the party and thus for countering other, less desirable local affiliations.[30] In Tibetan Rebgong, however, the urban community worked to formalize top-down urbanization, complementing the market-based scaling up of land use rights with the (stealthy) scaling up of management authority under CCP auspices. In this, Jima was again subsumed in an administrative unit not unlike the Maoist commune in scale and function.

In 2005–8 when I was there, the new urban community and its administrative aspirations seemed to be laughably irrelevant to the vast majority of Jima villagers. Most I spoke with had not even heard of it, and the office was just the former village residence committee office, a tiny one-room building next to the old, neglected village prayer temple. But Tshering's worldly loanwords as he described the new system exposed his insider access, so that even as he portrayed himself as a passive trainee in mandatory meetings and complained about his expanded duties, he came across as knowing what most villagers did not: the Jima Urban Community replaced the former post-Mao village residence committee altogether, obviating the need for any village-level representative (the old village head position) who, since reforms, was supposed to have been independently chosen by villagers as evidence of their grassroots autonomy. As such, Tshering's state authority was now translocal and urban-based, as he presided over nonlocal underlings in charge of land use management in the new district. Despite his caveat above, Tshering by the mid-2000s was most definitely the State's official. When he pronounced to me the end of Jima dewa as a rural administrative unit, his knowing and matter-of-fact tone in this context contrasted sharply with the dread and despair he had voiced throughout the rest of the interview as Tshering the farmer:

> Now we have no village status. We have none, you know. Jima has none. Jima has been subsumed into the prefecture city [Ch. *chengshi*]. . . . Now it's the urban community [Ch. *shequ*].

The Voices of Dorje: The Rise and Fall of the Activist Deity

> All you attentive protector deities, we exhort you to stand up and get to work! Amnye Shachong, go to the enemy! Shachong's soldiers, go to the enemy! Expand your troops and brandish your weapons! . . . Fill up the enemies' lands with your troops! Destroy their fortress walls from the foundations! Pulverize the enemies' life force and chop it to bits! Feast on the enemies' blood and flesh! Cut off the enemies' lineages at the roots! Loot and feast on all their possessions!
>
> —Exhortation section of Jima village prayer entreating
> the mountain deity Shachong

I was never able to interview Dorje; in many ways he remained an enigma to me. However, as a singularly controversial deity medium, villagers I spoke to had closely observed him since he was chosen in 1991 to replace his father Lodray, the only Jima deity medium to have survived the Maoist labor camps. Dorje's on- and offstage moves since then had shaped villagers' increasing ambivalence about the presence and implications of the deity Shachong in Jima. By the 2000s it had become imperative for Party Secretary Tshering to distance himself from the state-business collusions that many villagers felt were responsible for the loss of Jima lands. He did that by positioning himself as a paternal figure working for and voicing the dewa—a moral commensurate with Amnye (lit., "Grandfather") Shachong. But throughout the conflict, Dorje's Shachong countered Tshering by claiming the moral mandate of the collective dewa, as he had been through Lodray in the triumphant early 1980s, the only real oppositional (and Tibetan) voice of Truth.

Dorje, however, like the young lama Shartshang who had first authenticated him, had grown up at the vanguard of the post-Mao generation of Tibetans. The profoundly compromised nature of local Tibetan institutions by then meant that monologic Tibetan voices were much harder to pull off. Dorje's impossible task as Jima's deity medium in the 1990s and 2000s was thus to come across onstage as merely a physical animator and never the author or principal of Shachong's voice. Otherwise, the presence of Dorje, the self-interested villager, would leak through. This, I argue, was even more difficult in the mid-1990s when Shachong emerged in new ways as an activist deity in defense of Jima's lands. As the medium for Rebgong's divine regional king, Dorje's dilemma encapsulated those facing all Tibetans under post-Mao reforms—he rose to singular prominence even as Shachong communicated in unprecedented silence.

In the early 1980s, after the triumphant tour of the tenth Panchen Lama, the trauma of the Maoist years' appropriations had made the return of

Shachong imperative for Jima villagers, not primarily as a symbol of familiar folk custom but as a ferocious foundation owner whose favor authorized
dewa elders to guard ancestral heritage and collective fortune grounded in
the land. Indeed in my conversations, with older villagers across the valley, they routinely referred to the Household Responsibility System (HRS)
that broke up the Maoist communes simply as "dividing the land" (Tib. *sa
bgod bcos pa*), meaning returning to households fields they had previously
owned.[31] For many rural residents, HRS was simply land restitution, not a
shift to a newfangled "contract" system for land use rights. In the valley,
Jima was in fact the first village to dare to stage Lurol again, and after villagers rebuilt Shachong's temple, the first to feature a deity medium inhabited
by the deity. As provincial and prefecture officials flocked to Jima's revived
Lurol to celebrate state support for local ethnic or folk custom, Dorje's
father Lodray rose to unprecedented prominence in the valley as Shachong's medium.

In his recollections of that time, Gabzang portrayed Shachong's voice,
through Lodray, as echoing the admonitions of the tenth Panchen Lama:
"When he returned from the labor camps, Lodray was excellent at hosting
Shachong! He spoke so well, twice as good as before! He spoke the truth,
he told us to spread Buddhism and listen to the policies of the government."

FIGURE 9. Rebgong main valley floor with farm fields prior to expropriation, 1990. Photo by
Lawrence Epstein.

As such, Lodray's Shachong was in part supporting the Panchen Lama's vision of yang dar counterdevelopment on Tibetan terms. The deity fiercely claimed Jima's new post-Mao status as an "administrative village" (Ch. *xing-zheng cun*) to be the triumphant return of the Tibetan dewa. But after Lodray died, and as the pace of marketization quickened in the valley, villagers spoke of disturbing signs of inauspiciousness and disunity in the dewa. Thus, when the village held its first medium recognition rites in the temple since the 1940s, and Lodray's son Dorje was the one whom Shachong inhabited, villagers were greatly pleased and relieved, even though now Shachong refused to speak through him.

In fact, the vast majority of new mediums in Rebgong did not speak. Instead, in what to me seemed like a high-stakes game of charades, Dorje's Shachong and other deities most often communicated using an elaborate repertoire of gestures, facial expressions, and body language addressed to certain elders, who then relayed to spectators what the deity was saying. In post-Mao Rebgong, mountain deities had gone mute; their presence as divine sovereigns was thus weakened. That is, Shachong's new silence marked the loss of Tibetan speech and ritual genres, a loss that had transformed post-Mao deity mediumship in the valley. Dorje grew up attending public schools and never enjoyed the long apprenticeship with other mediums or the close lama-disciple relationships that were common in the past. Perhaps despite himself then, in his practice Dorje blurred all-important distinctions between mediums' different local personas and thus between the roles of animator and author onstage (see figure 10). In this way, his practice raised the question of deity presence and proper dewa authority at a time when major changes were underway in Jima.

In the highly managed forms of Rebgong deity mediumship, mediums' shifts to formalized speech genres and behavior allow for the emergence of the deity's presence as a uniquely monologic voice. Unlike Party Secretary Tshering, the deity, especially through his use of traditional speech styles, tropes, and allusions, claims authority as an author and never as an animator. Such processes of entextualization, as Keane (2001, 2008a) and others have argued, are crucial for creating "tradition," relatively durable media forms that cross spaces and times and thereby distance a voice from present speakers. Mountain deities from this angle do not just protect, they reauthor the Tibetan grounds for dewa collective fortune. Crucially, the split between author and animator, between the voice of the deity and that of the medium, is effected in the performative split between body and speech—the medium's body, aided by dewa men, is overwhelmed and out of control onstage. Indeed, the deity's very material presence is said to so overmatch

		Frame space (Goffman)			Participation roles (Goffman)		
	Local persona	Social position	Formality	As speaker	As addressee and figure		
sa steng / earth / human	*Thongru* Everyday person, worker or cadre.	Mundane, polluted, offstage. Never player in central dewa affairs. Innate abilities to host deities or demons. Ideally young, handsome man from good lineage.	Relatively informal, code inconsistent.	Taken variously as author, animator, and principal, uses wide variety of speech genres. *Voices interests of self, household and personal networks.*	Addressed if respected as lha pa, with title, referred to as thongru, or with his given name or nickname.		*Villager's voices: informal offstage*
mundane / polluted	*Lhawa (lha pa)* A social role played by *thongru*. Prepares human body for deity presence, guards it against demonic attack.	Purified intermediate status. Onstage at dewa events, but peripheral to central activities, defers to elders. Trained by senior *lha pa* or lama.	Relatively formal, code consistent. Formal dress for events, strict decorum to prepare.	Shifts toward animator and principal, commands traditional repertoire of oral and written genres. *Voices interests of whole village.*	Addressed and referred to by villagers as lha pa, with honorifics.		*Decreasing heteroglossia*
increasing formality	—Buddhist lamas recognize—	"ontological gap" (Keane); very difficult to communicate across—		—Dewa elders translate—			*Shift responsibility to new speaker*
sa bla / heaven / deities / transcendent / more pure →	*Leeden (lus rten)* Empty bodily "support" or vessel for the invisible body of the deity.	Consciousness and agency of *thongru* is absent. The deity is the public persona, onstage in specific ritual events, king or military commander of a specific village and region. Pronounces on status of the dewa, disciplines villagers, consults on illnesses, mediates conflicts.	High degree of deference from others while onstage. Code consistent, speech genres nonordinary, traditional. Uses repertoire of known hand gestures, facial expressions, bodily shaking, and puffing. But also unpredictably wild, angry, physical power indexes absolute rule.	Body is physical, but not willful animator. Deity is author; whole dewa as principal. Addresses whole village, occasionally specific villagers. Makes pronouncements, no reported speech. *Voices and reauthors dewa values and power.*	Thongru not present as addressee. Deity addressed as "grandfather" or "ancestor" in everyday reference, most often with titles and honorifics in ritual speech. After offerings, commanded to protect and enhance Buddhism and village fortune.		*Increasingly monologic* / *Deity's voice: formal onstage*

FIGURE 10. Voice shifts and deity medium personas in human-mountain deity communication practices in Rebgong

the mediums' physical capacity that his face and chest can swell enough to burst blood vessels and buttons. Emptied of the medium's consciousness, the body is nothing but a physical animator for the deity's authorship.

This shift to communication across the difficult human-deity divide is only credible, however, in the context of the medium's proper comportment and deference offstage. In practice, I found, Rebgong deity mediums must manage multiple personas. In everyday Tibetan reference, there are in fact three ideal personas for mediums: the *thongru*, the mundane villager offstage; the *lhawa* (Tib. *lha pa*), the specific social role he plays at particular events; and the *leeden* (Tib. *lus rten*, lit., "bodily support"), the physical medium onstage.[32]

For a person to be a credible and authoritative medium over time, all three personas must be performatively distinguishable and all three must be taken to be detached, in favor of the deity and elders' leadership, from decision-making in mundane village affairs. In this, the lhawa persona is crucial. As a liaison between mundane and transcendent realms who is not yet inhabited by the deity, the lhawa's relative formality for key events (abstaining from impure food and behavior, formal dress, long braid down, mastery of traditional oratory, deference to elders and lamas) signals both his capacity to purify and prepare his body for habitation by the proper deity and his status as representing dewa interests (and not his self-interests as the thongru).[33]

Significantly, Dorje's mediumship all along narrowed the participation roles of the lhawa and the leeden in unprecedented ways, thereby blurring distinctions between his ordinary and extraordinary personas, and weakening the credibility of his communications as Shachong. Thus by the mid-2000s when the conflict erupted, many villagers routinely referred to him only by his given name, and not by any titles or honorifics that had once been due a respected lhawa. Of course, given the secularization of their upbringing, Dorje and other mediums of his generation could not but live more as thongru. In that light, his and others' incapacity for deity speech could appear as deliberate avoidance: without mastery of traditional oral speech genres, to speak as the deity risks sounding too ordinary, too much like the presence of the thongru. Given recent state anxieties about the threat of charismatic yet scheming "evil cult" (Ch. *xiejiao*) leaders, such a risk would be all too great.[34]

However, in part due to the unprecedented state and dewa emphasis on Jima's Lurol after reforms, Dorje's mediumship pushed the envelope in ways his counterparts in other villages did not. As such, Dorje's Shachong accommodated state efforts to confine and tame deity presence within the folk ethnic spectacle of Lurol even though he would eventually refuse that confinement in particularly threatening ways. For one thing, as a lhawa, Dorje increasingly focused his participation on Lurol only, eliminating traditional roles as consultant in household affairs and opting out of some traditional visits to other villages. For another, Shachong's status as a particularly tamed (Buddhist) deity of the "white side" allowed Dorje's Shachong to appear as less fierce and wild than other deities; he rarely disciplined or addressed specific villagers. Unlike other mediums, whose frightening wildness and feats of self-mutilation compensated for their lack of speech to establish the deities' presence (see figure 10), Dorje's leeden was the most subdued in body language, most often only shaking slightly and puffing rhythmically as he gestured commands. Finally, unlike all other mediums I witnessed, Dorje did not keep his thongru persona offstage during Lurol. Instead, he limited the exhausting times of deity habitation to key ritual tasks only, frequently shifting from leeden to the casual thongru, slumping, spitting and smoking in plain sight on the temple veranda, laughing along with others at the antics of comedy routines.

All along then, but increasingly into the 2000s, the necessary split between the voices of Dorje and that of the deity did not come across as well; the thongru, along with his special interests, was emerging onstage, even when he was supposedly fully inhabited by Shachong. Dorje's mediumship thus facilitated the overall shift in Jima to a more skeptical relationship with the deities that elders so lamented to me in the 2000s. People were less certain that Shachong voiced the moral interests of the collective dewa. However, Dorje's unprecedented prominence in the early reform years reflected Shachong's renewed mandate as an activist defender of Jima's revived claims to collective autonomy. After all, as the excerpt above suggests, in the ritual texts Shachong is exhorted to battle on behalf of the dewa as a move to (brutally) take and incorporate demonic others' land and wealth. Villagers had watched helplessly as most of their valley floor farm lands had been expropriated piecemeal during the 1970s. But the state's prominent support for Jima's Lurol in the 1980s opened the way to an activist deity to whom still-fearful villagers could defer that battle as urbanization pressures increased.

In this, Dorje's Shachong worked closely with dewa elders, claiming the rightful autonomy of a (rural) administrative village, even after villagers were officially given urban status. The deity's most significant salvo came in 1994, before Tshering was reappointed as Jima's party secretary, and just as state enterprises began to fail and the fate of Jima's former lands was uncertain. On the annual day of dewa preparation for Lurol that summer, when the medium hosts Shachong in the temple to choose Lurol leaders, Dorje's

Shachong for the first time also chose a new village head. That move effectively routed and humiliated Gabzang, whose career as Jima head had begun during the Maoist years, and replaced him with a respected Jima patriarch with no experience as a Maoist official.

I was told that villagers were stunned; this was after all the first time the deity had acted so independently of elders. Still, villagers strongly supported the shift as definitely the will of Shachong because it was taken as a righteous defense of Jima's lands. Gabzang, I learned, despite his protests was suspected of colluding with the state to sell off Jima's lands during his tenure before and after reforms. Dorje's move as Shachong was thus a collective effort to regroup the dewa against encroachment, to retake the village head position as a dewa representative morally cleansed of the State. Emboldened by dewa support, Dorje's career as Jima's medium peaked in the late 1990s in close concert with dewa elders, the new temple keeper, and the new village head, just as the last Jima households gave up farming. That was when the new village head, along with Gabzang and Tshering, submitted petitions to the town government seeking the return of Jima lands from bankrupt state firms—to no avail. That was also when Dorje's Shachong called for and presided over the massive renovation of his temple made possible by the incomes of Jima's new urban landlords.

The magnificent temple was finished in the summer of 2000, just as the Great Open the West campaign was launched. By then, conditions were already in place for the fall of Jima's activist deity, a process, I argue, that culminated in Jima's fateful conflict five years later. Despite Shachong's best efforts, Jima's farmland had been delinked from the dewa's foundational heritage and transformed into a marketable commodity in sales to outsiders. In effect, the social contract with the state under which the initial land transfers had occurred was retroactively changed to a binding contract of sale. With that, the grounds for collective action in Jima and hopes for a return of dewa autonomy dissipated, pushing villagers to focus on the gains of their own households and networks and highlighting the relative wealth of new state officials and landlord households.

Indeed the risk all along of post-Mao state-local diplomacy in Lurol's ritual hospitality events was that they threatened to publicly collapse the moral distance between the dewa and the state. As provincial and prefecture officials focused on Jima's Lurol as a model of state-sanctioned folk tradition, those spectacles threatened to highlight the actually amoral nature of both Shachong and local state officials under capitalist reforms, emphasizing the declining relevance of dewa elders in capturing collective fortune. Villagers in fact tended to conceptualize state and divine authorities as part of the same, hierarchical universe, with themselves positioned at the bottom of the chain of command. The popular recognition was that post-Mao state officials shared the voracious appetites of mountain deities, and that their support of villagers, like that of deities, was not a moral guarantee (as in the Maoist socialist ideal), but a temporary boon captured by the well-placed gift. Gabzang, for example, was adamant in describing how, during those official visits to Jima's Lurol in the mid-1980s, for the first time Jima villagers were required to "serve and entertain" (Ch. *zhaodai*) state dignitaries with white offering scarves and all kinds of alcohol. "We had no such custom before!" he insisted.

For him, officials' presence at Lurol occasioned a comparison that denied the fiction that the Chinese state was anything but an extrinsic authority requiring hospitality and propitiation: "The meaning of Lurol," he stated, "is the same as dancing in front of state leaders like the prefecture head, to make the deities happy." Gabzang went on to contrast mountain deities' amorality with the moral stance of Buddhist lamas: "Mountain deities help thieves, after all! They will help whoever takes care of them well!" Dewa elders and younger Jima intellectuals in the 2000s thus lamented to me what they saw as elders' declining capacity to regulate villagers' interactions with Shachong in the face of gift inflation—counter to the Panchen Lama's hopes, quantity was eclipsing quality. Gabzang dismissed the now-massive amounts of offerings displayed at Lurol, commenting that the festival had become mere entertainment for tourists and a chance for villagers to show off their wealth. He brushed aside as inconsequential the increasing numbers of individuals making informal offerings to mountain deities to enhance their fortunes in household affairs, school exams, and business dealings. For him, the larger offerings and petty requests at Lurol did not guarantee a response from the deity; elders' ability to command his presence had waned: "Now the deity can't see human [i.e., dewa] affairs and sometimes he doesn't come at all [implying that the medium could be faking possession]."

The collective mandate of the 1990s, however, had insulated Dorje from criticisms of the altered forms of his practice, allowing for generous interpretations of his communications as Shachong. Thus, when Jima faced a new vacuum of authority in the early 2000s, and Dorje's Shachong once again attempted to intervene in choosing a village head, he failed spectacularly—the presence of Dorje the thongru had become too evident for villagers and state officials alike. The decisive moments had come several months before the showdown between Dorje's Shachong and the elders at the 2005 Lurol, and all hinged on the waning credibility of the village head position as urbanization pressures intensified. The village head Shachong had so startlingly chosen in 1994 had himself come under suspicion of using communal land to build a hotel in his own name. His and a subsequent village heads' resignations provided the ideal opening for county and town officials to put an end to Jima's de facto status as an administrative village and supersede dewa authority with the new urban community. Ironically, they did this by evoking the legal status of dewa collective autonomy.[35] In Gabzang's words:

> The village head must be elected by the People. That is the policy of the CCP [Ch. Gongchandang], you know. But the medium [Dorje] chose him. The prefecture and county officials all said that the medium has no role in choosing the village head, the People have to vote. You need the agreement of the majority. . . . So they came to investigate in the temple . . . and declared that the village head chosen by the medium was invalid. They said Jima had no village head! So in general they said Jima did not need a village head. They said this is because Jima is now an urban community under Longwu town.

In the name of democracy, state urbanization officials had challenged Shachong's collective mandate and eliminated Jima's village representative altogether, thereby attempting to put the deity back in his proper place in Lurol as merely a symbol of Jima's rural past. The loss of the village head made Tshering the de facto leader of all dewa affairs. Tshering was then rumored to have been the actual source of the criticisms that had led Shachong's village head to resign.

It was at this juncture in 2005 that a young Jima man, scion of a wealthy landlord family linked by marriage to Tshering, secured more foreign NGO funding to expand Shachong's temple yet again. In this ferment, the influx of outside capital brought long-simmering tensions to a head. We could see the next move of Dorje's Shachong as the last gasp of Jima dewa as a collective. On the day the temple expansion was to begin, Dorje came to be inhabited by the deity and gestured the construction to stop so that he could properly select leaders *and* reappoint the village head. For the first time, and in defiance of state authorities, Shachong attempted to reclaim the village head position (as evidence of his collective mandate) to challenge the ascendant elders. But his open defiance of elders exposed the breakdown of collectivity in Jima and thus highlighted Dorje's mundane persona as a villager with networks of his own: he came from a less wealthy household, but his prominent uncles and nine siblings were strong supporters. Thus the wealthy elders interpreted his gestures not as the voice of Shachong but as the self-interested voices of the thongru and of the men translating the deity, an opposing faction seeking control of the project; they ignored Shachong's instructions.

Dorje's riskiest move came next. He retired to the temple with some of his supporters. Then, even though officials had ruled the village head obsolete, Shachong commanded them to go from household to household and collect votes on two candidates for village head. According to several witnesses, when his aides dutifully inquired at households, villagers recoiled in fear and confusion and refused to vote, counseling them that such a thing was inappropriate and dangerous. Thus the aides dropped the effort and an election was never held. In this case, the effort of Dorje's Shachong to relegitimize the village head position by appropriating the state's election format blurred the voices of thongru and deity too much, and took him to the outer limits of his dewa mandate. Here Dorje's Shachong strayed so far beyond the realm of dewa ritual that he threatened the precarious silent pact among Tibetans. Indeed, as Gabzang put it, officials' threats during their temple investigation a few months earlier had been indirect, but pointed:

> If Dorje continues to be helpful during Lurol, then there's no problem. But he keeps getting mixed up in this and that . . . [investigators] said, 'all you retired officials,' (a few of them were involved, you know), 'you state officials don't need to be here—leave! You don't need to be mixed up in such things, you get salaries from the State!

Shachong's attempted election had defied such official efforts to separate state and dewa. Dorje thus teetered close to the edge of embodying the "evil cult" threat to regional party leaders—raising for the first time since the Maoist years the unacknowledged issue of the gap between Tibetan communities and Chinese state administrative units, the lie of Tibetan political autonomy under CCP rule.

The very public showdown between the wealthy elders and Dorje's Shachong at Lurol two months later was thus the deity's last-ditch effort to challenge a new party-led urban landlord and official elite in Jima. By ejecting the elders, he denied the morality of their temple service and linked their wealth and authority to the venal motives of the State associated with Tshering. In this, he appealed once again to dewa autonomy, but the grounds for Dorje's capacity to voice that monologically were gone—the elders questioned the very presence of the deity onstage, leading to the collapse of Lurol entirely and Dorje's departure in a self-imposed exile. In the ensuing months, the loss of the deity and dewa collectivity meant the specter of the State haunted all involved; no one could claim to legitimately represent collective interests in the dewa: "The elder faction just wants the dewa's power," asserted one supporter of Dorje. "There is a lot of dewa money and they are corrupt! [Ch. Fubai]." Their accusations were met with the same: "The younger men just want to take power from the elders!" a supporter of the elders told me. In that light, even the redistribution of massive Lurol offerings came under radical question, reducing temple gifts to alienable dewa capital: both sides privately accused the other of appropriating offerings for selfish enjoyment and gain.[36]

Conclusion: Faking Favor

Welcome the Olympics; Establish a New Trend; Be Civilized; Promote Harmony

—Postunrest slogan banner in Longwu town streets, July 2008

Jima's 2007 Lurol two years after the conflict erupted seemed to stage, once more, the triumphant return of Shachong. At Lurol, Dorje was again center stage as his medium, his silent gestures more wild and animated than I had ever seen him, an alluring spectacle for the hundreds of camera lenses pointed his way. The wife of one of the opposing elders I spoke with grumbled that nothing had changed, "It's just back to the way it was before [e.g., with Dorje and his supporters in charge]." "They're just leaders for three days only [e.g., during the festival]," replied her husband. His view pointed to the larger consequences for Tibetan villagers of the fundamentally altered conditions for public presence in Rebgong by 2007.

FIGURE 11. The deity Amnye Shachong inhabits Dorje (on left, in white) at the feet of the eighth Shartshang lama (seated), Jima temple veranda, summer 2007. Author's photo.

In this chapter, a Bakhtinian perspective on voice as contested presence allowed us to look beyond the freeze-frames of tourists' photos and scholars' ahistorical accounts of Lurol and Tibetan deity mediumship in the valley. Bakhtin's focus on the often agonistic dialogism at the heart of any claim to single-voiced authoritative presence gave us tools for understanding the actual dynamism and high stakes of Tibetan cultural revival and state-local relations under post-Mao reforms. Dorje and Tshering, both Jima men operating against the traumatic history of the Maoist conquest of the dewa, emerged as commensurate, yet highly compromised mediums voicing competing sources of authority. Through them, the 2005–7 conflict in Jima staged the presence, and thus the very existence, of the deity and the dewa against those of the CCP and the new urban community, as state-sponsored capitalism put Jima's ancestral lands into outsiders' hands.

In this light we can begin to grasp the heightened risks of hospitality for Tibetans in Rebgong, and the breakdown of silent pact diplomacy in the unrest on the valley floor that erupted just six months later in 2008. The Jima conflict coincided precisely with the watershed moment in the frontier zone when the socialist sleight of hand once again resulted in the widespread expropriation of Tibetan lands, only this time under the very different timespace idioms of capitalist "market integration." That is, when the very grounds of communal sovereignty and fortune are at stake, hospitality spectacles, like those of Maoist work teams offering free medical care or welfare gifts in the early 1950s (Weiner 2012), or of post-Mao officials attending Jima's reestablished Lurol to show their support for Tibetan "cultural revival," cannot easily mask tensions over the nature and jurisdictions of hosts and guests. In the early 1950s, CCP work teams offered Rebgong Tibetans socialist entitlements and promises of only temporary adjustments and voluntary choices in return for their incorporation into the nation-state. But those promises never made clear regional party officials' endgame: their plans to implement socialist transformation as land collectivization under CCP management, including plans for wide-scale settling of Tibetan pastoralists and immigration of Chinese settlers.[37] That led to rural Tibetans' open revolt when the endgame became clear in 1958. In the 2000s, however, the endgame (and the end of the yang dar years in Rebgong) was precipitated by the central CCP's Eleventh Five Year Plan for national development in 2006. Under that rubric, the twin campaigns of constructing a New Socialist Countryside and bolstering grassroots party presence were the practical manifestations of President Hu's calls for scientific development and harmony.

As Jima villagers discovered, that was when the new temporal and spatial terms of authoritarian capitalism became painfully apparent: its potential to overwhelm the diplomatic compromise between socialism and older Tibetan forms of authority that had been promised in post-Mao Tibetan autonomous governance. The new urban community, after all, now included as equal subjects under CCP leadership all residents, including Chinese and Muslim immigrants and newly settled pastoralists. Thus, the contested revival of Jima's Lurol and deity mediumship was, in the end, part and parcel of what was essentially a military conflict. It was a renewed battle for fortune in which, true to the legacy of Tibetan frontier politics, Tibetans' efforts to capture fortune at the expense of regional opponents by incorporating outside sources of authority resulted in the loss of the last legal vestige of Jima's collective autonomy.

From this angle, the return of Shachong in Jima's 2007 Lurol was far from a triumph; it signaled instead the death of the dewa as a landed community under Tibetan elders' rightful rule. The fall of the activist deity offstage meant that Dorje's Shachong was now a particularly compromised divine agent, leading the way back to the silent pact that allowed urban Tibetans not to directly confront the sources of their disenfranchisement. When he returned in 2007, Dorje's Shachong had miraculously and for the first time spoken before the lama to evidence his presence (see figure 11), but his return to silence during most of the Lurol festival signaled a collective retreat from public presence on Tibetan terms. He was particularly wild onstage that summer, but his role in Jima had been tamed in the face of state sanction; he was put back within the proper folk confines of Lurol's ethnic pageantry. Unlike in 2005, this time the presence of Dorje's Shachong was not publicly challenged, but neither was that of Party Secretary Tshering. In 2007, Tshering, his neck adorned with the white offering scarf, for the first time took up prominent positions on the temple veranda during Lurol. That scarf, I learned, spoke volumes to villagers on both sides of the conflict. When a deity, through his medium, places a scarf around the neck of an elder, he indicates for all to see the bestowal of his divine favor. Most villagers knew that Tshering's scarf faked that favor. Indeed, a supporter of his proudly told me how he had watched as Tshering entered the temple unbidden at the opening of Lurol and bestowed *himself* with the scarf. "That was good," said the supporter, "it showed them he's in charge!"

Thus when Dorje's Shachong capped Lurol with a triumphant closing speech, Tshering standing next to him, the party secretary's scarf framed and diminished them both. Shachong's speech was brief and limited to general pronouncements about the success of the day and directives to villagers to stay unified and avoid "fighting." Tshering claimed the last word, revoicing Shachong's speech for villagers, his unprecedented presence there embodying the now-direct rule party leaders asserted over Jima. "Did you notice that no one whooped in response?" an opponent pointed out to me later. Still, no one openly challenged him. Jima's 2007 Lurol thus culminated in the open secret of a counterfeit elder-divine partnership. Despite villagers' efforts to voice the State as an extrinsic other, the moral distance between it and the dewa had collapsed. Tshering's faked scarf indicated the loss of dewa elders' and the deity's mandate to protect collective fortune over the increasingly class-based interests of households. In this context, Dorje and Tshering's final dialogue onstage voiced the State above all; their speeches mirrored the silencing platitudes of state admonitions for citizens to remain harmonious while seeking middle-class comfort.

The triumph of the State in Jima had consequences that reached far beyond Lurol. As development pressures divided and pushed rural Tibetans off lands they had once controlled, by the summer 2007 rural regions across Rebgong were exploding with local skirmishes and protests, which police worked overtime to control—the ability of state officials to enforce local harmony was exceedingly fragile. Ironically, in Jima the state-enforced end of Shachong as the dewa's activist deity perhaps facilitated the final release of the deity from his role as a guardian of land-based collective fortune, freeing him to support the individual fortunes of the youth and businessmen clamoring for his attention in the urban community. The death of the dewa meant the loss of *yang* as the product of a Tibetan-controlled life-giving communal territory. This was not just a figurative death, but the loss of long-term, collective vitality on Tibetan villagers' terms.

Thus, when a few months later young Tibetan men across Rebgong participated in the unrest and public protests during the run-up to the 2008 Olympics and PAP troops were brought in to enforce martial law in town, Jima elders and officials were called on to be vanguard agents of the state. In those tense months, I heard some privately grumble that Jima men had refused to participate in the demonstrations; Jima was now the heart of "Chinese Rebgong" (Tib. *rgya gi reb gong*), they said. But Jima elders were cornered; they had to demonstrate their loyalty in their control over dewa youth. That April, after the worst of the street clashes with security forces, I watched on prefecture television as Tshering and other elders were admonished by prefecture officials. The elders' faces were shocked and grim, seemingly swollen as if possessed with all that they could not say. Tshering stood to speak, as if proud: "Jima Urban Community has a lot of officials; this is our advantage in conducting work. Our officials worked hard to influence people and thus no Jima person participated in the riots." Jima, apparently, had done its part to uphold harmony.

಼ | | CHAPTER 3

Othering Spaces, Cementing Treasure

Concrete, Money, and the Politics of Value in Kharnak Village School

In this chapter, we delve further into the dialogic nature of development encounters by heading up the Guchu River to explore the awkward dynamics of a primary school renovation project I helped manage in the rural Tibetan village of Kharnak. My offer to help fund a new courtyard wall for Kharnak's school turned out to be a much more complex undertaking than I had ever anticipated. Contrary to my original naive notion that I would remain in the background, my Tibetan male friends from Kharnak expected me to play key roles in the wall project as a fundraiser (they urged me to help broker a much larger donation from a foreign woman abroad), as a comanager (they expected me to attend all negotiation meetings with contractors), and as a symbolic overseer (they wanted me to conspicuously audit the construction process for quality). Foreign donors in secular development projects were in fact very problematic persons for Tibetan villagers. As empowered outsiders offering gifts, what jurisdictions did donors host? What obligations to them did recipients take on? Such hospitality dilemmas, I discovered, revolved around the contested meaning and value of seemingly mundane material media of exchange like concrete, offering scarves, and money. To meet the potentially community-altering timespace terms of development workers' gifts, Tibetan village leaders had to "capture" and convert both donors and gifts into mediums of value for their communities alone.

Unbeknownst to Drolma and Lobzang, the offering scarves I had brought into their household in the spring of 2008 had traveled some distance to get to their guestroom. After that conflictual summer of 2007 in Jima, I returned to Rebgong with my family that fall. But once we were settled in the Jima house, I was quickly swept up in the projects of other villages several kilometers upriver. I had mentioned to friends that as a way to "give back" while I conducted research on the impact of development policies in Tibetan communities, I was interested in funding some small projects in support of Tibetan schools. In my naiveté, I had somehow thought that that would be a "side" pursuit, and that as a giver I could stay relatively anonymous. Little did I know that those projects would define my time and personas in Rebgong (especially after the military crackdown), and that those problematic offering scarves would be key instruments of my capture as a donor for two rival villages in the Upper Narrows (Tib. 'phrang yar nang) of Rebgong's Guchu River valley: Kharnak (which I focus on here) and Langmo (the focus of chapter 4).

The Guchu River valley lies at the lowest end of that major tributary of the great Machu (Ch. Huanghe, Yellow) River,[1] which flows down to China's "interior" from the heights (up to 6,200 meters) of the Tibetan plateau. To the unfamiliar eye, especially when driving upriver on the new concrete provincial highway at the height of the summer, the upper valley in the early 2000s could look like the ideal rural respite from the noisy bustle and choking smog of lowland cities. Traveling with urban Tibetan friends of mine through that watershed often meant stops to lie awhile on grassy peaks dotted with colorful and fragrant flowers and herbs, and exclamations, in part for my benefit, at how "joyfully pleasant" (Tib. skyid po) it was. Indeed, the views from those spots were a feast for the eyes, the very vistas that drew thousands of tourists to Rebgong annually. Looking southwest from the long, wide oval of the main valley, the seat of Rongbo Monastery, urban density fades to farm fields of green barley or yellow rapeseed. There, the valley narrows upriver to a tight defile between mountain ridges that rise to three thousand meters before opening again into the wide, flat oval of Kharnak village's fields. On either side, earth-toned clusters of the square, adobe courtyard homes of Tibetan dewas are visible in the greens and blues of mountainsides and tributary valleys, tucked among the serpentine, stairstep sculpture of terraced fields and scattered juniper forests.[2]

I often marveled at how immersive it felt to be in those fragrant mountains, how their viewpoints, like the great promise of the three-dimensional virtual worlds of video games or of Google Earth's ever-mobile drone eye,

FIGURE 12. View of Upper Narrows mountains and highland villages, summer 2008. Author's photo.

seemed to offer immediate access to both a transcendent perspective and to an embodied experience of the region. But looks, as they say, can be deceiving. In fact, traveling upriver with Tibetans from the various villages of the Upper Narrows was always a bewildering process of being placed within half-hidden histories of divine and embattled abodes (Tib. *gnas*). In practice, the place name Trang Yarnang (Upper Narrows) is, recalling Bakhtin, a historically loaded idiom. The name carries with it a sense of perilous journeys through ambushable rocky gorges, a centuries-old echo of the fears of travelers leaving the relative safety of the lowland town. But under heightened state repression in the early 2000s, people often experienced car rides and mountain hikes upriver as journeys of relief, spaces of relative safety where Tibetan residents could break the silent pact and talk of their anxieties and resentments in the face of breakneck development and the specter of land appropriation ("the State owns everything," sighed one driver as we passed one of the small hydroelectric dams that now plied the river every several kilometers). Or they could gesture toward the now-unseen marks of the miraculous interventions of lamas and deities in their highland communities. Those trips with them then were often restyled pilgrimages, part and parcel of rival efforts to capture me on behalf of the projects of particular communities.[3]

This was abundantly clear during my first trip up to Kharnak village in December 2007 with Gendun, the small and wiry, fast-talking schoolteacher in his early thirties from Kharnak who first told me of the dewa's plans to build a new courtyard wall for their primary school. As our Tibetan driver headed the taxi upriver, Gendun passionately lamented the declining and marginalized state of Tibetan language education, linking that directly to the sinking status of Tibetans in general under recent development policies. Switching voices as we ascended, his rapid-fire stories from the backseat narrated the terrain we traversed not as the idyllic rural backdrop for a generic Tibetan folk, but as the specific home territories (Tib. *pha gzhis*, lit., "father-foundation") of fortune-seeking Tibetan dewa, networked across centuries of seething movement and strife that continue to this day.

Thus in the Upper Narrows, as elsewhere in the Sino-Tibetan frontier zone, the vast "natural" vistas of mountain views belied the density and unfolding history of human-nonhuman relations there. Over time, my senses would be tuned differently, to perceive every single topographic feature, square meter of cultivable or herdable land, and built environment as spoken for, inhabited, and fraught with (mis)fortune. As a particularly consequential container of fortune, Kharnak village, with its cluster of some 185 households and one thousand people,[4] is centrally located in a wide and flat bowl, perfectly situated as a gateway to the grasslands of the Guchu River's upper reaches, where Tibetan farming dewas give way to transmigrant pastoralist ones. There on a level shelf carved into a hillock directly above the new highway that bifurcated the village was Kharnak's primary school. At first glance, it looked like most other village schools I had seen in a context where concrete was still rare and expensive; the school consisted in just a few brick and concrete buildings in a dirt courtyard surrounded by crumbling packed-earth walls. Next to the scraped and patched aluminum and brick gate was a faded County Education Bureau slogan in Chinese from the 1990s, painted in red on peeling stucco clinging precariously to the earthen wall: "Universalize compulsory education; Improve the quality [Ch. *sushi*] of the population!"

But this was no mere tour, where I could simply look at inert objects that never look (much less talk) back, and thereby remain free to give and get out. Instead, the politics of presence became palpable for me as soon as I crossed the threshold of that gate and entered a Kharnak village hospitality event as a Very Important Guest, a potential donor. There waiting to greet me were the smiling project leaders, headed by Gendun's Kharnak age mate and counterpart in this story, Drakpa, who was the Tshothang school district head and a CCP member. To my eternal embarrassment, in a gesture that would lay

FIGURE 13.   Kharnak school wall 1990s County Education Bureau slogan: "Universalize compulsory education; improve the quality [Ch. *sushi*] of the population!" winter 2007. Author's photo.

the template for many such encounters in his school district, Drakpa led the others in draping white offering scarves around my neck as they welcomed me to the school. I knew the drill, from the televised hospitality spectacles of official visits "down to the countryside" (Ch. *xia xiang*). But I never felt so awkwardly onstage as when I stood under the captivating touch of scarves loaded with the uncertain hopes of villagers. I soon discovered that I could be anything but an anonymous donor choosing to be generous on my own terms.

As we saw in chapter 2, by 2007 the new terms of authoritarian capitalism in Rebgong meant top-down urbanization pressures down in town. In the Upper Narrows, those pressures played out as a deepening assault on the material shape and value, or "quality," of rural life. In that context, the Kharnak school wall project, like all other dewa-based construction projects upriver, was in fact another battle for fortune. That is, on the threshold of Kharnak's school grounds, I was drawn into a different kind of counterdevelopment effort, in which the sovereign presence of a Tibetan community was again vitally at stake, and yet (as we will see, ironically) the conditions, natures, and futures of gifts and their recipients were particularly obscure.

This time, in stark contrast to Jima village's class-based and intergenerational factionalism, the politics of presence in Kharnak were manifest in a partially stealthy, yet aggressively expanding neosocialist communalism, one in which the proper scale of the home community (and container of fortune) was nonetheless in question. During the wall repair project, those tensions came to a head in the rift that opened in our management team, between the charismatic and rebellious teacher Gendun on one hand and on the other, the staid and careful education official Drakpa. And everything, it turned out, the very future of the village as well as Gendun and Drakpa's own positions and relationship, revolved around the nature of concrete as a particularly problematic medium of supposedly modern value.

Concrete Heterotopias: Materiality and Mediating Value

My beloved fatherland, the Golden Realm of Rebgong!
Your perimeters are adorned with mountains and valleys.
Wealth and riches swirl around the mountains and valleys like clouds.
The rushing sound of the Guchu River voices a praise song for you,
My fatherland, The Golden Realm of Rebgong!
The education that develops our nationality expands from here.
The calligraphy pens of the nationality's scholars spread from here.

—Refrain from popular 2000s Tibetan language song,
"The Golden Realm of Rebgong"

In chapters 1 and 2, I introduced a linguistic anthropological approach to human-nonhuman relations in Rebgong.[5] Mikhail Bakhtin's perspectives on the embodied dynamics of chronotopes (historically loaded idioms) and voice (linguistically performed personas) in communicative events gave us ways to understand language and semiotics as inextricably intertwined with—indeed constitutive of—people's experiences of material or palpable presence, human or not. In this chapter, we consider the construction of school grounds as particular kinds of built environments, and we delve further into the politics of presence by looking more closely at the contested nature of certain material objects (scarves, money, and especially, concrete) as pivotal media of value. That is, those objects, in their circulation, are meant to actively imbue places and people with highly prized qualities. Gendun and Drakpa's project, after all, was not to build any old enclosure for Kharnak's school, but a gorgeous stone, brick and concrete wall, complete with a Chinese-style gate resembling that of a Buddhist temple. Here, I situate the wall and gate construction in the broader politics and hazards of hospitality events. We thereby come to see how the politics of presence play out at key junctures in which people work to capture and convert slippery objects and unclear value across media and events (scarves to money, money to scarves, money to concrete, concrete to quality students, donors to guests, recipients to sovereign hosts, statist school to Tibetan abode).[6]

We already saw in chapter 1 how Tibetan offering scarves in the early 2000s in Rebgong were positioned as a kind of antimoney, a material exchange object that promised to convert the potentially amoral quantities of monetized commensuration to the specifically Tibetan qualities of moral exchange. Here, I emphasize again that the specific formal features of objects, and thus their capacities to shape or to encourage action, are both material and semiotic. That is, like how the soft silkiness and whiteness of offering scarves were associated with specific experiences of altruistic Buddhism and Tibetan reciprocity, or how I came to sense Tibetans' mountainous landscapes differently from my earlier visual impressions, people in fact sense objects as bundles of selected qualities, themselves linked (iconically, in relations of likeness, and indexically, in relations of cause and efficacy) to the qualities of other desired or undesired objects, timespaces, and persons.[7] Yet, recalling the scalar slipperiness of exchange objects in hospitality encounters, their qualities will not necessarily be sensed (and thus valued) by others in the same way—objects offer no sheer presence to human interlocutors. From this angle, we can look beyond the charismatic rhetorics of modernizing development and understand value not as inhering in the essential substances of persons and things, but as emerging in an ongoing interpretive politics that is embedded in particular histories of power and hierarchicized exchange.[8]

To hone in on these dynamics specific to built environments in statist development projects, in this chapter I turn to Michel Foucault's notion of "other-spaces" (heterotopias) (1967, 1). By that he meant built environments, including two-dimensional artifacts like carpets, movie screens and wall surfaces, but quintessentially schools, prisons, public housing complexes, or even shopping malls, that are meant to counter, disrupt, alter or improve key aspects of existing social spaces and times. That is, other-spaces for Foucault are materially and aesthetically specific social engineering projects. Thus here, I take up Foucault's concept of heterotopias in order to complement Bakhtin's approach to the temporal and spatial dynamics of personhood in discourse practices.[9] These are built environments specifically aimed at extending or distributing certain agencies (like those of deities, the state, the party, or the dewa) and thereby positioning inhabitants in historically charged timespaces as valued or devalued social figures.[10]

This then helps clarify why concrete is such a pivotal medium of value, and why the meaning and efficacy of its various qualities were particularly problematic for Tibetans in Rebgong's Upper Narrows. As the key building material in modernist and nationalist other-spaces, concrete in China, as elsewhere, has been the stuff of dreams. For development planners since the advent of the PRC, it promised spaces for ideally hygienic and ordered lifestyles, and completely knowable and responsive citizens. And under meteoric urban construction since the 1990s especially, the assemblage of materials, practices, and industries that constitute the amalgam we call "concrete" has become so pervasive as to be utterly mundane. Yet the sheer weight of its presence speaks to the fantastic excess of China's reform-era development "miracle"—concrete bonds and finishes massive, nation-building infrastructures;[11] it enables the economies of scale and standardization practices fueling the recent state-sponsored housing construction boom;[12] and the industries that create concrete now generate the record-setting air pollution choking the very cities it builds.[13]

From the perspective I'm developing here then, we would have to consider concrete not as inert, artificial stone, but as a shifting and high-stakes medium of value. In other words, it is a pivotal artifact with a set of sensuous qualities that, in particular contexts, evoke desired potencies, states, and timespace scales of human (and nonhuman) agency.[14] In practice then, there is no inherent difference between concrete and other kinds of ritual implements with which people strive to naturalize meaning and efficacy to various ends. That is, there is an uncertain magic to concrete; it is a kind of alchemical process seeking to transmute or convert a variety of substances and a wide range of people and practices (in our case, especially donors, the money they offer, and the students they supposedly support) into the elixir of modern life and the profits of canny investments. As such, the meaning and value of concrete in particular situations is radically open to risk and contestation. Indeed, as Chinese planners increasingly tout urbanization as an ultimate good and the gateway to ideally integrated markets out west, concrete forms have evoked for residents and visitors alike both the soaring heights of modern progress and the crushing depths of failure and decrepitude.[15]

As I discovered in the Upper Narrows, the meaning and value of concrete in rural Tibetan school building projects was anything but a marginal concern. In the midst of our wall repair project in Kharnak, the devastation of the massive Sichuan earthquake (May 2008) just south of us, and especially the thousands of children crushed to death in shoddily built schools there, raised the issue of low-quality concrete to the level of national- and global-scale moral crisis. In the earthquake zone, the piles of crumbling and unreinforced concrete rubble revealed rural schools as quintessential "tofu dregs projects" (Ch. *doufuzha gongcheng*).[16] For protesters and contrite officials alike, those concrete tombs embodied the most reprehensible form of what Melanie van der Hoorn (2009, 1) has called "corrupt architecture": schools built with the messy remainders of time, materials, and money after multiple stages of disinvestment, graft, and shortcuts.

That disaster belied the promise, reflected in the peeling slogan on Kharnak school's earthen wall, of central state, UN, and NGO campaigns since the 1990s, touting the importance of funding universal primary education in rural China:[17] that high-quality (Ch. *zhiliang*, Tib. *rgyu spus*) concrete school grounds would necessarily call forth and shape high-quality (Ch. *suzhi*, Tib. *spus tshad*) students, as national citizens and future market subjects. The specter of the collapsed schools in Sichuan reframed concrete instead as a key material sign of collapsed socialist values and, in the context of renewed anticorruption campaigns, as a threat to CCP legitimacy.[18] The rubble revealed the tragic reality, something Gendun and Drakpa knew well, that in practice rural education out west was at the bottom of both administrative hierarchies and development priorities. As the optimistic yang dar era peaked by the mid-2000s in Rebgong, the rescaling of state development authority to urban centers entailed decentralized education funding, heightening pressure on regional school officials to find resources for their own districts and incentivizing them to charge fees or to demand household contributions.[19]

In this, I learned, Tongren County and Kharnak dewa teachers and officials struggled with the particularly problematic nature of interethnic relations and the status of Tibetan language and culture in the modern futures they hoped for. In the Upper Narrows, secular schools were built in a few villages, including in Kharnak, only after the CCP takeover in the early 1950s. By the 2000s, Longwu town was the site of the prefecture's three main Tibetan high schools, and, as in the praise song above, Rebgong had come to be known across Tibetan regions and into the diaspora as the center of a flourishing Tibetan culture and intellectualism.[20] That reputation in turn was taken up by prefecture and then central tourism officials, touting Longwu town as a Model National Culture City (Quanguo Lishi Wenhua Mingcheng).[21] The Rebgong Culture Concert, which celebrated that status in 2006, even performed the final lines of the praise song lyrics above, by opening with a dance in which a Tibetan boy is ceremoniously handed a calligraphy pen, with which he then reverently dances.

By the time I got caught up in Gendun and Drakpa's plans for Kharnak school, the gap between that vision for Rebgong Tibetan education and the dismal reality of Tibetan primary schools had in their accounts reached crisis proportions. Funds were scarce, teachers poorly paid, attendance rates low and Tibetan high schoolers could not compete with the most prestigious prefecture high school, which was dominated by the children of Chinese state and business elites. In that context of interethnic and state-local tension, I realized, Tibetan village primary schools were particularly fraught other-spaces. They were sites of confusingly overlapping and competing efforts to revalue and rescale people and places in the face of top-down urbanization pressures across the valley. Our beautiful new concrete wall, in turn, was a key medium for an ongoing battle for fortune over the relevant scale and value of the altered space it was supposed to demarcate and contain. On it, Gendun and Drakpa, along with village leaders, forged their hopes for an ideal amalgam of neosocialist and Tibetan regionalist aspirations—first and foremost on behalf of Kharnak village, their home territory.

Rivers to the Future: Capturing the Donor in the Battle for Fortune

As for the outer container, the environment:

> To the west, Choje Dongrub Rinchen taught and tamed the dewa's birth god, the great conqueror of enemies, King Makgol, who in an instant first established the land as a fortress and a material support [Tib. *rten*] for this dewa.

> To the east, on the regional deity Chazey's mountain, the deity resides in his palace of a beautiful white pine forest.

> and there, amidst cool streams and the singing of the blue cuckoo bird, sits the Buddhist hermitage of Jetsha, where the melodious sound of the chanted Dharma echoes throughout the valley, and the bright light of blessing-power [Tib. *byin rlabs*] shines like many pearls scattered across the ground.

> To the north, at the intersection in the shape of a vajra cross, the blessing-power of the Amdo mani stone pile and the Great Liberation Stupa is widely renowned.

As for the inner contents, the sentient beings:

> Like a golden rosary of Geshes who obtained authority through Buddhist learning and realization, many scholar-lamas such as Losal Nyima came from this village.

In particular, nowadays the dewa is also home to many thinkers rich
in wisdom who have made great achievements and provided role
models in developing secular education everywhere.

Further, the clever ones who have traveled out and mastered
cosmopolitan knowledge cherish the lives of us [Tibetan]
mountain-dwellers, and during their glorious careers strive
for the light of wisdom.

—Excerpt from place eulogy poem describing Kharnak dewa,
used as voice-over in the village's New Year video, 2008

To get at the actual scalar slipperiness of school grounds for Gendun and
Drakpa, we cannot consider the materiality of built environments separately
from the dialogic nature of language in practice.[22] Recalling the three major
historical idioms of exchange and fortune in the frontier zone that I laid out
in chapter 1 (lama-lay leader alliance, Maoist socialism, and New Socialism or
authoritarian capitalism), Gendun and Drakpa's counterdevelopment vision
for the school was not an atavistic, reactionary traditionalism, the revival of
an ancient Tibetan ontology. Instead, like the Panchen Lama, they sought to
position Kharnak in a complex, if ambivalent, hybrid modernity that dialogically appropriated aspects of each of those three main visions for translocal
exchange. And in so doing, they could at times performatively overcomply
with expectations for personhood and value that they attributed to powerful
outsiders (like state superiors or foreign donors). And a vital part of that process was capturing and converting me, through the dynamics of verbal persuasion, from a distanced donor to an intimate patron dedicated to Kharnak.

In that multilingual locale, where most rural Tibetans spoke only regional
dialects of Tibetan, I was often struck by how most foreign development
workers and donors entered into complex transactions and hospitality events
in a near-total linguistic blackout. Foreigners I met, all of them well intentioned, coped with the dilemmas this posed for communication in various
ways. Some sheepishly admitted their limits and relied heavily on translators. Others seemed blithely unaware of any deficit or even claimed that
knowing the language would get in the way of a more visceral empathy
for Tibetans. Yet in the often-condensed time frames of their visits, the vast
majority could be unconsciously casual about their linguistic limits, evincing
folk theories of language as a simply transparent medium of communication, easily converted to others (like gestures, or the shared bodyspaces of
festivals or meals). By contrast, Tibetans like Gendun and Drakpa had a passionate sense of the historically charged nature of the Tibetan language—its

precious irreplaceability. Indeed as we'll see, the stakes of our school wall project were, in a sense, all about language.

I came to realize that linguistic avoidance (conscious or not) is part and parcel of the occultness, the enabling opacity, at the heart of transnational development encounters.[23] This is because, in hierarchical exchanges enabled by the mediating presence of translators, the linguistic blackout allows foreign givers to remain relatively insulated from the sometimes painful complexities of social relationships. They can thereby manage the timespace terms of their own presence, maintaining a safe distance from reciprocal obligations that keeps them quasi-absent, transcendently mobile. Meanwhile, in the now-global requirement to audit transfers of goods and cash for efficient and proper use, development workers must presume (or pretend) that "transparency" is possible.[24] For example, in the ubiquitous rituals of project contract-signings, or for illiterate Tibetans, fingerprintings, development workers must seek signs of recipients' sheer presence, their authentic (and innocent) intentioned agreement. Thus, to uphold the missions of their organizations across vast distances and linguistic gaps, development workers can get drawn into what Arturo Escobar referred to as the development industry's "gluttony of vision" (1995, 192). In other words, development workers can fetishize the visible (versus seeking information beyond the reach of the eye) as quasi-scientific access to self-evident objects. For them, seeing is supposed to be believing.

My dialogic approach to ethnography, however, compels me to explore instead the consequences of listening, that is, rendering myself in part vulnerably present on interlocutors' own linguistic terms. As Susan Harding put it, referring to her ethnographic research among Christian evangelicals in the United States, "If you are willing to listen . . . you have begun to convert" (1986, 178).[25] This was not an instantaneous or one-way process—the welcome scarves at the old school gate were in fact only an opener. In our long, in-depth conversations and planning sessions over the subsequent months, we reciprocally vied for presence as the men worked to voice themselves in ways they thought I expected. Over time I came to better understand the charged and problematic nature of foreigners' presence in the valley: potential recipients of their gifts competed to counter foreigners' godlike mobility and opaque origins and motives by emplacing them as once and future guests.

Prefecture and county education officials, for example, would proudly show me their collections of outside visitors' business cards (including those of eastern and overseas Chinese), and boast of how well they had feted them.[26] And most important, in the 1990s and early 2000s Rebgong residents often construed foreigners as substitutes for both lost lamas and absent state officials. In the waning years of yang dar, the presence of foreign donors could seem to counter the perceived loss of Buddhist-socialist compassion. Thus, in the escalation of hospitality spectacles across the valley, foreigner givers (especially non-Chinese ones) could be taken as counterstate agents, intrinsically compassionate and pure of corruption precisely because of their willingness to help unknown others. As officials' careers were increasingly pegged to their ability to bring in outside revenue (see below), the presence of foreign bodies on their visits to constituents could work to rebrand officials themselves as caring socialists.[27] That process in turn was materialized in the proliferating media of gratitude and achievement: the now-ubiquitous donor plaques and awards for official achievement adhered to school and office walls and gates.[28]

My own conversion process began in the opposite direction of Kharnak's school. In a trip that indicated the widening scale of Kharnak men's development efforts, we drove downriver to Gendun's new apartment in the growing suburbs north of town—"we don't call these 'homes,' [Tib. *yul*]" he said in the car. "We say they're 'Chinese houses' [Tib. *rgya khang*]." There Drakpa, along with the bespectacled Tashi, Kharnak's passionate school principal and himself a CCP member, were waiting to greet me. Over the next two hours, they laid out their case for themselves and the school wall project.

Tibetan salaried state workers, as representatives of Tibetan communities under the silent pact, have to be expert scaling agents, artfully and diplomatically shifting among often-clashing timespaces. Indeed in that and many subsequent conversations, the Kharnak men attempted to ally with me as cosmopolitan and compassionate modernizing agents. Yet as they also sought to attract the elusive attention of their state superiors, it was clear that Gendun and Drakpa especially were negotiating obligations to multiple scales of communities and levels of state bureaus. The two were lineage affines and peers who grew up together in Kharnak village upriver, but Gendun was a teacher at a middle school in another lowland district, and because of his charisma and (rudimentary) English skills, he had just been appointed to a yearlong fundraising position for the Tongren County Education Bureau (serving thirteen school districts and more than fifty schools). Meanwhile Drakpa was responsible for managing and fundraising for the twelve schools of his rural school district in the Upper Narrows, with his office based at the Tshothang township seat upriver. And both of them reported to Shawojia, the notoriously harddriving Tibetan head of the Tongren County Education Bureau down in town.

Both men thus had to grapple with the moral dilemmas of their positions within the vertical administrative hierarchies of the old socialist state, pivoting between the demands of their superiors and those of the disillusioned and suspicious Tibetan "Masses" at the "grassroots." Drakpa for his part presented himself to me as the ideal socialist official, and even though, he opined, such a stance was "old thinking" (Tib. *bsam blo rnying pa*), he said he worked tirelessly to fundraise and efficiently distribute cash and goods to provide free services to poor Tibetan villagers.[29] As Drakpa put it with some irony, using a term for "entreat" or "plead" that Tibetans often used in prayers to lamas and deities, "my job is to entreat [Tib. *zho byed*] superiors on behalf of my schools." Meanwhile, he portrayed education policies and, with Gendun and Tashi chiming in, school curricula, as "pressed down" on them from above (Tib. *gnan dang thal*). By contrast, in his many passionate soliloquies over multiple cups of grain alcohol, Gendun's grand visions, drawing on his time online and his friendships with foreigners, evoked the dangerous scale of a transregional Tibetan nationalism. He worked to promote pride in a general, indeed globalized Tibetan culture, especially through supporting the Tibetan language curricula that Rebgong teachers had worked so hard to develop.

But this school repair project in their own home village had brought Drakpa, the stalwart veteran of many school construction projects, together with Gendun the zealous novice. In our initial planning conversations, they along with principal Tashi, were close collaborators. As they sought to convert me into a patron, they also recruited me to share in their experience of what Julie Chu (2014) has called a "politics of disrepair," a larger crisis they saw as affecting *all* Tibetans in the PRC: the discriminatory defunding and neglect of Tibetan schools and the looming specter of state-mandated Chinese-language curricula. "The situation has gotten worse and worse for Tibetans!" insisted Tashi, "and we are beside ourselves with anxiety over it." In the end, they argued, the only way to stave off complete assimilation was to advocate for exclusively Tibetan-language education until high school. But now primary school students were forced to study Chinese *and* English as well. Situating themselves in this way at the grassroots of a Chinese-dominated state hierarchy, they could portray themselves as almost totally powerless. Ironically, Tashi's culminating lament to that effect unconsciously instantiated the very process they decried. Despite himself, Chinese loanwords crept in, and in such a strikingly subtle way that I involuntarily laughed in response: "The *burden* [Ch. *fudan*] is just too great!" he cried. "Yet to not teach at all would be *even* [Ch. *geng*] worse!" (emphasis mine). Gendun's own response was swift, the extreme speed of his words mirroring the pace of the changes he heard registered in Tashi's hybrid speech:

> Seriously, we . . . now we are being swept along by a wave! We . . . We Tibetans are being swept along on a *wave* down the Machu [Yellow] River! We're being carried away so fast we can barely stand!

But when they sought to ally with me as a potential end run around such forces sweeping them downriver ("To tell the truth," said Gendun, "we pray for a rich American to come!"), that portrayal could clash with an ideal image of themselves as aggressively powerful. Tashi's story, with Gendun and Drakpa chiming in, of his heroic diatribe aimed at the new Chinese County Education Bureau head the year before was the crux of my conversion in that light. In it, Tashi narrated himself risking demotion to challenge pervasive gift inflation in Rebgong and break with the silent pact diplomacy of hospitality spectacles for superiors. Crucially, as he voiced himself baldly exhorting the new bureau head, he was pivoting between the narrated event in the official's office and the present one in Gendun's apartment, addressing (as "you") *both* the hapless official and me, the potential donor. And in his telling, I was drawn into playing the part of the bureau head by supplying the ideal answers to his rhetorical questions:

T: Last year, when the new Tongren County Education Bureau head took office . . . we two had been co-workers, you know. So I went to his house and . . . a lot of my friends were there, taking all kinds of things [as gifts] for him. I had taken no such things. All I took was a single offering scarf. And I said to him, Now if you look at this, it looks like a single offering scarf. But I have come to you with pure intentions, like the saying, "My offering scarf is small but it is a divine gift." And you have enough experience as a director of both Chinese and Tibetan education to know: *there is a disparity between the two!*"

CM: Yes!

T: You know there is!

CM: Yes!

T: So as for our Tibetan education, you *have* to *rescue* it! It's awful!

CM: mmm [emphatically]

T: [louder, higher pitch] As I said those things, I got so angry I couldn't control myself! The more I talked the angrier I got! and I said whatever came to me, whether or not it was appropriate!! Then, at a later meeting the new leader held with the district's school principals, I was so angry I scolded the principals, even though I don't really have the authority to do that: "[shouting] Speak up!! You *see* that Tibetan education is declining! If you really care about it, *say* something!! But even if you did, it wouldn't make any difference!"

DP. He spoke all day!

T: The leader told me to sit down and he would speak, but I still had more to say and told him, "You wait, I'm speaking! You talk of 'human quality education' [Ch. *suzhi jiaoyu*]. But don't Tibetans have their own 'human quality education'?"

CM: Yes!

T: Our Moral Lessons books [Tib. *legs bshad*] are all about "human quality education"! Our scholars from ancient times have talked of good morals. So you don't have to tell us any more about it! Our textbooks are all about 'quality.' You talk and talk of "human quality," but we have known about that since ancient times. *Why are we Tibetans in this current situation??* It is *because of the people in charge*!!

DP: We said all this last year, now the Education Bureau leader has changed again [to the Tibetan Shawojia]. We all worked together to tell him these things clearly.

Tashi's outspokenness, they told me, chuckling ironically, did indeed lead to his demotion, which was why he was now the principal of their lowly village primary school. But Drakpa's final summarizing statement framed Tashi's diatribe not as the voice of an unruly maverick, but as the communal voice of "Tibetans," and especially of Kharnak dewa. Here, Tashi claims the authority of that voice (versus that of the State) to directly challenge the unspoken racist premises of state-sponsored "human quality" discourse (e.g., Tibetans are inherently "low quality" and thus "lag behind"). He reclaims the notion of quality instead, by contrast with his charge of state neglect of Tibetan education, for a morally Tibetan socialism. This then was the battle for fortune in which they sought to capture me on behalf of Kharnak: "Now you know the main ideas in our heads," summed up Gendun. "They are precious [Tib. *rin po che*]—hold them in your mind like a ball!"

That effort to capture me in 2008 was only the latest salvo in a much longer contentious process. Since the Maoist years in Rebgong's Upper Narrows, as elsewhere, secular school buildings had been instruments of what Katherine Verdery (1996, 40) called "etatization," time and space-seizing projects to reorient and settle Tibetans as citizens of the PRC nation-state. But as the place eulogy poem about Kharnak dewa at the beginning of this section makes clear, such statist other-spaces intervened in places where history-making was essential in the creation, protection, and ongoing vitality of Tibetan communities as sovereign containers of fortune. That poem was in fact written by Akhu Gyamtsho, a Rongbo monk from a prominent Kharnak family, and it leads the voiceover narration of a New Year video village leaders distributed in 2008. It also figures importantly in the village history book Akhu Gyamtsho authored around the same time, in part, he writes, to redress the impending crisis of a loss of dewa history as elders were dying off like "the sun setting behind the mountains" (GDKS 2012, 4). The two parts of the poem (container and contents) assert the presence of invisible Protectors and link the materiality of the environment to righteous human and divine action—dewa history for Akhu Gyamtsho is heroic, divinely favored patrilineal settlement over time. And those battle victories are enabled by the metanatural force of Buddhist blessing-power, the "bright light" of discernment that is wielded by lamas and contained and reactivated in the "material supports" of trained people and built abodes: monks, hermitages, and especially, the Great Liberation Stupa (Tib. *mchod rten*, lit., "support for offering") placed at the threshold of Kharnak territory.

That stupa embodied another kind of consequential other-space in the valley: Kharnak villagers' histories of the stupa trace dewa leaders' timespace scaling efforts as the battle for fortune upriver intensified into the eighteenth and nineteenth centuries. As many scholars have pointed out, despite the rise of the Geluk Shartshang lamas at Rongbo Monastery (seventeenth century), the Geluk sect was never able to achieve the kind of hegemonic influence in Rebgong that it did elsewhere.[30] Instead, Geluk efforts to expand into the Upper Narrows, claiming mountain sites already renowned for the tantric activities of ancient yogins, were met with a thriving and partially oppositional Nyingma and nonsectarian movement.[31] When I talked with him about village history in 2011, Akhu Gyamtsho the Geluk monk seemed slightly embarrassed to note that Kharnak had lineages of lay tantric priests. And the three main altars of their old village temple reflected the village's eclectic recourse to both Geluk and Nyingma lamas.[32] Thus, as Tibetan-Mongol conflicts over land heated up under Qing overlordship and more settlers moved into the region, the eighteenth and nineteenth centuries in the Upper Narrows were marked by the vigorous travels of competing lama gift masters who allied with lay patrons through teachings, offerings, and Buddhist building projects (like Jetsha Hermitage mentioned in the praise poem above, on the mountainside facing Kharnak).[33]

Stupas are key historical idioms and sites for such efforts. They are in fact three-dimensional reliquaries, containers of actual pieces (indexes) of Buddha and lama bodies and their various accouterments. As such, their blessing power is supposed to render Buddhas' minds, their powerful omniscience, enduringly present, thereby extending lamas' capacities to perceive and thus protect the fortunate conditions of any container's contents. As da Col points out, Tibetan notions of containership and fortune presume that the interiors of persons and places are inherently shifting, obscure to ordinary humans' mundane vision (2012a, 92). Stupas are thus a kind of supercontainer.

They are other-spaces meant to instantiate an all-seeing wisdom eye on behalf of human patrons.[34] Once properly consecrated (lit., "vivified," made into a divine abode), they are supposed to aid and protect all sentient beings. But in practice, they are most often invoked as protectors of the jurisdictional claims of particular gift masters or hosts (like Kharnak dewa); stupas materialize particular lama-lay leader alliances.

Akhu Gyamtsho features the Kharnak stupa on the cover of his book, and in his preface he even likens the book itself to a "golden stupa erected for my homeland" (2). But in his narrative, the stupa is a moving presence. The vicissitudes of its reconstructions map village leaders' exceedingly proactive efforts, amidst shifting relations with other dewa, to ally with ascendant lamas and make Kharnak a sovereign center of the Upper Narrows and gateway to the Tibetan highlands—all the way to Lhasa. The wood and stone stupa was supposedly first built by one of the founders of Rongbo Monastery in the fourteenth century. But the site had been tamed and empowered long before, when yogins paved the way for Kharnak ancestors, who were, they say, part of the Shuk sublineage of a famous minister from central Tibet, to "capture" (Tib. *bzung*) and settle the place. Dewa men would proudly tell me that the stupa site was so empowered, pilgrims would launch their journeys to Lhasa there. However, according to Akhu Gyamtsho, starting in the eighteenth century and speeding up into the twentieth, the stupa was renovated, rebuilt, and reconsecrated at least *eight* times, always by Kharnak villagers under the auspices of the various Geluk lamas reclaiming it.

Perhaps the most spectacular of such events in Akhu Gyamtsho's account was in early spring of 1935, when the stupa was the central ground for Tibetan villagers' organized revolt against the predations of the troops of the ascendant Muslim Chinese (Hui) regime based in Xining. After the fall of the Qing, overlordship in the name of modernity came to Rebgong and the Upper Narrows in the form of the Muslim chief Ma Bufang's efforts to solidify control of taxation and corvee labor obligations there. His efforts to build garrisons and develop Longwu town, ostensibly as a county seat of the Chinese Guomindang state, led to renewed attempts to establish an administrative hierarchy and demand taxes from Tibetans upriver.[35] In Akhu Gyamtsho's telling, the "three tribal federations" (Tib. *shog kha gsum*) in the Upper Narrows, including the Shuk lineage federation to which Kharnak belonged, revolted after hundreds of residents had been brutally forced to cut lumber to float downriver. Enraged at reported beatings and rapes,

everyone agreed that the three tribal federations would gather at the Upper Narrows mani pile and stupa and powerfully unite. They blocked off the valley so that not one Chinese or Hui could enter it. They refused to provide corvee labor, illegal taxes, grain, grass, silver, horses or cattle, sheep, wool, leather, sheepskins, lambskins, or leather and yak hair ropes. Resisting the Ma bandits, they called themselves a People's Militia, with 150 people, every household pledged one gun, and all men over 15 years were put in the militia. As the saying goes, "if we rise up together we'll make it to the top, if we fall, we fall together," they resolved to share all happiness and suffering, and they decided to set up border stations and guards. (GDKS 2012, 164)

The stupa was then the site for a massive communal offering ceremony in which the invited lama invoked divine protectors to prepare for battle and turn away enemies. But that protection would not last long. According to Akhu Gyamtsho, in 1938 Ma Bufang ordered a two-pronged attack (from the west and south) to take back the Upper Narrows, and after an allied dewa, key lineage fellows, broke vows and surrendered to Ma's troops, Kharnak men were left alone to bravely fight them off at the border barrier as villagers fled to the highland forests. Akhu Gyamtsho's prose nearly trembles with rage as he narrates the tragic aftermath: the stupa and Kharnak village burned down and looted,[36] whole families killed, and the severed heads of Tibetan rebels from across the valley collected at Kharnak and loaded onto cattle by Tibetan "running dogs" (Tib. *rgyugs khyi*) of the Ma's, in order to be presented downriver to the Muslim district leader and then hung along the town's main road.[37] But as in other accounts of such battles, once that brutal pacification had been accomplished, Ma's troops withdrew. That in turn set the stage for what was really a first yang dar (Buddhist restoration) in Rebgong's Upper Narrows, four decades before the post-Mao visit of the Panchen Lama: lamas and laity allied to quickly rebuild and reconsecrate the Buddhist abodes destroyed by Ma troops. In the 1940s, on the eve of the CCP victory, writes Akhu Gyamtsho, the Kharnak stupa was rebuilt. And it was the seventh Shartshang lama himself who reconsecrated it.

Perhaps it was the devastation of that battle defeat, or the promise of CCP rhetoric of national democracy and "minority nationality" autonomy, that caused a shift of tactics in Kharnak. After Chinese Communist work teams and PLA troops arrived upriver in the early 1950s, instead of open rebellion, Kharnak leaders laid down a legacy of a kind of avant-garde countercompliance that I would say has lasted to the present. That shift is portrayed in the last two lines of Akhu Gyamtsho's place eulogy poem above, when the village's secular education officials and diasporic cosmopolitans take the idiomatic position of the Geluk lama-scholars the dewa historically produced.

That is, starting in the early 1950s, Kharnak men took the lead in embracing certain forms of CCP-led development while attempting to maneuver their village as a revitalized modern center and container of fortune. As Benno Weiner (2012) argues, early CCP reform efforts in the more remote pastoralist regions of the Upper Narrows met only reluctant or symbolic acquiescence from tribal leaders.[38] In reality, the presence of the new claimants to overlordship only exacerbated the battle for fortune upriver. Those early modern Buddhist restoration efforts continued into the Maoist years along with ongoing interdewa feuds and sporadic uprisings.[39]

In the frenzy of administrative scaling claims that unfolded in those years, Kharnak leaders attempted to position the dewa as a favored center, pivoting downriver to CCP superiors and upriver to their Shuk tribal federation.[40] In 1952, CCP leaders added a fourth administrative district to Tongren County that encompassed the farming dewa of the Upper Narrows, making the Shuk federation one of three townships, but placing the district seat in the rival federation of Tshothang's dewa upriver. Yet as Weiner states, these scaling claims were in name only; no material infrastructure yet existed (2012, 164). As Kharnak men proudly told me, it was Kharnak dewa that first built a statist other-space in 1953: the Upper Narrows' first secular primary school. And most prominently, three years later, Kharnak was the first rural Tibetan village in Tongren to establish an all-Tibetan CCP Party branch office, nonetheless serving all of Shuk township (TRXZ 2001, 38). But those countercompliance efforts could not protect the dewa after the 1958 military crackdown on a rebellion and after the radical restructuring of collectivization. In a dizzying array of campaigns, the dewa was subsumed as a "production brigade" under multiple communes whose seat was placed at Tshothang,[41] prominent men were arrested, the temple looted and made into a granary, and in 1966, at the beginning of the Cultural Revolution, the Kharnak stupa was once again destroyed.[42]

Kharnak never regained its status as a tribal or township administrative center. After the tenth Panchen Lama inaugurated the post-Mao yang dar years, decollectivization made Kharnak an administrative village under the old commune government seat of Tshothang township.[43] But in Akhu Gyamtsho's telling, as soon as decollectivization was made official in 1984, Kharnak villagers sought lamas to help rebuild the stupa. Importantly, the lead lama chose to heighten the stupa's blessing power by moving its foundation upriver a short distance to claim the empowered site where the tenth Panchen Lama had given a teaching during his 1980 visit. When the stupa was reconsecrated before a large assembly of villagers, monks, and lamas, it thus contained not only the Panchen Lama's throne, but his robes and image, along with those of the late seventh Shartshang (who died in prison in 1958). And despite the presence of lamas and attendees from across the valley, Akhu Gyamtsho now definitively claims the stupa not as the Upper Narrows Stupa, like during his account of the battle with Ma troops, but as the Kharnak Stupa.

The new stupa thus worked to position Kharnak in the Panchen Lama's post-Mao yang dar vision, literally laying the foundation for the dewa's future, that ideal hybrid of socialist modernity and a refigured lama-lay leader alliance to which Gendun, Drakpa, and Akhu Gyamtsho so passionately aspired. Indeed, in Akhu Gyamtsho's poem for the village above, the lines directly following mention of the stupa turn to describing the fertility and fortune its blessing power enables. As such, Akhu Gyamtsho directly counters Gendun's anxious wave metaphor for state-led education as the force driving of ethnic assimilation and emigration downriver. Here, the river, like the native education officials, flows from a particular, blessed, and fertile basin down to meet and incorporate the future on Kharnak terms:

> The good crops, heavy with the six types of grain, wave in the wind, while beside the village, the blue Guchu River, making the beautiful sound of "lhang lhang" as it continuously descends, knocks again and again at the door of future knowledge.

Indeed when I crossed the threshold of Kharnak's school gate that spring, I was immediately struck that this was no ordinary rural primary school. By the mid-1990s in fact, Kharnak had repositioned itself as the dewa producing the most salaried officials in the Upper Narrows,[44] and in 1996 elders and officials were able to fundraise from prominent households and a particularly charismatic young Geluk lama for a beautiful new two-story concrete classroom building for the school, complete with glassed-in outer hallways and a computer room across the courtyard. In the ensuing years, with Kharnak officials in charge of the school district and as fundraising efforts increasingly turned to foreign donors, Kharnak school became a model project site, attracting funds from a joint Qinghai Province–World Bank project (1996–2001) and then in the late 2000s, from a joint prefecture education bureau–UN project (2006–10).

The Economy of Appearances: School Grounds, Futurity, and the Crisis of Time

In today's society, the most important thing for both Buddhism and governance is education. Education is something not only individuals need, but it is also the root of benefit for the nationality and the State. In particular, this is a time in which society is surging forth on a wave of education. As for teens and children, *we can't waste their youth.* The ones whose responsibility it is to put them on the straight path, the great road to education, are the parents and the elders. You all must establish good habits toward your school and teachers, and work to support them. Teachers and students *should not waste time.*

—Excerpt from the eighth Shartshang lama's speech at there-consecration ceremony for Kharnak's renovated stupa, summer 2006

We can now go back and better grasp the stakes of school grounds as post-Mao battles for fortune in the Upper Narrows.[45] In the early reform years, the Kharnak school took on a heightened role in leaders' efforts to achieve the diplomatic compromise between older forms of lama-lay leader alliances and socialist modernity that had promised a quasi-autonomous dewa-based Tibetan governance. In practice, socialism in these parts was always a sleight of hand, in that the spectacles of hospitality and compassion under various CCP campaigns allowed for the simultaneous presence of multiple occult motives and unforeseen consequences. As we'll see, everyone claimed their projects for socialism. But in Tibetan regions by the 2000s socialism took on a different valence then back east in China. In part theater of discipline and welfare, and in part political concession to "minority nationalities," the Maoist state apparatus was still very much intact there. Meanwhile, as we saw in Jima village, post-Mao reforms brought a new emphasis on the dewa or village (versus lineage groups like clans or "tribes") as a sovereign community and administrative unit among Tibetans. And that process in turn reinvigorated intervillage tensions ("dewas are too strong these days!" lamented a young Tibetan urbanite I knew who had relatives among the county police).

In the Upper Narrows, the policy emphasis on universal primary education had led to a spate of school construction in highland villages in the 1990s and early 2000s.[46] Importantly, villagers I spoke to talked of that process in terms of the performative requirements of the old socialist state. That is, like rebuilt temples and stupas, new village schools also worked to reanchor dewas as quasi-autonomous communities. But villagers emphasized the need for school grounds to create a collective "face" (Tib. *ngo*), a visible and legible space to draw in state (and later, foreigners') attention and resources. They hoped to thereby demonstrate to state superiors and competing villages the power of their networks and the worthiness of their ongoing existence despite recent funding cuts. Thus, as Drakpa put it, trying to recruit me at our first meeting, state-sanctioned construction projects upriver, like schools, courtyard walls, and concrete roads, indicated the proper egalitarian attention and compassionate care of a socialist state, now sadly lacking in his rural school district:

> In particular, people who live in the cities and those in the grassroots are not equal. If urbanites were compared to those up here, we could say that in terms of rights, rural people have been placed a bit lower. That is how it is at the grassroots. Urbanites and rural people don't face each other equally; if they did, then state higher-up's would come to see, and they would build nice concrete roads! and there would be nice school buildings with courtyard walls, and school conditions would be good. But those things are nowhere to be seen, higher-up's don't come often, so there won't be any.

These exigencies of socialist presence and resource distribution further complicated the status of rural Tibetan officials like Drakpa and Gendun; such men embodied the great ambivalence of Tibetan villagers toward the Chinese state.[47] In the late 2000s, Tibetan officials were the object of, on one hand, great suspicion and resentment in the face of corruption scandals, and on the other, desire and aspiration as holders of the only secure career resulting from Tibetan language education. From the perspective of villages like Kharnak, as Akhu Gyamtsho's poem so amply illustrated, homegrown Tibetan salaried officials, nurtured in the secular school, metonymically stood for the native intelligence, collective power, or efficacy (Tib. *nus pa*), and thus future prosperity of the village. They were the ones with "voice and face" (Tib. *kha ngo can*), who most properly advocate for their home villages to state bureaus (and foreigners) downriver. By contrast, as Drakpa put it, the poorer villages further upriver who had no one to be their voice and face had no recourse but to rely on him to find funding for school repair and resources.

Hence the great pressures on Gendun and Drakpa when we began the Kharnak school wall project. As native son officials of Kharnak they were supposed to operate as advocates for the village alone, yet their broader-scale official obligations meant they had to avoid appearing to other Tibetan villages to use their positions to favor Kharnak. In terms of the pervasive anti-corruption rhetoric Tibetans across Rebgong used, that could come across as "rotten" (Ch. *fubai*), as selfishly "eating" money (Tib. *sgor mo za*) for the benefit of improper scales of constituents. In the context of the mid-2000s urban construction boom, money, as we will see, was anything but a transparent medium of value.

As I mentioned in chapter 2, under the new national development push starting in 2007, central leaders' twenty-first century version of the socialist sleight of hand was encapsulated in the New Socialist Countryside (NSC) campaign. But in Rebgong that campaign in practice brought to rural regions the timespaces of authoritarian capitalism, along with its techniques and media for perceiving and auditing value or quality. The Maoist state had required elaborate performances of loyalty and face for citizens to capture and display distributions of resources. But with the NSC campaign in particular, the Rebgong region was subject to what Anna Tsing (2000, 2005) has called a capitalist "economy of appearances." That is, in renewed state and NGO meetings and propaganda efforts, all residents were called to participate in new kinds of construction and hospitality spectacles that worked to, in Tsing's words, "conjure" dreamlike future possibilities for audiences of profit-seeking outsiders (2000, 118).

In this, Tibetan officials and villagers alike were exhorted to counter both Tibetan historical idioms of sovereign containment and lama lay-leader alliance, as well as Maoist socialist idioms of rightful distribution. Under the economy of appearances, ideal preparation for long-term fortunes was not

FIGURE 14.   Western couple rides a ten thousand peso note into the sky: "Investing is for making a *Profit!*" Billboard ad for Lenghu Road Chief Finance Center, Xining, summer 2005. Author's photo.

sovereign subsistence or "lazy" dependence on the state. Instead residents were to display their "human quality" (Ch. *suzhi*) by orienting themselves to exciting futures just beyond the horizon, to aspire first and foremost to be subjects of a national- and global-scale integrated market. As "new" socialists, they were to be "self-reliant" and "entrepreneurial," to actively "compete for and capture" (Ch. *zhengqu*) not state entitlements, but private investment (including loans) from downriver.[48] Crucially, this sleight of hand turned on the carrot-and-stick enticements of the capitalist crisis of time—that the shimmering mirage of prosperous modern futures would be lost to others if one did not hurry to participate, or that one would be deemed low quality and subject to discipline if one failed to deliver the cash (or the project) on time.[49] This new experience of a crisis of time, the headlong rush downriver, I think, is what Gendun was trying to get at with his anxious wave metaphor during our first meeting.

Reenter concrete. In 2007 the NSC campaign set off a renewed "utopia of reconstruction" (Bakken 2000) that heightened the stakes of reading potential value on material surfaces.[50] In contrast to principal Tashi's diatribe about human "quality" as an ideally long-term process of moral training, that concept in actuality drew all participants, including foreign donors, into practices of visual auditing for signs of investability and risk. And that in turn promised precisely what Tashi's diatribe sought to stave off: the conflation of the quality of things with the quality (as potential monetary value) of people. In practice, Rebgong officials' NSC projects fetishized concrete other-spaces, especially the most public and visible spaces such as buildings and their facades, walls, pathways and plazas, as key signs of urbane modernity and high investment potential.

Here, the peculiar sensuous and social qualities of concrete, its initial plasticity and then hardness and durability, the networked labor and profit-making transregional industry it entails, are supposed to evoke (both iconically and indexically) the human ingenuity and ideally long-term, prosperous futures of wise investments in open markets. But just as in the so-called brutalist architecture of early modern cities elsewhere, the hard flatness, smoothness, and standardized forms of concrete under NSC auspices in Rebgong were supposed to effect a kind of sanitizing decontextualization associated with ideally ordered modernities.[51] Clean, hard, and smooth concrete is supposed to remove people and places from the disorderly roughness, stain and vulnerability to the elements of soft, yielding mud, local brick and even wood, the main building materials historically used in Tibetan domestic architecture (including in rural primary schools).[52] Amidst increasing state-local and interethnic tensions, in NSC rhetoric tropes of "dirt" evoked

FIGURE 15. Artist's montage of planned consolidated boarding school for rural Tibetan middle schoolers, floating above a golf course, Drakpa's office, Tshothang township seat, summer 2013. Author's photo.

Maoist moral categories for disloyal citizens, but now they evoked the (menacing) low quality of both antistate and antimarket subjects.

Thus, even as the construction boom raised the price of concrete, with competition for contracts among largely Chinese construction companies and contractors, harried officials focused on the appearance of villages above all. And they urged villagers to contribute cash and labor to "beautification" projects.[53] For example, prefecture government deputy head Dorje Tshering, speaking at a 2007 meeting on furthering the work of the NSC campaign, urged prefecture officials to work on improving the quality of farmers and pastoralists, as well as of rural cadres and party members. He went on to exhort them:

> We must focus on the work of renovating the appearance of rural communities. In farming regions, the main problem is rectifying the "6 chaoses" [Ch. *liu luan*]: chaotic housing construction, chaotic piling of muck and dung, chaotic stacking of wheat piles, chaotic throwing of trash, chaotic tossing of dirty water, and chaotic construction of animal pens. In pastoralist regions, the most important things are cleaning up trash, ordering animal pens and constructing sanitary toilets.

For officials of rural school districts, I found, these dynamics had already been set in motion with the new push under the Open the West campaign to achieve the mandatory nine years of education in minority regions. For example, the glossy posters I saw in the Tongren County Education Bureau office touted their achievements under that policy between 2000 and 2005 by highlighting their efforts to fundraise for and build "basic infrastructure." In the poster, "dangerous," or "derelict" school buildings (Ch. *weifang*) are repaired or replaced through the "loving charity" (Ch. *aixin*) of donors and officials, creating "broad and beautiful study environments" instead.

But by spring 2008, the NSC campaign had become a broad rubric for other directives to rural school officials, which in part responded to the dilemmas they faced, so passionately lamented to me by Gendun, Drakpa and Tashi, of increased pressures to expand primary education in the absence of guaranteed funds. Simultaneously with NSC directives, Tibetan school officials were also supposed to recruit villagers to participate in the state-mandated School Consolidation program (Ch. *xuexiao buju tiaozheng*). That central education initiative laid out a technocratic vision of an ultraefficient and productive allocation of school resources based on transparent auditing and reporting.[54] The policy notice on the wall of the prefecture Education Bureau head's office labeled the initiative "urgent," firmly placing it in the crisis of time:

> It is still extremely clear that the scope of the regulation of middle/ primary school distribution is limited, the effort expended is small, and we still find the situation in rural middle/primary schools of too many sites, small scope, high production costs, and low results. . . . Regulating the distribution of rural middle/primary schools is one of the most important factors for constructing New Socialist farming and pastoralist regions, as well as for promoting the development of a harmonious society.

These pressures compelled well-intentioned school officials to engage in the economy of appearances and, in a new kind of trompe l'oeil aesthetics of optical illusion, to focus on concrete buildings (and especially their smooth, painted façades) as sites of value creation (see figure 15). Contrary to concrete's value as an icon of modern durability, capitalist incentives to short-term profits and decision horizons in Rebgong had highlighted concrete's capacity as a medium for surface impressions and photo ops instead. For harried rural school officials operating on tiny budgets, concrete façades offered quick and easy ways to convert the good intentions of offering scarves and the murky circulations of money into signs of proper use and care. Indeed, I noticed that in the hundreds of photos Drakpa gave me of the school grounds in his district, photos he used in his fundraising efforts, none depicted a single person or interior shot. And in the County Education Bureau poster, the "broad and beautiful study environments" are represented exclusively by those same exterior shots. Building façades stood as signs in themselves, indicating projects successfully completed or needed. In that context, funding for less visible infrastructure, personnel, books, and ongoing maintenance and curriculum development was relatively scarce.

Importantly, despite ongoing criticisms of such practices (villagers and officials alike grumbled to me at times about the fetishism of surfaces in construction projects),[55] we cannot just dismiss façades in Rebgong as sheer "appearance" or "empty symbols." Instead they are themselves materialized other-spaces with real consequences for labor and social fortunes. In the Upper Narrows, they were key components of the new politics of presence that turned on access to infrastructure and displaying and auditing wanted versus unwanted buildings and even whole communities.[56] In tandem with the NSC campaign then, the School Consolidation program was supposed to "rationalize" the distribution of students and "economize" on expensive construction materials and infrastructure provision—which in practice meant spurring the rush downriver in an expanding effort to resettle and urbanize highland residents.[57] As Drakpa told me, school officials like him in fact had to help entice highland villagers to build new, orderly settlements at lower elevations next to roads and to send their children to consolidated boarding schools downriver,[58] even if it meant long travel times and young children away from home for weeks or months (and thus the loss of their labor).

In this, state support for school construction was both carrot and stick. As pressures increased to eliminate many of the upriver primary schools in the valley, the promise of a new dewa primary school in a resettlement site to help prepare children for the modern future—along with the refusal to provision older highland schools—was a powerful incentive to villagers to make the move down. In our first conversations, Drakpa presented the School Consolidation policy to me as a fait accompli, voicing the State to portray his decision to withhold donor funds to a recalcitrant village as evidence of his efficient use of money:

> Now all the villages will be moving down, but that village will not agree to come down. They took the state-funded houses [in the lower sites], but they said only the elderly and the children would live in them. The rest said they would stay in the highland village. I don't know why they

would do that. But they still want the school built above. There are a few donors who gave ¥100,000. But if they built it up there and the village moved down, then the donors' money would be wasted. I can't let that happen, so I told the donors, "You can't give the money now."

Ironically then, primary schools in the Upper Narrows were now positioned to spur the ideal evacuation of highland villages, to speed a process of dewa devitalization already under way: the "spectralization" of once-productive village land as primarily sites of welfare, absorbing the too-young, ill, injured, or elderly as everyone else was supposed to be out seeking sources of cash (Yan 2003a).

As we can now appreciate, in this new battle for fortune the relatively secure status of Kharnak dewa's school was no coincidence. Unlike primary schools doomed to close or be reduced to preschools upriver, in 2008 Kharnak school was able to keep its designation as a "comprehensive" K-6 primary school (Ch. *wanxiao*, Tib. *cha tshang slob grwa*), now slated to take students from neighboring villages. The school, I learned, was in fact the center of Kharnak leaders' own proactive scaling efforts under the economy of appearances, their latest countercompliance move to defend the dewa as a container of fortune. In 2006, on the eve of the NSC campaign, Kharnak leaders, along with a lama from the village, had raised funds to rebuild the Kharnak stupa with steel and concrete, adding eight small stupas to the site.[59] This time, the eighth Shartshang lama reconsecrated the Buddhist abode, capping the ceremony with the speech excerpted above. In part complying with the lama's (and the State's) vision of futurity and the crisis of time, in late 2007 Drakpa and several other male age mates (Gendun was conspicuously uninvolved) quietly established their own unofficial NGO, the Kharnak Village Uplift Foundation (KVUF).

The membership of village men (and a few women) vowed to fundraise for and promote high-achieving students and teachers, as well as universal access to school for Kharnak children. But the KVUF was about much more than the school. It was Kharnak leaders' own effort at a neosocialist communalism that on one hand sought to reclaim the dewa as the center of the old Shuk tribal federation, and on the other took up the cosmopolitanism evoked in Akhu Gyamtsho's poem to scale up the dewa to a global diaspora. The translocal and even transnational reach of the dewa was to include not only villagers living outside the prefecture and abroad but also myself. Thus later and with the solemnity of offering scarves draped around my neck, I was inducted into the KVUF under the watchful eye of the village's main mountain deity Makgol—the Kharnak men insisted that he was no ordinary regional god but a much-traveled king who was particularly amenable to protecting foreigners. And in the foundation's charter statement, the dewa is a "town" (Tib. *grong khyer*), and it lists among its members prominent villagers living abroad.[60] The statement frames the village's illustrious legacy of secular education in an emerging international-scale, entrepreneurial "battle for knowledge":

> Nowadays, the conflict inherent to the world is the result of conflict among contending national powers, and ultimately, this is a conflict among peoples who have knowledge. Thus it is a conflict over access to education. Consequently, it is certain that whoever gains the power [Tib. *nus pa*] of independent practices and innovative creations will necessarily triumph.

The charter portrays this advocacy as work to "develop the quality [Tib. *spus tshad*] of our people [Tibetans]" and "our lifestyles," but in line with Tashi's diatribe to the Chinese head of the County Education Bureau that year, it conspicuously portrays quality as the neosocialist ideal of ongoing social empathy in the midst of amoral market incentives: the charter includes the goal to raise funds for elderly villagers. Yet in my conversation with the charter's author, a former monk from Kharnak in his thirties, he described the goals of the group as deemphasizing their previous welfare work to prioritize the futures of village children. And that project, he insisted, laying out a kinship-based vision of moral exchange and solidarity that bypassed the state altogether, is best pursued by starting with dewa natives (Tib. *sa gnas gi mi*) and moving outward from there:

> The way I think of it is that one person has no power while with many people, we have power. First there is one's own household, then one's own siblings' households, then the dewa and lineages, then all Tibetans. Only then will one be well-positioned to turn toward the world at large.

Finally, the 2008 New Year video, the one that opened with Akhu Gyamtsho's poem, was a highly edited celebration of the KVUF's lavish coming-out party in Kharnak, to which they had invited village leaders from the Shuk tribal federation. According to Akhu Gyamtsho, that party, framed as an offering feast for Kharnak's deity Makgol, would set the precedent for annual hospitality exchanges within the Shuk lineage villages for years to come. The video itself, I learned later, became a medium of value: the KVUF presented it to villagers (and potential foreign gift masters) as an opening gift in their ongoing recruitment efforts. Kharnak leaders, it seems, had turned the economy of appearances to their own purposes.

The Wall as Precarious Threshold: Hospitality and Competing Conversions

In this ferment, I was surprised to discover that the new school wall itself was to become a particularly important medium of value. The shifting terms of the battle for fortune in the Upper Narrows meant that all along the potential value of material objects, built environments, and persons was anything but transparently readable. Yet, in 2008 the economy of appearances under the silent pact compelled all of us, in key encounters, to act as if it was (the wall project, after all, coincided precisely with the military crackdown on Tibetan unrest in town). In New Socialist practices for sensing and securing fortunate futures, schools were to be simple idiomatic replacements for stupas and temples, technocrats for lamas, sheer presence for invisible beings and motives.

But as we broke ground on the new concrete wall it became quickly clear that such modernizing conversions were always incomplete and contested. To the end, it was never really certain who was the gift master, who or what scale the wall was for, and what it was worth—to the point that Gendun and Drakpa, old friends, affines, and village age mates, completely fell out, their households thereby awkwardly separated for years to come. Here, we could take Kharnak's school wall, and especially its new gate, as a precarious threshold, a heterotopia in Foucault's sense in that multiple timespaces and aspirations for fortune vied for material presence there. To unpack this process, I tell the story of the wall project through four material-semiotic conversion efforts that unfolded as Gendun, Drakpa, and the KVUF men attempted to host competing gift masters to various ends.

Conversion One: Old School Grounds to Model New Socialist School

Gendun and Drakpa lived in fear of the wrath of their boss, Shawojia, the newly appointed Tibetan County Education Bureau head. As a CCP member who had a Masters degree in education, Shawojia was known for his dogged advocacy for Tibetan education and his no-nonsense acceptance of the premises of state-led scientific development. In the school districts of the Upper Narrows he was the quintessential New Socialist technocrat. His withering gaze during his whirlwind tours of schools could read lack of villager compliance as radically backward and even "dirty" low quality.[61] In his speeches to village elders and school officials that I attended, Shawojia's eyes would stare imperiously into an abstract distance, modeling the distant future he constantly exhorted villagers to see in their children.

To meet the gaze of Shawojia then, Gendun, Drakpa, and Tashi had to pivot among competing historical idioms of exchange and fortune under the sign of socialism. And my presence as the foreign patron could help to display their New Socialist compliance to Shawojia, while offering possibilities to pursue their own visions. Thus, in my first visits to the school, they frequently put me in the role of auditor, an extension in some ways of Shawojia's eyes. On that first visit, I had been struck by how well-appointed the classroom building was. But it was equally striking that the crumbling earthen wall of the school contrasted sharply with the well-maintained old village temple directly next door. In the face of villagers' seemingly different priorities, when they turned to me as auditor, the men could echo the premises of New Socialist quality that their boss Shawojia espoused. All three would complain of backward, ignorant, or superstitious Tibetan villagers in Kharnak and upriver who, in contrast to Chinese villagers, would refuse to "see" or trust the motives and projected outcomes of projects like school repairs while eagerly donating funds, labor, and resources to temple construction.

Yet in separate conversations I found that villagers in the Upper Narrows widely categorized schools as particular kinds of other-spaces that did indeed hold out the promise of certain worldly forms of fortune. But in contrast to Shawojia's vision, they drew on older socialist notions of statist infrastructure to conceptualize schools not necessarily as unimportant but as entitlements, the primary funding purview of lowland state officials. Indeed Drakpa had to fundraise so much in his school district because many rural Tibetans refused to pay fees for state services they felt entitled to.

For my benefit though, Gendun, Drakpa, and Tashi would portray villagers' insistence on "old" socialism as an antimodern stance. Yet recalling the recently reconsecrated stupa, the men's vision for Kharnak did not entail eliminating Buddhist abodes. Instead, in keeping with the tenth Panchen Lama's hopes for a Tibetan modernity, they sought to recalibrate the value hierarchy that placed Buddhist sites above schools for villagers: "Schools are more valuable [Tib. *rtsa che*] than temples," insisted Tashi in our first meeting. "Schools are where people are raised! Without educated people in them, temples are useless, even if there is nice stuff in them!" Gendun took that further to complain, "If we ask villagers for money for a school wall, they won't pay, but if we ask for funds for a monastery's walls, they will borrow in order to give—that's the big difference between ancient and modern people [Tib. *gna' deng gi mi*]." Thus to convert the old school grounds into a model

New Socialist school, their task was to demonstrate to me, and by extension to Shawojia, its incorporation into villagers' own values, to make it a display of the dewa's entrepreneurial and self-sufficient care—the very goals, ostensibly, of the KVUF. Hence on my first visit, their great pride in showing me the piles of huge river stones and sand that villagers, organized by them, had transported there in preparation for the new wall.

Conversion Two: Rural Tibetan Kids to "Successful" Modern Subjects

Under the capitalist crisis of time the appearance and quality of rural children in the Upper Narrows were increasingly touted as essential for villagers' future fortunes. In our initial planning conversations and tours, Gendun, Drakpa, and Tashi presented the urgent need and function of a new stone, brick, and concrete wall and gate in the New Socialist terms of modernist decontextualization and sanitization on behalf of village kids. The 1990s school building had in fact been built on a shelf carved into a steep hill next to the main road. The crumbling pounded earth walls on either side merged with the two-story mud embankment behind the main building, which was eroding with seasonal rain and snow. On the downhill side, a large crack in the concrete back wall of the (now defunct) computer room showed that the side building was slowly falling.

As we inspected the space, Gendun carefully photographing each stage, they portrayed the problem as both a technical one of needing to better shore up the grounds and buildings, and as a technocratic one of needing to better demarcate the grounds from the adjacent village and contain (thus rendering more visible) the children inside. A stone and concrete wall, they insisted, would keep out invasions of dirty, unruly livestock and keep young students safely out of the road and their minds concentrated on their studies. Hybrid notions of containment applied to the bodies and minds of village children as well. Drawing on popular Tibetan notions of bodies as porous material frameworks (Tib. *gzugs po*) for shifting mental processes and forces of fortune, Tibetan education officials often talked of students as containers (Tib. *snod*) needing to be filled up with knowledge. But in those circles, I learned, that historically loaded idiom could easily be turned to the service of the technocratic timespace scales of the economy of appearances.

In the context of increasing anxieties about access to higher education, Tibetans across Rebgong widely used the intransitive verb *chong* (Tib. '*khy ongs*) to refer to the successful striving of children (and their native villages or households) in transregional pursuits; it worked to position kids as ideally modern, entrepreneurial subjects fulfilling a destiny in a "free" job market.[62] In our initial conversation about the school wall, my fellow project managers were well aware of the implications of this market-based notion of materiality and value in Tibetan secular education. They saw how their superiors worked to audit material surfaces (bodies, school facilities) for future investability. Speaking of small upriver schools slated for closure, Gendun said, "If they have no impressive material facilities, then the county won't waste time or resources on them." Drakpa clarified sarcastically, "They'll say [such schools] have no product, like a factory, there'll be no final product and they'll say they're not needed. There's no way to argue against it."

But when they were moved to refute the racism of New Socialist notions of quality with older socialist emphases on the primary causal influence of learning environments, all three men would take up aspects of that capitalist rhetoric to assert that modern material facilities like those in lowland Chinese schools directly shaped kids' ability to succeed, converting them into modern subjects: "We don't have the conditions and material facilities required for success [Tib. *'khyongs spyad po'i rgyu cha*]," insisted Drakpa. "Without them [our students] can't succeed." In that light, they also envisioned the concretized other-spaces of renovated school grounds as ideal sites for disciplined transparency, as technologies and media for making exterior surfaces reveal inner contents. In Kharnak's school, just as in all the others I visited, painted concrete walls were framing devices for displays of state-issued guidelines, exhortation posters, and painted slogans, and Drakpa, Gendun, and Tashi would frequently point with pride to displays that set them apart from other schools: the accumulated academic merit and "progressive school" awards, as well as Tashi's new blackboard chart on which he daily recorded named students' merits and demerits.

Conversion Three: Money to Scarves, Donor to Guest

As we have seen, the heightened battle for fortune with the rise of authoritarian capitalism in Rebgong hinged all along on the erratic power and hazards of money as a medium of value. That is, ideally a sheer token of quantity, cash as (trans)national currency promises utter, transparent exchangeability in any time or space, a far-reaching superpower of agentive "flow" (e.g. its so-called "liquidity"). Such money, it would seem, wants to move and convert things, to extend the agency and fortune of its users across vast distances and times. Indeed money presumably has no value in its sheer presence. Instead its various material and digital tokens suggest unrealized value awaiting future transactions.[63] This in fact is how many of the foreign donors

I knew seemed to think of money, as a way to easily convert their good intentions into positive social change abroad. And I often joked with Drakpa that when I delivered into his hands cash I had promised for a school project, his and others' faces registered an uncanny, near-drugged bliss (recall figure 14).

However, as we have seen, the very scale-jumping power of money was also the source of its danger in Rebgong. As quantified value potential, money requires national- and transnational-scale social contracts, trust that its abstract value will be retained over time. But at the moment of transaction, tokens of cash are minicontracts supposedly shorn of any enduring social or ritual markers, allowing for quick and potentially hidden exchanges. The great moral dilemmas of money, and hence the economy of appearances, derive from its unique capacity for scalar slipperiness, its material and semiotic role as, in Bill Maurer's words, "a hinge between short-term and long-term transactional orders" (2006, 24). This peculiar magic of money, I found, was an essential component of the occultness of New Socialist development work in Rebgong. In practice the liquidity of money was not inherent to the medium, but situational. Like the abstract State, abstract money allowed for convenient deferrals of responsibility. There was never any money, or no one was ever sure where it went.

Thus, the transfer of the foreign donors' money was perhaps the most conflictual conversion process during our school wall project. In practice, the display of transparency (as hospitality) unfolded as competing efforts to capture and contain both the donors and their money, to publicly convert them to durable sources of fortune on behalf of particular jurisdictions. Drakpa had hired Mr. Zhang, a local Tibetan-speaking Chinese contractor he knew from long experience, to oversee the wall construction. At first, Gendun had enthusiastically participated in our elaborate negotiations with contractor Zhang, which included several inspection tours, and gifts of multiple meals, alcohol, and cigarettes while we pored over figures and carefully signed and fingerprinted contracts—all meticulously documented on camera by me and Gendun.

In those early meetings, both Gendun and Drakpa enthused that Zhang had great experience since the early reform years, building both state infrastructure and Tibetan Buddhist abodes like stupas. He had in fact, said Drakpa, built the Kharnak school classroom building in the 1990s. I was often struck by the sheer time and resources spent in our long negotiations with Zhang, the repetitive and flowery speeches about mutual good will, trust, and long-term friendship. But I also realized that this was the ritualized transparency required in good relations (Ch. *guanxi*) with business partners over time; it allowed all parties to agree on a much-reduced price for the project, partially under the table (e.g., tax free to Zhang, in exchange for ongoing contracts).

But those attempts at diplomatic transparency, it turned out, were not enough for Gendun. He had not been there when Drakpa, Zhang, and I had, in a flurry of receipts and photographs documented in the lobby of a county bank office, transferred my donated cash into Drakpa's official account. But later, Gendun told me anxiously that the transfer had been botched, and that we needed a "ceremony" to publicly perform the transfer in front of Shawojia, Kharnak leaders and KVUF members. Only then, he said, would we be able to stave off rumors about us selfishly "eating" the money. Two days later, I found myself the guest of honor in the front seat of an official black sedan, driving up to Kharnak with Shawojia and three of his underlings crammed into the backseat.

As Shawojia told me later, this was his first-ever visit to Kharnak village and he said he had never before seen such a money transfer ceremony. He emerged from the car like an old pro however, leading me through the routine of an official visit as village leaders greeted us in the road with white offering scarves, bestowing several on Gendun, more on Shawojia, and the majority on me. Groaning under the weight of the scarves, I could barely get up the steps to the school gate, but Shawojia deftly removed his and, walking slowly and regally while a KVUF member walked backward filming us, he gave me a brief history of the school. His eyes sweeping the construction site, he remarked with approval, "Now *this* is starting to look like a school!" As the village leaders watched respectfully and women teachers prepared tea and fried bread to serve us, Shawojia and I were installed on a small sofa in the school office, our knees touching the small table on which had been placed our food. But Gendun quickly had the food moved away so that stacks of cash, standing in for the donors' gift, could take pride of place. The neatly wrapped bundles of hundred-yuan notes, each wrapper stamped with the Chinese seal of the bank, had been withdrawn by Drakpa for the occasion.

With great urgency, Gendun and two KVUF members worked to arrange it in two stacks at the center of the table, one larger than the other. For this, they brought several of the most expensive kind of white offering scarves, shiny, clean, and bright, and whispering urgently to each other not to block the view of the cash, they lovingly positioned the scarves around the stacks and, for good measure, topped them off with 10-yuan notes featuring the face of Mao Zedong.[64] Cash in place, Gendun took the video camera from me and backed away respectfully. Then, with Gendun and the KVUF man filming, the stage was set for Shawojia's official oration. As I sheepishly played my role in the event, however, it was hard to keep track of who in

FIGURE 16. Donor money lovingly displayed with Mao Zedong-faced ten yuan notes and offering scarves, Kharnak school wall project meeting, April 2008. Author's video still.

fact was the gift master, and as the Kharnak men pivoted among the various contenders for that role, what the money was supposed to signify.

Here, the materiality of scarves, money and persons was crucial. The initial offering scarves, supposedly loaded with villagers' hopes and good intentions, by dint of numbers were supposed to capture and mark me off as the main donor. But in fact another foreign woman whom I had helped to contact had donated the lion's share of the funds. The two differently sized stacks of cash, strikingly portraying the exact amounts each of us had donated, stood in for the foreign donors on the table. Meanwhile, the villagers also sought the elusive attention of Shawojia, while village leaders had added scarves to greet Gendun as well. Finally, to stave off accusations of lazy dependency, all dewa recipients had to work to convert outside givers to guests, thereby reclaiming the status of agentive (and sovereign) host and attempting to bind the giver not to one-off gifts but to a longer future of exchange. The stakes of this were clear when Shawojia began to speak. In the monotonous tones of an official used to giving such speeches all over the county, he voiced the State to take the role of the far-seeing New Socialist technocrat and thus the ultra-gift master and host.

Shawojia began with an authoritative summary of the project, even though up till then he had had *nothing at all* to do with it. In his introduction, he named the key players and their responsibilities, highlighted the efficient and transparent use of money, and using the royal "we," he claimed me as a guest *not* of Kharnak village but of Tongren County as a whole:

> There is still much work to do beyond this project. As for maintaining our relationship with her, we must help her. She is a stranger to this region, and thus we are the hosts [Tib. *bdag po*] and she is our guest.

Shawojia then delivered the rest of the speech in the voice of the State's auditor, linking his approving gaze to the very future existence of the school under the impending School Consolidation program. "In the future," he lectured them, "schools will be closely scrutinized. We will be going through and comparing all schools. Starting this year, the county's eighty-nine schools will be consolidated into seventy-nine total." In this, Shawojia held up Kharnak as a model school for the district, claiming it (and our project) as an achievement for all of Rebgong (meaning his education bureau). Kharnak was a "correct and pure" school (Tib. *gra gra dag dag*) because its grounds and the presence of the KVUF evidenced the village's active commitment to nurturing secular intellectuals and officials. That was why, he added, the county was now helping them. But when he described "dirty," noncompliant villages (Tib. *sde rtsog*), his speech took on his most adamant tones, becoming louder and faster as he claimed the State's eminent domain over schools:

> We have said this often [to villages]: "if you have a good relationship with your village's school, if you know that your school has needs and you help with that, then when someone asks, 'Whose school is this?' we say, 'It belongs to the village.' And if you, . . . there are some really bad/dirty villages. If you don't even contribute a single shovelful of help in building the school, and still complain about the teachers' bad qualities, then if one asked 'Whose school is this?' we say '*It belongs to the State.*'"

Significantly though, even as Shawojia's speech peaked in vehemence his listeners seemed to have checked out, their eyes at half mast or wandering, the women chatting in the back. Indeed, Gendun's filming choices reflected his very different priorities for the event. At that very moment, he turns the lens away and documents the room and the presence of village leaders instead. He does not return the lens to Shawojia for a full six minutes, until the official begins to wrap up by admonishing them not to waste their children's future—implying that in an imminent world without entitlements or subsistence, children (as market subjects) would be *all* they had to rely on: "The real issue is that in the future, if Kharnak village wants to uplift itself, you must rely on the children. If the children are wasted, it's like wasting the dewa as a whole." And he depicted himself telling me the donor not to give soft, perishable gifts like food and clothing, but to invest in education, likening that money to the hard currency of silver that lasts into the future, converting itself into the self-sufficient "capital" (Tib. *ma rtsa*) of learning: "So if we feed all of our kids with this kind of silver, in the future they will be able to feed themselves, and they won't have to rely on anyone else."

But the cash before us, those flimsy paper tokens of quantity already transferred, was not yet hard currency in that way. When Shawojia finally finished speaking to polite applause, the real star of the show was neither him nor me but the stacks of bills on the table. As Gendun had put it, we needed to give Shawojia "face," but now they could pivot away and claim the money's unrealized value for the dewa. As the power of Mao's face on the stacks of cash before us suggested, in practice for Tibetans, money has never been a transparent medium of sheer quantity. In Buddhist and non-Buddhist practices for capturing fortune, money, like Mao, is both an icon (in the image of Mao's face on bills) and an index (a constitutive cause) of a volatile power, a vital force of distributed efficacy (as in the Tibetan term *nus pa*, "power" or "potency"). As a fortune-enhancing force, arrayed on home and temple altars, it is in some ways a mundane counterpart to Buddhist blessing power (Tib. *byin rlabs*).[65] This was clearly evident in the awed and careful way in which the men had handled the cash, and in how the offering scarves, repurposed from capturing me, now turned their captivating touch to the stacks of bills.

I was now urged to stand up and effectively erase myself (and the other foreign donor) by solemnly transferring the stacks into the hands of Drakpa and Tashi, the main project managers. Shawojia made the announcement, his honorific language formalizing the moment by placing me in the role of a high, even Buddhist, patron: "Next our donor will bestow upon us the money!" Gendun's lens zoomed in on the action, Drakpa's accountant made a show of counting the currency, and KVUF members photographed the two men posing with the money—even though the funds in fact were already at work in our project (Drakpa had already given Zhang his first payment). This dramatized transfer, the offering scarves that framed it with sincere intentions, was supposed to thereby convert the cash from scale-jumping abstraction to future fortune under the auspices of my Kharnak hosts. The event broke up quickly after that. Shawojia was escorted out and the money whisked away. I jokingly asked Gendun where it went, and he replied with great relief that that was not our concern anymore, it was out of our hands now.

Conversion Four: School Wall and Gate to Tibetan Buddhist Abode

Yet even that elaborate performance was not enough to contain the project's potential fortune in the KVUF's envisioned dewa. As soon as Shawojia was gone, the KVUF men came alive, and along with Tashi and Gendun, they enthusiastically began to discuss the need for another ritual at the site of the new school gate, one that would turn their hospitality from human guests to divine ones, and directly harness the metanatural force of Buddhist blessing power. For Tibetans in Rebgong, a wide array of threshold rituals (to auspiciously site a new space or to shore up an existing one) work to counter the scalar slipperiness of media of value like money. They evoke the aid of protector deities, Buddhas, and lamas in discerning the causes and conditions of fortune and misfortune.

In siting rites like this one, residents offer precious things, or "treasures" (Tib. *gter*), by burying them at emblematic junctures in both human and divine territories. In the Upper Narrows, treasures were most often composed of substances evoking the ideal fertility of the land: precise assemblages of grains, good dirt, good water, and juniper. As Sarah Jacoby put it

FIGURE 17. Purifying the *gter* "treasure" for the Kharnak school gate treasure offering, spring 2008. Author's photo.

(2014, 103), especially in contexts where humans disturb or extract things from lands (in pilgrimage "harvests," agriculture, or construction work), a treasure bundle or "vase," properly blessed and empowered by a lama and emplaced or "planted" (Tib. *sa 'debs*) works to restore an auspicious balance in human-nonhuman relations.[66] That is, a successfully implanted treasure vase creates an automatic link between the auspicious earth and its supported surface, and thereby works to (re)invigorate the vital essences (Tib. *bcud*) and thus sociomoral fortune (*yang*) that residents seek to contain. In the same way that monastic receipts for cash donations transform money into "material supports for faith" (Tib. *dad rten sgor*), treasure rites at key thresholds attempt to convert built environments into material supports for fortunate communities.

In Kharnak's school repair project then, the new three-door Chinese-style *paifang* gate (Tib. *rgya sgo*) was to become the key juncture for reconstituting that other-space on the KVUF's terms. The gate was a way to overcome villagers' old socialist hierarchy of values and fully incorporate the school into the dewa. In principal Tashi's initial drawing of the wall, he figures the gate at the center as disproportionately large and adorned with sloping tiled roofs. Importantly, he imagines the gate as the medium for renaming the school, not as the Chinese language "Kharnak Comprehensive School," but as the grand, even Buddhist templelike Tibetan language "Kharnak School, Sanctuary for the Dissemination of Culture" (Tib. *rig gnas dar rgyas gling*), and thus, like the first post-Mao Tibetan-language schools envisioned by the Panchen Lama, the gateway to specifically Tibetan knowledge.

At principal Tashi's urging, the men decided that offering a treasure at the base of the gate would be essential for ensuring a productive future for the school and its students, and Drakpa organized them to bring materials for an incense offering to accompany the burial of the treasure bundle early the next morning.[67] To me, Tashi explained, "a treasure is for ensuring that all the vital essence [Tib. *bcud*] inside does not leave, and that it will never be depleted." But as they portrayed it, the ritual was also for seeking increase. Gendun opined that they needed something to augment education and knowledge above all, and the men decided that, in contrast to the kind of treasure bundle usually offered by households seeking the increase of wealth, a treasure offered to the female Buddhist deity Drolma (Skt. Tara) would be most suited.[68] As Tashi enthused to me, "A Drolma treasure is about increase, so that the number of students would increase, and students' knowledge would increase. It would be extremely good for us!" And Gendun summed up, linking the ritual to the desire for market-based success on behalf of the village, "If we do that, then in this school many students will succeed [Tib. *'khyongs*] to the utmost. That is the goal."

Fear and Loathing in Concrete

We can now return to my arguments at the beginning of this chapter and understand how concrete came to be a particularly problematic medium of value in our school wall repair project. In New Socialist construction projects in Rebgong, the heavy durability of concrete after all was supposed to convert the ethereal good intentions of offering scarves and the capricious volatility of money into long-term fortune for communities. In Kharnak, that initial treasure offering at the school gate site worked to lay the foundations for that conversion in advance. As a ritual specifically aimed at increasing knowledge and not wealth, it sought to conspicuously differentiate the school, the repair project, and their leaders from the petty interests of households. In other words, the ritual sought to transmute certain substances and values entering the village (money, building materials, built forms) into clearly readable signs of collective vitality and communal knowledge. But as the wall and gate took shape that spring under the auspices of Mr. Zhang, that is not how it turned out.

Gendun, under great pressure to fundraise for the county education bureau that year,[69] even as he grew increasingly anxious about the status of Tibetan culture and language under the military crackdown, began to sense built forms, and especially concrete, in different ways. To the dismay of Drakpa and Tashi, Gendun's dawning knowledge of the actually decrepit condition of rural Tibetan primary schools across Rebgong led him to express increasing, and then adamant doubt, and finally despair and outrage about the quality of Mr. Zhang's concrete. In Gendun's ever-anxious and untrained eyes, the concrete mortar binding the wall's inner layer of bricks and the concrete stucco that would cover it were not easily readable, instead they hid the potential of deliberate neglect and diverted funds that could be taken (for years to come) as evidence of his own corruption and inadequacy.

Good concrete, in fact, is an intricate art. It consists in precise ratios of particular kinds of sand, rock or "aggregate," water, and cement powder, that must be geared to the type of project and to particular environmental conditions. Further, to avoid cracking or crumbling over time, it must be mixed, poured and cured in exact, time-delimited ways according to climate. Painting a smooth concrete surface requires procedures to prime and seal it so that the paint will adhere. Experts say well-made and maintained concrete can last thousands of years. But to the untrained, new concrete can be exceedingly hard to assess. Despite the office posters touting the education bureau's renovation efforts in the 2000s, in our tours of schools all over the county that spring many villagers and students tended to take for granted the cold, dirty, cracked and peeling concrete walls of their schools. In some ways, they had come to be naturalized as the inherent conditions of low-quality rural people and places. Villagers and leaders alike assumed extremely short lifespans for their built forms—a building that lasted more than ten years, like Kharnak's now shabby-looking classroom building, was often pointed out to me as evidence of *good* construction.

But as the construction boom heated up into the 2000s, villagers too began to look at concrete forms with new eyes. Stark juxtapositions of decrepit highland schools with beautiful household compounds or lowland school grounds led many to read them as signs of abject neglect and corruption, the betrayal of an (old) socialist social contract. This is what Gendun feared most. As the spring wore on and the wall went up, Gendun broke under the pressure of all the variables he could not discern—for him, it seemed, the attempted transparency of the money transfer ceremony had completely failed. Despite his lack of training and his job description as merely a fund-raiser for the county, he began to style himself as a kind of meta-auditor for all school construction projects in the Upper Narrows, pushing into the more experienced Drakpa's purview to do it. In effect, he was trying to enforce the impossible standards of a technocratic transparency, taking up the rhetoric of international development organizations to dispense with the delicacies of long-term ritualized relations and read built forms as the mechanical outcomes of contracts once signed. With idealist passion, he publicly upbraided and instructed contractors, workers, and village leaders (including principal Tashi) wherever he went.

Contractor Zhang's work on the Kharnak school wall thus increasingly fell short in his eyes. Gendun claimed that he never showed up to supervise his Chinese workers, and he brought me along as fellow auditor on multiple trips to the project site. Now, the mortar between the wall's foundation stones and bricks, chunky and messily laid, evoked deliberate neglect *and* the abject status of Tibetans in general. The conflict finally came to a head when Gendun tried to reclaim control of the project budget from Drakpa, attempting as well to reclaim the surplus cash KVUF members had agreed would go toward the school's first ever concrete playground. That move, starkly countering the public money transfer ceremony, threatened to disintegrate all the carefully laid material-semiotic conversions for capturing the project's value on village terms, the basis for Gendun and Drakpa's alliance. Most important, Gendun's challenge could portray Drakpa's status as a state official and party member, and his long-term collaboration with contractor Zhang, as inherently corrupt, immorally capturing value for the wrong scales. Indeed, in an irate text message to me, Gendun proclaimed that he "hated" Drakpa, and, hinting, asked me to consider why he "doesn't care about quality" (Ch. *zhiliang*). In the end, in an attempt to have Zhang fired and the wall completely redone, Gendun even brought in a government quality inspector, but to no avail. The work went on.

Meanwhile, in heartfelt conversations with me, Drakpa and Tashi were deeply wounded by Gendun's accusations and, they told me, contractor Zhang was angered and offended. To Drakpa, Gendun had alienated everyone by flouting all the "procedures" (Tib. *rgyud rim*) in place to monitor and manage projects, leaving Drakpa to mend fences socially. To me, Drakpa noted with irony that Kharnak villagers thought Gendun was a heroic "gift master" for bringing so much money to the village, but he insisted that he himself didn't care about such "face": "You know after a few years people will forget who you are," he said, "it doesn't last." Yet Drakpa also portrayed himself as a long-suffering silent protector of Gendun's "face" in the village and at work: it wouldn't help to bring in his boss Shawojia, Drakpa said, "because I am protecting [Ch. *baohu*] Gendun, Shawojia would fire him and I don't want him to lose that much face."

Ultimately, the concrete of the Kharnak school wall never did reveal its inner secrets. The stark division of labor between Tibetan residents and Chinese party leaders and contractors in the frontier zone meant that none of the Tibetan managers, even Drakpa, had the skills or the status to parse out the multiple variables and circulations involved in its creation, intentioned or not. Gendun finally quit the project in protest, leaving it to Drakpa to finish. As Gendun discovered, under the economy of appearances as it played out in the Upper Narrows, they could not in the end totally capture money in concrete, rendering its moral status and efficacy completely visible for the dewa. In the face of widening rural-urban and interethnic disparities in Rebgong, the circulations of money were always already opaque.

Conclusion: Concrete Gluttony

In this chapter, a linguistic anthropological approach to materiality and value gave us tools for understanding tangible things not as inert objects simply present, but as contested media of value embedded in an intensifying battle for fortune in Rebgong's rural Upper Narrows. In that light, Foucault's notion of other-spaces offered us a way to conceptualize rural Tibetan primary schools as aesthetically specific built environments in which the foundational timespace terms of personhood, development, and fortune were being centrally challenged. The story of Kharnak's school wall demonstrated that this was no clash of discrete ontologies, but a complex set of dialogues as competing gift masters sought to appropriate and convert various media of value on behalf of different scales of communities. Just as in Jima village, at issue here was the very vitality and future existence of Tibetan communities. In 2008, the New Socialist Countryside campaign, along with the School Consolidation program, took top-down urbanization upriver, threatening to devitalize rural villages in a grand vision of market integration. Here, this is not the planned "death of the street," as in James Holston's analysis of the modernist city of Brasília (1989), but the designed death of the unruly rural.

This is what Kharnak village's proactive leaders sought to stave off, even after Gendun and Drakpa fell out. By early July 2008, the school wall and gate were being finished. One of the reasons Zhang's workers had left the brick mortar messy was that it was to be covered with the clean, smooth exteriors of concrete stucco. That was when Drakpa texted me an invitation to a final treasure ritual, this one for the roof of the new gate. Only this time, said Drakpa, Gendun was not invited. I arrived around 9:00 a.m. to find Drakpa, dressed in a dapper suit, gathered with principal Tashi, several KVUF members, contractor Zhang and his four Chinese workers. School was in session and uniformed children, their red Communist Youth League scarves around their necks, watched and waited expectantly. The KVUF men had an incense offering ready on a nearby brick altar, with firecrackers and conch shells poised to call the deities to the feast. Beer, grain alcohol, tea drinks, and candy were prominently prepared to give to all who gathered there. Drakpa proudly showed me the palm-sized treasure bundle Tashi had had made: it was a cloth bag stuffed with "the five types of grain" and topped with a sprig of juniper (see figure 17). On it was sewn a handwritten ink prayer:

tshe ring nad med cing / yon tan rgya mtsho rgyas /
snyan grags nam mkhar khyab / bsod nams dar rgyas shog /

(Expand our health and long life and the ocean of all our inherent good
    qualities
May our fame spread far and wide, and our good karma flourish and grow)

Tashi put a ladder up to the gate roof for me to have a look: it was elaborately cast in concrete and rebar, ready for the final pour. The treasure was to be placed in the center, directly into the wet concrete.

Back on the ground, contractor Zhang greeted me politely in Tibetan and took the opportunity to reiterate to me the honorableness of his motives. He insisted that this was a very well-built gate, and that nowadays, with prices going up, you couldn't get such a gate built for less than thirty thousand yuan, but, as per the original contract, he had agreed to do it for Kharnak for ten thousand. He recounted how insulted and angered he had been by Gendun's scoldings, emphasizing that he had forty years of experience and had never been attacked in such a way. He had been so upset about it, he said, that he had contemplated quitting the project, but felt in the end that he had to honor the contract. This ritual was thus in part about Zhang and Drakpa recementing the value and morality of their working relationship for an audience of villagers and myself. Indeed the whole event was shaped by the temporal requirements of Zhang's concrete.

It began as Zhang's workers commenced shoveling the wet concrete up from the mixer below, while both Zhang and Drakpa conspicuously supervised. Zhang made a show of inspecting the mix, and then jumping up on the platform to direct its placement in the gate roof. Then, moving quickly before the concrete set, workers made a hole in the center, and Drakpa signaled to the men to begin the offering feast by lighting the incense fire and firecrackers. After purifying the treasure by passing it over burning juniper, and as Tashi recited a prayer to Drolma next to him, Drakpa lovingly placed it in the concrete, topping it with pebbles and a few pieces of candy, and framing it on either side with two white offering scarves, hung from the protruding rebar. While Tashi threw candy to the villagers, workers, and students below, Drakpa finally descended to complete the incense offerings by pouring grain alcohol around the smoking juniper and grains.

The hospitality spectacle of the final offering ritual at the school gate was a collaborative effort to recapture value for the village in the wake of Gendun's challenge to the project. In it, the qualities of well-made concrete and those of the treasure and offering scarves were supposed to be mutually constitutive: the presumed durability of the concrete drying and fixing the treasure bundle in place supposedly projects the multifaceted fortune of village bodies and minds into a future both mundane and supramundane. The concrete anchors it to the gate and to the blessed and vitalized earth of the earlier treasure at its foundation. In turn, the embedded treasure on top, framed by the culminating offering scarves, works to fill up and thus complete and purify the concrete gate (wall and school) as a whole. The ritual thereby claims them as part of the divinely guarded sovereign territory of Kharnak village, an auspicious opening to knowledge that will generate the fame required for ongoing prosperity. At that precarious threshold, the village men's various offerings to an array of gathered humans and invisible beings attempted to capture and convert the project donors' gifts of cash once and for all, thereby repositioning villagers not as vulnerable recipients but again as sovereign hosts. In this way, the final treasure ritual tried to reframe and fix the concrete wall and gate as both ideal amalgams and active generators of the qualities of Buddhist efficacy, socialist morality, capitalist wealth, and a specifically Tibetan purified landscape—the neosocialist communalism that the KVUF had pledged to create.

At first glance, their efforts seemed to have succeeded. By August, as the entire region remained under de facto martial law in the run-up to the Beijing Olympics, Kharnak's school grounds were awash in a gluttony of concrete—at a time when concrete was scarce and expensive. The completed wall and gate were literally breathtaking. Larger and more elaborate than any school wall and gate I had seen in rural Tibetan regions (even the central district consolidated boarding school), they were almost completely covered in concrete stucco. And, taking up the trompe l'oeil aesthetics of NSC construction, even the river rocks of the foundation, so painstakingly hauled there by villagers, had been virtually covered with concrete so that now they looked flattened and artificial. Drakpa had indeed used the project surplus to have the oversized playground inside done in poured concrete, so that no hint of mud could be seen. Now, the smooth surfaces of the wall and gate

FIGURE 18.   Painted Tibetan language wall slogan: "Holding fast to education, we must raise our people's quality [Tib. *spus tshad*]," Kharnak school, summer 2011. Author's photo.

were to be painted inside and out with the symbols of Tibetan culture: folk dancers, the eight auspicious signs, and slogans exclusively in Tibetan language: "Holding fast to education, we must raise our people's quality." As a whole, the school grounds for Drakpa and his fellow KVUF members were supposed to stand as a monument to the fully modern power, efficacy, and solidarity of Kharnak villagers and their leaders' transregional, even global, networking skills.

However, in the ferment of ongoing unrest in subsequent years, the value and meaning of that built environment was to shift in unforeseen ways. By 2011 when I visited again, Drakpa and Gendun, along with their households and lineage allies, were still in conflict (the issue of who had been the rightful gift masters had never been resolved: "We have no relationship whatsoever anymore," Drakpa sighed). And the once brightly painted gate was peeling, the concrete stucco on the walls stained and cracking. Drakpa's concrete playground, of which he had been so proud, was badly crumbling, a classic case of poorly finished concrete under freeze-thaw conditions. Finally, heightened surveillance in the valley had pushed Kharnak's communalist vision and the KVUF underground. Drakpa told me they had destroyed all the KVUF's charter documents, even as Kharnak continued its new gatherings with the Shuk tribal federation, and other villages within it had quietly started their own Uplift foundations. Drakpa seemed nostalgic about our collaborations three years earlier. At a recent KVUF-hosted village event, he said, the deity medium Shampa, entranced as Makgol, had suddenly blurted out, "One is missing!" "That was you," Drakpa told me.

While regional officials pushed New Socialist development as an antidote to Tibetan unrest, the entire county in the summer of 2011 had come to be enveloped in an unprecedented gluttony of concrete. The lower valley especially was a theater of competing other-spaces battling for fortune (see the epilogue). As I toured schools with a resigned and fatigued Drakpa, it was clear that concrete was now the key public sign and spectacle of authoritarian largesse. The state's gift of development, and the obligations it entailed, now far outstripped Kharnak leaders' attempts to capture and convert the gift at their school.[70] As Drakpa sheepishly put it, referring to the expense and struggle of putting in the playground at Kharnak three years earlier, "Now concrete is cheap." Indeed, most of the dirt courtyards of his district's schools had been covered with concrete. But they too had already begun to crumble.

◌ | | CHAPTER 4

The Melodious Sound of the Right-Turning Conch

Historiography and Buddhist Counterdevelopment in Langmo Village

In this chapter, we travel further upriver to the small and marginalized Tibetan community of Langmo, a neighboring village and rival of Kharnak. Here we explore the stakes and consequences of village history making as a dialogic process in the context of increasing state-led pressures on rural land use. I had met Langmo elders back in 2005, long before I knew Kharnak village leaders, when I was first looking for highland communities to research. Langmo elders, it turned out, had their own goals for our collaboration. Their counterdevelopment plans for the dewa meant "capturing" foreign donors and converting them to dewa patrons. Thus, just like in Kharnak, my naïve offer in 2008 to help fund Langmo's primary school roof repair drew me into deepening relationships with villagers I had never anticipated. And that meant taking a role as a key listener and medium for elders' oppositional accounts of Langmo history. In the face of resettlement pressures, elders insisted that the dewa's Buddhist history grounded the community's sovereign right to their former lands, even as the military crackdown brought state security forces' search for "Troublemakers" to the Upper Narrows.

In 2008, I was not fully incorporated as a patron of Kharnak village (the village we encountered in chapter 3) until after the completion of their school's stunning concrete wall, during the harvest festival season that July.

At Kharnak's celebrations, as we squatted with the women in the village temple and waited for the village's respected deity medium, the retired official Shampa, to make his annual pronouncements, Gendun suddenly rushed up to me, my husband Cain, and my friend Catherine (a well-known English teacher in her late fifties who lived in town), hustling us forward to kneel before the medium. Gendun's hands shook with excitement as he helped us hold up offering scarves to Shampa, whose body was violently inhabited by Kharnak's mountain deity Makgol (the one who likes to protect foreigners). Shampa-as-Makgol then dropped into our scarves the kernels of grain he had previously blessed by blowing on them. Gendun and Drakpa's eyes shone with delight as they helped us tie the grains into the scarves, exclaiming that this kind of gift from the deity himself was extremely rare. To this day, that golden scarf, the grains tied tightly in its middle, hangs in the front hall of my house.

But long before I had ever stepped foot in Kharnak, I had already been captured by an even grander divine presence on behalf of the rival village just upriver, the tiny neighboring community of Langmo. By 2008, the happenstance of my participation as a donor in both villages further problematized my personas and roles in the Upper Narrows. But over time those awkward relationships also helped me understand the nature and stakes of outsider-funded development projects for rural Tibetans in twenty-first century Rebgong. As I, like the education officials Gendun and Drakpa, had to pivot among multiple interlocutors and obligations up and down the valley, I came to grasp more deeply the ways in which residents' embodied experiences of the dewa, that vital communal unit and container of fortune, were shifting dangerously amidst intensifying intervillage competition.

But back in 2005 when I first drove up the valley on my way to Langmo village, crammed in a taxi with my friend Catherine; Tenzin, her young Tibetan assistant; and Gyalo, the tall and imposing Langmo elder who had invited us, I knew nothing of such things. Nor did I realize just how much Catherine herself had been drawn into playing the role of Foreign Gift Master in Rebgong's Upper Narrows and beyond. In subsequent years, in fact, she would rise (despite herself) to be a key figure in rural Tibetans' competing narratives about dewa fortunes. On the way up, passing unknowingly through Kharnak and crossing the Guchu River as the valley narrowed through steep maroon-red rocky cliffs, I had felt the relief and sense of expansive space offered by the rural idyll. Back then, before the optimism of the yang dar years had waned, the early summer countryside seemed to brim with peaceful prosperity, every inch of the valley floor lands and mountainside terraces awash in bright green fields of ripening barley. And

Catherine, she told me, had been busy helping with the ongoing revival of Tibetan Buddhist culture in Rebgong, brokering small grants from foreign NGOs and embassies for "cultural preservation" projects on behalf of Tibetan villagers.

That was why we were headed to Langmo, so Catherine could audit the progress of the interior painting in the village's new Buddhist temple, for which she had attained a grant from the Dutch Embassy. But when we arrived in the village, its neat adobe courtyard homes tucked against the steep hillside across from the river's bend, Catherine and I entered a hospitality event neither of us had bargained for. As I attempted to help translate for Catherine in my albeit rusty Tibetan,[1] I had to grapple for the first time with the ambivalent consequences of listening. Just as I would later find in Kharnak village, this was not going to be a tour in which I could remain an anonymous observer. In retrospect, I now see how the shifting timespace terms of the hospitality that day, the unspoken tensions around the nature and status of givers or hosts and their recipients or guests, were mediated by three key gifts of offering scarves to us. Those gifts from village elders were progressive efforts to convert Catherine, and then especially me, to render us present as once and future patrons for the dewa.

The first came at Gyalo's house over tea, when several village elders arrived to offer Catherine some ordinary nylon scarves, praising her "great compassion" and telling her that her Tibetan name (Lhamo Dorje) would be included on a plaque on the temple gate. They would hear none of it when Catherine protested adamantly that she herself was not the donor, the Dutch Embassy was. Such misapprehensions, I was to learn, were the source of great frustration and ambivalence for Catherine—even though she was deeply committed to promoting Tibetan culture in the region against what she saw as the looming threat of sinification. A meticulously respectful participant in Buddhist worship, she saw her role in Tibetan development projects as merely that of a neutral broker for the efficient flow of money. In her view, once money transferred, she should have no further obligations to either donor or recipient. But on that day, she could do nothing but accept the scarves. Her status as compassionate Buddhist patron thereby established, we were ushered up to the unfinished temple itself. The brick, concrete, and carved-wood hall, grandly dubbed the Temple of Primordial Auspiciousness of Samsara and Nirvana, was a magnificent presence for such a tiny village (only 229 people or 42 households, a third to a quarter the size of the neighboring villages).[2] Surrounded by high packed-earth walls, the main altar building, with its elegant Chinese-style tiled roof, had been positioned on the hillside with a commanding view of the village below.

Camera in hand and awkwardly self-conscious ("I'm no expert!" she whispered to me), Catherine was led into the unpainted interior of the hall to document the painter's first efforts for the Dutch Embassy. But when we emerged into the courtyard, she seemed surprised when Langmo elders explained that they needed more money to finish the side buildings of the complex. To her great frustration, that seemed to dredge up previous tensions over the project, in which, she had told me, elders supposedly ignored the terms of the contract with the embassy they had signed (and fingerprinted) and used remaining funds to expand the complex at the behest of a "monk." As the elders increasingly turned their vehement narrative to me, explaining that the temple would be their lama's rural residence and teaching quarters, Catherine remained vague, withdrawing into the background. The elders' second gift of scarves was thus the pivotal one.

Unbeknownst to either of us, villagers had drawn on meager communal funds to arrange a picnic feast for us in a festive tent down by the river. There, as Gyalo merrily drank a whole bottle of barley alcohol and Catherine and Tenzin busied themselves looking at photos, Gyalo focused his story of the village on me, addressing my Tibetan persona: "We have it so hard, Tshomo, we have very few salaried officials, and very little farmland. Many households don't have enough to eat, and jobs are hard to find!" As he got drunker, it finally dawned on me that I was now the targeted patron, that my indebtedness as a guest was supposed to challenge my naïve (and privileged) presumption of neutral distance and free mobility: "Lhamo Dorje [Catherine] has done her part," he pronounced, "now you have to do yours!" That was when elders brought their second gift of scarves, this time of the finest quality embossed white silk, topped with skeins of golden brocade cloth, an offering that far outstripped in elegance the meager opening gift over tea. This time, they made sure to give them to me.

The third and final gift of scarves that day, the one that supposedly effected my capture as a patron for Langmo dewa, came when the day culminated with a trip several kilometers further upriver to the centuries-old Geluk sect Tshema Monastery. The small and crumbling monastery, perched on a hill above its patron village, seemed to be an extension of home for Gyalo. "This is our main monastery," he explained. "Tshema and Langmo are one dewa!" Turning up the gravel road toward the village, Gyalo gave scant attention to the county's forest management station ("we're fined four to five thousand yuan if we cut one tree!"), and opposite it, the new hydroelectric dam and its workers quarters, built and run, he said, by Chinese companies based in Xining. But when we were greeted by the elderly monk caretaker in front of the monastery's main assembly hall, once again the nature of their hospitality was unclear to us. Catherine had hoped to visit the mother of a student of hers, but here again, it seemed, we were being emplaced as potential patrons.

On our tour of the grounds then, Catherine once again withdrew as I listened to the old monk's stories. He spoke proudly of the monastery's nine centuries of history since its founding in the thirteenth century, but he emphasized the difficulties the monastery now faced, especially after their main lama escaped to exile in 1958 and government "higher ups" had not allowed them to search for his incarnation after he died. The brick and concrete stucco stupas, hastily rebuilt in the early 1980s, were now disintegrating and villagers, he insisted, were too poor to help. We ended up in front of the three-story temple for the future Buddha Maitreya, and Gyalo suggested we take a picture to commemorate the occasion. That is where the old monk placed elegant white scarves around our necks, asking us to "strive hard" (Tib. *sra la byed*) on behalf of the monastery. Gyalo laughed heartily, pointing at me, "The deity has captured Tshomo!" (Tib. *lha yis mtsho mo bzung dang*), he cried.

Histories of the Future: Historiography and Auspicious Sovereignty

> This container, called Langmo Plain of Abundance, auspiciously formed as part of the Four Clans of Tshothang. It is the place where the fertile pollens of all kinds of flowers are continuously born. Here, the precious protector Buddhas enjoy the playful dance of the mountains and rivers. As the river, endowed with the eight good qualities, zigzags through the fields, the divine Protectors feast on the musical sound of crops heavy with nutritious grains.
>
> Today, the contents of this container, the people around whom swirl fortune and the signs of auspiciousness, gather together to offer a harmonious performance. This is the fortunate and wealthy dewa, where the rosary string of elders is longer than the faithfully flowing line of the river, and the branching petals of the youthful generations expand like the summer sea.
>
> —Excerpt from the opening speech at the Langmo village party celebrating
> the completion of their new temple, summer 2006

Back in 2005, I remember being perplexed about what Gyalo's talk of "capture" had meant (which deity? why?). By the 2008 New Year though, I had a much clearer idea ("it was the Buddha Maitreya who captured you," Gyalo had said when we met again). In the story of my deepening engagement with Langmo villagers, Gyalo's counterpart for me was Dorje Gyap, my principal host and interlocutor there. Both men were respected elders in their fifties, but in contrast to Gyalo's fiery brawn and imposing presence, Dorje Gyap was small and sallow-skinned, his battered fedora covering his long and thinning hair. In larger groups, while Gyalo's voice boomed, Dorje Gyap would fade quietly into the background. After an illness in the early 1990s, he told me, Dorje Gyap had become increasingly deaf, such that he was sidelined from his previous roles as village leader, and others now had to lean in and yell into his ear to keep him up to speed. But I came to realize that it was Dorje Gyap, pivoting between guiding the village and heading his own large household (he and his wife had eight children), who all along was the key thinker and visionary in the dewa's unfolding battle for fortune. It was he, more than anyone, who brought Gyalo's triumphant pronouncement of my capture to fruition.[3]

Over the next several years, I, like many guests of the village before me, enjoyed the hospitality Dorje Gyap and his wife offered, becoming a patron for both his household (sponsoring several of his youngest children's educations) and for the village (helping to repair the roof of their tiny primary school, and brokering an NGO grant for a running water system). But it was on a crisp and sunny February day in 2008, the second day of the lunar New Year, while Dorje Gyap and his wife were hosting my family and I in customary fashion, that the nature and stakes of my roles in Langmo shifted significantly, in part as a direct consequence of listening. That is, after weeks of my requests to hear about village "history," and as the winter gave way to a spring of unrest and crackdown, Dorje Gyap and other Langmo elders began to position me not just as a giver of money, but as a provider of access to the power of language. That is, they sought my help as a medium and advocate for their counternarratives of the dewa's past and future.

On that occasion in early 2008, we sat in the formal guestroom of Dorje Gyap's home, where guests were fêted in order to both share in and help ensure the auspiciousness of the New Year. The spacious, wood-paneled room itself seemed to manifest the household's ideal wealth and prosperity, contrasting starkly with the austerity of the family's everyday existence (that was the only time that I ever entered that room). Low tables were piled high with artfully arranged feast foods, and the wall next to photos of important lamas was adorned with a beautiful juniper branch "tree" hung with candies, flowers and a few Chinese one-, five-, and ten-yuan notes. Then, as a response to yet another of my requests to hear about village history ("you want me to talk *now*?"), Dorje Gyap played a video for me called,

"The Melodious Sound of the Right-Turning Conch," after the white conch shells that, when blown through, are supposed to call for and produce the auspicious and victorious sound of the Buddha Dharma. Langmo elders, he said, had commissioned the video to commemorate and celebrate the completion of their new temple (which villagers now called "the Assembly Hall") just a few months after Catherine and I had visited it in 2005.

Langmo's 2005 video was participating in the spate of Tibetan language media production across Rebgong that I mentioned in chapter 1. In the Upper Narrows, that new media amounted to emergent genres of especially dewa history. Dorje Gyap had collaborated with village elders and a couple of their monk sons (his own monk son, he told me, wrote the narrative voice-over) to create Langmo's video. In it, they work to contextualize the new Assembly Hall, placing it in a centuries-old Geluk sect Buddhist lineage via the village's historical role as a "patron community" (Tib. *lha sde*) for one of Rongbo Monastery's main incarnate lamas, one Arol Tshang. But when the video culminated with footage (from 2006) of richly dressed villagers partying at the lavish celebration in the new temple's courtyard, Dorje Gyap's face registered quick discomfort. "It must look like we're wealthy, but we're not!" he commented, chuckling ironically, his wife chiming in to support him. "Those things [the motorcycles, the fur-lined robes, the huge coral bead necklaces]," he insisted, "were borrowed from all over for the occasion. We were going to film it, right? If we filmed it, and it was not nice-looking, then that would've been bad!" For the rest of the afternoon, that was the refrain Dorje Gyap would return to: "Despite how it looked in the video, we're not rich!"

In the previous chapters, I drew on a linguistic anthropological approach to what I called a politics of presence in Rebgong, as a way to demonstrate how language and semiotics (as interpretive practice) fundamentally shape people's experiences of materiality, embodied personhood, and power under state-led development pressures. In this chapter, we delve further by exploring the nature and stakes of historiography in the Upper Narrows. Here, villagers' stories of the past are not the expression of a single, objective history, but they participate in a contentious narrative process that always entails selective memory and forgetting. As such, we could consider historical narration as perhaps the most fundamental and ubiquitous form of timespace scale-making. To put it in Bakhtin's terms, historiography is always dialogic. In their narratives of the past, people are always consciously or unconsciously addressing visible and invisible interlocutors (e.g., listeners, readers, viewers, human or not). Performances of such stories—emplotments of the past—are thus also attempts to position selves and others as types of persons, to plot them within the morally charged temporal shifts and spatial purviews of competing collectivities.[4]

Importantly, since the 1950s in the Tibetan communities of the Upper Narrows, historiography in the Maoist "new society" (Ch. *xin shehui*) has been all about contested sovereignties. That is, the traumatic rupture of CCP-led socialist transformation starting in 1958 hinged on mandatory performances of a new nationalist (and class) history of feudal suffering and modern liberation, a story that justified land collectivization under CCP-led communes.[5] This, in fact, as we began to see in chapters 2 and 3, is the very essence of the silent pact in Tibetan regions of the PRC: when public history is the purview of the State as the legitimate voice of the nation, and as ultimate owner of all land and resources, whose stories of the past, where-when, work to authorize long term land-use rights? On behalf of what scales of collectivities?[6] From the perspective on the dialogic production of social relations I have been developing in this book, we couldn't see this contestation over official stories of the past as just a top-down "national history" erasing a single or discrete, local Tibetan history. Instead, consider again the three main historical idioms of exchange and fortune I discussed in chapter 1 (lama-lay leader alliance, Maoist socialism, and authoritarian capitalism). Each of those figures in people's stories of the past carried differently scaled histories, with different implications for the social and moral grounds of human communities and their access to fortune over time.

In the various forms of historiography I encountered in Langmo, I realized, villagers brought those key figures of fortunate exchange and their entailed histories into dialogue with each other, pivoting among them depending on the type of hospitality encounter they were staging with powerful outsiders. That is, Langmo villagers' stories of the dewa's past were varying attempts to communicate "out" and "up." They were part and parcel of villagers' highly proactive efforts to appeal to superiors for "support" or "care" (Ch. *zhaogu*, Tib. *skyabs skyor*), in order to stave off what they saw as the accelerating marginalization and even potential erasure of the village and its rightful fortunes altogether. In practice, these were not stories of a singular, local community over time, but assertions about the very nature and timespace scale of the dewa as, yet again, villagers' embodied experience of their community shifted radically. Just like their rivals in Kharnak, Langmo elders discovered that the new crisis of time in the 2000s meant headlong futurity downriver, the ideal erasure of past (and present) in a race for the ever-receding distant horizon of well-earned wealth.

In contrast to the technocratic terms of the contract with the Dutch Embassy Catherine had brokered for the new temple, Langmo was no

FIGURE 19.   Billboard depicting artist's rendition of ideal pastoralist resettlement community on valley floor, Longwu town settlement construction site, summer 2011. Author's photo.

traditional Tibetan hamlet requiring "cultural preservation" in the face of market integration.[7] It was instead a radically displaced community. In a carrot-and-stick process that presaged by almost a decade the more recent push to resettle all Tibetan pastoralist populations in towns at lower altitudes,[8] between 1995 and 2001, Langmo villagers had led the way in moving the entire village from their historical site in the mountains down to the new highway on the valley floor. In the process, they sold most of their livestock and left behind the new primary school elders had just organized to build. Villagers were dismayed to find, however, that the move down had left them vulnerable to new land grabs by both state bureaus and the larger and more powerful neighboring villages (including Kharnak). For many Langmo residents, this was not a step toward a shining modern future, but a crisis of historical sovereignty that had greatly impoverished them. Villagers' historiography, across media forms and events, was thus most fundamentally aimed at claiming and displaying a dewa scale that spanned the spaces and times of both village sites. They thereby attempted to link the present lower village to the now-abandoned upper or "peak" (Tib. *kha*) village and its sovereign claims to an auspicious, indeed preordained, fortune—the "fortunate and wealthy dewa" (Tib. *g'yang sde phyugs mo*) of the elder's speech at the

Langmo temple opening party that begins this section. This was their counterhistory of the future.

This context of the crisis of time helps explain the rise in the production of
media portraying dewa history across Rebgong from the early 2000s on, and
why I found that such media for Tibetans was often carefully guarded, even
from fellow villagers, and deemed highly charged and (potentially) politically
risky. As we began to see in chapter 3, under the heightened pressures of the
economy of appearances that pitted villages and the relative human quality
of their residents against each other, dewa historiography competed for the
eyes and ears of powerful strangers. As such, narrators strove to lay down
the legitimating grounds for collective efforts in the battle for fortune. And
that battle, as we will see, could come to real blows. Here then, in contrast
to Jima village's class and generational factionalism, and to Kharnak leaders'
neo-socialist communalism, Langmo elders ultimately prioritized Buddhist
counterdevelopment efforts, grounded in particular claims to past and present lama-lay leader alliances.

Finally, historical narration, no less than the ritualized construction of
school grounds we explored in chapter 3, is a multimedia or multimodal
process (unfolding across a variety of media formats appealing to multiple
senses, often simultaneously). Hence, for example, the various kinds of histories Langmo villagers produced in 2005: oral and written stories of abject
poverty on one hand and filmic stories of auspicious wealth on the other.
Historiography is thus not just a matter of discourse, but as a politics of presence it is always also an embodied process that works to constitute inhabited
environments. Indeed in this chapter, as illustrated by the elder's praise speech
excerpted above, we expand on our exploration of built environments in chapter 3 to consider so-called "natural" environments as themselves key containers of fortune, the products of human and divine intervention. Yet in Tibetan
communities, where great prestige accrues to the written text, villagers strive
to entextualize their accounts of the past, reaching for but not always seamlessly imitating prestigious registers or genres. As Bauman and Briggs (1990)
point out, the "intertextual gap" between any performance and the ideal
generic model(s) it emulates allows for change and creativity despite claims
to unbroken continuity. I would add that intermodal gaps (e.g., between different kinds of signs, verbal, visual, aural) within even one text or media form
can allow for creative ambiguities that remain diplomatically unnoticed.[9]

As a way to tell the story of the rising stakes of historiography and place
making in Langmo into 2008 and beyond, in the coming sections, we explore
these dynamics in two complementary, yet dialogically conflictual histories
of the future that were presented to me by Langmo villagers. First, a short,

written story of the dewa's move down from the peak. That story awk-wardly emulated the statist terms of forward-looking development, framed in the modern genre of citizens' petitions to state superiors; and second, the 2005–6 video account of the dewa's Buddhist history, modeled on the pres-tigious Tibetan genres of place eulogy and, most importantly, lama biogra-phy (Tib. *rnam thar*). As we will see, despite their very different timespace terms, both forms of narrative (just like the elder's speech above) relied on a key historical idiom of social and spatial continuity for Tibetans, the lineage (Tib. *rgyud*). And, most importantly, both narratives navigated precariously shifting demands on rural residents to speak or to perform well (read: com-pliantly) for superiors, especially as the crackdown on Tibetan unrest that spring brought the search for "Troublemakers" to Langmo.

The Earnest Hopes of the Masses: Performing Poverty on the Valley Floor

> Our destitute and backward village, lacking scientific training and skills, education and knowledge, holds out the hope that you will kindly provide aid so that our people [Tib. *mang tshogs*, lit., "the Masses"] can apply all their energy to studying education and scientific knowledge, and thereby strive for the future [Tib. *mdun lam*, lit., "the path forward"].
>
> —Closing lines of elders' written history of Langmo dewa,
> February 14, 2008

As we saw in chapter 3, within the unspoken tensions of hospitality spec-tacles during development projects in Rebgong villages, the successful host claims the ultimate prerogative to speak, and to thereby set the terms of the largesse on display. Kharnak village leaders, as themselves salaried officials and even party members, could pivot between, on the one hand, their proper roles as listeners vis-à-vis their state superiors like Shawojia and on the other, their presumed roles as authoritative speakers vis-à-vis their rural inferiors like Langmo villagers. By contrast, Langmo leaders, as they were constantly reminding me, had very few salaried officials among them and thus they were often expected to play the role of mute listeners, passively witnessing the compassion of visiting officials and compliantly absorbing their policy admonitions. After months of passionate conversations with Langmo elders and ordinary villagers, I was often struck by how drastically they seemed to be diminished (or even erased) as interlocutors in the company of visit-ing officials and foreign VIPs. On such formulaic occasions, much rode for participants on maintaining a wide gulf in status between the old socialist personas of "the State" and "the Masses," such that villagers (cast as the Masses) could come across as less than human, resembling that widespread category of pitied others for Tibetans who lack the capacity to converse altogether—"dumb cattle" (Tib. *zog*).

Hence even Kharnak's Gendun, who in other contexts expressed some of the most fiery indignation at state bureaus' discriminatory treatment of Tibetans, could traffic in such terms. Over the course of that spring 2008, Gendun felt increasing pressure to demonstrate results from his official county role as school fundraiser, and he took it on himself to supervise the repair of the roof of Langmo's tiny school, built just four years earlier on the valley floor and now badly leaking. I watched in dismay as he would stalk about on our visits there, upbraiding the Chinese contractor (who indeed had tried to cut corners) and barking orders at elders. On one visit, embarrassed in front of a visitor at evidence of freshly peeling paint he thought Langmo elders had failed to maintain, Gendun exploded. "Stupid cows! Idiots!" he exclaimed, describing the villagers. Such apparent neglect for him seemed to be clear evidence of what he and other education officials saw as Tibetan villagers' backward indifference toward schools in favor of supporting their Buddhist temples.

But I found that Kharnak's education officials like Gendun never really recognized the uniquely precarious status of Langmo as a recently resettled dewa (remember that Drakpa had been charged with enticing mountain villages down to the road with the promise of new state-funded schools; Langmo's was one of the earliest of those). As I heard more of Dorje Gyap's, and then other villagers' stories of their in fact highly proactive efforts in the village's move down, I couldn't help but see Dorje Gyap's worsening deafness as a kind of uncanny metaphor for long-term, sociopolitical barriers to translocal communication and understanding. And those communicative barriers in turn were contributing to the marginalization of the very subjects that state-led development would ostensibly celebrate. From the perspective of Langmo villagers then, it was state officials who were inscrutable, unsensing interlocutors, their visits seemingly random, their motives opaque or arbitrary. As one elder adamantly insisted to me, "They refuse to see with their own eyes!" And another, "We can't speak to them, and even if we did, our speech wouldn't be valued!" Yet besides the risk of being reduced to the status of dumb animals, rural Tibetans like Langmo residents also faced the political risks of noncompliant speech. By that I mean, as principal Tashi had discovered, talk to state superiors that broke the silent pact and directly challenged the vertical hierarchy of appropriate deference and address. Indeed, as the crackdown on Tibetan unrest deepened that spring, Langmo villagers were increasingly haunted by the presence of another abject persona exiled from rightful state-local interaction: criminal "Troublemakers" (Ch. *naoshizhe*, lit., "those who create incidents by making noise").

Development agendas under the Open the West slogan since the early 2000s had, as elsewhere, heightened demands on Tibetans to present themselves as the rural "poor," worthy (not lazy) recipients of state and NGO aid.[10] But the overt militarization of compliance across Rebgong in spring 2008 made villagers' performances of innocent poverty mandatory. In the various stories of the dewa's past I heard, the main way that Langmo elders navigated these roles was to assert that, all along, they were a community of heroic recipient-patrons, not passive welfare dependents. Their dewa histories claimed an unbroken legacy of exemplary hospitality to superiors, with villagers striving to be sovereign stewards of fortune and, as state-local relationships were increasingly commodified, hard-working fundraisers. Yet that moral emplotment in Langmo was riven by intertextual gaps as villagers grappled with the disjunctures between their pasts and presents, between shifting state rhetoric and the reality of their lives on the valley floor. In this, villagers' own stories could embody the voice of the State, even as they worked to directly oppose it, portraying themselves as the Masses. Consider in this light the contrasting stories of Langmo's move to the valley floor I heard from Dorje Gyap on one hand (whose voice was strongly present in the elders' written history-petition) and, on the other, from his own stepmother Deji.

Dorje Gyap's stories of the move down were perhaps the most adamant and detailed of all. His impaired hearing often led him to gesture more strongly than others, gritting his teeth in frustration and acting out the commanding demeanor of uncaring officials. But he was perhaps particularly frustrated because he portrayed himself, and others looked to him, as the most entrepreneurial of villagers, the visionary behind most of the dewa's counterdevelopment moves since the mid-1990s. It was his emplotment, voicing both righteous defiance and respectful compliance, I think that most strongly structured the written history-petition Langmo elders eventually gave me.[11] And importantly, all along Dorje Gyap framed his histories for me as explicitly countering what he and other elders saw as the recent *theft* of their dewa history by another elder, one of Langmo's few salaried officials, who had taken their previously written history ("it was my own son the monk who wrote it!" Dorje Gyap said indignantly) for a prefecture government social history project on Rebgong. Dorje Gyap and the elders were incensed that his official version had edited out a lot, including all mention of Langmo's situation since the move down.

In the first version Dorje Gyap told me in early January 2008, the story was of the dewa as a sovereign community and land unit (encompassing both the cluster of houses and the fields and grasslands) linked to "500 years of history," via lineage relations to Tshema Monastery upriver, its famous lama, and its patron village: "Langmo and Tshema," he insisted, echoing Gyalo, "are one dewa." Then, Dorje Gyap skipped all the way to 1981, skirting the traumatic Maoist years to locate Langmo at its upper, peak site after the commune (based upriver in the large neighboring village of Dethang) broke up and all land and livestock were reallocated to individual households. As the opening lines of the written history-petition put it,

> In 1981, the commune was dismantled and all property redistributed. At that time, Langmo was one of the villages in the county that enjoyed relative wealth because the village had many fields and livestock. This is because at that time the village consisted of only 130 people and grass, land and water were plentiful.[12]

Those were the optimistic early yang dar years, when the revival of Langmo as a separate dewa supposedly manifested the ideally modern compromise between CCP-led socialism and Tibetan autonomous governance that the Panchen Lama had envisioned. Importantly, and in stark contrast to Gendun's disgust at Langmo villagers' apparent passivity toward their valley floor school, Dorje Gyap narrates the dewa's eventual move down as the outcome of the socialist sleight of hand. He framed the move in the State's repeated refusal to honor promises of care, despite elders' initiative and earnest compliance in fundraising for and building a new primary school on the peak.

In fact, according to him, their primary school was the very crux of conflict over the dewa's modern future. After Langmo's peak village lost its commune-supported school in 1981,[13] the community was without a school for fifteen years, even as local state bureaus turned in earnest to developing the Upper Narrows. Dorje Gyap said that when he was village head in the late 1980s (and still had his hearing), his requests for county funds for a new school fell on deaf ears, in part because officials were reluctant to extend infrastructure up to the peak. Instead, officials urged Langmo villagers to move down to the valley floor, where it would be more "convenient" for residents and they would have fewer hardships. In his telling, however, officials effectively split the village in two by offering the promise of a fully funded (140,000 yuan) school and aid for home building down below, enticing eight households to move. Those were the ones, not coincidentally, who had salaried officials among them and thus less land and livestock. Meanwhile, the

twenty households who subsisted on their fields and livestock herds, real-
izing there were few fields and no fodder down below, refused to move. For
Dorje Gyap, this challenged the very integrity of the village as a communal
unit, "Langmo dewa" for him was still on the peak:

> The ones who moved down early were all relatives. So we had a falling
> out. Thus two villages were made, and that was not right. I didn't say
> I wouldn't move down, but I said if the village comes I will come, if the
> village won't come I won't either.

Dorje Gyap then portrayed virtuous school building as a key act of (compliant) resistance. In a story of heroic communal effort I would hear many
times from Langmo villagers, Dorje Gyap told of the Eight Compassionate Elders, led by himself, who spared nothing to fundraise—from villagers,
from a Rongbo lama who was known to help Tibetan schools, and finally
from their own households—to build a small brick school and courtyard on
the peak. The history-petition put it this way, emphasizing the dewa's exemplary hospitality for approving officials,[14] using honorifics to liken them to
lamas:

> In 1996, 8 particularly motivated and altruistic men raised over 6,000
> yuan among themselves. They built a six-room Tibetan style build-
> ing and established a new primary school. Relevant education officials
> from the county, township and school district attended [Tib. *phebs gnang
> par*, lit., "gave the gift of their visit"] the opening banquet and greatly
> praised the school and the village leaders' initiative in founding it.

However, as quantities of cash increasingly served as key measures of state
favor, that paltry sum for the peak school could not compete with the
140,000 yuan promised for the lower school. In Dorje Gyap's and the history-
petition's accounts, the next four years unfolded as a kind of infrastructural
war of attrition as local bureaus refused to fund infrastructure on the peak,
the early movers on the valley floor reaped state benefits, and village leaders
began planning the construction of the lower school, including taking out
state loans for it. That was when, according to Dorje Gyap, the State (e.g.,
for him, county education officials distributing provincial funds) brought to
bear the crisis of time as an ultimatum, pitting Langmo against other compliant villages:

> So the State said, "If you don't build it this year we will not give you
> the money. We will give the 140,000 to [that other dewa that wants to
> move down] instead. You should not improve the school building on

the peak anymore; there will be no money for it. So if you're going to build a lower school, do it this year. If you're going to move down, do it this year. If you don't move down, there will be no money at all."

Households still on the peak however held out until 2001, when they finally conceded, taking promised state loans for new home construction, and carrying their property piece by piece, including bricks and wood from their houses, as well as from the peak school, down to their new sites.[15] But state bureaus' promises of aid in the form of a running water system and the 140,000 yuan for the new school (none of which, it turned out, were ever put in writing), never materialized: "The expectations of the Masses were never fulfilled," claimed their written history. This even though villagers yet again had worked hard to fundraise for and build a courtyard, playground, and walls for the lower school. The cheaply constructed lower building began to leak just three years later,[16] and county officials quickly reduced it to nothing but a preschool. Far from their lazy indifference then, the poverty of Langmo dewa on the valley floor, elders concluded, was due to the State's failure to provide the care to which they were entitled:

> Even though villagers regularly seek wage labor, their monetary income is insufficient to even buy food and clothing. For this reason, they are unable to make timely payments on the loans they carry from banks and other sources.[17] These are the main reasons that Langmo village has fallen into destitution [Tib. *dbul phongs su gyur*, lit., "become beggars"]. (Final paragraph of the history-petition)

The rise of my position as the elders' main listener and medium of dewa history was not without tensions. The two village heads in particular were concerned that the proper elders (e.g., certain men native to the dewa) control the narrative I heard. But early on I insisted on talking to others, including to some village women. Just a few days later then in early January, Dorje Gyap's stepmother Deji, an extremely sharp woman in her early seventies, told me a strikingly different story of the dewa's move down. In contrast to the elders' stories, which tried to voice the Masses betrayed by the socialist social contract, Deji's story voiced the compassionate State, operating under the premises of New Socialist authoritarian capitalism. As we sat next to the coal stove in her large and clean, yet strangely empty village house, her six-year-old granddaughter playing quietly nearby, she cradled her disabled seven-year-old granddaughter who had just had a violent seizure. Despite such humble surroundings though, in Deji's rapid-fire narration, and in the certainty with which she recalled dates, meetings, and policy speeches brimming with Chinese loanwords, Deji seemed to uncannily embody the figure of the State, so much so that I caught a glimpse of villagers' encounters with the county officials who had come to persuade them to move down.

Deji's household, in fact, was positioned on the other side of the conflict over the move down that had (literally) split the village; theirs was one of the early movers, whom she said had decided to relocate together back in 1995. And, in a twist that evoked dewa tensions extending back to the Maoist years, she told me, her voice faltering to a whisper, that her late husband, Dorje Gyap's father, had been a salaried official in the County Police Bureau (PSB). Indeed in her telling, his early status as a party member and security official during that tumultuous time benefited her household to this day.[18] The moral and timespace premises of Deji's story thus fundamentally challenged those of the elders. She positioned her household among the early movers as farsighted visionaries progressively complying with the modern advice of the State (e.g., for her, "commune" and county development planners). In the voice of the planners, whom she said had urged them to move down from their rain-fed "mountain fields" to their irrigated "river fields," the post-Mao Langmo dewa is a small, impoverished cluster of exclusively farmer households, each with individually allocated fields:

> It was the county officials, those people would say, "You all, you are a Special Needs village. You all settled on the mountain peak and on one hand you have water difficulties. On the other hand, you are located on the very top of a steep hill. And the road is . . . transport is very inconvenient. So you all should move down, if you move down, we can help you."

Crucially though, in Deji's telling, officials portrayed the move down as villagers' ideal opportunity to better listen to state policy—and thereby be converted to progressive ways of thinking. In this, the main historically loaded idiom distinguishing past and present (and "low-level" versus high-quality persons) was "the brain" (Tib. klad pa). For Maoist work teams in the 1950s, that term, with its highly corporeal connotations (versus "heart-mind," sems), had meant a modern revolutionary consciousness realized through collective labor. Now it was repurposed to signify a kind of strategic, entrepreneurial, and technocratic intelligence, open to officials' guidance. For Deji and the planners she voiced, the "faster" thinking of a proper "brain" came from the expanded horizons of travel down and out of the Upper Narrows, a transformation she/they portrayed as the dutiful agency of individuals preparing for the future by buying machines, seeking wage labor, and sending their children to school:

> Nowadays we have learned how to use our own brains, but in the past we didn't know how to use our own brains. Nowadays, we go out to other places, and come back having seen with our own eyes how high level the thinking is in other places, how much experience they have in farming. So everyone has gone all over and come back, and realized that we are behind, and learned how to use mechanized farm tools.[19] So what defines this era nowadays? It is that now people know how to use their brains to do wage labor and get money, to plant fields and to meet the obligation to send their kids to school.

In this telling then, the story of the move down is not of a communal dewa but of individual brains opening to the world, an emplotment that allows Deji to gloss over the loss of subsistence livestock herding, the elimination of socialist entitlements, or the differential benefits accruing to the early-moving official households ("it's not that there was ever any conflict, just that our thinking was different," she said).[20] She can thus blame the contemporary poverty of the late-moving Langmo households on their own backward lack of compliance. Indeed, according to her, when the remaining households finally relocated, their mistake was to ignore the advice of the State and establish their new houses on their valley floor fields, rather than on the hillside plots that "commune" (e.g., Tshothang township based in Dethang village) leaders had surveyed for them back in the mid-1990s. In her telling, state superiors noted Langmo's Special Needs (officially poor) status and compassionately waived the fine on the latecomers for building on arable land, while admonishing them: "So the higher up's said, 'Now you've put yourselves at a disadvantage. If you had moved to the hillside plots, you would still have the food from your river fields, you would still have a little bit of arable land.'" Deji acknowledged that valley floor fields were tiny, village population had nearly doubled since the 1980s, and thus villagers increasingly depended on cash to get by.[21] But in her telling, entanglement in debt signified the innocent poverty of those individuals who truly strive to succeed in the job market. And for her, that virtuous debt was epitomized by the tens of thousands of yuan in loans her own stepson Dorje Gyap had heroically taken out to fund his children's educations ("Our household used to be one of the wealthiest in the village," Dorje Gyap told me one day, "now," holding up his pinky finger signifying bottom rank, "we're reduced to this!"). Deji summed up in the singsong rhythm of those citing the formulaic refrains of New Socialist development rhetoric:

If the brain gets better, life gets better! If you say in your brain that you can do that work [Tib. *las ka*, lit., "manual labor"], then even if you can't now you'll eventually succeed. If in your brain you think you can do the work, but in your heart you don't really want it, you won't succeed. That's how it is.

The striking gap between these two accounts of Langmo's move down, each staging competing versions of the communicative gulf between the State and the Masses, illustrates the intertextual stakes of the elders' written history-petition. Presented to me publicly and with great fanfare two months later, that document was meant to keep such statist voices as Deji's at bay. My apotheosis as a different kind of patron in the village, as a medium of Langmo's counterhistory, came on March 3, 2008, at the dewa's annual New Year "health and longevity prayer rites" (Tib. *sku rim*). That multidimensional hospitality event, one of the rare occasions in which all villagers are obligated to participate (that was the first time I had ever seen villagers gathered in one place), finally brought home to me how the battle for fortune in the Upper Narrows was playing out on multiple fronts simultaneously. Held in Langmo's brand-new Buddhist Assembly Hall over five days, village headmen and elders recruit villagers as well as monks from Tshema Monastery to chant key propitiation and purification prayers aimed at strengthening the dewa's communal fortune for the year. Importantly, the texts and the number of iterations they must chant (in the thousands) are assigned to them annually by the eighth Shartshang lama, as was traditional for all the patron villages of Rongbo Monastery.

With increasing tensions over the specter of Tibetan unrest that spring, I realized, the 2008 event in Langmo was a vital effort in timespace scale-making. That is, it allowed villagers to position VIP human visitors (state officials, the foreign donor) under the purview of divine superiors (the Buddhas, protector deities, and Geluk lamas), hosting all as guests of Langmo dewa, the communal unit and fortunate landscape that spanned both peak and lower sites. Indeed, as we began to see in chapters 1 and 2, in Geluk Buddhist communities like Langmo, where human and divine superiors are ritually hosted on similar terms, the overarching, or metagenre, of hospitality is the "prayer for aid and protection" (Tib. *skyabs 'jug*), presented by patrons to Buddhist "fields of merit." In practice, that genre of submissive appeal can bridge mundane and divine timespaces, casting human superiors as godlike. It was thus arguably the very performative grounds of lama-lay leader patronage relations in the valley prior to CCP intervention. Langmo's annual prayer ritual was villagers' own meta-appeal for aid, where the huge numbers of assigned chantings indicated the weightiness and hard work of striving for fortune.[22] There, as the temple courtyard hummed with the voices of the village men chanting the texts, women cleaned hundreds of brass water offering bowls, and the courtyard oven sent clouds of incense offerings to the heavens, the massive quantities of prayers rivaled the large quantities of money circulating through the valley, working to clear barriers to capturing that cash and the scale-jumping fortune it promised for Langmo.

Yet that year, the prayer quota was larger than ever ("it's endless!" remarked Dorje Gyap). Just two weeks earlier, at the county's New Year festivities, Rebgong had seen its first unrest of the year, a street battle that broke out in a crowd watching state-funded fireworks. A dispute between a Tibetan teen-ager and a Hui merchant over buying a balloon had escalated into a skirmish between young Tibetan laymen and monks and unarmed local police. It ended with the detention and beatings of some of the rioters.[23] To help stave off further misfortune, Langmo elders told me, Shartshang had assigned villagers throughout the valley more prayers than usual for their annual rites. In Dorje Gyap's house that early March day, as we prepared to head up to the Assembly Hall, he told me, gesturing his wrists bound in handcuffs, that his own twenty-year-old son and another Langmo teen had been among the detainees at the February melee. His wife chimed in adamantly to establish her son's innocence, complaining that he had only gone to see the fireworks and was just a bystander. "He's okay," said Dorje Gyap, "he wasn't beaten much, and they were released the next day. He's up at the Assembly Hall right now chanting prayers." But his voice registered great indignation and fear as he continued. He said that the very next day officials had come to his home to register their son's name and their own:

> If one is found to have a background [as a Troublemaker], then they will stop that person from doing anything he wants, like if there were jobs available, they would look at his file and say they didn't want him. If he was an official, they would fire him, or take away his salary. If he wanted to take exams for school, he would be blocked from taking them.

"What does that mean for the future?" I asked. "We don't know," sighed Dorje Gyap. "We are just the Masses. And the Masses have no recourse."

That misfortune, they discovered, would continue to unfold over that spring and beyond. In fact, the very morning of my visit to Langmo's annual prayer rites, they told me, villagers were made to host a delegation of five county officials, who lectured them on state policy concerning such "incidents" and urged them to protect "social stability." Recall that March 3, as I mentioned in chapter 1, was the very night of my Jima host Drolma's bad dreams, when provincial officials were pressuring their Tibetan underlings to control their regions prior to March 10. "Perhaps I shouldn't go up to the Assembly Hall then," I offered. "Oh no it's fine now," said Dorje Gyap, "the officials already left." Unbeknownst to me then, the stage was set for my arrival at the Assembly Hall as the Truly Compassionate Foreigner, Langmo village's counterstate advocate.

Only later, when elders grandly hosted me for a meal at the village head's home in order to formally present their written history-petition, did I learn that villagers gathered for the annual prayers had been primed for my visit. Concerned to portray the document as democratically representing the view of the entire village, the elders insisted that they had read the entire thing aloud before gathered villagers the day before, asking them to raise their hands if they agreed with it and with turning it over to me. "Everyone agreed!" said the village head, "they all yelled, '*Yes!*'" Thus when I crossed the threshold of the crowded temple courtyard, the villagers, women on the left, men on the right, were ready. To my dismay, the village head, shifting to honorifics to present me as lamalike, called loudly to all, "Everyone stand up, Tshomo has arrived!" Three elders then came forward to present me with the most elegant offering scarves topped with expensive golden brocade cloth (the very scarves that would wrap the bundle to be expelled from Drolma's house the next day). I was then ushered over to sit with the elder men. It was there and then later at the elders meeting that I truly began to grasp the stakes and dilemmas Langmo villagers faced after their move down, the great communicative gaps within which they felt increasingly trapped.

My presence as a listener seemed to have brought this into stark relief for them: "I beg you for help, dear Tshomo!" Norzang addressed me in the high pitch of the desperate. "We are the main elders here, but we are illiterate. We are like dumb cattle!" The elders pointed to the men chanting on the veranda, "Those are the only ones who can do the prayer work, because most of them are former Tshema Monastery monks [e.g., they were the only ones with some literacy]," Norzang explained. Then, as they lamented to me their difficulties since the move down, I took out the old photo Dorje Gyap had given me of the first class of village students at the new peak school they had built together in the late 1990s. That drew a crowd of men and women as we looked at the photo and the elders pointed out which of the pictured children were now the young adults surrounding us—we were all performing a melancholy history as the younger ones smiled ruefully and the elders explained that none of them had been able to continue with school. Later, at the meal for me in the village head's home, elders were adamant about the absolute truth of the village's poverty on the valley floor: "Unlike some other villages who are actually rich, but pretend to be poor," insisted a former village head, "in this history-petition there are no lies whatsoever! Our poverty is the truth! You can see it with your own eyes!" Such a capacity to sense and act on the truth, explained Dorje Gyap, is possible only when the "heart-minds" (not "brains") of interlocutors intimately connect (in part, he implied, by sharing a language):

> There are many like you who come to help by giving money. But the most important thing is that you have to have an intimate connection with people. It has to come from the heart-mind. If there is no meeting of the minds, then there is no real basis for communication [Tib. *sems med na da kha ma yod ni ma red*, lit., "There is no real presence"]. . . . And the people who really need the money don't end up getting it.

Such reciprocal understanding for the elders contrasted sharply with the "trickery" (Tib. *mgo bskor*) of official visits. Villagers were particularly angry about the hospitality spectacle they were compelled to participate in just after their move down from the peak, in 2002. That was when, recounted the elder who was village head at that time, the County Education Bureau head had arrived to tell him that a delegation of provincial Civil Affairs Department officials would be hosted at Langmo's new village,[24] and he should make sure to take them to see the three most wealthy households, telling the visitors that they were grateful to the State and that the county officials were doing a great job. "I wanted to show them the three *poorest* households! We were really poor! But we couldn't say anything," he said, and "that's how they trick people!" Indeed, several village women I had spoken with said, chuckling sarcastically at the absurdity of it, that they had been told to wear their nicest clothes for the visit. "But we didn't have any! We had to borrow some for the event." One woman snorted derisively, "they made us look rich!" Villagers were convinced that the "trickery" of such spectacles, in which they felt compelled to remain silent, was responsible for the paltry aid they ultimately received (just a thousand yuan per household).

Authoritarian Lawlessness: Commodifying Land in the Upper Narrows

In a type of development spectacle widely utilized across China since the Maoist years,[25] county officials in 2002 had hijacked Langmo's new valley floor site as a backdrop for hosting their state superiors. And Langmo elders were wearily aware that, as before, speech to officials was only really "heard" if accompanied by "under the table gifts" (e.g., especially money). But what was new for villagers positioned on the frontiers of Open the West development and resource extraction was that the partially stealthy commodification and consequent parceling of rural land was drastically shifting their embodied experience of the dewa. That is, the 2002 Civil Affairs inspection visit—and Deji's narrative to me six years later—staged Langmo's valley floor village as a periurban cluster of houses for newly mobile individuals, a vanguard settlement modeling the benefits of state-led market participation.[26]

By contrast, elders at the annual prayer rites were most anguished to describe their experience of the move down as a radical narrowing of their horizons, their feeling of being trapped in both space (new boundaries) and time (new debts). Langmo dewa for them was not just a community of farmers, but one of mixed pursuits, in which livestock herds, as Dorje Gyap explained at our meeting, were their major form of "capital" (Tib. ma rtsa) and food security over long winters. And they described an ideal time before, when the mountain grasslands, and even the winter fields, adjacent to their small ridge were open for communal livestock herding and fuel gathering, an experience they glossed, in an oft-repeated phrase, as "no boundaries on land or water use" (Tib. sa mtshams chu mtshams med gi). Now, they complained, it was illegal to collect wood from "their" forests and the large neighboring villages of Kharnak and Dethang enforced strict boundaries on the lands they claimed, even fencing them and fining Langmo villagers if their livestock strayed across them. Those new restrictions on land use, and not the move down per se, they explained, were what compelled them to sell off their livestock. As one elder lamented, "the State said if we move down, we would have better opportunities. But since we got down here on the valley floor, we are stuck in one place! We're not allowed to move at all!" Another, chafing at new fees he said officials had promised would be waived, said he retorted to them, "Send us back to the peak then! I have no happiness here!"

As I showed in chapter 2, the increasing commodification of land-use rights and the rescaling of state authority to municipalities by the late 1990s had incentivized regional state bureaus to appropriate village land in Rebgong's urban center for sale to Chinese developers. Here in the Upper Narrows, Langmo villagers faced land appropriation because dewa leaders and state officials were competing to capture the profits of resource management and extraction. Villagers' experience of being trapped on the valley floor by

2002 illustrates how post-Mao urbanization pressures sweeping rural Tibetans downriver largely stemmed from technocratic land management in the highlands, as Chinese planners increasingly looked west for resources to fuel a hungry nation. That is, by the early 1990s in the prefecture, long before the official NSC campaign that fetishized the display of human quality in modern built environments, official planners drew on the internationally charismatic rhetoric of "sustainable development" to emphasize the need for high-quality (read: efficiently managed) natural landscapes in mountain forests and grasslands. Such spaces according to new conservation policies needed protection from the "degrading" practices of burgeoning populations of Tibetan pastoralists and farmers.[27]

Prefecture officials began urging Tibetan pastoralists just upriver from Langmo to build winter houses and fence their household grasslands in the early 90s, but they made fencing there mandatory in 1996 (just as Langmo elders were resisting official efforts to get them to move down). That policy, they said, would stave off increasing conflicts over land use (Ptackova 2013, 101).[28] Finally, once-lush juniper and spruce forests in the Upper Narrows had been largely denuded during the Maoist years, and massive downstream floods in 1998 made reforestation in the frontier zone a central policy concern. In what Emily Yeh (2009) calls the rise of the Chinese "environmental state," a suite of policies to "return" pastures and terraced fields to forests were brought to bear on rural Tibetans by the early 2000s.[29] Hence, Langmo villagers told me, the terraced fields of Gomar, the mountain village visible across the valley from them, were now green not with barley but with the tree saplings households had contracted to plant in exchange for cash compensation from the county government. And all around them, villagers encountered the "closed mountain" (Ch. *feng shan*) signs of the valley's forest management station.

Yet, as many observers have pointed out, the rapid degradation of high-altitude landscapes was not the result of Tibetans' "backward" husbandry, or of purely natural processes, but of Chinese state-led land reform and development during the Maoist years, and then through the post-Mao Household Responsibility System (HRS) that allocated land use rights first and foremost to individual households. Importantly, HRS thereby left the scale and legal status of larger landholding units (like villages) ambiguous or unclear to many. It is not that rural Tibetans had no sense of boundaries (or no land conflicts) before CCP intervention,[30] only that recent land reforms commodifying use rights (e.g., in cash "compensation" for state-appropriated land, or later, the capacity to privately rent or sell use rights to others) threatened to radically narrow the sovereign basis of fortune. That is, commodified use rights could pit households and villages against each other, and encourage shorter-term land-use decisions.[31] Yet as we have begun to see, for rural Tibetans, the great optimism of the early yang dar years was not about the revival of Buddhism per se, but the (partial) revitalization of lama-lay leader alliances that authorized lineage-based communal claims to fortune. Indeed, just as I found in Jima, in Langmo villagers' histories, they portrayed decollectivization not primarily as households' new contracts with the state, but as land restitution and the return of the dewa as a sovereign landholding unit in revived patronage relationships with particular lamas and monasteries (like Tshema upriver and Rongbo downriver).

But by the mid-1990s, I realized, most Langmo villagers were unaware of the particularly precarious nature of the dewa—its legal status as communal landholder had in fact been erased with militarized collectivization in the Upper Narrows in 1958. That was when villagers' embodied experience of the dewa was first radically transformed. The village on the peak, Dorje Gyap told me, had in fact been forcibly emptied in 1958 when male leaders were arrested in the crackdown on Tibetan resistance, all property confiscated and "given to Dethang" (e.g., the new commune seat), and all remaining villagers were made to move across the valley to live in Gomar as a "production team" of the new commune, not to return until 1960.[32] In the ferment of administrative rescaling in subsequent years, smaller villages in the valley in this way lost out in the new nexus of state-local authority that privileged large villages as administrative seats. And that process in turn would both co-opt and strengthen the communal power of particular Tibetan lineage groupings (like the Shuk tribal federation to which Kharnak belonged) over others. Hence, as mentioned in chapter 3, Dethang dewa upriver became the seat of the commune, and then of the post-Mao Tshothang township, while the dewa itself became a production brigade, and then a post-Mao administrative village (and thus a legal, "collective" landowner). Langmo villagers in fact recognized the Maoist origins of Dethang's contemporary sovereignty; they routinely referred to that dewa, using the Chinese loanword, as "the commune" (Ch. gongshe).[33] Meanwhile, Kharnak dewa had also emerged from decollectivization as a legally sanctioned administrative village.

But the terrible truth for Langmo was that collectivization had erased their sovereign claims as landowners vis-à-vis the state; they had no legal status as a separate "village" at all. "See," said Dorje Gyap, showing me his household's land contract one day, "the name 'Langmo' does not even appear. We're just listed as 'Team Number 6' of Dethang village!" In effect, the Maoist commune, premised on scientific notions of land as

the inanimate medium of human production, had privileged fixed, contiguous space in the valley over the shifting, noncontiguous spaces of rural
Tibetans' lineage-based experiences of sovereignty.[34] Dethang dewa in fact
was located between Langmo and Tshema upriver (recall elders were adamant that Langmo and Tshema were in fact "one dewa"). Dethang's rise
as administrative seat in the Upper Narrows had cut Langmo off from its
lineage fellows, isolating it between Dethang upriver and Kharnak downriver. Thus, as the monetization of land and resources sent rural Tibetans
scrambling for access and profits by the mid-1990s, Langmo villagers faced
not the fair distribution of an ideally socialist state or the orderly progress of
"scientific development," but a version of what Anna Tsing (2000, 132) has
called "authoritarian lawlessness": alliances between regional state officials
and powerful villages that were both legally grounded and secretly extra-
judicial. That, some Langmo elders knew, was the reason why they had no
"presence" (Tib. *kha ma*) with the State: "The State sometimes says there
is a strategic development plan," scoffed one elder at the prayer rites, "but
in reality they don't have one. Only if a dewa has powerful officials will the
State listen to them." The flipside of that however was another elder's assertion. Lamenting Langmo's small size in the battle for access to resources, he
said, "If a dewa is big and powerful enough, the State's policies can't control
them; they can do whatever they want!"

Langmo elders found that their lineagelike assumptions about loyal solidarity did not apply when Dethang leaders received profits from pasture
rentals or county payments for infrastructure or compensation for land and
water appropriation (like the new Chinese-run hydroelectric dam in 2006
that shunted water straight through Langmo). Relating this history to me
at our meeting, elders used the old Maoist term, and not the Tibetan term
dewa to describe their relationship to Dethang: "We are one collective, but
they take all the benefits!" In fact, given Dethang's legal status as collective
landowner, and the increasing demand for pastures from upriver pastoralist
households now locked out of communal lands by mandatory fencing, it
could well have been Dethang officials' plan all along (under the auspices of
the township/commune) to move Langmo villagers down from their peak
site in order to claim their mountain grasslands and fields for rent to others.[35]
And such a plan would have jibed well with county officials' lack of interest
in funding infrastructure to the peak village.

Langmo villagers, it seemed, had not planned to give up livestock herding when they moved. But as soon as they did, elders said, Dethang villagers began sending their animals onto Langmo fields. And even though
many Dethang villagers had themselves sold their livestock, leaders would

FIGURE 20.   Dorje Gyap contemplates former Langmo lands planted with tree seedlings, summer 2008. Author's photo.

not allow Langmo villagers' animals onto their formerly communal grass-lands; they were rented out to others. That led to a series of brutal fights. "The State never formally authorized those boundaries, they just took it," explained Dorje Gyap, "but when we went to complain to commune leaders, they just said, 'Tough luck, you deserved it [e.g., for not taking their offer of aid to move down].'" Langmo villagers' efforts to defend their access to land had also given them the reputation of noncompliant Troublemakers with higher state bureaus downriver.[36] That reputation then worked in Kharnak's favor, when in 2003 county planners tried to annex hillside lands for tree planting. According to the elders, Kharnak leaders had complied, taking the cash compensation, while Langmo leaders refused. Yet the fenced-off land ultimately included key pastures that Langmo villagers had used (punish-ment, they opined, for their lack of compliance). That too resulted in bloody battles between Kharnak and Langmo village men when Langmo herders tried to go across. Dorje Gyap summed up their predicament in this new battle for fortune:

> The central government's policies are really good. If you have money, whatever you want to do, wherever you want to go, if you have a clever

brain, you can get rich. What is not good is that small villages get forcibly crushed. Now we really can't set foot on those lands. People were
killed and much money changed hands, they were killed and no one
speaks of it!

We can now return to the elders' written history-petition and their pre-
sentation of it to me at the annual prayer rites, and better appreciate the
intertextual gaps and tensions they navigate as they perform their poverty on
the valley floor. The voices and the timespace premises of the document do
not in fact seamlessly cohere. That is, it attempts to simultaneously address
different categories of transcendent human patrons (an abstract State and
faceless rich foreigners). As such, the petition crafts an awkward hybrid of
development rhetoric that maps the shifting policy terrain villagers encountered upon their move down. Like the Chinese petitioners who in increasing
numbers in the 2000s took desperate journeys to Beijing to plead their cases
with central authorities,[37] here Langmo villagers stage a dialogue through
me with powerful outsiders, as a way to circumvent the local authorities who
claimed to speak for them: "We are tired of lying! We want to tell the truth
even if it means our arrest!!" yelled the village head at the end of our meeting. But unlike those individual petitioners in Beijing, the biggest intertextual
gap here is elders' insistence on the sovereign presence of the communal
dewa, even as the commodification of land and labor privileged household
and individual interests above all.

That is, as epitomized in Dorje Gyap's own hybrid vision, elders sought
to stave off a new evacuation of the village in its total proletarianization,
the reduction of villagers to "beggars" for wages in menial or manual labor.
Indeed, as his elderly stepmother Deji's own isolation ironically illustrated,
the Langmo dewa I knew in 2008 emptied out for almost half the year. The
majority of villagers were joining highland Tibetans across the plateau in a
new market-based nomadism: seasonal moves upriver in search not of pasturelands but of the coveted "caterpillar fungus" (Tib. *g'yar rtsa dgun 'bu*) to
sell to lowland brokers for much-needed cash.[38] Thus unlike the highly asser-
tive tone of the Kharnak Village Uplift Foundation's manifesto we encountered in chapter 3, Langmo elders' history-petition is ultimately framed, as
in the epigraph above, as an awkwardly submissive prayer for aid, appealing
to compassionate superiors in the face of socialist betrayal and the amoral
brutality of authoritarian capitalism. Voicing the dewa as the collective perspective of the citizen Masses, the petition's story begins with direct con-
demnation of official neglect of their (communal) socialist entitlements,
but ultimately pivots away from that dangerously "Troublemaker" stance. It
ends instead with abject compliance with New Socialist values of exemplary

striving for their children's futures: they request monetary aid not as an entitlement, but as the just reward for their entrepreneurial ambitions. Only then could the truth of their poverty come across as heroically innocent.

Auspicious Sovereignty: Performing Wealth in the Mountains

> All you assembled spectators, you people of the snow mountains, descendants of the same lineage,
>
> here in Arol Vajradhara's pure patron dewa, Langmo, the Plain of Abundance, the wealthy and fortunate village,
>
> this celebration of the Temple of Primordial Auspiciousness of Samsara and Nirvana
> and this song and dance performance like the melodious sound of the right-turning conch,
> are about to end.
>
> Now we pray that:
>
> To the native lands of the great Tibetan brothers of this cool snow mountain region,
> and especially to Rebgong, the origin of wisdom,
> May the auspiciousness of timely rain and excellent harvests come,
>
> To all the snowland regions may the auspiciousness of increase in wealth come,
> May all have abundant prosperity and happiness!
>> —Closing prayer at the Langmo village party celebrating the
>> completion of their new temple, summer 2006

We can now go back and better grasp the tensions around the auditing gaze of state officials and foreign donors as Langmo villagers performed their wealth in their new valley floor Assembly Hall. And we can better appreciate how the elders' filmic history of the new temple both complemented and countered their own written history-petition in the context of a crisis of sovereignty. Dorje Gyap and his family were nervous about me viewing the performance of village wealth in Langmo's 2006 video because I was not part of the audience the video sought to address. Captured as the village's advocate to secular superiors for scarce cash, my presence could elicit anxious performances of ideally innocent poverty. By contrast, as the closing prayer cited above and featured in the video indicates, the film was meant for a place-based Tibetan Buddhist audience, including especially Langmo villagers themselves. To paraphrase Terence Turner (2002, 87), as a new medium of dewa historiography in the valley, such videos for rural Tibetans were not just about passively recording events. They were meant to performatively constitute a social reality and project it into the future. As such, the video (which unlike the history-petition never mentions money) was supposed to both demonstrate and help create the intrinsic wealth of the dewa as the historical product of yang. That was the generative, life-giving fortune emplaced in Langmo's landscape by the tantric ritual prowess of three incarnations of the village's Geluk preceptor lama, Arol Tshang.

The video was thereby part of Langmo villagers' most important effort in the mounting battle for fortune in the Upper Narrows. This history of the future was an explicitly Buddhist counterdevelopment project, marshaling the persuasive force of multisensory signs and prestigious genres of Buddhist narrative in order to restore dewa sovereignty in the wake of its radical displacement. Buddhist place-making played key roles in intersectarian and state-local relations in Rebgong. Such place-making never entailed merely creating abstract, "sacred" spaces, even during the post-Mao yang dar years.

FIGURE 21. The third Arol Tshang, Lobzang Longdok (right) (1888–1959), displayed next to lineage montage of Rongbo Monastery's eighth Shartshang lama, Langmo village headman home, summer 2007. Author's photo.

Instead, as in the placement of stupas or the burying of treasures, the creation of Buddhist places has always centered on embedding the purifying and vitalizing force of specific lamas' blessing power within certain landscapes as the highest—and most generative—of values.

Such practices work to extend the lama's tantric ritual agency, his capacity to tame demons and deities and animate indigenous fortune (yang), beyond his present body. The lama's presence thereby endures, not only as the ongoing life of the Buddha Dharma, but also as the spontaneous rising up and flourishing of the conditions for fertile life in general. That is how, as in the elder's opening speech above, the nonhuman environment comes to coalesce as itself an auspicious container for particular communities. From this angle, Langmo villagers' new temple was not the reactionary impulse of conservative rural "locals" defending a bounded domain. Instead, positioning themselves as heroic stewards and patrons of the blessing power of specifically Geluk lineages of lamas, villagers were, as before, working to reclaim and recenter the displaced dewa in an alternative translocal timespace, one, however, that was not necessarily incompatible with capitalist agendas.[39]

Here I emphasize that Tibetans' efforts to capture or "indigenize" fortune by emplacing the lama's blessing power are most importantly carried out through the performance of historical narratives that lay or impose the bodies and biographies of lamas onto places. Such narratives thereby craft lineages of incarnations that extend lamas' emplaced power across unbroken time.[40] In Bakhtin's terms, in the Buddhist ritual and narrative genres of place eulogy and lama biography featured in Langmo's video, the embodied figure of the incarnate lama is the key historical idiom linking fortunate pasts with auspicious futures. Yet, like the elders' history-petition, their elegant 2006 video is fundamentally shaped by intertextual and intermodal gaps as it tries to redress the dewa's Maoist and then post-Mao displacements—the video is a great reaching-up for this tiny, embattled community. Narrated by a Tshema monk in the most hypercorrected prestige register of Amdo Tibetan he could muster,[41] the video counters the radical narrowing of the dewa on the valley floor by scaling up Langmo's new temple from the humble prayer hall of the peak village to a full-blown Buddhist abode or "power place" (Tib. *gnas*), consecrated by high Geluk lamas from downriver (hence its hyperbolic name). Most important, in awkward computer-edited audiovisual montages, the video counters villagers' exile from communication with state superiors by filmically laying the bodies and biographies of important lamas across Langmo's former territories, and by claiming nonverbal signs (especially sounds) as auspicious evidence of villagers' proper hospitality for and ongoing communication with Buddhist divines.

The video in this light makes clear why Langmo leaders, in contrast to Khar-nak's, were prioritizing temple building over school construction. Recalling the Langmo official's "theft" of their written history on behalf of the State, vil-lagers' move to the valley floor had loosened their already precarious hold on sovereign history. In contrast to Chinese state historiography, which presents dated events in linear series, the lineage histories of Tibetan villages make time a function of spatial conquest and the unbroken settlement of male ancestors. Lineage narratives thus are not strict chronologies with dates. Instead they highlight stories of ancestors' triumphs, in what seems to be the far-distant past.[42] But as an autonomous dewa, Langmo, despite elders' assertions about their "long history," had less clear claims to such a lineage heritage. It was instead perhaps the youngest settlement in the Upper Narrows. And it was the Arol Tshang lamas who had put Langmo on the map, linking the dewa to their tantric projects of purifying retreat. Langmo originated when the second Arol founded Jetsha hermitage in 1855 and asked three households from Tshema dewa to settle nearby and serve as its cooks and fuel gatherers.[43]

For Shampa, Kharnak village's deity medium (the one whose body had been inhabited by Makgol to give me the blessed grains), Langmo's relatively recent history, and the nonheroic way in which, he said, three "poor" house-holds from Tshema had come over at the behest of the lama, disqualified them from any sovereign status separate from Tshema. That, he claimed, was the root of the 2003 land conflict between Kharnak and Langmo. In our interview that summer, Shampa got to the heart of the matter, acknowledg-ing that my role as a medium of Langmo's history was a threat (I had not told him anything about my work in the neighboring village, yet village leaders on either side had long since heard):

> What we two villages don't agree on is that we say they just came over temporarily from Tshema. They belong to Tshema. Langmo just came over temporarily, so from that perspective there is no need to tell their history. In fact the essential history, the true one is that that is Kharnak land. They themselves say they are of Tshema, so they don't need a history. Isn't that what you all are doing?

This explains why Langmo elders insisted on their link to Tshema as "one dewa" despite their spatial separation, and even as they insisted on their his-torically autonomous status as a patron dewa of Arol Tshang and Jetsha. The main work of their 2006 video then was to reclaim the privileged status of the peak village on lands once appropriated (and retamed) by the second Arol.[44] With tenuous claims to heroic tribal heritage, Langmo's strongest claim to sovereign history were lineages of Geluk incarnate lamas and their Buddhist place-making efforts. Thus in the video's history, the lama's blessing power trumps all values (including money), while lineage alliance trumps both chronology and contiguous space. The voiceover narration, as the verbal backbone of the video's emplotment, is grounded in the biographies of the Arol lamas, starting up on the mountain with Jetsha and ending down on the valley floor with the new Assembly Hall. The video culminates with the first-ever visit in 2006 of Rongbo Monastery's head lama, the eighth Shartshang, and then Langmo's elaborate celebration party that summer.

The Arol lineage of incarnate lamas, it turns out, was itself a relatively new intervention in the valley, emerging only with the advent of Geluk hegemony in Rebgong. In fact, legend has it that the first Arol Tshang, Drakpa Gyamtso (1740–1804), was one of three (body, speech, and mind) incarnations of the famous first Shartshang at Rongbo (d. 1739). Born in a village called Arol in the Upper Narrows, he was in fact passed over as the second Shartshang in favor of another candidate, but he studied at Rongbo and ended up as abbot of Tshema Monastery. All three Arol's before the Maoist years were particularly long-lived. The lineage rose to great prominence when the second, Lobzang Longrik Gyamtso (1806–86), became the main teacher of the sixth Shartshang and other major lamas at Rongbo. The third Arol rose to abbot of Rongbo and then in 1915 its regent after the death of the sixth Shartshang.[45] Langmo's video narration, however, skips over the first Arol and begins with the life of the second as the founder of Jetsha. Moving quickly over the traditional highlights of a Geluk monk's scholarly career at Rongbo, the story focuses on his intensive ritual work in hundreds of meditative retreats, which inspires him to found the hermitage upriver:

> Then during the first month of 1854, the lama had traveled to the forest of Jetsha, where he stayed in meditation for several months. His students then asked him if they could build a residence for him there. The Precious One generously agreed. Thus in 1855 the retreat abode of Jetsha, Auspicious Fortress of the Dharma, was built.

When he gets to the third Arol, Lobzang Longdok (1888–1959), the video's narrator says he was born to the Tshema lineage, and emphasizes that he saw his predecessor's prophecy come to fruition by making Jetsha a "mother monastery" (Tib. *ma dgon*) of a network of monasteries in and outside of Rebgong, including founding Drelzong Monastery (south of Qinghai Lake) in 1926.[46] The third Arol's efforts were most likely supported by patrons and students garnered when, as the video puts it, "the Precious One traveled to Buddhist seats across the Tibetan plateau, widely turning the wheel of the Dharma."

Importantly, we have to see the prolific efforts of the second and third Arols as themselves Geluk counterdevelopment projects in the midst of intensifying sectarian competition and outside encroachment. And those pressures led Geluk lamas increasingly to the mountains. Tantric ritual, in fact, was the very crux of the battle for fortune in the Upper Narrows throughout the early modern era.[47] As Yangdon Dondhup points out, with the rise of an organized Nyingma movement upriver, by the nineteenth century influential Nyingma lamas and their disciples gained a reputation for protective powers that challenged Geluk monastic authority. At the same time, the close relationships of Geluk lamas with lowland regimes and businesses, as well as the increasingly brutal predations of the Muslim chief Ma's troops, jeopardized not only Geluk jurisdictions, but also the crucial moral purity of Geluk monastic renunciation. Consequently, Rongbo lamas frequently spent time at mountain retreats, as a way to purify their practices and reclaim the generative blessing power won in tantric rituals on behalf of their jurisdictions. Langmo's video narration is thus careful to emphasize the Arol lamas' ascetic prowess:

> At the retreat abode of Jetsha, the third Arol did many practices, such as spending much time focusing exclusively on the yoga of one-pointedness. Everyone could see his dedication from his prominently emaciated body.

But the biggest disjuncture the video must work to repair is that of the empty throne, the legacy of Maoist attacks on lamas beginning in 1958. The voiceover lays the biographies of the second and third Arol incarnations across footage of Langmo's old and new landscapes in the story of Jetsha hermitage. Yet the great third Arol Tshang had died in 1958 in a Chinese prison (GDKS 2012, 59). And his incarnation, the fourth Arol, recognized in the region of Drelzong Monastery only after post-Mao reforms, had stirred great controversy in the early 1990s when he left monkhood at Drelzong for lay life in Beijing. He eventually married, took a position as a county official back in Qinghai, and became wealthy as a producer of popular Tibetan music.[48]

Langmo was not only bereft of land and herds, but like many dewas in the Upper Narrows (including Tshema and Kharnak) they were bereft of a central lama whose unstained blessing-power could both generate and shore up the sovereignty they had once claimed. This then sheds light on Kharnak deity medium Shampa's disdain for Langmo claims to their land, even though Langmo's settlement story was not actually categorically different from Kharnak's. In the absence of a powerful lama to extend the Arol lineage's hegemony over the lineage's monastic network, Kharnak leaders could look to the new state-local nexus of authority to authorize their retaking the land (and Jetsha hermitage). County efforts to annex land for tree planting in 2003 gave Kharnak grounds for fencing off Langmo from Jetsha forest (see figure 20). Indeed in his 2012 book, Kharnak's Akhu Gyamtso proudly claims the second Arol as a Shuk tribesman and insists that Kharnak leaders were among the elite students (versus Langmo's "poor" servants) who had first helped build Jetsha hermitage (GDKS 2012, 59).

Thus, recalling the tensions Catherine encountered when we visited Langmo's unfinished temple in 2005, as soon as everyone had moved down in the early 2000s, Dorje Gyap had led Langmo elders in seeking aid for a new, expanded temple complex from a new Geluk lama. That was one Denzin Gyamtsho, a dashing young monk and sworn ascetic (Tib. *ri khrod pa*) whose scholarship, Chinese language skills, and charisma had attracted a sizeable following of wealthy inland Chinese disciples. Langmo villagers had met him when he first visited Jetsha to give teachings in 2001. Denzin Gyamtsho, it seems, was a lama perfectly suited for the waning years of yang dar optimism in Rebgong, when the long-prophesied final degeneration of Buddhism in Tibet seemed to be at hand. In a career trajectory that directly countered that of his age mate, the fourth Arol Tshang, he had chosen to become a Geluk monk and sworn ascetic only after attending the state-run Nationalities University in Xining (e.g., he chose a Buddhist monastic career over a potentially privileged one as a state official). Excelling in his studies with famous lamas at Labrang Monastery in the 1990s, he spent time in Shanghai before returning to monastic studies in Amdo. By 2008, rumor had it that he was very wealthy and lived in Xining at a residence purchased for him by Chinese students.[49]

At Langmo's 2008 annual prayer rites, elders downplayed any conflict with Catherine over temple funds and insisted to me that it was Denzin Gyamtsho who had encouraged them to make the temple an "outstanding one," giving them the confidence to fundraise among Tibetans up and down the valley. But in our conversations, Dorje Gyap portrayed himself as the initiator and visionary, planning for a large temple site all along, touting his great faith in Denzin Gyamtsho and, just as the second Arol's students had done, suggesting to the lama that villagers build him his own teaching hall and quarters in the new temple. Indeed, just like the Arol incarnations, Denzin Gyamtsho was a lama in search of a seat. Langmo's new Assembly Hall expanded his patronage sphere up into the mountains where so many famous lama-ascetics had reached the heights of tantric yogic achievement. It was he who, after a visit to Langmo in 2002 with several of his Chinese disciples, raised seventy thousand yuan from his Chinese students for the expansion of the temple, a sum that villagers discovered still proved insufficient to complete it (hence their request to Catherine for more money in 2005).[50]

In Langmo's video celebrating the temple, the unresolved disjuncture of the empty throne is evident in the intermodal gap between the voiceover narration and the audiovisual footage it supposedly complements. That is, the video attempts to repair the disjuncture by laying the body (but not the biography) of Denzin Gyamtsho under the narrated biography of the Arol lamas and over gorgeous footage of Jetsha and Langmo's peak village site. The video thereby makes the new lama heir to the Arols' former Buddhist realm. And it extends Langmo's rightful jurisdiction over their historical territory as dutiful patrons of both the old hermitage above and the new temple below. The voiceover in turn binds the awkward juxtapositions together at key junctures by asserting the presence of auspicious signs of the lamas' blessing power. In so doing, the video works to evidence Dorje Gyap and other elders' deepening conviction that Denzin Gyamtsho was in fact the real fourth Arol Tshang, enthroning him as transcendent gift master for Langmo, even though he gave less cash for the temple than did the Dutch Embassy, and despite his lack of formal recognition by either the Geluk monastic establishment or the state.[51] In the video, the new lama's blessing-power trumps money as the ultimate, and foundational gift.

For example, at the video's opening, the triumphant cacophony of monastic *gyaling* horns, signaling monks' hospitality for Buddhist divines in prayer rituals, accompanies a montage of lama photos taken from the new temple's altar room. The photos fade in sequentially over loving footage of Jetsha hermitage, framing the video and the place in the hierarchy of Geluk timespace, from the most abstract and transcendent (Avalokitesvara stands in for the Dalai Lama, then the first Shartshang and the tenth Panchen Lama), through the Arol lineage to the present day. Importantly, the image of the third Arol fades directly into that of Denzin Gyamtso, both of which hover over Jetsha. Then, as the voiceover narrates the achievements of the Arol incarnations, the footage is of Denzin Gyamtsho, bestowing blessings at his home monastery, visiting Jetsha, and ultimately, enthroned in Langmo's new temple.

The most important moments of juxtaposition come early in the video. That is when the voiceover describes the tantric ritual prowess of the second Arol positioning himself as a Buddhist sovereign (Tib. *dgon bdag*), not only over the hermitage and its lay patrons, but also over the surrounding nonhuman environment. That is precisely when the first footage of Denzin Gyamtsho, seated on a throne and giving blessings to monk disciples in 2004, is edited in:

After his Retreat residence was finished, the lama arrived to give many kinds of tantric empowerments to the renunciants and monks there. He also gave many beneficial oral instructions for handling crimes and declared that no one should hunt or harm the birds and animals of the Retreat's lands. In sum, the Great Protector Vajradhara, in practicing so many forms of the Dharma, fulfilled the wishes of all faithful beings.

Here, the traditional ellipsis of incarnate lama biography renders the subject of the actions ambiguous; the passage could indeed be describing Denzin Gyamtsho. Successive lama incarnations after all are in part the same transcendent persona. The next montage then works to bind Denzin Gyamtsho to the Arol lineage by asserting the presence of auspicious signs, as lama bodies literally cover Jetsha's lands. While the footage attests to Denzin Gyamtsho's own blessing power, the voiceover describes how the second Arol's new retreat center attracted all the greatest Geluk lamas and scholars of the region, "so many," the narrator says, "it was as if the heavens covered the earth" (Tib. *gnam gyis sa bkab ba*).

Now, the footage features the expansive view from the hermitage and Langmo's peak village site, editing in close-ups of ripening grain, flowering trees and clear spring water flowing over rocks. Finally, the footage fades back to Denzin Gyamtsho on his throne giving teachings, just as the narrator asserts that such a confluence of great lamas at Arol's retreat had produced "multifarious auspicious signs of blessing power." In this way, the spontaneous emergence of auspicious signs attest to the vitalizing blessing power of both the second Arol and Denzin Gyamtsho, paving the way for later in the video when such signs are claimed for Denzin Gyamtsho's own 2005 visit to Langmo's new temple.

That is when the video's montages shift from the lama as transcendent host, to Langmo villagers as faithful patrons, empowered to host Buddhist divines on his behalf. Footage of Denzin Gyamtsho's enthronement in Langmo's temple is keyed to the voiceover description of the reestablishment of Jetsha during the 1980s post-Mao yang dar years, linking him to the great optimism of Buddhist regeneration. Then, the cacophony of the monks' horns that had opened the video are replaced with the celebratory cry of Langmo men's conch shell horns. As Robert Beer notes, Buddhists adapted the symbol of the right-turning conch from its ancient origins in India as a battle horn.[52] With its loud tenor call and bright white shell, it is an icon of sovereignty and the moral supremacy of the Buddha Dharma; the Buddha, says Beer, is supposed to have a conchlike voice. Here, the footage is of Langmo men staging a grand offering feast for deities in the temple courtyard. As conch shells voice the Dharma and call the protector deities, and younger men whoop and spray beer, elders proudly carry offerings out of the Assembly Hall to place them in the smoking incense oven, topped with elegant offering scarves. Meanwhile, the voiceover finally seals the relationships between Jetsha and the new temple, between Langmo and Denzin Gyamtsho through Arol Tshang, by claiming the new lama's arrival as the preordained, auspicious outcome of the Arol lamas' tantric prowess:

> Before, when Arol Vajradhara came and established his seat here, he developed a profound dharmic relationship with the dewa called Langmo. For over one hundred years, this pure patron dewa, correctly carrying out all rituals for the Retreat, upheld the ancient customs without fail. The great work of the lamas, monastic scholars and yogins of Arol Vajradhara's seat came to fruition at precisely the right time, and through the great compassion of our glorious lama, the venerable Denzin Gyamtsho, an auspicious time has arrived.

As final evidence of Langmo's newly heroic status as agents and stewards of Buddhist regeneration, the video then edits in another lama's visit to the now-complete temple, that of the eighth Shartshang, in order to consecrate the new temple in the fall of 2005. That first-ever visit of Rongbo's head lama and his monk retinue to such a tiny community conspicuously reclaimed it under the wider purview of Rongbo. But Langmo villagers' elaborate procession leading Shartshang's white Land Rover up the valley also positioned him in their battle for fortune. In an updated version of the traditional cavalry charges (Tib. *chibs bsu*) used to welcome and send off lamas, the video carefully documents the long line of Langmo men preceding Shartshang's jeep, dressed up in their borrowed ceremonial clothes and ornaments, and riding borrowed motorcycles bedecked with flowers and victory banners. On the way up, the procession motors through Kharnak dewa and conspicuously stops at Kharnak's newly renovated stupa, the very place where, as we saw in chapter 3, a few months later Shartshang would preside over its consecration and give his speech about striving for the future. Langmo, it seems, had beaten Kharnak to the punch.

Conclusion: Mourning the Mountain

In this chapter, we delved further into the politics of presence in Rebgong's Upper Narrows by considering historiography as a dialogic practice riven by what I called, following Bauman and Briggs, "intertextual gaps." This approach allowed us to understand Langmo villagers in the early 2000s not as lazy welfare dependents or as mute and stupid "cows," but as a rigorously striving rural community whose elders positioned it as an ideally Buddhist patron dewa in the face of the village's radical displacement and proletarianization on the valley floor. In the striking contrast between the 2008 written history-petition and the 2006 video, we found no single, discrete "history" describing a static local past, but a variety of multivoiced stories aimed at projecting a refigured sovereign dewa into the future. As villagers' prayers for aid attempted to host and capture multiple gift masters, their multisensory appeals to the varying moral terms of lama-lay leader alliance, Maoist socialism, and authoritarian capitalism produced ultimately irresolvable gaps in their stories. Yet the 2008 written history-petition harkened back to the elegant 2006 video (both of which strongly reflected Dorje Gyap's vision), pitting the twenty-first century State against the modern Geluk lama who, in contrast to the State's socialist betrayal, promises to carry on fulfilling the needs of the faithful.

Thus, as against the Civil Affairs Department visit to Langmo in 2002, in which county officials staged rural wealth as the just rewards for striving for cash, Langmo elders' Buddhist place-making was a countereconomy of appearances. They staged wealth not as accumulated cash, but as a multifaceted and vitalizing fortune, one that was both immanently generated (as a tantric battle victory) and eminently moral, to the peril of all who would attack it. They thereby defend the dewa as auspiciously sovereign, a site for the creation of qualitative fortune, and not for the mere extraction of quantitative value. The figure of my host Dorje Gyap, the hard-of-hearing visionary, was emblematic in this story. His entrepreneurship embraced the utopic aspects of state-sponsored market rhetoric, yet all along he was dedicated to the communal dewa as a sovereign unit. We could thus see Langmo elders' Buddhist development efforts, guided by Dorje Gyap's vision, not as anticapitalist, but as a kind of antiurban naturalism countering the headlong rush downriver.

As the opening song of the temple celebration party featured at the end of the video claimed, Langmo villagers' heroic stewardship ensures that the entire nonhuman environment remains a pleasing offering feast for Buddhist divines. Here, the relationship between human communities and the material, nonhuman world is modeled on that of a Buddhist temple: the supported and their supports (Tib. *rten dang brten pa*), the contents and their containers (Tib. *bcud dang snod*). In contrast to other Geluk Buddhist efforts in Rebgong as described by Jane Caple (2011), in which monks and lamas increasingly portrayed monasteries in terms of the rational pursuits of secular schools and even businesses, Langmo elders sought to reclaim and modernize the uncanny tantric ritual power gained in mountain retreats. As Kharnak dewa retook Jetsha hermitage above, Langmo elders created a new Buddhist destination down in the lower village. They thereby reached out through Denzin Gyamtsho's students to an ideally transnational diaspora of compassionate foreigners: "The Precious One has many foreign students!" enthused Dorje Gyap's old uncle hyperbolically.[53]

Hence the stark difference between Langmo's tiny and crumbling concrete primary school and the beautifully painted, wood-floored teaching hall in the new temple. By 2008, and even more so in 2011 when I visited again, villagers could not send their children to their own school. In the wake of the School Consolidation policy, the vast majority were sent downriver to different schools wherever relatives or friends could be found to house them. As against the flow downriver then, villagers saw the temple as absolutely essential for anchoring the auspiciously sovereign dewa in the Upper Narrows. They thus channeled any cash gained from their annual caterpillar fungus digging to purchasing the Buddha images and texts to reside in the temple. They prioritized those purchases over repaying house construction loans or even the loans needed to cover digging access rents. Most such cash in hand for them was actually debt, subject to the crisis of time.[54]

Yet by spring 2008 signs of inauspiciousness abounded as the crackdown on Troublemakers expanded in anticipation of the summer Olympics. Indeed, that March day in the temple courtyard, leaders had had to scold absent villagers for their lack of attendance and idle village boys for loitering, gambling, and smoking. Then, just three weeks later, after protests broke out across Tibetan regions, including upriver from Langmo, Dorje Gyap's son and other young men first arrested in February were rearrested, to be detained for months. Since that was when I had retreated to Xining, Dorje Gyap's wife anxiously filled me in when I returned, describing how they had heard that sons could avoid beatings if they came and peacefully turned themselves in. Now, instead of being urged to send kids downriver to school, parents were compelled to send them down to prison. She herself had escorted their son down to the PAP base, where over the next several weeks she met anguished Tibetan parents from highland villages across Rebgong, hurrying to bring their sons food.

By June, Dorje Gyap was looking increasingly haggard, especially after he returned from a meeting in town. Working his thin hands and curling his upper lip over his teeth in that characteristic way he expressed frustrated anger, he said Tibetan village leaders in the prefecture had been called down to sign contracts saying their villages would not "rise up" (Tib. *yar blangs*) before the Olympics. Then, in the midst of all this, the unthinkable occurred. Gyalo's fifty-year-old wife was found dead in the forest. Apparently, she had tragically fallen while on a secret foray to gather fuel, alone because the rest of their household was off digging for caterpillar fungus. At her funeral rites in the village, presided over by Tshema monks, the family was devastated, and the once-strapping Gyalo now seemed bent and defeated ("I have terrible karma," he sighed, his eyes brimming with tears). For weeks afterward, the whole village was in mourning for his wife, and many I knew took ascetic vows and chanted extra prayers to help her navigate the journey to her next life.

It was during those tense summer months that, on two occasions, I was finally able to hike up to the abandoned peak village site with Dorje Gyap and several other elders. Those hikes finally brought home to me just how much time is emplaced in land, and in the experience of ascent. Already at the March prayer rites meeting, elders had mentioned my desire to go up the mountain, but that had immediately evoked for them a mournful sense of irreplaceable loss. The feeling of loss was not only for the place of their child-hoods, but also for the capacity for an expansive and empowered communal vision: "It's nice up there in the summer!" said one elder, "down here it's not

FIGURE 22.   Ruins of dismantled houses amidst ripening barley crops, abandoned Langmo peak village, summer 2008. Author's photo.

that pleasant, you can't see anything from here." The village leader chimed in, "down here you can't see who's planting what. Up there you can tell things, you can *know* things." Then, quietly, and with a loud sigh he added, "It's *useless* here, I swear." Another summed up, gesturing up the mountain, "Up there, it's . . . amazing. I've been up there a few times but, I get so sad that I just can't *do* it!"

Our summer hikes traced that sadness up the mountain and back in time. Rest stops were occasions for narrating the loss of lands, as well as the ongoing danger of encroachment ("You have to see it with your own eyes!" they kept saying). Dorje Gyap took the opportunity to point across the valley at Gomar dewa, where a county-funded road for accessing their tree saplings had encouraged Gomar men to try to extend the road across the river and into Langmo territory, in search, elders feared, of scarce pasturelands or timber. And young Langmo and Gomar men, he recounted, had come to blows that April when Gomar leaders met with Dethang leaders to ask permission for the bridge, bypassing Langmo altogether. I remembered then how Langmo men had met in the new Assembly Hall to chant prayers to their protector deities in preparation for the battle. When we finally reached the ruins of the village, the empty packed-earth walls of houses and of the old prayer hall now enclosing nothing but small plots of barley, I felt a haunting sense from my companions of aching nostalgia and simmering anger at the death of the erstwhile dewa. "We miss it so much," said Dorje Gyap, pointing out the remains of what had been his brand-new house. In those strikingly recent ruins, the earthen walls themselves became mediums of dewa history. Dorje Gyap pointed out in the adobe mix hundreds of blackened, charred chunks of wood, repurposed after Ma's troops had burned the village down in retaliation for Tibetan resistance in 1938.

But elders were more circumspect when, on our first hike up, I pointed to what was a much more recent use of the remnant walls as media. They seemed surprised and sheepish to see, on a former house's earthen wall next to the main path, freshly carved graffiti meticulously drawn in formal Tibetan calligraphy. At first, I thought the foot-high letters said, "Tibet" (Tib. *bod*). But only that first word had been fully carved in the mud; the rest of the phrase had only been lightly outlined. It read, "Freedom for Tibet" (Tib. *bod rang btsan*). Dorje Gyap just chuckled awkwardly at it and walked on past; the others did not comment. I was left with no clear sense of what the graffiti meant to them. But when we returned a month later, just a few weeks before the Olympics were to begin, the entire phrase had been carefully filled in.

There, we sat above Dorje Gyap's old house and looked down and across the valley at the saplings on Gomar's former fields. Ever the visionary and, as it were, reading the writing on the wall, Dorje Gyap now saw those lands as cash-in-the-making, and therefore Langmo's only hope for the future: "The State now needs to 'greenify,'" he said, referring to recent environmental protection policies, "so they thus must 'buy land' [e.g., compensate villagers]. I told everyone to sell their lands and remaining livestock so that we can all get official urban residence status." He thought, wrongly harkening back to the urban entitlements of the Maoist years, that that would bring compliant villagers cash subsidies from the State for life.

THE SPECTACULAR SOCIAL OF THE RIGHTFUL STATE CHURCH

❧ | CHAPTER 5

Spectacular Compassion

"Natural" Disasters, National Mourning,
and the Unquiet Dead

In this chapter, we return from the Upper Nar-
rows to the lowland town of Longwu to explore the most far-reaching
stakes of development encounters in Rebgong. As the state of emergency
escalated in the spring of 2008, I retreated inside my tiny cement-block
apartment. Troops replaced residents in public spaces and streets while the
television spectacle of central and provincial news and slogans filled the
silence inside and out. I spent many a day and night scouring TV and online
media for information about the unrest and crackdown outside the valley,
but nothing prepared me for news of the devastating earthquake that hit
western Sichuan province just south of us on May 12. The collective misfortune and mass death of both the crackdown and the earthquake, events that
belied the triumphalism of the Olympics campaign, brought to the fore once
again the widest-scale battle for fortune in Sino-Tibetan relations: the contentious dialogue between Tibetan Buddhist monks and central state leaders. In the eyes of national and global audiences, which transcendent agent
of fortune would prevail as the supreme gift master?[1]

For most Rebgong Tibetans I knew, misfortune, even in the case of Gyalo's
poor wife, was never a mere accident, an occurrence innocent of past deeds
and future implications. Instead, as I came to realize in the spring and summer of 2008, misfortune indicated the loss of auspicious sovereignty—the

possibility of the loss of divine favor and therein the dissolution of vital containers of fortune. The anguished aftermath of any misfortune was thus fraught with ambivalence and fear as people sought help in trying to grasp the relevant causal factors: which types of agents (human? demon? deity?), moral forces (this-worldly corruption? longer-term karma? shorter-term pollution?), and containers (an individual body and karmic biography? a broader environment or collectivity? how broad? what kind?) were at issue? As we saw in chapters 1 and 4, surrounding natural environments, tamed and blessed by Buddhist lamas, become larger-scale containers of fortune for human communities. And thus, as in the monk author Gendun Palzang calling the violence of the Maoist years a "world-destroying tornado," "natural" disasters (storms, floods, droughts, epidemics) are key historical idioms and important causal signs (indexes) of the most transcendent of divine agents, the most powerful and indeterminate of destructive forces, and the widest of collective misfortunes. In the ongoing battle for fortune among Tibetans, there is no such thing as a "natural" disaster separate from the interventions of sentient beings.

That sensibility might explain my own feelings of raw despair and surreal vulnerability when, on the afternoon of May 12, just as de facto martial law had come to be woven into everyday routines across the valley, a massive earthquake hit just south of us in China's southwestern province of Sichuan. The 7.9-scale quake, the strongest the frontier zone had seen for some sixty years, rattled buildings even in Longwu town and was felt as far away as Beijing. The sheer scale of the disaster was overwhelming. It devastated that mountainous region to the south, leaving some ninety thousand people dead or missing. Yet up in Rebgong, the national cacophony of the media response to the Sichuan earthquake reverberated against the taut surface of state-mandated public silence. In that context, the very timing of the disaster in my own life there seemed uncanny to me. As the first images from the quake zone reached us in Rebgong, it seemed to eerily reveal the larger consequences of the suppressed misfortune I had just witnessed on my tours of Tibetan rural schools.

As we have seen in the previous chapters, for residents of Rebgong and other Tibetan county seats, disaster had already struck weeks before the earthquake in the form of the military crackdown on protest. When I returned from Xining city in early April to settle in my new apartment in town, it was strikingly clear how much had changed in the presence of troops. I remember being surprised during the New Year season to see local, unarmed Tibetan police patrols conspicuously circling town. But now it seemed, helmeted Chinese men in different kinds of uniform, armed with assault rifles, were

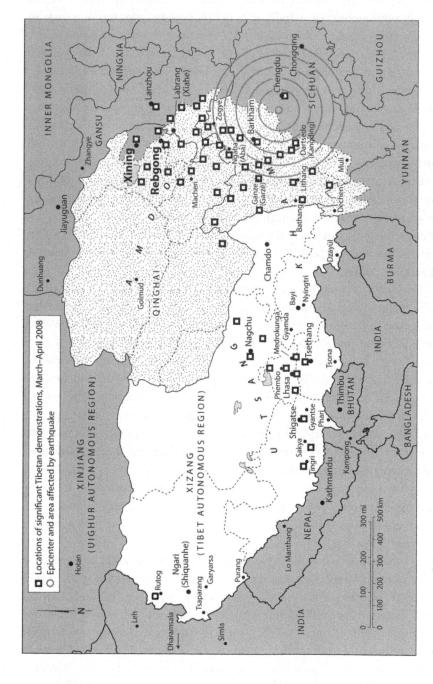

FIGURE 23. Map of Tibetan protests relative to Sichuan earthquake, spring 2008. Based on a map by Atelier Golok.

everywhere. There were so many that residents struggled to distinguish among them (blue local police, green infantry PLA from Lanzhou, dark blue Special Forces PAP from Henan, I was told), and over time rumors escalated as to their numbers (hundreds? thousands?).

Several squads of greens had camped in the town stadium by early March. A month later they were joined there in daily antiriot exercises by squads of dark blues. Hotels in town were full of green and dark blue bodies. Squads of both were staying in the courtyard just beneath my apartment windows.[2] On the streets, dark blues and greens staked out major intersections at night, stopping cars at random. During the day, they circled the monastery, sometimes blaring patriotic music, and every noon hour, they stood, truck lights flashing, at the main intersection in town to supervise Tibetan primary and middle school students as they emerged for lunch. Daily errands became routinized with averted gazes and sidelong glances at ubiquitous patrols and passing radar and personnel trucks. Once, back during the New Year season a young Tibetan policeman I knew had fallen out of line from his patrol as I passed to greet me warmly. Now, my eyes rarely met those of the tense (frightened?) and strikingly young Chinese men under their too-large helmets, holding their assault rifles barrel-up, tightly across their bodies as if to warn against attack. The TV offered no respite. News and special interest reports featured troops being inspected by provincial and prefectural leaders and conducting antiriot exercises. Meanwhile, periodic mass text messages on my phone from various security forces urged continued social stability and harmony.

In contrast to the conveniently remote figure of the abstract State we encountered in chapter 2, for town residents the military presence required personal dances with defensive distance—when policy is "fiercely implemented," Tibetans' metaphors for the State turn concrete ("The State is a rock and you are an egg," Lumoji's older brother once admonished her. "How can you break it?"). But I had been struck in early March by how my Tibetan urbanite friends at times seemed to brush off the arrival of troops, expressing support for disciplining the youthful "Troublemakers" who had fought with local police in February, teasing me about my own conspicuous visibility as a foreigner ("You should dye your hair black!" they teased, "I couldn't hide my nose!" I would reply), or joking about the soldiers sarcastically: "Maybe you should go out and yell 'Freedom for Tibet!'" my host Drolma said to her stepdaughter as she was about to leave. We had just been discussing the new presence of military street patrols, and everyone laughed heartily.

As it turned out, however, the military presence in Rebgong, as elsewhere, did not forestall further conflict, but escalated it. And that in turn raised newly painful dilemmas for such "comfortably well-off" Tibetan urbanites and officials. As the Olympics loomed ever closer, the military crackdown, they found, was an unfolding disaster that threatened to engulf them as well. Thus, with unaccustomed fear and uncertainty that April, my urban friends whispered stories of detained and beaten monks, lamas, lay friends, and relatives, and rumors flew of paid spies and disappeared bodies of hundreds of Tibetans said to have been shot by security forces during the unrest across the plateau.

In chapter 4, I described how the first February unrest in town, originally quickly defused, had been retroactively escalated after the March protests when young men who had been briefly detained in February were rearrested. Scaling up that town skirmish to a national-level ethnic conflict in turn directly precipitated the most disastrous street clash for Tibetans that spring. On April 17, a group of young Rongbo monks left the monastery on their way down to protest the arrest a few days earlier of three of their comrades, now charged with "masterminding" the February unrest. Meanwhile that same day, I heard, almost all the Tibetan students at the high school down the street staged a demonstration in their school courtyard, shouting "Release the prisoners!" "Army go home!" and "We want a peaceful society!" They attempted to march up the street but were blocked by Chinese PAP troops. Up by the monastery however, the monks' demonstration was more violently blocked by troops and the ensuing melee was a terrible spectacle of bloody beatings and arrests. In the brawl, troops targeted not only the young monks, but also older lay Tibetan bystanders and an elderly Rongbo lama, the highly respected former abbot and leader of the monastery's reopening back in 1980, all of whom had tried to intervene. Tibetan officials (including lamas) I knew now found themselves on a razor's edge. Pressures on them to earn their salaries and control youthful protesters had been building all spring. By late March, all officials had found their time seized in daily political education meetings, teachers were given central government-approved syllabi for teaching about the Lhasa "riots," and teachers had told me of taking shifts guarding the doors of school dorms at night. But now, recalling Jima village's party secretary Tshering at the end of chapter 2, their very futures depended on displaying their control of Tibetan youth.

That was the context in which my own roles in the valley narrowed most radically to that of Foreign Donor on Display. In late April and early May, I found myself accompanying Shawojia, the Tibetan County Education Bureau head we met in chapter 3, on his whirlwind tours of Tibetan rural schools. The spring thaw signals the beginning of the very short travel and construction season in those parts, and Shawojia was determined to take advantage of my presence and go despite the crackdown. Perhaps the mountains offered him and his underlings some relief from the endless political meetings he said had recently consumed him. But he also had to demonstrate to his own superiors his willingness to personally discipline the Tibetan villagers and students in his jurisdiction. My role, I realized later, was to be his softer, socialist face, representing his compassionate fundraising prowess and the promise of future development gifts to compliant dewas. In other words, my presence was supposed to help reposition Shawojia as ultra-gift master, a benevolent avatar of the state.

Those exhausting, all-day missions (our jeeps visited some fifteen primary schools and three central boarding schools, sometimes more than once, over ten days of travel to the most remote pastoralist communities in the county) showed me how pervasive were the inequalities between urban and rural communities, and between well-connected and marginalized dewas. Those were the inequities we encountered in chapter 3 that so characterized relations between Kharnak and Langmo villages. As our jeeps took hours to navigate precariously steep gravel and crumbling cement roads, I glimpsed how grueling must have been the tasks of Chinese work teams sent to "win over" rural Tibetans in the early Maoist years. But now, it seemed, every inch of the highland landscape was being vigorously exploited for conversion to cash and capital (or conserved for such). We drove past brick factories, quarries, and copper mines worked by Chinese crews, a national forest nursery and conservation area marked by ubiquitous "closed forest" and fire prevention signs, and finally, multiple yak or donkey caravans, pickup trucks, and camps of rural Tibetans preparing (legally or illegally) to head up into the mountains seeking caterpillar fungus.[3]

Seeing Shawojia in action at his meetings with school officials and dewa leaders, I also glimpsed the heightened stakes of the School Consolidation Policy discussed in chapter 3: the military crackdown had brought authoritarian capitalism to a head over the future of rural Tibetan youth. Throughout our tour, the broad contours of the story were the same. Dewa elders defending their efforts to continue making a living in their mountain homelands argued for keeping their schools and kids close to home. Meanwhile, in his speeches Shawojia scolded them for their backward thinking and urged them to send their kids down to boarding schools. Only now, his auditing gaze and his warnings about the crisis of time and the consequences of noncompliance were doubly charged with the threat of military might. In another village upriver from Langmo, the dignified and well-spoken leader admitted that many children had stopped attending once the county had defunded their village school and reduced it to a preschool.

And he complained that every relevant county bureau was urging them to move the entire dewa down to town. Shawojia's response, however, was to blame backward parents for losing control of their youth: "These days the minds of these kids who don't attend school are so loose and empty that they can't succeed." He went on to admonish them:

> Thus in your village there's interhousehold conflict, and even those who cut or kill each other. Hanging around like that, wasting time and being idle, that's what they will fall into doing. So you should send those kids down to school and fill them up with knowledge, then in the *future*, your village will succeed. If you don't send them, they'll be feeble, as they say, "unable to wipe their own snot," with no poise. The truth is, future villagers will have to rely on these kids. If you don't rely on them, there will be *nothing* to rely on.

In that context, Shawojia and his underlings held out any funding for school repairs as future rewards for policy compliance. Most of the crumbling and leaky concrete buildings we saw were less than a decade old ("The roof isn't dripping," insisted elders at one school, "it's *pouring*"). The county and township officials earnestly explained to me, however, glossing over the infrastructural war of attrition and widespread rumors of corruption, that this was due to the "extreme climate" at such high altitudes. "Lower down," explained Shawojia matter-of-factly, "school buildings will last ten years or so, but up here only five or six."

In the early afternoon of May 12, I had just returned to my apartment from my final tour with Shawojia, and I fell into bed, exhausted. That is why I slept through the earthquake. I awoke to frantic emails from home and rushed to the television to watch the first CCTV news images of the devastation to the south. Like many others, I was transfixed by the footage of the state-led relief efforts that now dominated both provincial and central television. But I choked up as I took in the graphic images of grieving survivors, of buildings reduced to concrete rubble, and most stunningly, of children's bodies being pulled out of collapsed schools by frantic parents, shocked bystanders, and PLA soldiers. I leaned against my own apartment's concrete wall in shock and looked up at the cracking ceiling: I felt I knew now why those children had died.

And yet, as I watched those first horrible images of the earthquake's aftermath, I actually found solace in the apparent efficacy of central state-led rescue and relief efforts portrayed in the Chinese and global news media. In the first couple days, I watched impressed as Chinese premier Wen Jiabao exhorted the relief troops in the disaster zone, and I found myself feeling

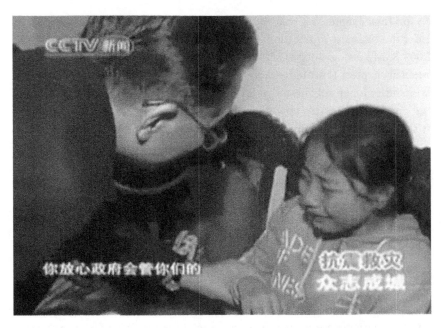

FIGURE 24. Premier Wen Jiabao comforts crying orphan girl: "It'll be alright. The government will take care of you all." Sichuan earthquake zone, May 2008. CCTV news still from YouTube.

heartened along with stricken survivors, as the kindly Wen held a crying orphaned girl's hand, camera bulbs flashing, to whisper to her,

> Don't cry . . . it'll be alright. The government will take care of you all. The government cares about your life.

That feeling of mine, however, did not last long.

The Management of Life and Death under Olympic Time

> Let our love light up this dark night
> Distance cannot stop our heartfelt concern
> Your pain is also our wound
> The quaking earth cannot disperse
> The power of love.
>
> —"Ai de Liliang" (The Power of Love), song for quake victims
> composed by Hong Kong songwriter Cecilia Lau, May 2008

The previous chapters have taken us on a journey of ascent, following my shifting roles as an interlocutor, a guest, and a foreign donor in Tibetan communities, from Rebgong's central valley floor to the Upper Narrows and beyond.

In this final chapter, we return to Longwu town and the valley floor to consider the broadest implications of the battle for fortune among Tibetans in 2007–8. My dialogic approach to personhood, power, and state-led development in chapters 1 through 4 demonstrated that communities in these regions were never inherently bounded locales or poor, peripheral margins. Instead, we can now appreciate how the contemporary marginalization of Tibetans is the result of a contentious process of material and semiotic scale-making, as the battle for fortune escalated under authoritarian capitalism in the first years of the twenty-first century.

However, recalling the one-year countdown clock on Beijing's Tiananmen Square that opened this book, in 2007–8 the battle for fortune in Rebgong was scaled up by a new historically loaded idiom: the ever-impending Summer Olympics. Recalling Bakhtin's notion of the chronotope, common idioms and objects people invoke that are charged with presumptions about moral times and spaces, the Beijing Olympics was embedded in a joyous narrative of the longed-for arrival of a united and modern nation as host to the world. That story in turn had brought the auspicious sovereignty of the CCP-led nation-state itself into stark relief over the calendar year. That is why I took to calling it "the Olympic Year," and, like others, came to see that time as a watershed moment in the history of the PRC.

Olympic time had begun years before. The state-led Olympic media campaign had offered to finally deliver the glittering future that had been held out to rural Tibetans as the promise of New Socialist reforms under the Great Open the West slogan. In the state media campaign, the grand spectacle of the Olympics was supposed to demonstrate to all PRC citizens and the world the CCP's prowess in creating a "moderately well-off," "harmonious and stable" Chinese society. But the temporal claims of the Olympic campaign also sought to anchor CCP sovereignty in the otherworldly, even sacred legitimacy of a millennia-old imperial past. Drawing on long tradition in China of Confucian statesmanship and the numerology of calendrical events emblematic of auspicious rule, state leaders and propagandists scheduled the opening of the Beijing Games around the auspicious number 8 (8/8/08, at 8:08 p.m.) (see figure 1). The sense of national anticipation and expanding, "global" scale then played out across specific times and spaces for PRC communities and transnational netizens in ubiquitous countdown practices and,[4] most importantly, in the great Chinese citizen-state-diaspora collaboration of the largest-ever transnational Olympic torch relay that spring.[5]

Yet for many observers, that year seemed to present an impossibly stark juxtaposition of ecstatic nationalist triumph and traumatic natural and social disaster. By early summer 2008, Rebgong residents joined bloggers and news media in and outside of China in enumerating and debating the significance of an uncanny series of natural disasters that year—a once-every-fifty-year snowstorm over the New Year, the deadly Sichuan earthquake, crippling June floods, and devastating locust swarms in July. But commentators also talked of equally disturbing social and financial disasters that year: a massive train collision, a falling stock market, record-high inflation, and most important, the Tibetan unrest and military crackdown that brought international media scrutiny and fueled angry confrontations abroad between pro-Tibet and pro-China demonstrators during the torch relay.[6] In 2008, Olympic time was anything but secular and abstract. Instead, in practice it was strongly millenarian. That is, the chronotopic premises of Olympic countdown practices aimed to monumentalize and sacralize links between national welfare, social order, and CCP rule, tying them to a precisely timed, utopic arrival. But such practices thereby ironically opened the way to alternative interpretations of auspicious rule in the face of perceived crisis—despite the best efforts of central leaders, monologic state media could not stave off the voices of subjects excluded from participating in Olympic triumph.[7]

In this final chapter then, I consider the Tibetan unrest and the Sichuan earthquake as particularly emblematic disastrous events in the PRC, linked by a high-stakes biopolitics that challenged the very legitimacy of CCP rule. By "biopolitics" I mean, following Foucault (1990), state leaders' claims to the moral management of life and death as the sovereign right and duty to optimize the "natural" or biological existence of national populations. Such claims of modern statehood, we can now understand, were part and parcel of both Maoist socialism and New Socialist development policies in Rebgong, even as individuals were increasingly urged to take responsibility for raising their own "quality" (Greenhalgh 2005, 4). But in the wake of widespread disillusionment with official rhetoric of socialist care and individual responsibility, the crises of 2008 gave rise to new, competing figures of transcendent care and hospitality. In the spotlight of state and international media, this new biopolitics of the state of emergency came to a head in opposing forms of spectacular compassion: the humanitarianism of PRC leaders refigured as paternal helmsmen of a "disaster relief state," versus the universalized Buddhist humanitarianism of embattled Tibetan monastic communities. In Bakhtin's terms, here we encounter the most macroscale dialogue shaping not only Sino-Tibetan relations, but PRC national and international relations: the mutually constituting voices and figures of the State and Tibetan Buddhist monks as rival gift masters.

Tibetan monks and lamas emerged that year as particularly problematic national Others because their Buddhist authority as both state agents and potential dissidents resisted the mundane timespaces of statist biopolitical relief, thereby highlighting state leaders' own precarious recourse to sacralized authority. Indeed, in the emotional days after the earthquake, both Chinese state leaders and Tibetan Buddhist monks and lamas in the PRC fundraised for quake victims and staged rituals for the earthquake dead. And Tibetan monks in exile followed the Dalai Lama's example in offering prayers for the quake dead, even though the constant drumbeat of Chinese state media since the March unrest had been to vilify and blame the Dalai Lama and his "separatist clique" for instigating it.[8]

Interestingly, that year the infamous admen of Benetton Group, the Italian clothing retailer, also asserted the linked nature of the Tibetan unrest and the Sichuan earthquake in the context of Olympic time. The August 2008 issue of Benetton's graphic arts journal, *Colors*, titled "Victims," was deliberately timed to launch on the opening day of the Beijing Olympics. Editors had recruited Tibetan Buddhist monks and lamas abroad to pose as they prayed for earthquake victims. The magazine issue then juxtaposed characteristically graphic news photos from the Sichuan quake with eye-catching photomontages of the Tibetan monks praying for victims.[9] Those montages in fact worked to support the corporate diplomacy expressed in the magazine's centerfold advertisement, which was in turn reproduced on T-shirts for sale. Under a huge masthead reading "Victims," the ad depicts a praying Tibetan monk mirrored by a Chinese "soldier" dressed to evoke the thousands of PLA troops sent to the quake zone as relief workers. The centerfold thus frames the events in an ethnonationalist conflict between "Tibet" and "China"—resolved here in common concern for suffering humanity. As a Benetton spokeswoman for the ad put it, "We absolutely don't wish to take sides for China or Tibet. It's a universal message of peace, tolerance, and peaceful coexistence between people."[10]

However, anthropologists, drawing on theorists like Giorgio Agamben, have recently argued that such claims actually participate in the new forms of biopolitics that emerged in the 1990s with the rise of transnational networks of "humanitarian" organizations seeking to provide apolitical relief or aid to distant trauma victims.[11] Agamben famously saw international humanitarianism as deeply complicit with state interests. This, he argues, is because relief workers' (and corporate ad campaigns') advocacy of abstract compassion for apolitical suffering bodies can shore up the very basis of state leaders' claims to biopower: their recourse to the "state of exception" that allows leaders to stand both in and outside of the law and ethically treat certain lives and bodies (e.g., military enemies, criminals, dissidents) as killable with impunity. The state's Other for Agamben is this "bare" or "banished" life, stripped of

FIGURE 25.   Benetton *Colors* magazine "Victims" issue centerfold ad, August 2008

a citizen's legal rights and protections, an asocial figure to whom nothing is owed (1998, 12, 78). Thus, as Miriam Ticktin, has argued (2006, 42), in an age of the capitalist retreat from entitlements in favor of "free" markets, state-sponsored humanitarianism as a mode of governance positions abstract compassion, state leaders' pure generosity, as a new kind of state of exception in the face of massive reform and new crises of sovereignty.

Anthropologists like Ticktin and others caution us, however, not to take as given the foundational modernist dualisms (e.g., bare/biological versus political/ideological) that shape state and international organizations' rhetoric and cast aid recipients as helpless victims.[12] From the perspective of an anthropology of humanitarianism and biopower, bare life is not apolitical biology, but the specter all citizens face of state-sanctioned extrajuridical vulnerability. Further, the nature and form of that vulnerability are always shaped in practice by particular politics of presence, contested understandings of the very limits of the human and the nonhuman (e.g., other sentient beings and various "natural" or supernatural forces). As Jean Comaroff put it, "While the will to power or the effects of structural violence might significantly sever life from civic protection and social value, no act of sovereignty . . . can actually alienate humans from entailment in webs of signs, relations and affect" (2007, 209).[13] From this angle, the state of exception in humanitarian governance is not just the temporary suspension of law for instrumental reasons of maintaining secular order, but it is also a claim to the routinized yet transcendent authority to mediate human-nonhuman divides.[14]

In the PRC, the unanticipated tumult and tragedy of the Tibetan unrest and the Sichuan earthquake in 2008 raised the specter of the margins for all citizens that year—not only of the impoverished western regions but also of all those citizens left behind in China's meteoric market reforms. All along, post-Mao Chinese leaders had responded to foreign critics of "human rights" abuses with what Aihwa Ong (1999, 77) describes as a Confucian-inflected "Asian humanitarianism" that touted the state's duty to maintain social order and citizens' human right to (state-led) economic development above all.[15] But as increasingly vocal critics in China and abroad pointed out, the 1989 crackdown on the Tiananmen Square protests had ushered in a new era of authoritarian capitalism, withdrawing much of the socialist state's welfare apparatus and privileging state-business alliances and the privatized lifestyles on display in the cosmopolitan eastern metropolises. With the rise of cell phones and social media, the 2000s thus saw a proliferation of popular organizing efforts in NGOs, labor protests, and in the east, calls for human and civil rights and the rule of law.[16] By 2008, the very Maoist legacy of the CCP as a legitimately popular sovereignty, paternal rulers representing and nurturing the People above all, was for many in grave doubt.

Not surprisingly then, China's Olympic year, especially after the Sichuan quake, saw the apotheosis of charity or compassion (Ch. *aixin*, lit., "loving heart") under the state-led "disaster relief" (Ch. *jiuzai*) campaign, a campaign I take to indicate this new biopolitics of the postsocialist PRC state in crisis.[17] Most important, the postquake disaster relief campaign attempted to reconcile the tensions, so evident in the Olympic campaign, between the values of international liberal humanitarianism and those of China's statist Confucian humanism by framing quake victims as filial Chinese citizens above all.[18] Further, state leaders worked to harness the unprecedented surge of interest in voluntarism and NGO organizing among Chinese citizens after the quake by linking themes of both universalized and Confucian-inflected spectacular affect ("love," "warmth," but also "brotherly concern") on one hand with militarized state management on the other. Central leaders deployed almost 150,000 troops to the quake zone, in some cases diverting them from duties patrolling nearby Tibetan regions. This, as Nirav Patel notes, was the largest PLA deployment since 1979 (2009, 13).[19] State coverage of relief efforts prominently featured PLA and PAP troops working tirelessly to rescue people trapped under building rubble.

Finally, the disaster relief campaign was framed in part as a response to critics of the military crackdown on Tibetan unrest, complementing state media coverage portraying violent monk rioters' and the Dalai Lama's seemingly illegitimate claims to Buddhist compassion. For example, the Chinese novelist Yu Hua, one of the best-known critics and satirists of contemporary Chinese society, wrote an afterword to Benetton's *Colors* Victims issue. In it, he refutes the premises of the entire magazine issue by denying any link between the Tibetan unrest and the Sichuan earthquake. Still, he conflates state and citizens to assert that the "Chinese" response to the earthquake refuted Westerners' ill-informed "anti-Chinese criticism" after the military crackdown on Tibetans. Echoing the Confucian terms of ubiquitous postquake slogans touting Chinese "traditional morality" (Ch. *chuantong meide*), he lauds the "traditional collectivity" and organizational efficiency of the disaster relief campaign. Meanwhile, state media coverage of the Lhasa unrest had depicted monk participants and the Dalai Lama in the most extreme terms as violent, inhuman, or savage "separatists" (Ch. *zangdu fenzi*), "wolves in sheep's clothing" attacking innocent bystanders. In the evil and selfish efforts of the Dalai Lama clique to instigate such violence, argued the *Tibet Daily* just two weeks before the earthquake, "We see no evidence of the [Buddhist] compassion to help all beings."[20]

The massive scale and immediacy of the postquake trauma allowed state leaders in this way to further arbitrate the moral (and legal) consequences of a human-nonhuman divide, heightening the stakes for all citizens of the proper performance of innocence. Drawing on the ancient premises of Confucian morality, President Hu Jintao's ubiquitous slogan defined humanity as (state-mediated) empathy or love in contrast to unfeeling, ruthless nature, placing him in the position of the sage-king charged with extending his humanity to the margins: "The earthquake is ruthless, but humanity is loving" (Ch. *dizhen wu qing ren you qing*) (Møllgaard 2010, 128). The disaster relief campaign thus presented China's citizens with a newly stark contrast between two types of extrajuridical persons demanding state response: ruthless, wild Tibetan separatists versus innocent sufferers of disaster (Ch. *zaimin*, i.e., victims of both the Tibetan rioters and of the quake).[21]

As we wrap up our consideration of the battle for fortune in Rebgong, in these final sections of the book I focus on the management of death as a way to get at the contested and situated nature of these new humanitarian claims to a state of exception. During the Olympic year, Chinese leaders, as before, were faced with staving off the return of the margins in the form of the unquiet dead. My dialogic approach to development encounters requires us to take seriously people's embodied experiences of personhood and otherness (what I have been calling "the politics of presence"). We would thus have to treat the dead, just like divine beings, as potentially present persons and interlocutors for the living. I take death rituals to be among the most high-stakes of scale-making practices. They are dynamic transactions that work to re-create essential timespaces in the face of the perceived loss of socially embedded persons.[22] As such, they are often the occasion for the communal performance of both heightened affect and hyperobligated hospitality and generosity, as kin and community moral economies are settled, reevaluated, and extended vis-à-vis the radically altered status of the deceased. Death rituals thus work to manage the intense liminality of the dead as both social intimates and potentially alien Others, staging yet never fully containing the emotional excess of grief.[23]

Ironically, the patriotic imperative to acknowledge the untimely dead after the quake opened space onstage for the competing spectacular compassion of the state's emblematic Other, Tibetan Buddhist monks and lamas, providing the only occasions that year in which Tibetans in China could legitimately address national and international audiences.[24] In the context of the state-sponsored prominence of Tibetan Buddhism in post-Mao China, we could see state leaders' and Tibetan monks' postquake death rituals as harkening back to the politics of the premodern patron-preceptor relationship between Tibetan lamas and imperial lords. Those Ming- and Qing-era elites, argues James Hevia, "vied to transcend each other" at court (1995, 48), even as they collaborated in each others' jurisdictional interests (e.g., in the reciprocity of imperial seals exchanged for lamas' Buddhist teachings and regional loyalty).[25]

However, given the profoundly compromised position of Tibetan monks and lamas under the PRC since the radical disjunctures of the Maoist years, as well as more recent lay concerns about venal lamas and the moral degeneration of the Buddha Dharma, I consider postquake death rituals in 2008 to be scenes of encounter in which both sets of officiants sought to restore sovereignty as oppositional states of exceptional generosity. That is, in ministering to the dead, both central state leaders and Tibetan monks and lamas sought to claim a refigured status as ultra-gift masters for broadened constituencies. In this light I take state leaders' and Tibetan monks' public rituals for the dead not as evidence of common engagement in a universal humanitarianism, but as high-profile scale-making projects that worked to establish competing transactional orders and grounds of moral transcendence.[26] State-led mourning in fact attempted to delimit or silence the deceased as asocial deaths in a nation forever oriented to the future. Meanwhile, Tibetans' Buddhist rituals portended the return of the still-social, indeed unquiet dead in a reinvigorated, pan-Tibetan landscape marked and polluted by state violence past and present.

Silencing the Dead: Post-Quake Statist Mourning

We will always engrave this mission on our minds: We must fight to achieve the mighty revival of the Chinese nation. Disaster can attempt to capture our homelands and lives, but it will never capture our confidence and courage. . . . Facing a clear goal, and with staunch determination, let us advance! advance! advance!

—Qinghai Province party secretary Qiang Wei
speech at May 19 national mourning ceremony, Xining city

In modern biopolitical states, which stake legitimacy on the transcendent and benevolent power to optimize life (and delimit death), the subjects and grounds of public grief and mortuary transactions can become matters of intimate state regulation. In the PRC, where citizens accepted such regulation in exchange for the gift of state-led development and welfare, oppositional mass mourning for popular yet officially disgraced leaders (e.g., for Zhou Enlai over Mao after both died in 1976, and for Hu Yaobang in 1989) marked key crises in CCP sovereignty because such displays highlighted the gross failures of the benevolent, socialist state.[27] Those moments elicited determined repression by central leaders because they risked exposing suppressed death as the product of a national-scale state of exception under CCP auspices. That is, recognizing mass deaths could evoke the violence and impunity to which most citizens were subject during the Maoist years especially. Indeed, for all CCP leaders since, the triumphs of Maoist and then post-Mao development have always rested uneasily on an unacknowledged "funereal landscape" (Das 2007, 13): citizens' unrequited mourning for those killed and scarred in Maoist campaigns and especially in the unprecedentedly massive tragedy of the Great Leap Forward famine (1959–61).[28]

China's Olympic year was another such pivotal moment when the dead threatened to return. It was not coincidental that 2008 saw the publication of major dissident writings by Chinese elites that rejected party-line explanations for Maoist atrocities as the results of inexplicable mass "chaos" or "natural" disaster and laid the blame squarely on CCP leader's policies. Most poignant perhaps was the publication, the very month of the Sichuan earthquake, of former party member Yang Jisheng's appropriately named book, *Tombstone* (Ch. *Mubei*). That massive tome, now banned in the PRC, is the

first-ever comprehensive study by a Chinese insider of the causes and consequences of the Great Leap Forward.[29]

The decades-long Olympic campaign had highlighted the transcendent
nature of the CCP's guiding agency in national development.[30] Thus after
the Sichuan quake, it was actually exceedingly difficult for local and central
officials to represent that mass death and suffering as a "natural" catastrophe and not a manmade disaster demanding moral retribution (Oliver-Smith
2002, 24). This was especially true given the immediately apparent graphic
contrast between, on one hand, the rubble of shoddily constructed primary
and middle schools in which thousands of children died, and on the other,
safely intact party and government buildings.[31] Local officials' technocratic
response to the quake as a "natural" disaster, as well as central leaders' Confucian paternalism, both of which worked to shift attention from disaster
preparedness to disaster relief, was then challenged not only by rageful grieving parents.[32]

As rescue efforts gave way to recovery, leaders also encountered the oppositional Confucianism of citizens' rumors and blogs about the causes of the
quake that took up the imperial cosmologies so prevalent in Olympics brand
campaigns (e.g., in the five Olympic mascot characters) and presumed the
deep link between natural harmony and virtuous rule that was the Mandate
of Heaven (Ch. *tianming*). As China scholars have noted, earthquakes have for
centuries been taken as evidence that central rulers no longer maintain the
proper moral balance between heaven and earth, human and nonhuman.[33]
Traditionally the number eight is taken to be auspicious because the Chinese
term for eight, *ba,* rhymes with *fa,* for "fortune" or "wealthy." Yet for many
observers, the massive scale of the earthquake retroactively reframed all
other misfortunate events that year. Chinese netizens and ordinary residents
alike began to wonder whether the events of 2008 had rendered the number 8
unlucky instead. With the imminent Olympics in mind, people anxiously
noted that the numerical dates for the three major disasters that year, the
January snowstorm, the Tibetan uprising, and the Sichuan earthquake, all
added up to 8.[34] Further, bloggers began to read the five Olympic mascots as
omens (e.g., as both indexes or causal signs and icons or signs of likeness) for
each of the disasters of that year, including the earthquake (panda mascot,
symbol for Sichuan) and the Tibetan unrest (Tibetan antelope mascot, symbol for western minorities). Meanwhile, state media condemned such talk as
"superstition," and internet censors were quick to remove related posts and
attempted to prohibit such keywords as "anger by heaven."[35]

Importantly, such anxieties over the causes of misfortune and inauspicious
rule could shape radically different experiences of the quake's aftermath for

Tibetan and Chinese citizens. In part due to the (temporary and expedient) privatization of service provision via NGOs, and the unprecedented upsurge of interest in charity among Chinese urban elites, many Chinese intellectuals and netizens, even the most penetrating of critics like the novelist Yu Hua, experienced quake relief voluntarism and public mourning as the optimistic rise of a virtuous Chinese "civil society."[36] But as Yu Hua's comments above demonstrated, in the millenarian context of Olympic time, such public displays of "Chinese" virtue and solidarity could come across as a kind of defensive ethnic nationalism that jibed well with central leaders' interest in conflating nation and state. And crucially, despite emerging criticisms of state officials' relief efforts at the time, their strongly humanitarian premises vis-à-vis mass death and suffering brought Chinese citizens onto shared ground with the authoritarian state.

In this context, postquake official mourning just three weeks after the crackdown on Tibetan unrest in fact came across to many Tibetans not as joyous "catharsis" (Bin Xu 2014) but as a new and powerful form of humanitarian discipline. In Rebgong, even as Rongbo Monastery remained on partial lockdown; monks, rural villagers, and local officials underwent "patriotic" and "legal education"; and military patrols continued their rounds, commemoration activities and fundraising for earthquake victims became mandatory for work units and students. In provincial and prefectural decrees, on television and in traveling photo exhibits on the Lhasa riot, the disaster relief slogans of "loving hearts" and "traditional morality," directly calqued in Tibetan, were explicitly linked to postunrest slogans calling for social stability. For the first time that year, the transcendental trauma of so-called natural and untimely mass death brought a diverse array of competing voices under the sway of Chinese central leaders' humanitarian sovereignty. In other words, in the immediate aftermath of the quake, the only publicly legitimate signs of common humanity and objects of universal compassion across the PRC were the apolitical suffering bodies of quake victims, figured nonetheless as lost or bereft Chinese citizens.

State media never acknowledged security forces' use of deadly force against Tibetan protesters during the unrest, even though multiple witnesses reported such events to foreign media, and the only number of dead reported were the twenty-two killed in the March 14 Lhasa riot, eighteen of whom were Han Chinese, most in burning buildings.[37] Though Tibetans in Rebgong were convinced that hundreds of Tibetans had been killed and secretly disposed of, foreign observers counted 140 Tibetans killed by security forces. By contrast, in his foreword for Benetton's *Colors* Victims issue, the well-known Chinese writer Acheng lauds the newly enlightened "transparency" of PRC leaders in their prompt reports of the death toll after the Sichuan earthquake, even though such reports still refused to clarify how many students had died in collapsed schools.

Immediately after the quake, domestic and foreign media colluded in sweeping all dissent, and especially the international outcry over the military crackdown on Tibetan protest, off the public stage. For example, in new vigilante online search practices, Chinese netizens tracked down and hounded young Chinese urbanites whose posts did not show the proper "respect" for quake victims. And not unlike the depoliticized shock montages of Benetton's *Colors*, in graphic slideshows and videos of crushed bodies and sobbing quake survivors, Chinese bloggers admonished Tibet supporters to silence their protests out of "compassion" for China.[38] Meanwhile, international media coverage of the Tibetan unrest all but ended as foreign leaders offered condolences to PRC leaders and praised their disaster response. Even the Dalai Lama's government in India issued a statement exhorting exiled Tibetans to refrain from protests outside Chinese embassies and express "solidarity" and fundraise for Chinese quake victims—even though the quake had hit Tibetan regions as well.[39]

Thus, amidst the chaos and shock of the first days after the quake, official mourning was the key practice by which CCP leaders attempted to recentralize a moral economy by reinvigorating the biopolitics of life management under the disaster relief state. They thereby expediently narrowed the timespace parameters of recognizable humanity to the biological, the mundane, and the secular. Statist mourning worked to appropriate both the intimately local and problematically public online grief of citizens that year and sacralize the moral superiority of national-scale abstract compassion under CCP auspices instead. Further, state officials' own highly publicized mourning practices in Tibetan regions and across the PRC elevated charity over obligation, the innocent living over the dangerous dead.[40] That is, their performances emphasized innate, paternal affect toward suffering survivors (i.e., *zaimin*, lit., "disaster people/citizens"), not the dead, as the ideal form of state largesse, all the while positioning the state (through the Civil Affairs Bureau) as the proper mediator of charitable funds and donated resources.[41]

Within hours of the quake, the tearful Wen Jiabao was the face of statist grief in the quake zone.[42] And just two days later, central officials matched the massive popular outpouring of support for survivors with the high spectacle of ceremonial fundraising for quake relief on central television.[43] The May 14 CCTV news montage, dutifully aired in Rebgong, marked the launch of those "offer loving heart events" (Ch. *xian aixin huodong*). It thereby set the stage for official and business charity that would play out in similar events

FIGURE 26. Montage of CCTV news stills of CCP-led official postquake fundraising campaigns, May 2008

across the country for months to come. The montage featured officials at all central bureaus lining up to donate money in prominently displayed red collection boxes (Ch. *juankuan xiang*) and tearfully professing faith in the party's leadership. In Rebgong a few days later, the prefecture party committee organized a gala fundraising event in front of the town cinema. On camera, the Chinese woman deputy director of the county shouted her compassion at the reporter: "When brother citizens of China are suffering, then all of our hearts bleed!"

However, amidst the extreme emotion and controversy of the nationwide fundraising effort and the ongoing march of the Olympic torch,[44] national collective mourning rites were moments of state-led fixity. That is, especially in the emblematic moment of silence, they were highly circumscribed occasions for collective participation in and regulation of the moral nature and timespaces of national transactions. In this, the rites were key sites for citizen-state collaboration in humanitarian spectacular compassion, setting the stage for the apotheosis of the modern Chinese nation-state in the coming Olympics. That is, the national mourning rites attempted to elevate or sacralize the ordinary dead and radically limit their social presence, cordoning them off from the celebration of state-led life management in the disaster relief and Olympic campaigns. One-minute moments of silence were observed at Olympic torch relay events right after the quake, but solemn hiatus became national mandate precisely seven days postquake when, according to Bin Xu (2013a), prominent Chinese bloggers called for a halt to the torch relay and petitioned central leaders to stage a nationwide moment of silence for quake victims. Heeding their petition then gave state leaders the opportunity, in the face of corruption rumors, to stage their abstract compassion as national spectacle. The State Council hastily declared the opening of a three-day period of national mourning (May 19–22). The period was to begin with a nationwide three-minute moment of silence at the precise moment, 2:28 p.m., that the quake hit.[45]

The May 19 three-minute "silent mourning" (Ch. *mo'ai*), led by President Hu Jintao, made state-mediated silence truly monumental. In those moments the cacophony of human voices and the bustle of everyday market activities (including that of the nascent stock exchanges, which suspended all trade) were replaced by air-raid sirens and vehicle horns sounding across the country to mark the beginning of the ritual hiatus. State media crews had been mobilized so that CCTV aired live footage of nationwide observances. And awed citizens privately filmed the event from high-rises while others voluntarily forced traffic and pedestrians to stop as people stood with heads bowed.[46] In citizens' videos posted online however, as soon as the three minutes were up, traffic, pedestrians, and official formations immediately scattered, quickly returning to everyday pursuits.

Despite unprecedented popular participation, those national mourning rites in fact drew on a long legacy of CCP efforts to intervene in local mortuary practices and manage death on behalf of the nation. As many observers have pointed out, unlike imperial elites, the new biopolitics of Maoist leaders envisioned state-mandated funerals that would radically narrow the relevant subjects and timespaces to the human secular (versus vast pantheons of deities) and most importantly, eradicate the dead as social beings and guests, that is as transactional partners in ongoing material exchanges hosted by the living (e.g., as ancestors or ghosts). In this, local officials were to usurp the roles of ritual specialists who helped mediate those exchanges, channeling the wasteful hospitality and affiliations spent on the dead to the nation-state instead. During the Maoist years, cremation, as opposed to the Chinese preference for burial and long-term relations with ancestors at gravesites, was touted as an egalitarian practice linking all as first and foremost national citizens and sealing the finality of death as mere biological cessation.[47]

The ideal Maoist funeral was thus pared down to an exercise in nationalist testimony, a brief "memorial" service officiated by local cadres in the work unit (Whyte 1990, 295). In this way, Maoist death rituals sought to reduce the deceased to a mere referent of testimony, an inert object or catalyst for proper exchanges among the living. But CCP funeral reform arguably never eradicated the unruly dead, and mandatory mourning went national when the return of the dead was most menacing: upon the death of Mao Zedong.[48] As a way to require solemn respect for the now-embattled leader and his party legacy, Mao's elaborate funeral services included the PRC's first ever three-minute national silence, complete with air raid sirens meant to indicate the grief-stricken wails (Ch. *ju'ai*) of the nation for Mao.[49]

State-led national mourning during the Olympic year was thus an unprecedentedly populist effort that put lost citizens in the place of sacralized leaders.[50] As the writer Acheng enthuses in his *Colors* foreword, "It was the first time in sixty years that the government paid tribute to the common people." But postquake national mourning, I would say, especially the initial moment of silence, was the opening salvo in the consolidation of the postsocialist disaster relief state. As a humanitarian gesture, it was not for the "common people" as socially embedded residents endowed with rights, but for the innocent lives of quake victims as anonymous "compatriots" (Ch. *tongbao*), always already recipients of the state's transcendent generosity.[51] Leaders in that context shed no tears. Instead, as the slogan invoked from Mao's funeral exhorted, "Transform grief into strength" (Ch. *hua beitong wei liliang*), leaders modeled disciplined grief meant to leave the dead in the past and show unmatched resolve for the living.[52] The three-minute national silence was not after all an actual moment of silence. Instead the air raid sirens were supposed to replace all other sounds as the object of mandatory contemplation. Recalling the monastic horns and conch shells from chapter 4, here the sirens were an urgent call addressing the nation, the rising pitch and continuous, echoing cry voicing the rightful managers of the (permanent) state of emergency. Grief as national affect was thus not only innate compassion in the face of universal trauma, but also solemn awe for the biopower of the united nation-state moving into the future.

In that context, the sirens signaled not just grief-stricken wails, but the enigmatic state of emergency, and the great gift of the military and relief infrastructure built and mobilized under CCP control.[53] Such a gift, the sirens asserted, transcended, indeed constituted and enabled, the generosity of all citizens and foreign supporters that year.[54] We could thus see the three-minute national "silence" during the Olympic year as the interposition and embodiment of the postsocialist state of exception, state leaders' claim to a new or revived popular sovereignty that would put down any disruption of the torch relay and carry the nation to its utopic arrival in the Games.

In a culminating moment of what Teets (2014) euphemistically calls "consultative authoritarianism," CCP leaders collaborated with local officials, Chinese intellectuals, and netizens to enforce the immobility and extreme time-boundedness of those few minutes, during which nothing material was supposedly given or received. Together, they recruited all citizens to experience the pure gift, the spectacular compassion, of the humanitarian nation-state. As a liminal moment of reflection and state-mediated attention focused for the first time on lost citizens, leaders tried to fix the statist gift outside of everyday time (and law) as a state of extraordinarily abstract and unidirectional good intention alone. In Agamben's terms, in the silent state of exception quake victims both living and dead were supposed to be rendered "bare." They were not transactional partners (i.e., with legitimate claims to rights and the gratitude of leaders) but inert recipients testifying to the state's loving capacity to give (and take) life at will.

The Return of the Dead: Tibetan Oppositional Mourning

Yea . . .
That year of 1958
That was the year the black enemy arrived in Tibet
That was the year they arrested the lamas.
That was the year we were terrified.
That was the year we were terrified.

Yea . . .
That year of 2008
That was the year they beat innocent Tibetans.
That was the year they killed citizens of the world.
That was the year we were terrified.
That was the year we were terrified.

—Traditional style Amdo Tibetan folksong by Tashi Dhondup, summer 2008

Meanwhile in Rebgong, Tibetans' experiences after the spring unrest epitomized the swiftness with which the figure of the apolitical innocent victim could shift to that of the state's menacing Other.[55] The previous chapters have demonstrated that state-led development efforts under reforms made "poverty-stricken" Tibetan regions emblematic sites for the display of post-Mao state, business, and NGO generosity. But the 2008 spring unrest and state media coverage of it seemed to reveal Tibetans as emblematic ingrates instead, refusing the New Socialist hospitality that justified ongoing CCP sovereignty in those regions.[56] That challenge to the depoliticized terms of humanitarian giving in turn mobilized long-simmering ethnic tensions, in which Chinese urbanites on- and offline attributed negative stereotypes not just to Tibetan "Troublemakers," but to all Tibetans. During the March turmoil in Rebgong, for example, Gendun, the county education official from Kharnak charged with fundraising for rural Tibetan primary schools, told me that several of his Chinese donors in the east had contacted him to say that they were no longer interested in funding Tibetans because they were "terrorists."

Officially managed public affect in Tibetan regions thus predated the quake by several weeks—spectacular compassion requires spectacular gratitude from citizen-recipients. Hence in televised hospitality spectacles that March and April, Tibetan offering scarves were once again conscripted for Maoist-style photo ops of Tibetan officials, monks, and villagers welcoming military officers and troops. And in the weeks after the Lhasa unrest, I watched as CCTV featured young Tibetan detainees expressing remorse. One teen-aged girl cried as she sat alone at a press conference, and apologized for her lack of gratitude for all the state aid she had received to attend school. Thus by the time of postquake national mourning, Tibetans were

FIGURE 27.   Tibetan Buddhist lamas (left) greet PLA troops with white offering scarves in Huangnan prefecture, March 2008. Huangnan TV news still by author.

doubly silenced under the legal and illegal violence of de facto martial law.[57] In Rebgong, Tibetans alone were subject to military checkpoints, arrests, beatings, and seizure of property.[58] And even as national quake mourning exhorted citizens to assemble for the three-minute silence, Tibetans across the valley were banned from all public gatherings. As one old village man I met on the mountainside put it, his red eyes watering with his own personal agony (he was on his way to deliver food to his son, who he said had been wrongly detained at the PAP base downriver), "Villagers are too terrified to come to town before the Olympics." The ascendance of the disaster relief state after the quake had widened the moral gap between properly innocent victims and dangerously dissident citizens.

But the military crackdown in Rebgong also scaled up Tibetans' own sense of a specifically Tibetan collective misfortune, reactivating deep ambivalences about the nature of collectivity and sovereignty under CCP rule. CCP-led "autonomous governance" had offered residents a state-sanctioned, pan-Tibetan "nationality" identity (Ch. *Zangzu*) and certain forms of collective affirmative action. Yet, as we have seen in the previous chapters, the battle for fortune under authoritarian capitalism in the 2000s exacerbated the older, frontier zone contrapuntal dynamics of internecine conflict and strategic incorporation that outside regimes could handily exploit. And under the silent pact, Tibetans' competing efforts at dewa and interdewa community building had to be kept under wraps. Recalling my urban Tibetan friends' defensive gestures in the presence of troops and their expanding fear of hidden spies, the crackdown was in some ways deeply fragmenting, compelling people to protect containers of fortune closest to home. Indeed, the escalation of the February skirmish in town had exploited long-standing fears of misfortune in the loss of state favor, pitting elders against the young, officials against nonofficials, urban elites against the rural disadvantaged. When I returned in April, for example, I saw people anxiously reading street notices from prefecture police, the same ones I found on my cell phone and on TV, offering cash in exchange for residents' incriminating photos of participants in the February street clash.

But terrified fragmentation simultaneously produced an expanding sense of abstract Tibetan collectivity and communal affection. The presence of faceless Chinese troops in the valley gave flesh to an implacable, transregional authoritarian state, but they also further ethnicized and polarized the conflict on the street.[59] Thus, my urban Tibetan friends' initial support for disciplining "Troublemakers" gave way to disbelief, anger, and inchoate grief when Chinese troops' beatings and detentions extended to peaceful Tibetan demonstrators and bystanders. That is why the April 17 street clash that opened this chapter was a watershed event for Rebgong Tibetans. Unlike the crackdown on previous clashes that year, which urbanites could attribute to immature lay and monastic youth, on April 17 lay and monastic, rural and urban, old and young Tibetans were beaten and manhandled together, all for an audience of horrified Tibetan onlookers. I myself did not witness the melee; I was on the next street over being detained by Chinese and Tibetan police (I had unknowingly wandered into the siege of the monastery and tried, in vain, to retreat).

On April 17, 2008, Chinese troops spectacularly disciplined Tibetans *as* Tibetans. That disaster would elicit the deepest sense of shock, inauspiciousness, and grief I heard from Tibetans that year, evoking stories of the unquiet dead across time (back to the repressed historical idiom of 1958) and space (extending across the plateau). Drolma, my former host from Jima, did not dare to contact me until a week later, when she nervously visited me in my apartment. As a female official who grew up under reforms, Drolma had never spent much time at the monastery, but witnessing the brutal treatment of monks and their lay supporters that day, she said, was too much for her. "It made my heart hurt" (Tib. *sems khu dang*), she insisted, invoking that internal space of the heart-mind that, as illustrated in chapter 4, is the locus of the most intimate and authentic of emotions. Her stepson was in shock at home, she told me, after he had been called in to translate for the monks at the detention center and watched as soldiers beat them at his feet. Then, lowering her voice to a whisper, she lamented that this was the worst state repression she had ever experienced: "This is a bad year, a *very* bad year," she concluded. And she repeated the rumor I found most Tibetans now accepted as fact—that elsewhere that spring more than one thousand Tibetans had actually been killed by security forces.

Over the ensuing weeks just prior to and after the Sichuan quake, Tibetans' stories of the April 17 clash became even more polarized. Up in Langmo in early May, Dorje Gyap and his wife described those events in extreme terms. His wife talked of her and other parents' rough treatment at the hands of Chinese troops on the day of the melee when they had tried to return from visiting their detained sons. She described being kicked out of town entirely and having to detour all the way around the valley to return home. Dorje Gyap chimed in to express his frustration. "The monks weren't 'rising up,'" he insisted, "they just wanted their friends released!" His version of events, characteristically mimed even though he himself had not witnessed them, depicted the Chinese soldiers being gleeful in their brutality, clapping and cheering when each monk was handcuffed and thrown into trucks. "Even women and old men were beaten!" he spat in disgust, the others chiming in to agree. And he too then evoked the unknown Tibetan dead as compatriots: "You know they shot and killed many monks in Lhasa. But you won't see their bodies, or their crying families on TV." He summed up with his usual sigh of resignation, only now, "Tibetans" as an ethnic group replaced the disadvantaged "Masses" as a class: "We Tibetans have no recourse!"

I did not see my former teacher Lumoji, whom we met in chapter 1, until early June, when she finally bucked up her courage to invite me for tea in a restaurant. There, she was nearly paralyzed with fear at finding herself in public with a foreigner. In hushed tones, she told me she had in fact stood on the sidewalk that day in April as monks and bystanders were beaten. Her eyes squinted shut as she described the violence, unconsciously throwing her arm up to mime the attacks, and then, wiping her face and neck, narrating the blood running down monks' faces. For her, despite the vitriol she had previously aimed at corrupt and lazy lamas and monks, this called forth the old historical idiom of lineage or tribal communality that imagined Tibetans across regions as kin: "They were my *brothers*! [Tib. *spun zla*]," she lamented, "but I could do nothing but stand there and cry." "So now," she went on, glancing up and out the window, "if you look around, it might look like everything's fine and peaceful, but in reality we are extremely tense and upset," pointing to her chest, "our hearts burn inside" (Tib. *sems nang tshig gi*). Then, describing the desperate terror of her own young daughter witnessing troops' brutality that spring, she opined that these events would impact Tibetans far into the future:

> We older people will all die, but these young people will be around for a long time, and they won't be able to forget what this was like. All this state violence is seriously harming any chance for "nationality unity," and now kids like my daughter will forever look at Chinese people and recoil, thinking, "Oh that's what Chinese are like."

Hence the great difference that year between Tibetans' and most Chinese citizens' experiences of postquake mourning. In Qinghai province's capital city Xining, provincial officials and thousands of Chinese citizens gathered in the central square to observe the May 19 moment of silence. After the sirens abated, provincial party secretary Qiang Wei addressed the crowd. He was in fact the boyish-looking Chinese official who, a few weeks earlier, had been so prominently featured on prefecture TV reviewing the troops in Qinghai's Tibetan regions and thanking them for coming to safeguard stability during the unrest. In a rousing speech using Maoist military metaphors, Qiang Wei represented the postquake state of emergency as the beginning of a party-led nationalist revival, one, he implied, that would conquer the attacks on the body politic of both the quake and of Tibetan separatists:

We will always engrave this mission on our minds: We must fight to achieve the mighty revival of the Chinese nation. Disaster can attempt to capture our homelands and lives, but it will never capture our confidence and courage. . . . Facing a clear goal, and with staunch determination, let us advance! advance! advance![60]

Yet across Tibetan regions in Qinghai and elsewhere in the days following the quake, public squares did not fill with Tibetans spontaneously observing national silence. Instead, most major Buddhist monasteries, especially Geluk ones such as Rebgong's Rongbo Monastery, organized prayer assemblies for the quake dead. As we saw in chapter 1, for many Tibetans a sense of the inauspicious waning of the yang dar years had already been building for several years. Postquake national mourning, however, allowed Geluk Tibetan monks and lamas to reclaim the transcendent power of Buddhist compassion under the state of emergency. And that move, in ways similar to the tenth Panchen Lama's early reform-era vision for a modernized Buddhism, opened a strategic dialogue with both PRC state and international humanitarianism. By that time, most monasteries in protest sites had been closed and occupied by security forces and work teams, while all assemblies and ritual services to laity were forbidden and many monks were still in detention.[61] Prayer rituals for the dead were thus the first time since the spring unrest that Tibetan monastic communities had been able to assemble publicly for Buddhist practice. Postquake monastic prayer assemblies thereby seemed to highlight Tibetan monks' capacity to transcend mere ethnic tensions and redress the fundamentally human suffering of unknown others.

PRC state media coverage of such assemblies represented the monastic officiants as ideally subordinate and filial minority citizens, modeling the party-led abstract national compassion of the humanitarian state. Tibetan monks and lamas praying for the quake dead supposedly demonstrated the truly abstract Buddhist compassion (Ch. cibei) that protesters and the Dalai Lama lacked.[62] Most important however, in unprecedented footage of monks lining up to place cash in red boxes, state media represented Tibetan monks' prayers as mere supplements to the primary humanitarian gift of state-mediated charitable fundraising for quake survivors. Monks and lamas, asserted the headlines, "fundraised and prayed for blessings" (Ch. juankuan qifu), while the deliberately bland phrase "pray for blessings" evoked the abstract and mundane good intentions of the philanthropist.[63]

FIGURE 28.   Montage of CCTV news stills of Tibetan monks' postquake prayer rituals and fundraising, May 2008

Further, the Tibetan translation of the postquake national value of "charity" or "loving heart" (Ch. *aixin*) urged Tibetans to "offer a mind of affection" (Tib. *gces sems 'bul*) for quake victims. That phrase in fact dialogically evoked and attempted to preempt the age-old Buddhist claim to transcendence: the foundational notion of *bodhicitta* (Tib. *byangchub sems*), the bodhisattva's altruistic mind of enlightenment that, in Geluk doctrine, grounded the transcendent power of monks and lamas to alleviate the suffering of all sentient beings. At Rongbo Monastery, where monks had been locked down or imprisoned since April 17, the bespeckled young Shartshang lama spoke to a Xinhua reporter about Rongbo's observances for the quake victims on May 15. In Chinese, he dutifully framed monastic generosity as emulating and supporting that of the state:

> We saw on TV how Premier Wen Jiabao personally went to the disaster zone to direct the rescue. We Tibetan monks and laity were greatly inspired by this, and we realized the greatness of China's CCP and government. . . . We pray and hope for the people and we take this 34,474

yuan and 3000 kg of flour and . . . send it through proper channels into the hands of the people of the disaster zone.[64]

However, in reasserting their essential role as death specialists under the state of emergency, Geluk Tibetan monks and lamas were also participating in their own politics of the apolitical, claiming the very practical and material efficacy of their universal compassion as exemplars of and conduits to Buddhahood. The Buddhist conquest of death on the path to enlightenment (often figured in military terms as a glorious victory over demons), is after all, the basis of the bodhisattva's transcendent compassion and omniscient capacity to arbitrate time across lifetimes.[65] From this angle, the primary gift was decidedly not the donations sent to the quake zone, but the omniscient guidance, purification, and protection bestowed on both living and dead in the face of catastrophic misfortune. In contrast to imperial-era monastic-state relations, where for example Chinese Buddhist monks tended to the mass dead on behalf of emperors,[66] in the context of the 2008 military crackdown, Tibetan monks' postquake prayer assemblies amounted to an "oppositional practice of time" (Mueggler 2001, 7) that challenged the narrow confines of statist biopolitical mourning and the millenarian march of Olympic time. They worked to address and assist, rather than erase the dead as still-social Buddhist subjects, migrating through the frighteningly infinite timespaces of better and worse deaths and rebirths.

Thanks in part to the Dalai Lama's efforts to universalize and depoliticize Tibetan Buddhism abroad, Tibetan monks' strategic appeals to their sovereign compassion in this role could resonate strongly with international supporters (pace, e.g., Lafitte 2010). Thus, even though the exiled monks featured praying for Chinese quake victims in Benetton's *Colors* took complex, indeed political, stances there vis-à-vis Chinese citizens and the Chinese state, the issue reduces their prayers to abstract good intentions commensurate with those of its assumed cosmopolitan readers. In their own play for transcendent compassion, the editors exhort readers to hang the pages of the magazine as prayer flags—they invite international readers to experience universalized Tibetan Buddhist prayer as a Benetton brand experience.

However, to really get at the stakes of Tibetans' death rituals in this context, we have to see Tibetan Buddhist funeral prayers not as chanted good intentions, but as a situated politics of presence participating in the ongoing battle for fortune. As the Tibetologist Giuseppi Tucci noted with some irony long ago, Tibetan Buddhism in practice was not just about abstract "social compassion" (1980, 210).[67] Just like in other tantric rituals of taming and purification, in funeral rites lamas and their monastic disciples claim the position of ultra-gift master hosting deities on behalf of the deceased and for the specific communities the dead leave behind. Lamas and monks thereby promise to shore up containers of fortune when they are most endangered by the dissolution of death.

In Geluk monastic jurisdictions like Rebgong's Rongbo, the collective fortune of all patron communities was traditionally ensured for the year only through the proper completion of an auspiciously dated calendar of tantric purification rituals, especially those of the annual New Year Prayer Festival (Tib. *smon lam chen mo*). The first street clash in Rebgong in fact broke out that February during the Prayer Festival, on the very day of Rongbo's annual monastic dance (Tib. *'cham*). That is the intricate public ritual in which masked monks perform as wrathful Buddha Protectors (including Palden Lhamo the Warrior Queen herself) to tame and kill (aka, "liberate") misfortune-causing demons for the year. Yet several of the monk dancers were among the detainees that night, and for the first time since the seventh Shartshang had revived the practice in 1953 (perhaps as a way to shore up Rongbo's sovereignty under CCP rule), monastic leaders faced the great inauspiciousness of the event's cancellation.[68] So important was it that the performance happen on its auspicious date that Rongbo lamas negotiated the monk dancers' release that very evening and the ritual was held for the first time ever at night.

Thus, as the specter of death increasingly haunted Rebgong Tibetans after the earthquake, Buddhist lamas and monks could take the position of masters of time itself. As in chapter 3, the omniscient "wisdom eye" of a charismatic lama supposedly allows him to perceive the relevant time frames and scales of responsible agents, and prescribe the proper gifts to demons and deities in order to stave off or purify the pollution of inauspicious events.[69] Indeed, by June 2008 the disastrous misfortune of the year for many Tibetans unfolded as an experience of deepening temporal oppression, enforced by central leaders' and Olympic organizers' determination that the Olympic torch relay continue as planned. Early that month, my urban friends and I remarked on a feeling of increasing tightness, as village leaders like Dorje Gyap were called down to sign contracts banning protests, and state media once again took up anti–Dalai Lama and social stability rhetoric. As it turned out, the last week of June (21–24) was when the torch was slated to run through Lhasa and then through Amdo Tibetan regions of Qinghai, and leaders feared further unrest. I remember my own dark mood and fatigue toward the Olympics starting to mirror that of my friends in town ("I have never felt so oppressed by an event in my life," I wrote in my field notes). I shouldn't have been surprised then when the enforcement of Olympic time in Rebgong was backed by a military warning—the series of booming artillery explosions from the PLA squad in the town stadium that first sent me through the roof on June 19.[70]

The battle for national fortune had seemingly come to a head in Longwu town, even as a new disaster of massive floods hit southern China, fulfilling for some Chinese bloggers the final omen of the Olympic mascots, the fish.[71] That was the context in which Tibetans I knew in town began to explicitly link the 2008 string of disasters together as causal signs of inauspicious human-nonhuman relations under CCP rule. Their anxious rumors about collective misfortune echoed the themes of Chinese bloggers, but drew instead on already prevalent Buddhist discourses prophesying an era of moral degeneration accelerated with the Chinese Communist takeover. Some even read the earthquake as both karmic and demonic retribution for state leaders' recent policies in Tibet.[72] That was also when I first heard Tibetans across the valley talk of plans for collective mourning of the unknown Tibetan dead, even though as far as I know no Rebgong Tibetan was killed in either the military crackdown or the quake.

The stage was set then for a new kind of transcendent role for Geluk monks and lamas as mass death specialists. Traditionally, Tibetan monks and lamas intervened in the more intimate scales of household mortuary rites as protectors and guides of the mobile, unpredictable life forces and fortunes of both living and dead, acting as essential mediators of their exchanges. However, in practice, Buddhist exegesis on the importance of nonattachment and calm acceptance of the inevitability of death and separation comes up against the unruly "material entanglements" (Langford 2009, 683) of the living with the dead—the fear, inconsolable grief, and deep sense of obligation to the dead of those left behind. The dead for ordinary Tibetans are thus potentially still-present subjects and household members who demand care and protection. Driven in part by the karmic force of their past deeds, the deceased are embarked on terrifying journeys out of their bodies and households and on to unknown future lives. The untimely dead, so catastrophically polluted by their misfortune, especially risk falling into miserable, low rebirths, or worse the liminal loneliness of hungry ghosts.

Thus in funerals, monks and lamas attempt to manage popular grief by both modeling and providing preparation for the all-important good death. In contrast to the horrifying asocial life of the untimely dead, a good Buddhist death is a chosen, well-accompanied, and divinely protected journey of the consciousness (Tib. *rnam shes*) through precisely timed stages of separation from the body and the household. In the process, both corpse and household are progressively purified and the corpse then ideally eliminated as a gift to hungry demons or animals. Thus unlike in Maoist funerals, for Tibetans, cremation marked not mere biological cessation but a purified offering traditionally reserved for the bodies vacated by high lamas and trulkus.

Further, for laity, the inexorability and extreme time-boundedness of Buddhist transmigration—forty-nine days' interim period (Tib. *bar do*)—lends a sense of urgent necessity to monks' and lamas' intervention in mourning. It is monks' incense offerings that transfer food and merit for the deceased at critical moments, and it is their chanted prayers, along with those of the officiating lama, that both instruct the deceased on the journey and recruit deities to help purify his/her karmic sins, clearing the way to better rebirths.[73] Ultimately, the forty-nine-day mourning period, during which relatives ideally refrain from recreation, washing, or wearing finery, should complete the deceased's journey. There should be no remainder save the purified bones or ashes of the corpse that, in emulation of the relics of lamas, are taken to sacred and pure sites and dispersed as a last meritorious gift.[74]

Unlike for ordinary people, the relics of Geluk incarnate lamas, entombed or cremated and then placed inside demon-pacifying stupas, retain the intrinsic blessing-power of the enlightened being's compassionate conquest of death. Recalling the story of Kharnak dewa in chapter 3, stupas thereby work to create and anchor larger-scale containers of fortune like dewas or Buddhist "power places" like monastic polities.[75] Lamas' relics in this way encapsulate the only proper ongoing social life of the deceased: as protective power against misfortune. In Geluk communities then, Buddhist funerals attempt to appropriate for the ordinary the ideal deaths of lamas, staving off the horror of untimely death by sending living relatives on journeys across empowered reliquary landscapes centered on monasteries. Thus in Rebgong, a properly transmigrated loved one is meant to be gone; people are not supposed to even utter their names or keep their photos. But the loss of a beloved incarnate lama channels collective grief for whole worlds of guidance and protection.

In this light, Geluk monks and lamas' postquake assemblies in the midst of the military crackdown did not just manifest the abstract compassion of international or PRC state humanitarianism. Instead, the ethnic nature of the crackdown and the massive human losses suffered in the Sichuan quake under CCP auspices had implicated the transcendent scale and long-term time frame of Tibetans' collective misfortune that monks were uniquely positioned to address.[76] We could thus see those Geluk assemblies as efforts to reposition and scale up compromised monastic institutions and central lamas as protectors and mediators for both erstwhile jurisdictions and broadened constituencies of patron-subjects.

That is, the alternative transactional orders of Geluk monks' postquake death rituals both refigured lost Chinese citizens as Buddhist subjects and called forth the Tibetan dead in the face of their desecration under CCP rule. In the Geluk context especially, this was not just the unacknowledged deaths and disappeared corpses of Tibetans during the spring crackdown. It was also the unacknowledged desecration, during and after the Maoist years, of the lama-centered reliquary landscape that had linked Tibetan regions in monastic networks across the plateau. Indeed, in Rebgong as elsewhere under the reform-era silent pact, residents had had little chance, save a rare 1980 prefecture government memorial service for the seventh Shartshang and several other ruling elites, to publicly mourn the untimely dead of the Maoist years.[77] Instead, as in the 2008 song cited in the epigraph above, those unfortunate deceased haunted our conversations during the military crackdown in the form of stories of desecrated lamas. My monk friend Akhu Tenzin for example spoke of stories he heard of Tibetan villagers, organized by Chinese Red Guards during the Cultural Revolution to desecrate Rongbo Monastery's main temple, pulling down the funeral stupas containing the mummified corpses of revered lamas. And he voiced the Red Guards, referring to the belief that the lamas' still-present vitality would keep a body's heart warm, mockingly asking Tibetan participants to feel the corpses, "So, are they warm or not?"[78]

In the unprecedented coordination of monastic assemblies for the mass dead after the 2008 quake, monk officiants positioned themselves most importantly in contradistinction to the Chinese state leaders who presided over the national moment of silence. Their assemblies could thus be seen as an indictment of the pretensions of the state's exceptional gift, pointing up the national moral disaster of the unnurtured, untimely dead, Tibetan or not. As such, they attempted to redress, with compassionate tantric prowess, the unacknowledged deaths of both the seemingly innocent and the dangerously dissident, refusing the terms of statist humanitarianism that would so starkly distinguish—and extinguish—them all.

By the end of April in Rebgong, the military crackdown on Tibetan unrest had actually helped to produce its Other: a renewed awareness of absolute alterity and essentially ethnic vulnerability and pride that linked Tibetans across generation, region, and class. That awareness, I found, was manifest not only in a consciousness of the bottom-line significance of the monastic community. But most important, it emerged in a sense of searing, but silenced grief, as some younger Tibetans like Drolma and her own children finally began to understand the loss their elders had experienced during the violence of the Maoist years. Just as had their elders decades earlier, I heard, young men rashly proclaimed they wanted to go "fight the Chinese," and like their elders, new Tibetan pop songs stealthily channeled a collective grief into anguished laments for the long lost salvific presence of the Dalai Lama.[79]

In that context, monastic death rituals reemphasized monks and lamas' vanguard position as mass death specialists. The rites embodied the collective scale of the misfortune, implicating all disappeared Tibetans (dead or imprisoned) as lost kin. They thus set the postunrest grounds for practicing ethnic bonds that transcended generational, urban-rural, or state-citizen divides. Beginning that June, unprecedented collective mourning practices emerged among Tibetan laity as well, as a secret and largely silent recognition of the state of exception to which all Tibetans were subject under state violence (Das 2007, 216). In those practices, Tibetans reclaimed interhousehold and interdewa links that had been downplayed under post-Mao reforms and, like Lumoji, put into practice the lineage idiom of "brotherhood" so prevalent in popular Tibetan songs in the 2000s. Thus Tibetans in town applied practices of mourning avoidance usually reserved for lost household or lineage members to ordinary, unknown Tibetans as well, and to the consternation of regional officials, opted out of, or curtailed both summer festival and New Year celebrations that year: joyous worldly hospitality must be suspended when the dead demand nurturance.[80] As a Rongbo monk put it to me in July, "In general, when someone in the family dies, we do not participate in parties. That is why people do not celebrate this year; it is mourning."

In this context, the postquake Geluk assemblies for the dead positioned particular monasteries and lamas to intervene in Tibetans' translocal oppositional mourning, lending new weight to their authority. For example, like the newly populist efforts of postquake statist mourning, one lowland dewa's silent gesture for lost Tibetans during the summer harvest dances was to have the lead female dancer wear a white offering scarf on her hat in emulation of the ancient practice for mourning recently deceased high lamas. In wealthy Jima village, despite state-sponsored public festivities for the New Year, few Tibetans attended and most families curtailed the household-based conspicuous consumption and mutual feasting that was supposed to display and shore up household wealth and prosperity, channeling offerings instead to the monastery. So strong was this sentiment, I learned, that when several households displayed customary posters of the Chinese god of wealth, their front doors were furtively defaced by village vigilantes with the black marks denoting pollution and collective betrayal.

And even in regions where the roles of monasteries in lay communities had been severely compromised under reforms, Geluk postquake services stepped into the void of unsanctioned collective fear and grief, providing desperately needed recourse. After all, the week of postquake national mourning in May came within forty-nine days of the worst of the violence during the Tibetan unrest. State media touted the May 19 national mourning day observances at Kumbum Monastery, seat of Geluk founding lama Tsongkhapa and now Qinghai province's figurehead tourist center. Such media praised interethnic collaboration in humanitarian mourning, perhaps as way to entice Chinese tourists back (the usually bustling tourist site, I learned, was in fact largely empty of Chinese visitors). Kumbum monks, enthused the state report, fundraised and offered prayers for quake victims after the national moment of silence, while Chinese tourists prayed at the monastery's eight stupas "symbolizing sanctity and harmony."[81]

But that morning, it says, hours before the official launch of national mourning, another rite was held that corresponded with the monastery's own ritual calendar: the unfurling of a massive appliqué banner of Tsongkhapa on a steep slope facing monastic grounds. At his feet, over ten thousand Tibetan laity and some four hundred monks made offerings and prostrations. In that context, Tibetans were not, as the state report had it, merely praying for quake victims. Under the state of emergency, when the sight of even ten Tibetans together in public was cause for consternation, thousands had traveled to gather before the lama seeking his protection, a pale echo of the monastic polity Kumbum had once controlled. In the light of the lama's blessing-power, mediated by the monks' prayers, the unsanctioned Tibetan dead could also find true relief: purification and passage to new life.

Conclusion: The Return of the Dead, Again

In this final chapter, we returned to town from Rebgong's Upper Narrows to consider the ways in which the military crackdown on Tibetan unrest scaled up the battle for fortune there in the context of postquake disaster relief and the inexorable march of Olympic time. China's Olympic year marked the emergence of "loving compassion" as a revitalized biopolitics of the PRC refigured as a disaster relief state. In this, statist humanitarianism worked to bracket the moral implications of Confucian humanism for leaders by defining and delimiting the lives and deaths of citizens as biological subjects, even as state led capitalist development exposed the disproportionate vulnerability of the marginalized. Yet under the quasi-millenarian Olympic campaign, the series of large-scale disasters that year had highlighted not the technocratic state as a mere facilitator of "moderately well-off" lifestyles, but the enigmatic and transcendent nature of state sovereignty—central officials' claim to sacred status as both life-givers and life-takers.

Despite the irrepressible multivocality of that spring we saw here, state-led disaster relief and mourning in the spring and summer of 2008 succeeded in preserving the grounds of the CCP's auspicious sovereignty, at least provisionally. The Olympic Games opened on the long-awaited day of August 8 and seemingly went off without a hitch. Amidst the mind-boggling pageantry of the opening ceremonies, televised for a record audience of hundreds of millions of domestic viewers and billions of viewers abroad, the promised apotheosis of the Chinese nation-state came to fruition in the "Bird's nest" stadium in Beijing during the joyous flag-raising ceremony. Under the direction of the famous Chinese filmmaker Zhang Yimou, a more dramatic performance of the voluntary conjoining of nation and state under central leaders' paternal care could not have been dreamed up. As a cute little "Chinese" girl, resplendent in a red dress matching the color of the ten-foot-long PRC flag, lip-synchs a soft and sweet version of the patriotic song, "Ode to the Motherland," and spectators sing along in a rising crescendo, fifty-six children dressed in colorful folk clothing representing each of the recognized ethnic nationalities (the little "Tibetan" boy was right up front) hold hands and smilingly carry the flag across the stadium to the pole. There, they hand it off to straight-faced, goose-stepping, adult male PLA soldiers, who move in exaggerated military unison to solemnly raise the flag under the approving gaze of president Hu Jintao and other central leaders.

That culminating ceremony worked to infantilize and depoliticize the nation's multiethnic "People" in the wake of a tumultuous year. It thereby embodied for transnational audiences the Confucian terms of consultative authoritarianism in the PRC—this is what "harmony" is supposed to look like. Indeed, the CCP's auspicious sovereignty in that light was no mere spectacle. Back in Rebgong, the militarized control of Tibetan young people played out on the ground simultaneously with the Beijing Games. Just days before the games were to begin, Tibetans across the valley spoke of young monks from Rebgong being shipped back to town from all over the Tibetan plateau so that they could be held in detention there (receiving "legal education") until after the games. So many were detained, I was told, that the prison was full and the overflow was sent to a boarding middle school to stay in the dorms. Relatives were allowed to bring food, but no one knew whether they would be released once the Olympics were over. In that context, the games felt to many like unending ethnic repression: "We Tibetans don't want to watch the Olympics," a young village man told me, unself-consciously adopting the first person plural, "Before we would root for all the Chinese teams. But now we want them to lose!"

Thus, despite the Olympic spectacle, the millenarian promise of the games did not necessarily play out over time in China. Just as in the ambivalent aftermath of Mao's funeral, the great gift of state-led mourning in the spring of 2008 could never fully neutralize the voices and personas of citizens who remained out of the reach of state discipline (and thus refused the limits of biological cessation): the untimely dead. In fact, humanitarian discipline after the Tibetan unrest and the Sichuan earthquake had elevated, rendered hypervisible, Tibetan Buddhist monks and lamas as both marginal Others and as death specialists—rival supreme gift masters in the face of collective loss. In that context, Tibetan and Chinese citizens were not, as Benetton's *Colors* or the Olympics opening ceremony would have it, fundamentally divided by ethnicity only to be linked as innocent victims or humanitarian givers. Instead, as protesting parents of the Chinese schoolchildren crushed in the Sichuan earthquake joined Tibetan dissidents in illegal detention that summer and beyond, Tibetans and Chinese were linked first and foremost as subjects of CCP leaders' claims to the state of exception.[82]

In this, state officials' efforts, so similar to those of their imperial predecessors, to recruit Tibetan monks and lamas as supporters of state humanitarianism and as aides in "crossing over" (Ch. *chaodu*) (and thus eliminating) the untimely dead were in vain. As evidenced by lay Tibetans' unprecedented oppositional mourning practices, Tibetan monks' death rituals in the face of renewed state violence in fact for many evoked suppressed histories of polluted landscapes and unrequited collective grief. Hence, by 2010 the disaster relief state of China's Olympic year had set a template for an increasingly routinized response to the ongoing disaster of untimely death in Tibetan regions. Indeed, unprecedentedly, state leaders declared two more national days of mourning in 2010, both for "natural" disasters in Tibetan regions: April 21, for the thousands crushed in collapsed buildings during the April 14 6.9 magnitude earthquake in Yushu, Qinghai Province, and August 15, for over two thousand buried in massive mudslides in Zhouqu, Gansu Province on August 8, exactly two years to the day of the launch of the Beijing Olympics.

Despite even Chinese academics' warnings about the increasing vulnerability of those mountainous regions due to rapid urbanization and unchecked deforestation,[83] the 2010 disasters triggered new waves of humanitarian discipline within and outside the PRC.[84] Predictably, state media and supporters vilified as selfish, unpatriotic rumor mongers those who publicly suggested such events were not wholly natural. Meanwhile, a renewed round of state ceremonial fundraising was followed by tightened restrictions on NGOs that mandated channeling citizens' donations to state coffers.[85]

But in the mountainous prefecture of Yushu, where over 90 percent of residents are Tibetan, the majority of whom were highland pastoralists, the sheer Tibetanness of the earthquake's catastrophic aftermath belied the state's disaster relief template. Just as in 2008, tens of thousands of Chinese troops and relief workers were mobilized to the scene, and as before, both Hu Jintao and Wen Jiabao made visits to the epicenter to be photographed with crying victims and to offer condolences for "deceased compatriots" (Ch. *yunan tongbao*). However those efforts to frame the disaster as a national-scale event merely highlighted the vast gap between central leaders' perspectives and those of Tibetan residents. State media coverage of Yushu quake relief played down the Tibetanness of that remote county seat, staging it instead as a virtual remake of the Sichuan campaign focused on heroic state relief workers and uniformed troops. But this quake scene uncannily brought the efficacies of state and Tibetan Buddhist humanitarianism into direct confrontation over the fate of the Tibetan dead.

The Tibetanness of the new disaster zone defied statist humanitarianism not only because the nationwide coverage revealed the poverty and shoddy building construction that humanized Tibetans and linked them to the Chinese victims of the Sichuan quake.[86] More important, in that high altitude region, it was Tibetan Buddhist monks from surrounding monasteries who were the most immediate rescuers and death specialists for residents. As state relief workers struggled with the altitude in the first few days, hundreds of monks and nuns arrived to help search for survivors and tend to the dead. Unbeknown to local officials, hundreds of corpses were taken to monasteries that now, just as several had during the 2008 unrest, doubled as morgues. Though monastic leaders seem not to have taken a systematic count of the dead, they soon began to question official death tolls that estimated a little over two thousand killed, citing numbers between eight and ten thousand to reporters instead.[87]

In April 2010, the clashing transactional orders of statist and Tibetan Buddhist mourning confronted each other in the rubble of Jyekundo (Ch. Jiegu) town. In the days after the quake, monks held unprecedented mass cremation ceremonies for thousands of Tibetan dead, assembling on the hills above the flames to chant prayers accompanied by grieving laity from across the prefecture. Footage and images of those events, circulated via social media and cell phones among Tibetans in and outside of the PRC, were a stunning contrast to state media coverage of national mourning a few days later, in which monks, now ordered to leave the quake site, rarely appeared.[88]

That event was in fact the first time since the tenth Panchen Lama's early 1980s tours that Tibetan collective grief had been so graphically and publicly displayed, turning Yushu, historically far east of the Dalai Lamas' seat in Lhasa, into an emblematic funereal landscape that now encompasses the entire plateau. As the unspecific death tolls cited by monks pointed up, the misfortunate dead here called forth all the unacknowledged deceased who yet demanded nurturance and purification only Buddhist monks could provide.[89] And the scale of this new misfortune prompted anguished calls for the blessing power of the highest lama of all—the Dalai Lama. Within two days of the quake, a petition was sent to President Hu thanking the state for its relief work but claiming that only the Dalai Lama could nurture and "cross over" the Tibetan dead (*Boxun* 2010). The petition went unanswered but the Dalai Lama's presence could not in fact be thwarted: rumors had it in Yushu that the Dalai Lama had actually flown in a plane overhead to send his prayers down to the victims.

Epilogue
The Kindly Solemn Face of the Female Buddha

The six types of sentient beings are our parents,
Nonviolent peace is our innate mentality;
Heroic courage is our hearts' inheritance;
This people living in the snowy mountains,
The first settlers of the high plateaus,
is us, the red-faced Tibetans of the snowland.

Oh! brothers, Tibetans,
We come remembering your profound love and affection,
Today we perform a dance before you,
Oh! brothers, Tibetans,
This is the circle dance you taught us,
This is a gift to greet and honor our brothers,
Oh! brothers, Tibetans (repeats)

> —Wildly popular anthem and cell phone ringtone in Rebgong,
> performed in the town stadium by the four most
> famous Tibetan male singers, summer 2006

In the winter of 2007, just after Jima village's harvest festival had come to its ambivalent conclusion, Li Xuansheng, Huangnan prefecture's rotund and entrepreneurial Chinese party secretary,[1] published one of the lead essays in the prefecture's inaugural issue of *Rebgong Culture* (Ch. *Regong Wenhua*), a glossy magazine aimed at Chinese investors and consumers (see figure 3). Li's essay, entitled "Develop the Rebgong Culture Industry, Construct a Harmonious 'Cultural Huangnan,'" (Li 2007) in fact repackages prefecture development planning documents, ramping up the rhetoric to sell an audience of outsiders on the great "economic value" of Rebgong's "cultural resources" (Ch. *wenhua ziyuan*). The energetic party secretary, it seems, had had big plans for the prefecture ever since he took the position in 2004.

Born in 1956 just south of Xining city, Li came of age at the end of the Cultural Revolution, and quickly left a middle school teaching job to begin an official career in a prefecture Commerce Bureau, becoming a CCP member in the process. With post-Mao reforms then, Li was well-positioned to be an influential promarket technocrat. But he found his true calling in 1999 when he became the head of the Qinghai Province Tourism Bureau. That position in turn was his springboard to the paramount leadership role in Huangnan prefecture in 2004, just as the Great Open the West program was underway. Development planning in twenty-first century Rebgong bore the unmistakable stamp of Li's (commodity) vision. His essay in the new magazine is thus a veritable blueprint for New Socialist capitalism in the valley, one that envisions culture as the "dragon's head" of the prefecture's tertiary industry and the leading export product of a national and global scale "Rebgong brand" (2007, 10).

Li argues that sellable culture, including the nationally recognized Rongbo Monastery and historical town, the famous Rebgong Buddhist thangka art, village folk culture like the harvest festival, as well as both natural ("wild and pristine" mountains, rivers, and forests) and built environments (monasteries, stupas, and plazas), is the linchpin for harmoniously integrating market principles and state planning and regulation. Only by providing incentives to businesses and households to invest in the "culture industry," he insists, will the prefecture achieve a utopic state of socialist prosperity and peaceful civilization:

To develop Rebgong's culture industry is to promote socialist culture under the market economy. It is an important way to satisfy the masses' demands for spiritual civilization. Even more important is to transform superior cultural resources into competitive economic superiority. . . . To create cultural competitiveness [e.g., by "upgrading" the Rebgong brand] is to manifest sustainable development. We must comprehensively and completely practice a scientific perspective on development, and according to the requirements of a socialist harmonious culture retain the best aspects of traditional culture and construct an advanced socialist one. (2007, 13)

With the ardor of an evangelist riding the wave of yang dar optimism in the valley, Party Secretary Li asserts that this vision for Rebgong culture will position the prefecture as the number three Qinghai tourist destination behind Qinghai Lake and Kumbum Monastery, and make it the premier provider of Tibetan cultural resources both provincially and nationally. But he also envisions the culture industry as the way to position Rebgong and Longwu town as models for development governance enriched by multiple sources of investment. Such a scheme, he enthuses, will produce "an ethnically united progressive city" at the center of the prefecture's "civilized villages and towns, civilized households, and civilized workplaces, all of which will create long-term mechanisms for providing paid work" (15).

From the dialogic perspective on frontier zone development encounters that I have been developing in this book, we can't take Li's utopic vision here as either the monologic voice of the State or as mere empty rhetoric. Instead, in my story of the partially unforeseen and tragic consequences of state-led development in Rebgong, I relied especially on Bakhtin's counter-intuitive approach to human communication as constituted first and foremost by multivoiced and potentially contentious dialogue. To put it simply, Bakhtin's approach to dialogic communication amounts to the empirical assertion that all human meaning-making, including that of the ethnographer, is absolutely inextricable from the reciprocal dynamics of embodied interactions. Through the analyses of various encounters in the previous chapters, this paradigm shift allowed us to grasp how types and scales of persons and values in development projects were fundamentally contested. Further, Bakhtin's concept of chronotopes, or historically loaded idioms that people evoked (not always successfully) to organize and orient persons in time and space, offered us a way to analyze the politics of presence in face-to-face development encounters as linked to wider-scale historical legacies of unequal political and economic exchange.

From this angle, we are better positioned to understand how Party Secretary Li's 2006–7 development plan for a Cultural Huangnan in fact launched the New Socialist battle for fortune in Rebgong, one that would compel Tibetans to break the silent pact and openly protest despite (and because of) escalating military discipline. What Li and his prefecture underlings ultimately produced was the very opposite of their glossy utopia—far from a model of interethnic harmony and prosperity, Rebgong in 2008 and beyond became a center of Tibetan protest and routinized military crackdown.[2] By the end of 2012, after a year of particularly intense unrest, Li Xuansheng found himself purged from office, unable to see to fruition many of his projects for the prefecture's culture industry.

Returning to 2006, then, the great success of the unprecedented Tibetan pop music concert that summer, in which enraptured Tibetan audiences packed the town stadium and cheered the famous Tibetan singers performing the song "Heartfelt Return" cited above, would have seemed to prefecture planners like Li as the ideal "cultural event" to put the Rebgong brand on the map. But the battle for fortune, as Li's plans defined it, would come to revolve around the very timespace premises of Tibetan culture itself. Back in the summer of 2007, Tibetans I knew spoke of the song "Heartfelt Return" not as mere pop media but in reverent tones as an anthem of an ascendant, pan-Tibetan pride and sovereignty. The song's emergence for them was a culminating event in the prefecture's post-Mao yang dar cultural revival, built as it was on the promise of Tibetan "autonomous government."

Indeed, unlike other forms of Tibetan place eulogy we have seen in previous chapters, this song was baldly addressive and assertively masculine, directly addressing all Tibetans as "brothers" (Tib. *spun zla*) linked by their common origins in the divine (Buddhist) landscape of the high plateau.[3] The accounts of chapters 2 through 5 demonstrated that culture for Tibetans in twenty-first century Rebgong was bound up with highly fraught efforts at community building in the face of capitalist development pressures. But for Party Secretary Li, Tibetan culture was most properly an abstract commodity, a set of recordable experiences and portable objects (like the Warrior Queen Palden Lhamo on the cover of his magazine in figure 3 above) served up to Chinese and foreign buyers. Further, as we will see, this new culture industry was in fact planned to be the onstage face of the new economy of appearances. That is, Rebgong Culture was supposed to attract outside investment that would ultimately revitalize the prefecture's less openly touted resource extraction industries.

Only by orienting the entire prefecture to that notion of culture (e.g., in the transformation of the main valley into a "Rebgong Culture Corridor"), Li insists in his 2007 essay, can we hope to finally bring rural Tibetans into the modern era. Repurposing the old Maoist CCP civilizing project, he goes on to assert that Chinese tourists' interactions with Tibetans would help "broadcast and glorify the superior aspects of nationality culture," (12) providing opportunities for visitors to engage in "economic, cultural and technical help and exchange" in order to "open up" the region. Further, Li explicitly links his plan to sell Rebgong culture to the central and provincial CCP's calls we encountered in chapters 2 through 4 for building grassroots party presence and implementing New Socialist Countryside reforms in rural Tibetan communities. Farmers and pastoralists were to be integrated into this economy of appearances and encouraged and trained to serve tourists by selling art and food, and providing experiences of "vacation farming," and "landscape viewing."

In his essay, Li admits that this plan for producing apolitical and sellable culture, while already underway, was still nascent. Indeed, in the internal Tourism Bureau annual report I obtained that year, the writers had diplomatically complained that "culture" and "tourism" were not working together enough. For an audience of outside investors in the magazine, however, Li portrays his development vision in much starker terms as requiring a chronotopic fight, a new Cultural Revolution:

> We must help the rural masses break into the market, and encourage them to *smash the temporal and spatial limitations* of their traditional folk behavior . . . [we will] thereby abolish those dregs amidst traditional culture, the obsolete and backward customs and habits that hinder the construction of spiritual civilization and economic development in Huangnan. (emphasis mine, 15)

In 2006–7, Party Secretary Li laid out the front lines of this new urban-rural battle for fortune in Rebgong at the very threshold of Rongbo Monastery itself: the huge new concrete and stone tourist square he ordered built in front of the monastic complex, complete with a magnificent Chinese-style gate and a railing of carved white marble imported from the east. In his plan for the town, the new plaza, dubbed Culture Square (Ch. Wenhua Guangchang), was to mark the monastery as a tourist destination linked to the new northern section of town (where tourists stayed) by a colorfully rendered Tibetan-style shopping avenue. Li's plans seem to have quickly borne fruit. He and the Tourism Bureau report more than 3 million tourist visits to Tongren County alone that year, more than double the number of the previous year.[4]

Yet the new square was also to be integrated into the monastery as a Buddhist space, with grand new prayer wheel galleries and temples extending the length of the monastery visible to the main avenue, and most importantly, the central presence of the nine-meter-high, golden bronze statue of the female Buddha Drolma (Skt. Tara). The statue's stele, carved into the white marble pedestal, begins with a direct quote from the Tourism Bureau's annual report (minus their claim that the square would help to "upgrade the status of the Rebgong brand"):

> *The Merits and Virtues Stele*: In 2006, in order to promote nationality culture, encourage ethnic unity, and beautify the city's environment, the

FIGURE 29. Drolma statue and Tibetan circumambulators, Drolma Square, Rebgong, March 2008. Author's photo.

prefecture government constructed the Rebgong Culture Square and the divine figure of Green Tara, the goddess who delivers all sentient beings [from misfortune]. The deity's statue is 9.369 m high, with three faces emanating kindly and solemn expressions.

Tibetans across the plateau have long venerated Drolma, but she had never had such prominent presence in Rebgong as she did in the early 2000s. Recalling chapter 3, when Kharnak men buried the Drolma "treasure" at the threshold of their new school gate, the "green" emanation of Drolma is associated with protecting against mundane misfortune and ensuring or increasing (enlightened) achievement. Further, the female Buddha Drolma offers analogies to the Chinese female bodhisattva Guanyin and thus suggests a strong appeal to Chinese Buddhist devotees whom, as we have seen, had become increasingly interested in Tibetan forms of Buddhism.[5]

Drolma was presumably the ideally hybrid Buddha for twenty-first century Rebgong. But by giving the female Buddha such prominence opposite the monastery, Party Secretary Li also exploited the rich iconography of gender as a way to reinvigorate the battle for fortune and deepen the commodification of Tibetan regions. That is, as a divine feminine presence in the new square, the kindly and solemn Drolma is supposed to embody the spectacular compassion of the state. In that context, she is an avatar of the socialist sleight of hand. Her presence works to feminize both Tibetan culture and the CCP-led state while diverting attention from the rise of authoritarian capitalism in, as we saw in chapters 2 through 4, expanding land appropriation and resource extraction. In 2007, a young urban Tibetan friend of mine, expressing his admiration for Party Secretary Li's concern for Tibetan culture, his wide networks, and capacity to get things done, remarked that "no one knew how he paid for it, he just showed up on the new square with the statue in a truck."[6] But Drolma's stele provides a clue: it lists as donors, along with two wealthy Chinese devotees, two corporations, the private Beijing-based tourism landscape design and development firm Creative Views (Ch. Chuangjing Shidian, a subsidiary of Chuangjing Tianxia, lit., "Make All under Heaven A Tourist Site"); and, donating the lion's share of 3.7 million yuan, the multibillion-yuan state-run, Xining-based Western Mining Corporation (Ch. Xibu Kuangye).

During the Maoist years CCP-led resource extraction firms literally occupied Rongbo Monastery's space, turning central monastic halls into storage and distribution outlets (provincial and prefecture mineral prospecting and excavation companies were housed there). But now, the new square and Drolma figure allowed the prefecture CCP to keep resource extraction offstage. In the new square, prefecture planners appropriated the silent pact diplomacy of Tibetan Buddhist hospitality spectacle and posed, along with Chinese corporations, as ultra-gift masters. Prefecture CCP officials thereby claimed via divine favor to be the only ones capable of delivering truly fortunate futures. Tibetan patrons were drawn into the economy of appearances there, as wealthy families vied to donate funds for the fancy prayer wheels along the front, their names duly recorded on plaques for all to see.[7] And Drolma provided a nice circumambulation site for Tibetan villagers, especially women barred from entering the monastery during the traditional summer retreat. For them, the square became known not as Culture Square, but as Drolma Square (Tib. sgrolma thang chen).

As it turned out, however, the square did not deliver on its promise to anchor a harmonious culture industry as the compassionate face of the State. In fact, Party Secretary Li's development plans all along categorized Tibetan culture as just another industrial resource to extract.[8] And the 2007 issue of *Rebgong Culture* touts other contracts Li was busy signing (to the tune of some 90 million yuan), including with another Chinese mining company to invest in the construction of a Rebgong Culture Palace in town, presumably in exchange for prospecting and mining rights in the prefecture. Drolma Square itself encapsulated the conflicts and dangers inherent in stealthy resource extraction. In 2006, the square was appropriated from a steep shelf of land in front of the monastery, historically called The Middle Table (Tib. cog tse bar ma), that by the late nineteenth century had separated the monastic complex from the profane market town far below it. The new square thus would require engineering prowess to stabilize it against the steep hillside; at the time it was the largest concrete pour in the valley.

But in the early spring of 2008, just as tensions were beginning to rise, an urban Tibetan friend of mine was lamenting, as had my friends in the Upper Narrows, the seemingly sudden acceleration of development construction across the valley. And he took me to see Drolma Square as an example of bad construction under the auspices of officials' rushed "show projects." That was when I first learned the phrase "tofu dregs construction." He pointed to the gravel ground, and the piles of patio stones nearby. "See that," he said, "That's an example. Two years ago, the prefecture party secretary had this constructed extremely fast, and within a few months when it froze, the patio stones had come right up." He pointed out how Tibetan pilgrims had peed all over the marble railings, and worst, he showed me the car-sized chunks of concrete and stone where an entire side of the massive, thirty-foot-high retaining wall had fallen down within months of its construction, destroying

FIGURE 30. Rongbo Monastery and Drolma Square (post-collapse concrete patch and house demolition site visible on right) from across the valley, summer 2008. Author's photo.

a village house below. I told him that I had seen the retaining wall already cracking the previous summer. He explained that his friend lived in one of the houses below, had noticed the cracking and even taken pictures of it to alert officials, to no avail. And he described how villagers still talked about the huge roar of the wall coming down that night. "They rebuilt the wall," he said, "better this time, a bit slower," pointing out how they needed the wall to clear the way, along with the many houses they had demolished, for the new concrete road they planned to put in at its base. "Did the families go voluntarily?" I asked. "Oh yes," he replied confidently, "they were all compensated." So were, he went on to explain, the Tibetan landlords on the main avenue from the square, whose shops were to be destroyed to make way for new two-story, Tibetan-style concrete buildings.

In practice then, Drolma square illustrates the "double movement" we have seen unfolding down and up the valley in the 2000s:[9] the escalating, reciprocal process of place-destroying capitalist commodification met by Tibetans' counterdevelopment efforts to (re)build communities and ensure their auspicious sovereignty, to safeguard specific containers of fortune for future generations of kin. As we have seen, tantric Buddhism under the auspices of Rongbo Monastery could be mobilized to defend those containers in the battle for fortune. The kindly, peaceful Drolma, after all, never came near supplanting the intense lay-monastic hospitality aimed at the fierce and dreadful Warrior Queen Palden Lhamo. And in terms of spatial position, Drolma sits on a raised dais opposite the monastery's Great Assembly Hall, in the very place where, prior to CCP intervention, a massive weapons cairn (Tib. *lha tho*) invoked the protection of the most hypermasculine and transcendent of warrior mountain deities, Machen Bomra, Lord of the highest mountain in all of Amdo.[10] It was there that Tibetan village men from the Upper Narrows first gathered in the mid-1930s to perform a "universal incense offering" (Tib. *'dzam gling spyi bsang*) to prepare them for the battle against Ma Bufang's troops described in chapter 3 (GDKS 2012, 165).

That was the same threshold that returned monks and lamas, along with Tibetan villagers, had reclaimed and purified when the "door to the Dharma" was first reopened in 1980, inaugurating the yang dar years in Rebgong. Lumoji told me she was a child then: "I remember that day [when the Assembly Hall grounds were officially returned to monastic control]! My mother went to work on it, to clean it. People were sweating, working so hard, and it stunk so bad! It was so toxic, many people died from breathing it! They would cover their faces with cloths." But my monk friend Akhu Tenzin, who had been collecting oral histories of the monastery in 2007, recounted the initial battles that ensued on the threshold of the Assembly Hall when, on an auspicious day of the New Year, Rongbo monks finally hosted rituals again. Everyone, he told me, knew well the Tibetan "activists" who had collaborated with Chinese officials and helped to organize the destruction of monastic property and deity images during the Cultural Revolution. When one of them, who had returned to being a monk, tried to attend those first assemblies and purification offerings and arrived at the main gate of the Hall, laity there stopped him and dragged him back. Akhu Tenzin voiced the monk's opponents, *"You helped the Chinese destroy things back then! There's no way you can come to the assembly!* They dragged him back twice!"[11] Later, he said, when another former activist known to have been particularly brutal tried to join the reestablished assembly as a monk, monks there kicked him out: "Back at home, he was so depressed that he killed himself." And Akhu Tenzin concluded matter-of-factly, "that's karmic retribution. Otherwise, no one would ever want to bring about one's own death like that."

As we wrap up our journey across Rebgong's Guchu Valley, we can now understand that the end of the yang dar years there, Tibetans' heightened sense of foreboding, moral degeneration, and loss, coincided with Li Xuansheng's new drive, in line with central and provincial priorities, to finally push capitalist development upriver and into the rural patron dewa of Rongbo Monastery. That in turn unleashed new opportunities for authoritarian lawlessness among Tibetans, in which powerful lineage-state alliances could disenfranchise and silence weaker, poorer communities. Yet as chapter 5 illustrated especially, the subsequent protests and military crackdown in 2008 led Tibetans across the valley to link the loss of culture and language to the inauspicious, untimely death of both persons and whole communities.

In Rebgong, as elsewhere across the Tibetan plateau, the successful close of the Beijing Olympics did not eliminate the presence of the untimely Tibetan dead. And many (most?) of the deceased, it turned out, were from highland rural regions. Indeed, sadly contradicting Akhu Tenzin's confident declaration about self-inflicted death among Tibetans, on March 9, 2009, Akhu Sheldrup, one of the Rongbo monks originally detained and beaten on that terrible day of April 17 the previous year, found a new use for offering scarves and hung himself with them in his quarters in the monastery. Given the date (on the eve of Tibetan Uprising Day and the one-year anniversary of the beginning of the 2008 unrest), and the white offering scarves' suggestion of sincere intent, we could take Akhu Sheldrup's death as a form of immolation, a sacrifice that made his body a medium for a now-suppressed pan-Tibetan public.[12]

In ways similar to the aftermath of 1958, the 2008 unrest and crackdown had in fact opened the way for CCP leaders' redoubled efforts at community busting among Tibetans in order to push through development reforms. In a striking reversal, postunrest development policy downplayed the disgust with villagers' "lazy" dependency I had often heard in education officials' New Socialist rhetoric and repurposed a Maoist-style spectacular compassion in the form of massive central state subsidies that required direct displays of gratitude and loyalty to the officials who distributed them (foreign donors, it seemed, were now irrelevant, their NGOs banned or starved out).[13] As the PAP squad's artillery blanks exploded above town that June 2008, both Party Secretary Li and his Tibetan deputy Dorje Tsering echoed central and provincial directives in impassioned speeches urging underlings to speed up the implementation of their 2006–7 development plans and compete for "bigger" projects like dams and mines.[14]

Meanwhile, in an internal report to party superiors I obtained on Tongren County's mining industry, the writers tout tens of millions of yuan in investments in copper, zinc, and lead mining and processing by Chinese companies.[15] But they also complain of the "extremely wide" gap between mining planners' and contractors' rhetoric and the reality: a lack of financial and safety oversight, rampant false reporting, and overdevelopment where mineral resources are in fact limited.[16] Yet they urge prefecture officials to "sweep away" all obstacles to the construction of mining projects, including multiple disputes with Tibetan villagers over land use and the scope of mining rights. In this, they argue, officials in the culture industry should push forward as the "advance preparatory work" of attracting investment that would benefit the "follow-up" stage of opening up the resource extraction industry.[17]

Thus beginning in 2010, Rebgong saw renewed protests among the very constituencies CCP leaders had most sought to educate and control in 2007–8: rural Tibetans, and young students and monks. Directly countering the 2008 message that any public gathering of Tibetans was a threat, Drolma Square now became the space for the "peaceful demonstrations" of a reclaimed Tibetan public, the primary stage for the fractious rural-urban interface that, as elsewhere across the PRC, state-led capitalist development had produced.[18] In 2010, responding to rumors that the long-feared elimination of Tibetan-language curricula would finally be pushed through, Tibetan middle and high school students (many of whom, recalling chapters 3 and 4, were from rural regions throughout the prefecture) poured out of classes and gathered at Drolma Square, where they were joined by some monks. Then, ignoring the military trucks and holding signs and shouting for "equality among nationalities" and "keeping Tibetan education," they marched through town streets. Their protests were echoed by other student protests both up- and downriver, as well as in Beijing.

Those 2010 protests, however, would seem to have been quickly defused.[19] Meanwhile, Li Xuansheng soldiered on, scaling up and crystallizing his original development plan for Rebgong. That year, his Beijing and Xining partners in tourism design were busy planning and building huge tourism destination sites in town under the Rebgong Culture brand.[20] And in 2011, he linked his plan to the new central state demand, under the twelfth Five Year Plan, for ramping up mineral resource extraction out west while pursuing "environmental protection." Li now called for establishing Huangnan as a showcase for sustainable development. Under the new party rubric, Rebgong culture could be more openly harnessed to be the advertising arm for enlightened resource extraction. Li now envisioned Rebgong as "a national-level, top-grade experimental Tibetan cultural ecology site and Tibetan culture base," in which six "model industrial parks" would produce and sell cultural products modeling the ideal balance between sustainability and extraction.[21] At the contract signing for one of those culture parks in the prefecture's new Kanbula National Geopark, Li addressed managers at the state-controlled construction corporation that owned both the geopark and an open-cut coal mine there, warning them that, "due to exogenous factors" the project's progress had met "definite problems." And taking up old Maoist military metaphors, he urged them to "unleash an invincible army that would dare to fight a hard battle" and see the project through.[22]

By the summer of 2011 when I visited again, the lowland valley was awash in the gluttony of concrete I mentioned at the end of chapter 3, as urban residents (including many Tibetan families) sought to benefit as best they could from the development push. At Rongbo Monastery, Li's new multistory concrete apartment building for monks, blocked by the monastic assembly in 2007, was complete and freshly painted to mimic traditional Tibetan monastic architecture, while crews had broken ground on a new PAP base next door. At Kharnak's school, teachers were so resigned to the imminent loss of their Tibetan language curriculum that they urged me to take a set of their textbooks as souvenirs: "We certainly won't be needing them," sighed one. And up at Langmo's abandoned peak village, the ruins of village households' packed-earth walls had become stealthy social media for anonymous villagers debating the future of Tibet and Tibetans. The original, tentative declaration of "Freedom for Tibet" (Tib. *bod rang btsan*) I had seen in 2008 had provoked a range of vigorous responses, such that graffiti now covered that wall and spilled onto others. It was now clear to me that the original graffito should be rendered more specifically in English as "*Independence* for Tibet," because someone unhappy with (or afraid of) that claim had tried to erase the final word in the phrase.[23] Someone else then redrew the word on top, only to have it crossed out again. A smaller version of the phrase below it had also been crossed out, and yet large and small copycat versions of the phrase had proliferated all across the wall and onto others. And, away from the fray, someone had scratched an admonition to the others across a dismantled house's foundation stones:

> bod rang btsan byed pa las bod bran g'yog byed mi rung pa ni / bod mi tshang mas shes na 'grig

> (All Tibetans should know that it is better to pursue independence for Tibet than for Tibetans to remain as serfs.)

As tensions unfolded that year and beyond, this time in the run-up to the eighteenth National CCP Congress (during which Xi Jinping took over as China's new party leader and President), open protest, spearheaded by rural Tibetans, would once again engulf Rebgong's central watershed. Between 2010 and 2013 Tibetan regions across the plateau saw increasing reports of mining-related land disputes, as well as of safety and ecological disasters,[24] and in their wake, escalating Tibetan protests and military crackdown. That was when a new form of social media, aimed at multiple addressees, emerged among Tibetans as a response to tightening state repression. This genre of media would tragically bring untimely death out into the open: the unprecedented spate of self-immolation by fire protests that began south of Rebgong in Ngaba (Ch. Aba) prefecture and spread across Amdo regions especially.[25] Virtually unprecedented as a Buddhist practice among Tibetans, the immolation by fire protests were initiated by young monks and nuns and later taken up by mostly young, rural laity. Now immolators used the spectacle of their own flaming bodies in public spaces to amplify protest messages that emphasized their nonviolent, Buddhist sacrifice. In this case, neither Tibetan lamas' and urban intellectuals' mediating interventions, nor security forces' routinized procedures for military crackdown could stem the tide. So heartrending was this new turn of events for Rebgong Tibetans that on November 19, 2012, all lamas from every monastery in the region reportedly signed and widely disseminated a Tibetan-language petition urging Tibetans not to resort to this form of protest:

> *Petition Expressing the Regret and Great Hopes of Our People's Young and Old Monks and Laity.* This wonderful human body is precious, and is the result of previously accumulated good merit, so that this is a rarely found single chance. Don't [sacrifice it] due to sorrow and suffering. You must instead encourage yourself to be able to use it to benefit yourself and all sentient beings for a long time. . . . Please immediately

stop this tragic situation, which piles on suffering for both you and others. Instead, have love for society, love for human life. We kneel on the ground with pure motivation, our hands clasped at our hearts and request this of you with our purest, unstained hearts.[26]

To no avail. By the end of 2012, ninety-nine Tibetans had burned themselves in protest across Kham and Amdo regions, peaking in frequency during November 2012, just as the CCP Congress was underway.[27]

Mid-morning on March 14, 2012, four years to the day of the 2008 Lhasa unrest, Akhu Jamyang Palden, a Rongbo monk in his early thirties, stepped out of the monastery and set himself on fire on Drolma Square. In so doing, he brought Akhu Sheldrup's sacrifice out from behind closed doors and, at that contested threshold, publicly reclaimed the battle for fortune in Rebgong as a matter of life and death. His act, which came just days after Tibetan middle school students in town once again took to the streets to protest new Chinese-language textbooks, would set in motion a tragic crescendo of immolations by fire in the valley leading up to and beyond the CCP Congress that November. As they become increasingly ritualized, each new immolation in turn called forth mass mourning (only now the untimely dead were from Rebgong Tibetans' own communities), further youth protest, and state discipline. "2012," my friends Drolma and Drakpa would tell me later, "was worse even than 2008!" In the fray, Party Secretary Li (who was off on another business junket during the most intense time of protest in November) was not the only one to lose his position. So too did county education officials like Shawojia.

Importantly, Akhu Jamyang Palden's choice of Drolma Square laid a template for scaling up that space as a stage for petitions or prayers for aid, not primarily to Rongbo's Shartshang lama nor to prefecture officials, but, in a rejection of a regional party-led future, up and out, to central party leaders, foreign and Tibetan supporters abroad, and ultimately to the Dalai Lama himself (many of the Rebgong immolators and their mourners called for his return).[28] Further, as many urban Tibetans retreated to the silent pact after 2008, the 2012 Rebgong immolations were a significant reversal of the urban-rural hierarchy of deference we saw in chapter 4, in which marginalized rural Tibetans were exiled from state-local communication. All fifteen of the immolators that year, including the monks and nuns, were from rural communities (at least nine of whom were from the more remote pastoralist communities in the Upper Narrows).[29] Now they brought their petitions to public spaces in flames, demanding the attention of all.

But that year it was Drolma Square that became the main site for the pan-Tibetan public, led by young monks as death specialists, that emerged in response. Three of the immolators chose to burn there, and at least four of their bodies were brought there for mass prayers before being taken to the ridge above the monastery to be cremated in a site usually reserved for high lamas. All of those events drew huge crowds. But it was Akhu Jamyang Palden's immolation (he survived for several months before succumbing that September) and then that of his good friend three days later, the forty-four-year-old farmer Sonam Dargye, that drew perhaps the largest-ever gatherings of Tibetan mourners and protesters in Rebgong. After Sonam Dargye shouted "Let the Dalai Lama return to Tibet!" and burned himself to death down the street from the square, mourners carried his body to Drolma's statue and laid it at her feet. There, as thousands of lay and monastic Tibetans from across the prefecture converged on the plaza to pray for him, white and gold offering scarves and brocades swathed him like a cremated lama, while framing his blackened head on all sides were placed photo montages of the Dalai Lama, his hands clasped in prayer. Now the kindly female Buddha Drolma, her transcendent compassion and promise to protect from harm, was meant to act not as an avatar of the State, but of the Geluk Buddhist sovereign.

My return visit in the summer of 2013 felt like mourning. The 2012 crackdown on unrest had in fact taken the gloves off the culture wars Li Xuansheng had launched back in 2007. Now new rules, laid out by the new party secretary (Li's replacement) at a prefecturewide meeting and widely promulgated, explicitly criminalized as "separatist" any support (including public mourning) for self-immolators and their families and threatened to cut off the State's gift of welfare and development aid to immolators' households and whole villages. But the new rules also provided sanction for criminalizing key forms of community building among Tibetans, including "using the excuse" of protecting Tibetan language, the environment, or most vaguely, any "outside affair" to fundraise, conduct incense offerings, or chant "scriptures."[30] Thus the months before my return saw multiple arrests of young students (including some middle schoolers), monks, and some villagers for their roles in the 2012 unrest.

This visit thus had to be quick and careful, as Tibetan friends moved gingerly in the shadow of new skyscrapers and surveillance cameras in town. State repression, it seems, had reduced me to auditing surfaces. In Jima village, deity medium Dorje had apparently found common cause with his former opponents the wealthy elders by securing a national-level title as a model performer of "intangible cultural heritage." Meanwhile the village itself had garnered multiple "Model Village" awards for its entrepreneurship and eye-catching, tourist-friendly temple. For the first time that summer, I heard, Chinese tourists joined, uninvited, into Jima's harvest festival dances as if they were the popular "folk" circle dances with Tibetans that they expected in town plazas or tourist destinations.[31] Up in Langmo, the little primary school stood weedy and in disrepair. The students, I was told, were now sent down to town at first grade. Yet villagers had managed to bring their long hoped-for stupa to fruition, and their celebratory feasts, one of which I awkwardly attended, brought back villagers and lineage allies who had been scattered across the region seeking caterpillar fungus and wage labor.

At Kharnak's thriving school, CCP slogans in Chinese had replaced the inspirational Tibetan quotes on the courtyard wall, while inside the new rules criminalizing Tibetan "separatists" were prominently displayed for primary school students who played under new surveillance cameras. Yet unlike Langmo, Kharnak party officials had taken their avant-garde compliance efforts to new heights, scaling up the vision from the school grounds to the entire dewa, including plans for a massive new gate at the opening of the valley next to the Kharnak stupa, only this time designed to evoke the formidable stone lines of ancient Tibetan fortresses. Their efforts to establish Kharnak as the eco-tourism destination of the Upper Narrows had garnered them "Model Village" plaques from both the prefecture and the province. That summer, even as construction crews broke ground for a new CCP head-quarters and "cultural center" in the very middle of the village, villagers were busy renovating their households with government funds, erecting the man-datory painted concrete walls to face the road. Now the smooth white walls were adorned with posters touting elders' plans for an "experimental village" at the head of the valley that, just as Party Secretary Li had envisioned, would museumize rural lifestyles for tourists and offer restaurants, hotels, an archery ground, exhibition hall and tent resort.

My friend Gendun, the Kharnak education official, tried to put on a good face for my visit. But his manic gregariousness and party-boy exuberance seemed dampened and forced. His grand plans for developing Tibetan cul-ture and language had been reined in (he was no longer permitted to fund-raise for schools and, he told me, he had spent time in detention for his online activities). For Cain's and my last day, Gendun valiantly organized a picnic on a ridge above the hydroelectric dam, corralling a couple of village bud-dies, contractors working on Kharnak household renovations, and Shampa, Kharnak's deity medium we met in chapter 4. As clouds darkened upriver, and the wind began to pick up, the men set up the umbrella, fire and pot for boiling mutton, and then settled down to survey the new construction in the village below. Gesturing at the storm clouds, Gendun mustered his old bravado for our benefit, "There's no way it'll rain on us," he joked, smiling broadly at Shampa, "We have our mountain deity Makgol here to divert it!"

We were soon joined by Lubum, one of Kharnak's officials and party members, who slowly puffed his way up the hillside to the ridge and plopped down. His swollen face and body were so miserable and unhealthy that I silently dubbed him "death's door guy." The men made an effort at joyous hospitality, but as they took to sharing the usual cups of grain alcohol, the gathering quickly lost its veneer of exuberance and devolved to the brink of violence. Ever drunker, Gendun and his two construction friends began to tease and harass the ingratiating Lubum about his status as an official, their jokes becoming more barbed and personal with each round of drinks, until they were directly challenging him as to why he "served the party" when so many Tibetans had less privilege than him. By then, Lubum, his eyes nearly swollen shut, was swaying silently on his mat—until suddenly he exploded in rage, lunging at Gendun and throwing his drink in his face. All of us jumped back in shock as Lubum sat down heavily and turned his back to us. As the rain began to come down in earnest, the men quickly moved to placate him. Shampa broke into a traditional song, while the others feigned rapt appreciation and murmured mollifying words to the drunken official.

Cain and I knew it was time for us to leave, but the men weren't ready to go. Even as the clouds opened over us, Gendun vowed that they would stay up there all day, no matter what. Racing the storm down the muddy road, squeezed on the back of a village boy's motorcycle, we left them there on the ridge, determined to brave it out.

འཇམ་དཔལ་དཔའ་བོས་ཇི་ལྟར་མཁྱེན་པ་དང་། །

Just as the warrior Mañjuśrī and

ཀུན་ཏུ་བཟང་པོ་དེ་ཡང་དེ་བཞིན་ཏེ། །

Samantabhadra realized things as they are,

དེ་དག་ཀུན་གྱི་རྗེས་སུ་བདག་སློབ་ཕྱིར། །

to follow their perfect example,

དགེ་བ་འདི་དག་ཐམས་ཅད་རབ་ཏུ་བསྔོ། །

I dedicate all these merits in the best way.

དུས་གསུམ་གཤེགས་པའི་རྒྱལ་བ་ཐམས་ཅད་ཀྱིས། །

Just as all the victorious Buddhas of the three times

བསྔོ་བ་གང་ལ་མཆོག་ཏུ་བསྔགས་པ་དེས། །

praised dedication as the best [practice],

བདག་གི་དགེ་བའི་རྩ་བ་འདི་ཀུན་ཀྱང་། །

now I dedicate all these roots of virtue

བཟང་པོ་སྤྱོད་ཕྱིར་རབ་ཏུ་བསྔོ་བར་བགྱི། །

so that all beings might perform good works.[32]

NOTES

Introduction

1. See Wu Hung 1997, Hai Ren 2004.

2. Chinese authorities had been anticipating Tibetan protests during the Olympics, largely due to activists' calls for action abroad, and military presence had been beefed up in central Tibet as early as the summer of 2007. However, evidence suggests that central leaders as well as local authorities in Tibetan regions had not anticipated the timing, the vehemence, or the wide scale of the unrest that broke out in spring 2008. The vast majority of protests consisted of peaceful demonstrations. See Smith 2010.

3. The yearbook also claims a huge increase in the percentage of the provincial population registered as urban compared to 1952 estimates (the first year of PRC census taking), up from 5 percent urban in 1952 to 40 percent urban in 2007.

4. As June Dreyer (2006) and others pointed out, however, the hoped for foreign investment did not pan out. The majority of investment was from the central state in the form of direct subsidies to provincial development bureaus and indirect subsidies to Chinese companies from outside the province (see below). See also Goodman 2004a, 2004b; Holbig 2004; Lai 2002; Oakes 2004; Fischer 2009a, 2009b.

5. While Tibetan friends sometimes spoke darkly of a sense of the increased presence of non-Tibetans in town in the early 2000s, reliable statistics on migration patterns in China are notoriously hard to come by. Official Yearbooks did not begin tracking those numbers until recently, and they do not report the ethnic status of migrators. The 2008 Qinghai Province Yearbook suggests a pattern of dynamic "churning" in Huangnan Prefecture, in which people, including Tibetans, moved in and out, mostly within the province. See Fischer 2008.

6. For more on the ambivalent and even detrimental effects for Tibetans of the postunrest deployment of state-led development in Tibetan regions, see especially Emily Yeh 2013. See also Fischer 2009a, 2009b, 2012, 2013.

7. For a description of "Olympic Education," sympathetic to Chinese state views, see Brownell 2009. See also Brownell 2008.

8. For commentary on the significance of 2008 as a watershed year in China, see Lam 2008; Liang Jing 2008; Moore 2008; Smith 2010; Schneider and Hwang 2014; Hubbert 2014; Bin Xu 2014, 2013a, 2013b, and especially Merkel-Hess et al 2009.

9. See also Schwartz 1994 and Barnett 2006 for insightful analyses of their experiences as accidental witnesses to the 1987–89 Tibetan protests in Lhasa.

10. In the past several decades, anthropologists have increasingly turned away from the colonial-era mission to seek out "exotic" others and instead devote themselves to analyzing and helping to address some of the most pressing sociopolitical

issues facing humans. See Nordstrom and Robben 1995, MacClancy 2002, Trouillot 2003, Das and Poole 2004, Coronil and Skurski 2006, Scheper-Hughes and Bourgois 2004, Das 2007, Martin 2007.

11. See Schwartz 1994, Barnett 2006, Yeh 2013, and especially the blog posts of the famous Tibetan dissident Tsering Woeser, translated on the blog *High Peaks Pure Earth*, http://highpeakspureearth.com.

12. For overviews, see especially Fabian 1983, Tedlock and Mannheim 1995, Visweswaran 1997.

13. This, for example, in contrast to journalists from all over the world who rushed to Tibetan regions in 2008 to report on "incidents," making heroic efforts for a few days to sneak past military checkpoints outside Tibetan towns before returning to their metropolitan posts. See especially as an example Kristoff 2008.

14. In the 1980s, Deng's economic advisers were engaged in intensive consultations with economists and policymakers in the United States and elsewhere (including Joseph Stiglitz and Milton Friedman) who were touting various versions of capitalist market liberalism as the key to China's post-Mao "reform and opening up" process (see Ong 1999, Naughton 2002, Wang Hui 2004).

15. See especially Cooper and Packard 1997, Graeber 2001, Power 2003, Edelman and Haugerud 2005.

16. See also Oakes and Schein 2006, Li and Ong 2008, Yeh 2013.

17. See also Oakes 2004, Li and Ong 2008, Oakes and Sutton 2010, Tenzin Jinba 2014.

18. Note that this contestation does not simply boil down to forms of "separatism" or claims to national "independence" among Tibetans, nor does it simply align with the political terms of "indigeneity" movements elsewhere. See chapter 1.

19. See especially Fischer 2009a, 2009b, 2012, 2013.

20. See Goldstein 1997, 2009, 2013, and Tsering Shakya 1999 for accounts of this fraught process of negotiation in the early 1950s.

21. By the 1990s, of all Tibetan regions in the PRC, Qinghai had both the highest rate of rebuilding of Tibetan temples and monasteries and the highest rate of Tibetans in bilingual secular education (Kolås and Thowsen 2005). These trends were epitomized in Rebgong. With its revitalizing Buddhist monastery, its eclectic range of Buddhist and non-Buddhist lay ritual practices, and its famous schools of Tibetan Buddhist art, it was arguably the main eastern center of Tibetan counterdevelopment efforts in the province (HNZZ 2001).

22. See Yeh 2013 for the most in-depth analysis of the cultural politics of Chinese state-led development as gift in Tibetan regions.

23. See Abrams 1988, Coronil 1997, Das and Poole 2004, Ong 1999.

24. For the Dalai Lama's Zone of Peace proposal see TEW 2005. For the Chinese State Council's 2005 white paper see IOSCPRC 2005.

25. For anthropologists analyzing contestations over the nature of socialism in a "post-socialist" era, see Verdery 1996, Ong 1999, Yurchak 2005, Li and Ong 2008.

26. See Harrell 1995, Schein 2000, Makley 2007 for overviews of these "nationality" (Ch. *minzu*) relations in the PRC.

27. See Sun 1922; Perdue 2005; Rohlf 2003, 2016.

28. Gregory Rohlf's 2016 book is the most comprehensive discussion of these development efforts in Qinghai as Chinese state-building under Mao. See also Naughton 1988; Rohlf 2003; Yeh 2003a; Fischer 2008, 2009b.

29. See *Guide* 1988, Wang and Bai 1991. Fischer (2009a, 39) argues that the historically Tibetan regions of Qinghai and the TAR "had been the worst cases of economic lagging in China from the beginning of the reforms years until the mid-1990s."

30. See Goodman 2004b.

31. See also Oakes 2004, Holbig 2004, Yeh 2009, 2013, Makley 2013, Ptackova 2013.

32. HNZZ 2001, TRXZ 2001. See Bass 1998, Lin Yi 2005, Postiglione et al. 2005, Fischer 2009b.

1. The Dangers of the Gift Master

1. See chapter 3, in which I take up Foucault's notion of "heterotopia" in more depth.

2. I refer here to students of Boas like Gladys Reichard and Zora Neale Hurston.

3. See also Hymes 1972, Dwyer 1979, Fabian 1983, Briggs 1986, Tedlock and Mannheim 1995, Visweswaran 1997, Trouillot 2003, Bilu 2015.

4. See especially de Castro 1998 and programmatic statements in Henare et al. 2006, and their critics, Keane 2009, 2013; Laidlaw 2012; Course 2010; Bessire and Bond 2014; Bessire 2014; Kohn 2015. This approach applied to Inner Asian peoples was associated especially with Caroline Humphrey and her students at the University of Cambridge. See their special issue of *Inner Asia 9* (2007), Empson 2011, Pedersen 2013.

5. See for example Sahlins 2000, Das 2007, Hansen and Stepputat 2006, Mahmood 2005, Trouillot 2003, Chakrabarty 2000.

6. See Wagner 1977; Strathern 1988; Carsten 2000, 2003; Stasch 2009.

7. See for example the influential "actor-network theories" of Latour 2005 and his critics and reformulations, as well as Gell 1998, Deleuze and Guattari 1987.

8. See especially Silverstein 1976, 2004; Bakhtin 1981; Hill 1986, 1995; Hill and Irvine 1993; Irvine 1979; Tedlock and Mannheim 1995; Engelke 2007; Stasch 2009; Keane 2003, 2009, 2014; Blommaert 2015.

9. For more on the notion of performativity in linguistic anthropology, see Silverstein 2004, Goffman 1981, Bauman and Briggs 1990.

10. See especially Goffman 1981, Lempert 2013 on addressivity, also Agha 2007 on recipient design.

11. See Lassiter 2005.

12. Though I was officially registered with the local PSB, I never had officially assigned handlers.

13. Sadly, due to ongoing state repression, I cannot name and thereby personally credit my Tibetan research collaborators. I identify them in the acknowledgements with nicknames and initials instead.

14. A Sanskrit word meaning both thunderbolt and diamond, a *vajra* (Tib. *rdo rje*) is the main symbol and ritual implement of Vajrayana, or tantric, Buddhism. It is most often manifest as a small, two-sided, hand-held scepter and wielded to demonstrate the indestructible nature of the Buddha Dharma.

15. See Goffman 1981; Tsing 2000, 2005; Stasch 2009; Agha 2007; Keane 2014.

16. See Keane 2003, 2009, 2014; Engelke 2007.

17. See LZDD 1997, RG et al. 2005, CGDJTR 2006.

18. See especially Lempert 2012 for a linguistic anthropological analysis of Geluk monastic debate practices in India.

19. Early Tibetologists like Nebeskey-Wojkowitz (1956) or Stephan Beyer (1973) were outliers in the field, but in the 1980s and 1990s anthropologists like Sherry Ortner (1978), Lichter and Epstein (1983), Samuel (1993), Blondeau (1995), Macdonald (1997), Karmay (1994, 1998), and Huber (1999) began to focus more on Tibetans' complex relationships with deities. In religious studies, scholars also began to focus more on ritual practice and deity cults to rethink Buddhism in practice (Lopez 1997b, Lopez 1998). This has led to a most recent flourishing of scholarly efforts to rethink the nature of Tibetan politics, violence and statecraft, lay-monastic relations, and the complexities of Tibetan notions of personhood, kinship, fortune, and economics (Mills 2003; Bell 2007; Makley 2007; da Col 2007, 2012a; Diemberger 2007; Cuevas 2008; Dalton 2012; Smyer-Yu 2013; Zivkovic 2013; Yeh 2013; Jacoby 2014).

20. The best scholarly analyses of these fundamentally dialogic relations between lay and monastic, Buddhist and non-Buddhist ritual practices among Tibetans historically are Mumford 1989, Samuel 1993, Huber 1999 and Jacoby 2014.

21. See da Col 2007, 2012a, 2012b; see also Ortner 1978, Mills 2003, Jacoby 2014.

22. Indeed the Tibetan term often translated as "universe" is *snod bcud* (lit. "container-essence, environments-and-sentient beings").

23. See especially Ohnuma 2005, 119; as well as Derrida 1992, Klima 2002, Mills 2003, Makley 2007, Langford 2009, Dalton 2012.

24. This nexus of relations I would say is what Weiner (2012) argues was definitive of "imperial" relations in the frontier zone, which persisted into the twentieth century and even all the way up to the CCP's 1958 "democratic reforms" (see below). For the early modern period then, after the fall of the Qing dynasty, Weiner, following Bulag, refers to this political nexus as "subimperial" relations.

25. See Weiner 2012, Yangdon Dhondup 2011, HNZZ 2001, Stevenson 1999.

26. See JMTC 1988, 731; GGLMTR 2002, 37; GDLT 2002; LZKR 2005; Gendun Palzang 2007.

27. See chapter 3 for more on treasure vases and place-making.

28. According to Pu Wencheng, the monastery housed up to 2,300 monks in its heyday in the eighteenth century, but by the time CCP work teams surveyed the region, they counted 1,712 monks, and 43 resident incarnate lamas. By then, monastic grounds occupied some 380 mu (~62 acres) and included 3 monastic colleges and over 35 temples and assembly halls (1990, 154).

29. Note that non-Geluk lamas in Rebgong also wrote critiques of what they saw as the immoral behavior of Buddhist practitioners and other pretenders. See Stoddard 2012 for an account of the Rebgong Nyingma community's founding lama rig 'dzin dpal ldan bkra shis' (1688–1743) diatribe about unscrupulous, boastful and false monks and tantrists in the ferment of the early eighteenth-century Rebgong.

30. See Weiner 2012 for the most detailed account, based on close readings of Chinese-language documents, of CCP-led socialist transformation in Rebgong in the 1950s. Also see NTNDLZ 2007; Goldstein 2009, 2013; Goldstein et al. 2009.

31. Rumors abounded in Rebgong about the suspicious nature of the young eight Shartshang's recognition, and the allegedly dishonorable uses of offerings to his estate by his older male relatives. The fact that he received a Chinese-language secular education until he became a monk at age eleven didn't help.

32. This was the Tisamling College, one of three at Rongbo Monastery. It was founded in 1630 by the first Shartshang lama. Since Rongbo came under the jurisdiction of the Geluk Shartshang lamas, the majority of monks have belonged to this college. It is now subject to state quotas on numbers of monk entrants.

33. See Caple 2011 for a detailed account of the cultural politics of this process in post-Mao Rebgong Buddhist monasteries.

34. See especially Tuttle 2005 for a detailed account of the ninth Panchen Lama's struggles with the Dalai Lama and his government in Lhasa. See also TIN 1997 for more on the tenth Panchen Lama's life.

35. See Harris 2001.

36. See Barnett 1997.

37. See Caple 2011, 39; also GDLT 2002, Gendun Palzang 2007.

38. See also HNWSZL 4 1997.

39. According to CCP work teams surveys in the 1950s, Rongbo Monastery directly owned only 1000 mu of farmland in the valley (~165 acres, relatively little compared to other monasteries in Rebgong and elsewhere in Amdo), as well as 1000s of head of livestock. In 1980, prefecture officials returned only a part of the land comprising the monastic complex to monastic control. It is now confined to a one-kilometer-long campus along what was the main road in Longwu town (Pu Wencheng 1990; also see Stevenson 1999, Caple 2011).

40. For the most in-depth discussion of this tension between palpable divine and demonic presence and abstract symbolism among Tibetan Buddhists historically, see Dalton 2012. See also Harris 2001.

41. See Jean and John Comaroff (1999) on "occult economies" in contrast to recent advocates of "multiple ontologies" like Pedersen (2013) who claim the Comaroffs' use of that phrase reduces ritualized exchange to political economy. While I see merit in Pedersen's critique, he himself still seems to treat only "shamanism" as "occult," and he seems to miss the Comaroffs' arguments that neoliberal capitalist exchanges in practice can be just as occult, hidden, or mysterious as such ritual transactions.

42. See Makley 2007 for a detailed account of this process in the famous Amdo monastery town of Labrang.

2. The Mountain Deity and the State

1. Chapter 2 is a revised and expanded version of my article, "The Politics of Presence: Voice, Deity Possession, and Dilemmas of Development among Tibetans in the PRC," CSSH 55, no. 3 (July 2013): 665–700. Reprinted with Permission.

2. The opening invocation given above is from "dkar phyogs skyongs ba'i yul lha se ku bya khyung la dbang gi 'phrin las gtso bor bsgrub par bskul tshul gyi cho ga 'dod dgu'i char 'beb shes bya ba bzhugs so" (Procedure for entreating the virtuous regional deity Seku Shachong to use his powerful action to shower down all wishes). All subsequent excerpts are from this text.

3. Nagas (Tib. *klu*) are ancient serpent demons who control underground water sources.

4. See especially Das and Poole 2004. See also Tsing 1993, Anagnost 1997, Coronil 1997, Mueggler 2001, Hart 2004.

5. Deity mediumship practices among Tibetans, especially those involving non-Buddhist deities, have been portrayed by scholars and officials as antimodern since the early twentieth century. The Tibetan exiled intellectual Jamyang Norbu (2005), in his diatribe against Tibetans' irremediably "superstitious" nature, in addition to disparaging the "fruity" young Tibetan exiled woman recently claiming to be possessed by mountain goddesses, mentions the newly exiled Dalai Lama in 1964 sending his Tibetan state oracles to greet and dismiss the mountain deity who had spontaneously possessed a Tibetan man, telling him that mountain deities were no longer needed with the advent of modernization. Melvyn Goldstein, Ben Jiao, and Tanzen Lhundrup (2009), in their analysis of the famous Nyemo incident during the Cultural Revolution in the TAR, reserve the terms *hysteria* and *imagined worlds* only for the Tibetans who claimed to be inhabited by deities and not for the fanatical Red Guards who waged brutal battles against each other in the name of Mao (see Makley 2009b).

6. Hence also, as suggested by the term *spirit*, in the common phrase "spirit possession," psychological or medical approaches that pathologize such practices but maintain the sovereignty of the self by reducing them to the altered mental states of a nonetheless singular person (see Mills 2008, 139), or sociological approaches that dismiss the presence of invisible beings by diagnosing the underlying causes of any form of possession as the unconscious confirmation of or resistance to practitioners' positions in hierarchical societies (e.g., Lewis 1971). For more recent anthropological debates, see Boddy 1994, Ong 1987, Lawrence 2000, Comaroff and Comaroff 1999, Taussig 1993.

7. See especially Nagano 2000; KTG 2005, 2006, 2009; Buffetrille 2008.

8. See Feuchtwang 2004, Chau 2005.

9. See Makley 2005, 2007, also Anagnost 2004, Mazard 2011, Weiner 2012.

10. For an important introduction to Bakhtin from the perspective of linguistic anthropology, see Hill 1986; also see Hill and Irvine 1993, Hill 1995, Tedlock and Mannheim 1995, Keane 2001. In Tibetan studies, Stanley R. Mumford (1989) was the first to systematically apply Bakhtin to an analysis of contestation between Tibetan Buddhist lamas and their "shamanist" rivals in a rural Nepali community. However, Mumford never fully explored the ethnographic implications of Bakhtin's work on linguistic form in sociopolitical contexts.

11. Versus, for example, the essays in Feuchtwang and Wang (2001).

12. See Diemberger 2005 for an account of such pollution causing the evacuation of a divine lake.

13. See Stuart et al. 1995, snying po rgyal and Solomon Rino 2009, Xirejiancuo 2008, KTG 2009 for accounts of this process of embodiment.

14. The missionary ethnographer Robert Ekvall for example noted in the 1920s and 1930s that ritual practices targeting deities of the land were much more elaborated among Tibetan farmers than among pastoralists (1939, 65). Although forms of deity possession are found among Tibetans across regions, Rebgong is the only Tibetan region where male mountain deity mediums play such central roles in village life and annual Lurol festivals led by mountain deity mediums are so predominant. However, the twenty or so dewa that hold Lurol are all farming villages located in the lower reaches of the valley. None of the higher mountain villages observe it. Some local historians argue that Lurol arose among farming dewa on the Rongbo

valley floor because it was originally about propitiating the underground serpent demons (Tib. *klu*) who controlled essential water supplies for river and spring-fed irrigation—hence the name of the festival. See ri gdengs 1994; Stuart et al. 1995; Epstein and Peng 1998; Stevenson 1999, 2005; Nagano 2000; 'brug thar and sangs rgyas tshe ring 2005; KTG 2006, 2009; snying po rgyal and Solomon Rino 2008; Buffetrille 2008; Xirejiancuo 2008.

15. See Chau 2005, Perry 2011.

16. See Rohlf 2003, Yeh 2008.

17. From here on, I use the terms *village* and *dewa* interchangeably. According to local historiography, Tibetan communities coalesced as seven dewas on the Rongbo valley floor (Tib. *rong bo sde bdun*) at the time of the first Sakya settlers in the thirteenth century. But the dewa unit took on new administrative importance in the early eighteenth century under the second Shartshang lama when he incorporated neighboring villages of the now-Geluk Monastery as patron villages, grouped under larger tribal rubrics (Tib. *shog*), with obligations to support the newly founded annual Monlam Festival (the so-called 21 smon shog). See Gendun Palzang 2007, JBGP 2009, Yangdon 2011, GDKS 2012.

18. Significantly, Jima scholar mkhar rtse rgyal (KTG 2006) argues that Lurol dances re-create and commemorate ancient battle victory celebrations when Tibetan imperial troops in the region were powerful enough to force Tang dynasty troops to sign a treaty in the ninth century. From the late nineteenth century on, Rebgong's central Rongbo valley saw the beginnings of significant settlements of Chinese and Muslim traders, as well as the first occupations by Qing and then KMT forces, and American and European Christian missions. But it was the forced taxes and depredations of the Muslim warlords under the Xining-based Ma clan beginning in the 1920s that most Tibetan elders still talk about as the first radical disjuncture in the life of the valley (see chapter 3). See Stevenson 1999, SBPG 2007, Xirejiancuo 2008, HNWSZL 3 1996, Weiner 2012.

19. See Carrasco 1959, Blondeau 1995. Robert Ekvall noted the remarkably unitary and communal nature of Tibetan farming villages in Rebgong, likening them to "miniature states." According to Ekvall, only authorized dewa subjects, those fully ensconced in networks of reciprocal exchanges, could cultivate fields. Elders also worked to harmonize cultivation schedules and adjudicate use of dewa common lands and resources. Further, opening new fields required communal permission and sale of lands to outsiders was anathema (1939, 34; 1954).

20. I am particularly inspired here by Erik Mueggler's work (2001). Hereafter, I use the capitalized epithet "the State" to refer to this abstract agent in the way Tibetans invoked it in everyday speech as an active, intentioned, social persona. Similarly, I capitalize such uses of commensurate figures like "the People" or "the Masses."

21. Official prefecture and county historiography tell versions of this story, while more recent Tibetan histories offer alternative accounts. See HNZZ 2001, TRXZ 2001, HNWSZL 3 1996, HNWSZL 1 1992, NTNDLZ 2007, Stevenson 1999, Weiner 2012.

22. Xirejiancuo (2008) claims that prior to 1958 Jima villagers owned a total of 3,400 mu (~226 hectares, ~560 acres) of cultivated fields, 1,400 irrigated or valley floor and 2,000 mu on the unirrigated, terraced mountainsides. Other Jima elders

I spoke to insisted that Jima villagers owned some 2,200 mu of fields on the valley floor alone. A monk historian I spoke with who was interviewing elderly monks about Rongbo Monastery's pre-CCP economy insisted that monks and monastic managers used forms of usury (indebtedness engineering) to claim ownership of some valley floor lands (euphemistically called *dkor zhing*, "offered / donated fields"), including some in Jima. But if CCP work teams' surveys are to be believed, the monastery did not ultimately accumulate huge holdings relative to other monasteries, perhaps due to the particularly solidary nature of the Tibetan dewa there, many of which (versus in Labrang for example) predated the founding of the monastery or at least its conversion to the Geluk sect. See Nian and Bai 1993, 155; Pu Wencheng 1990; JBGP 2009.

23. See also Guo 2001, Cai 2003, Li Zhang 2006 for similar processes of land expropriation occurring throughout the PRC by the late 1990s and early 2000s. In his 2009 study of those processes, George Lin says that the most profitable form of land development was the conversion of rural collective land to urban commercial real estate, due to the large price differential between those categories of property. The most important source of profit, he goes on to say, were the "land conveyance fees" (Ch. *churang jin*) that commercial land users paid to local officials. Those fees were most often collected and retained by municipal and county bureaus; little of it was remitted to the central state, and none were shared with rural collectives (9).

24. This was true in other Tibetan towns and cities as well. For analyses of the situation in Lhasa, see especially Barnett 2006; Yeh 2008, 2013; Fischer 2005.

25. I am especially inspired here by Talal Asad's essay in Das and Poole 2004. Note that Weiner, in his detailed account of increasing state-local tensions under early CCP state-building efforts in Rebgong in the 1950s, recounts how CCP work teams called for Tibetans to stand up in the new nation-state as "masters of their own homes," yet internal reports lamented how Tibetans still had a backward "guest" mentality (e.g., they accepted their status as patrons and subjects of Tibetan lamas and lay leaders). Meanwhile Tibetan officials complained to party inspectors that in reality "Tibetans do the housework, [but] the Chinese are the masters" (2012, 387, 392).

26. Beginning in the 1950s, Tibetan translators worked hard to invent new terms to convey the alien concepts of CCP state ideology to locals. Today, entire departments are devoted to such work. Typical phrases are direct calques of Chinese slogans and are exclusively used in official contexts and media. See Tsering Shakya 1994, Tournadre and Brown 2003.

27. I had not mentioned the topic of land expropriation before this moment. My interview with Tshering was tape recorded with his permission. It was conducted in Amdo Tibetan, but Chinese loanwords figured prominently in his speech. In all subsequent excerpts from the interview, I provide some of the original Tibetan terms he used in order to highlight those categories, but I note all uses of Chinese loanwords by providing the original Chinese.

28. I was told that by the mid-2000s, the richest of these Jima households owned several commercial buildings and brought in over 100,000 yuan/year, while most Jima building owners averaged about 35,000 yuan/year in rental income. This contrasted sharply with per capita incomes of rural farmers and nomads, as well as with poor households in Jima, who received only several 100 yuan/month in welfare subsidies.

29. Elizabeth Perry notes that the national NSC campaign (2006–7) was the first time since the Maoist years that every county official was required to attend week-long training sessions (2011, 40). In direct contrast to the goals of its original design-ers, who sought to shore up rural autonomy in the face of market reforms, Perry cites evidence that the national campaign amounted in many places to land grabs by local cadres and forced resettlements of villagers in urban apartments, all in the name of "village beautification" (42; cf. Day and Hale 2007, *Xinhua* 2007).

30. See Kojima and Kokubun 2002.

31. HNZZ 2001 recounts and dismisses the initial criticisms of the proposal to break up the communes and implement a so-called Household Responsibility Sys-tem by some old Maoist leaders: "Some responded that '[we] have been working collectively for 30 years, and in one night [we'll] return to the way it was before liberation.' They mistakenly thought that the responsibility system was just 'dividing fields and individually farming' (Ch. *fentian dangan*)." Yet that is precisely what many Tibetan villagers felt it was (2001, 298).

32. The origins of the term *thongru* in Tibetan are obscure. The Rebgong Tibetan scholar mkhar rtse rgyal speculated that it is of Tibetan origin (KTG 2005), while the Russian Tibetologist Roerich argued it was a Chinese loanword, the Ming- and Qing-era term *tongshi* for Tibetan interpreters who worked for local imperial officials (1958, 92–93). I thank Larry Epstein for calling my attention to the latter.

33. See Judith Irvine's discussion of multiple types of formality in speech events (1979).

34. See Makley 2013.

35. In 1998 new central laws were passed ostensibly to protect rural village autonomy by calling for formal elections of village leaders.

36. I could never get an accurate sense of how the conflict broke down demo-graphically. Some asserted that only a few households were actually directly involved, and their supporters broke out primarily along kinship lines. It seemed however, that the majority of villagers supported the return of Dorje as Shachong's medium, but not necessarily for the same reasons as his closest supporters. The routed elders came from wealthy landlord households, but there were also (but fewer) well-off state officials and landlord households among Dorje's strong supporters. The main differ-ence seemed to be that Dorje's most prominent supporters were almost exclusively of younger generations than the elders they opposed.

37. Benno Weiner, in his detailed account of that time in Tsekhog (Ch. Zeku) County, Rebgong, describes a 1952 speech in which a visiting party superior tells local work-team members not to inform Tibetan tribal leaders of their tribes' planned disappearance. And, after Mao's "High Tide of Socialism" launch, he describes an internal 1956 report that lays out plans to settle all Tibetan pastoralists while bring-ing in 100s of 1000s of Chinese farmers to turn the grasslands into farms (2012, 366). See also Rohlf 2003, 2016 and Yeh 2003a on the establishment of state farms in Qinghai as one post-1958 response to Tibetan unrest. Rohlf states that between 1954 and 1959 750,000 Chinese moved into Qinghai, concentrated in urban areas (2003, 462). HNZZ 2001 describes two periods of state-sponsored immigration to Huangnan Prefecture: 1958–61 when at least fifteen state farms were established, and a post-Cultural Revolution influx of Han Chinese to run new state factories (335). As Rohlf put it: "Resettlement is an enduring component in the Party's efforts at

social engineering and must be understood within an unbroken geopolitical arc that links Mao, Deng and Jiang" (457).

3. Othering Spaces, Cementing Treasure

1. Longwu town is at about 2,500 meters above sea level.

2. The 2000 census reports a registered population of 23,294 for Longwu town, versus only 6,440 for Tshothang township, the first rural township in the Upper Narrows. That small township included some twenty farming and pastoralist or semi-pastoralist villages.

3. For more on the central importance of pilgrimage practices among Tibetans both before and after CCP intervention, see especially Huber 1999, also Chenaktsang 2010, Ramble 2014, Buffetrille 2014.

4. This number of villagers is only an estimate of officially registered inhabitants in 2008 based on 2000 census data; it does not reflect the reality of people actually living there full-time (see below). As far as I knew, there were no non-Tibetan residents. Statistics reported by village leaders in 2013 claimed 195 households and 1,061 people.

5. Lyrics to "The Golden Realm of Rebgong" were written by Dorje Thar. Sung in the modern operatic style of Chinese pop songs, the song was famously sung by the well-known Tibetan singer Dragpa Tshering in the early–mid 2000s; it was performed at the televised New Year concert in Rebgong in 2003 and was frequently played on the radio.

6. In linguistic anthropology circles, this process of conversion has been referred to as "transduction," a material-semiotic process of shifting among different embodied forms that is ever-present in human communication and complementary to processes of "translation." It is another way to talk about the practice of what I have called "striving for indexicality." See Silverstein 2003, Handman 2014 .

7. See especially Keane 2003, 2009; also Fehervary 2013.

8. See especially Graeber 2001, Maurer 2006, Keane 2008b.

9. In fact, contrary to how some of Foucault's translators interpreted his notion of heterotopia as an exclusively spatial politics, Foucault was explicit that such other-spaces entailed (or attempted to make manifest) "other-times" ("heterochronies") as well (1967, 6). Thus I find this earlier approach of Foucault's to materiality and built environments more useful than how his later essays on the disciplinary nature of built environments have been interpreted. See for example Faubion 2008. Also see Holston 1989, Lawrence and Low 1990, Zukosky 2007, Dehaene and Cauter 2008.

10. Notions of distributed agency have been central in anthropologists' efforts to counter Westerners' presumptions of a universal intentioned human subject or self (see Strathern 1988). Alfred Gell (1998) most famously developed this view in relation to material artifacts, yet he still tends to assume universal cognitive structures in human perceivers.

11. China's Three Gorges Dam holds the world record for the largest concrete pour for a single project.

12. By 2011 China was consuming over half the world's cement. See Mi Shi 2013 for more on the costs of central planners' push for nationwide urbanization through "integration of rural and urban" policies (Ch. *chenzhenhua*).

13. According to the World Bank, by 2007 sixteen of the world's twenty most polluted cities were in China (World Bank 2007). When I drove across Amdo Tibetan regions of Qinghai province in 2013, it was clear that such concrete production-related pollution had found its way there. Concrete factories had sprung up at regular intervals along all major rivers, and even county towns now lived under a haze of smog.

14. Here I am inspired by theorists drawing on phenomenology to rethink the nature of concrete in architectural design and practice. See Lawrence and Low 1990; Melhuish 2005, 2007; Thomas 2006; Van der Hoorn 2009; Fehervary 2013.

15. See recent reports of Chinese government crackdowns on "illegal" buildings (Daub 2010), resident protests over forced demolitions (Li Zhang 2006, Qin Shao 2013, Chu 2014), and 2011–13 scandals over the use of subpar concrete (cheaper sea sand) in major construction projects in China's eastern cities, including failed high-speed railways and skyscraper projects stalled midway due to safety concerns. See Verdery 1999, Humphrey 2002, Van der Hoorn 2009, Pedersen 2013, and Chu 2014 on the cultural politics of failed infrastructure and disrepair.

16. That phrase was coined by Chinese premier Zhu Rongji in 1998 to describe a poorly constructed bridge, and it took on national prominence in the wake of the Sichuan earthquake school collapses. The earthquake occurred during school hours; the total number of students killed in collapsed buildings remains under debate. Chinese state media officially claims 5,335 dead. Others estimate up to 9,000 students and teachers killed. See chapter 5.

17. In the Tongren County Education Bureau, this was reflected most prominently since the early 2000s in the pressure on education officials to demonstrate progress in implementing the "Two Fundamentals" (Ch. Liang Ji) education campaign: universalizing nine years of compulsory education, and eliminating illiteracy among young people. As with other such policy campaigns, Tibetan regions lagged behind Chinese regions for years in implementing them. The Great Open the West campaign in 2000 brought renewed emphasis on finally carrying out such development goals out west.

18. Hence the harassment and illegal detentions of parents protesting shoddy school construction practices after the earthquake. See chapter 5.

19. This was in fact a renewed effort to decentralize education funding. Since the mid-1980s local school districts in Rebgong had been urged to "take responsibility" for raising revenue (HNZZ 2001). For more on this in Tibetan regions, see Bass 1998, Upton 1999, Bangso 2004, Kolås and Thowsen 2005, Postiglione et al. 2005.

20. The best in-depth English-language account of this process in Amdo Tibetan regions is Upton 1999. See also Pema Bhum 2008 and Hartley and Sciaffini-Vedani 2008.

21. See Lin Yi 2005. According to the head of the prefecture Education Bureau in 2007, Huangnan had more than one hundred schools, while the five main high schools were located in Longwu town. Two of the five were designated "standard" (nonnationality) schools, which were dominated by Han and Hui students respectively.

22. Geshes, mentioned in the epigraph above, are monk-scholars who have completed the entire curriculum in the major Geluk monasteries.

23. Indeed I was struck by how many highly well-intentioned and committed foreign development workers, willing to live in the region for months and even years at a time, never learned to speak Chinese, much less Amdo Tibetan, well enough to converse.

24. The spread and elaboration of "audit culture" and its consequences for both development workers and recipients in international development and philanthropy has been a central concern in the anthropology of development and humanitarianism. See Escobar 1995, Strathern 2000, Scherz 2014.

25. I would add that such effort at communication in others' languages is precisely what is entailed in the anthropologist Johannes Fabian's call (1983, 32) for theorists to move beyond older notions of the (scientific, modern) superiority of Western notions of timespace that denigrated non-Western others as "primitives" and enter into "intersubjective time" with interlocutors instead.

26. It became clear to me in 2007–8 that the officials of the Huangnan Prefecture and Tongren County Education Bureaus in Rebgong were in fact competitors for revenue to fund projects and thereby aid their careers.

27. According to statistics I obtained, in spring 2008 in Tongren County alone, the Education Bureau was directly managing fifteen school construction or repair projects, a total of 4,658,300 yuan, two-thirds of which came from foreign and private domestic donors. Those numbers do not include all the projects the thirteen school district heads were managing, including the Kharnak one.

28. "Donor plaque inflation" was widespread in temples and monasteries as well. In the reform-era rebuilding process, Tibetans had always recorded lists of Buddhist donors, but since the late 1990s especially even individual prayer wheels had plaques. See the Epilogue.

29. In fact, I found that in the absence of many state services, schoolteachers and grassroots education officials were often acting as de facto social workers, taking on duties far beyond their school-related work (connecting rural Tibetans with clothing, medical care, food, stoves, etc.). For example, in the increasing numbers of boarding schools, it was women teachers who were doing the lion's share of care for young students, being called on to act as de facto mothers, even as many had their own young children in villages or towns far away.

30. See for example Makley 2007, Nietupski 1999 on Labrang Monastery.

31. Recent years have seen the rise of a vigorous Tibetan and international scholarship investigating the history and ritual worlds of the nonsectarian tantric movement that came to be called the Rebgong Community of Many Yogins (Tib. *Rebgong sngags mang*). See Yangdon Dhondup 2013, Stoddard 2013, Sihlé 2013.

32. The temple, sandwiched between the school grounds uphill and the party office downhill, was more than seventy years old, having been burned down in the 1930s when the Muslim chief Ma Bufang's troops attacked the valley (see below). It was saved from destruction during the Cultural Revolution because it was used for grain storage. The Jowo or Sakyamuni Buddha, flanked by Padmasambhava and Tsongkhapa, take pride of place in the central altar. They are guarded on either side by the old Sakya sect Buddhist protector Gur and by a pantheon of village mountain deities (Chazey, Makgol, and Nyanchen). The village's root lama, gser khri tshang, was a Geluk trulku and teacher of the current Rongbo ruling lama Shartshang before he died.

33. The great Nyingma lama Shapkar is perhaps the most famous of these traveling lamas, but Geluk lamas from Rongbo followed suit, including the seventh Shartshang and the third Arol Tshang who gave teachings and redistributed offerings in the Upper Narrows up until their arrests in 1958. See chapter 4.

34. In Nepal and Bhutan stupas in fact often have massive painted eyes on their peaks.

35. In part because the Ma "warlords" or "bandits" (Tib. Ma jag) were enemies of the ascendant CCP, Tibetan oral and written history in Rebgong is particularly eloquent on that subject. Indeed, I found that under the post-Mao silent pact the Mas, most often depicted as monstrous predators, in many ways come to stand in for the CCP in Tibetans' historical accounts. See Weiner 2012, HNWSZL 1 1992, SBPG 2007.

36. Note that Akhu Gyamtsho states some households escaped this fate by pleading with their "friends and relatives" among the Ma troops to spare them—as elsewhere, the attacking troops included Tibetan soldiers, some of whom were mercenaries, others had been conscripted as part of a Ma-imposed "militia tax."

37. Note that the eighty-year-old Gabzang, himself a former official in the Ma regime, in our first long interview in Jima village said donkeys and cattle from Jima were confiscated and used for this purpose. He remembered the severed heads displayed in town.

38. Recalling Tibetans' rage at the Ma regime's claims to their corvee labor for construction downriver, Weiner notes that when CCP work teams organized the construction of the Zeku County seat upriver in 1955, Tibetan tribes in the Upper Narrows were required to provide 1000s of head of pack cattle for transporting wood, cement, and food upriver (2012, 332).

39. Importantly, in some ways it was the tenth Panchen Lama's predecessor, the ninth Panchen Lama who helped inaugurate the early modern Buddhist restoration in Rebgong. On a tour to Rongbo and Labrang Monasteries in June 1936, a year before Ma Bufang's counterattack in the Upper Narrows, he initiated into the Kalacakra mandala several high Geluk lamas who would go on to be important Buddhist advocates and abode-builders, including the seventh Shartshang, the third Arol tshang, and the sixth Gongtang. Those three lamas went on to hold many of the massive Kalacakra empowerment ceremonies for monastic and lay audiences across Rebgong (including many in the Upper Narrows) and Labrang regions in the 1940s and 1950s (see GDKS 2012, Gendun Rabsal 2013). Further, Weiner notes that between 1953 and 1958 Zeku County just upriver from Kharnak "witnessed the greatest period of monastery building in the area's history" (2012, 350). Weiner eventually concludes that the region was not in fact fully pacified until the early 1960s. See also Tuttle 2005; Pu Wencheng 1990, 481–90.

40. The three sections of the Shuk federation (Tib. shug lung pa gsum) included two large dewa's on either side of Kharnak.

41. In 1958, the Shuk and Tshothang townships were lumped together under Hongxing Commune. In 1959, they were merged with the pastoralist Xingfu Commune upriver. In 1961, they were separated into two communes again, only to be rejoined in 1966 (TRXZ 2001, 39–48).

42. Under the post-Mao silent pact Akhu Gyamtsho's history conspicuously avoids narrating the Maoist years. I do not have much information on how Kharnak

villagers fared during those decades, who may or may not have joined the rebels, and who, in fact, was made to destroy the stupa. As Benno Weiner notes, the first open rebellions in 1958 were spearheaded by men from more remote nomadic tribes upriver (2012, 412). Akhu Tenzin told me of an elaborate system during the early months of the Cultural Revolution when Chinese Red Guards assigned Tibetan villages to destroy particular temples in Rongbo Monastery. He insisted that the leaders were Chinese but the vast majority of destruction was carried out by Tibetans (most under duress, but some, he said, were ideologically or opportunistically motivated).

43. In 2008, villagers still routinely referred to that village, always using the Chinese loanword, as the "commune" (Ch. *gongshe*). See chapter 4.

44. Teachers and officials from Kharnak were playing important roles upriver, including in the neighboring county of Zeku.

45. Source for epigraph of this section GDKS (2012, 114). Emphasis mine.

46. Numbers of primary schools fluctuated widely from the late 1970s to the 2000s with the vicissitudes of education policy. HNZZ reports a peak of 526 primary schools in HN prefecture in 1977, down to 366 in 1980 and then 178 in 1990 (2001, 1043). A new spate of primary school building emerged after the Great Open the West campaign and renewed campaigns to promote universal education (like *liang ji*, 2 basics) in collaboration with IGO's and foreign and domestic NGOs (like Project Hope, Spring Buds, etc.).

47. In the 2000s, the vast majority of rural Tibetan officials were men. Educated women tended to end up as (lower-paid) school teachers.

48. Note that this new rubric was a reemphasis on rhetoric and practices already in place since post-Mao reforms (e.g., in the shift to a "responsibility system" and the move to decentralized education funding) (HNZZ 2001, 1042). But the 2007 NSC campaign placed greatest emphasis on moving away from socialist spectacles of showing good use of entitlements to demonstrating worthiness for state funds first. In prefecture deputy head Dorje Tsering's 2007 speech about NSC work, he urged officials to annually increase the amount of capital in the form of loans to help farmers and nomads with construction projects.

49. See Verdery 1996 and Guyer 2007 for more on the anthropology of capitalist time politics.

50. In many ways, Maoist state-building and development all along consisted in a series of utopic reconstruction projects; recall the huge other-spaces out west of state farms and communes, especially after the "study Dazhai" movement in the 1970s.

51. See Melhuish 2005, 2007; van der Hoorn 2009; Fehervary 2013.

52. According to HNZZ 2001, before the 1970s, the vast majority of buildings in town were one-story pounded earth and wood compounds. The first concrete apartment and state office building boom in Longwu town began in the 1970s.

53. In Rebgong's periurban and rural villages this meant a prefecturewide campaign to cement village pathways, to which households were supposed to contribute three hundred yuan each. As the Tibet Heritage Fund blog pointed out, the NSC campaign had led to a widespread devaluation of Tibetan traditional architecture, as well as the loss of knowledge and appreciation among Tibetans of traditional construction techniques and their unique advantages in that region (THF 2010).

54. Like most major policy initiatives, this School Consolidation Program was first used in Chinese regions to the east and only later made mandatory for school officials in Tibetan regions. As usual then, implementation there has had different implications for Tibetan communities. See Yang and Wang 2007, Martinson 2008.

55. Huangnan prefecture deputy head Dorje Tsering, in a 2007 speech admonishing officials to do better work in construction projects, offers a litany of criticisms, including too rapid building, little research, and neglect of local conditions. Further, during the unrest in 2008, he took a tour of schools and admonished officials to stop pursuing what he called "show projects" or "cadre achievement projects" and focus instead on "People's" (Ch. *minsheng*) projects like education advancement. Caple (2011) in her fieldwork among monks in Rebgong between 2008–10 also notes monks' frequent complaints about the superficiality of new painted facades.

56. Chinese investigative reporting on primary schools in the late 2000s under new school consolidation policies revealed the conflicts and corruption at the heart of those efforts in Chinese regions. For example, in one region, angry villagers and donors discovered their new foreigner-funded Hope School buildings abandoned, repurposed, and the equipment redistributed or sold off after students were made to attend schools far from their home villages. See Martinson 2008.

57. This process in highland farming villages predated and in some ways laid templates for the resettlement of pastoralist communities further upriver, which greatly accelerated after 2008. See chapter 4.

58. Enticements included promises of subsidies for housing construction, low-interest loans, and (one-off) compensations for lost livestock.

59. Revealingly, the 2006 renovation was an intervention to repair the crumbling, inferior concrete and stucco tiles used in a renovation of the stupa just six years earlier, in 2000 (GDKS 2012, 112).

60. This impulse to scale up the dewa could help explain why some village leaders seemed to inflate numbers of villagers in our conversations. I estimated only about one thousand current residents, while some, like Kharnak's deity medium, estimated double that, in part because he was imagining Kharnak (hyperbolically) as a global diaspora, and explicitly counted people living "outside" in his count. Village leaders were proud of the translocal reach of the dewa and expected villagers elsewhere to maintain close relations with their home community.

61. Indeed by late spring 2008, I began to hear from education officials at various levels complaints about the work of Shawojia. Several of his underlings complained about his impatience with ritual niceties, saying that they experienced his leadership as cold and even cruel. One woman official who had conducted research for the prefecture that summer confided that his county had registered their lowest-ever scores on the university entrance exams. Meanwhile, she said, all he cared about was constructing shiny new buildings.

62. Not coincidentally, the term 'khyongs in Tibetan carries connotations of filling something up to capacity, and thus "fulfilling." Tropes of completeness in this way are strongly linked to notions of auspiciousness and good fortune for Tibetans, as in how the stages of the waxing (auspicious) and waning (inauspicious) moon structure the lunar calendar and all astrological divination practices.

63. I am most inspired here by recent anthropologists of money and value who are rethinking older theories such as those of Simmel. See especially Maurer 2006, Keane 2008b.

64. In lay Tibetans' amulets and household posters, Mao Zedong is often associated with wide-reaching (karmic) power (Tib. *dbang thang*), similar to that attributed to money. See da Col 2007.

65. Hence in contrast to the ways in which Chinese "spirit money" is used as a parallel currency in direct transactions with deities, Tibetans' household altars display national currencies in symbolic amounts only. Thus in Tibetan offerings to deities, number (amount of cash) is not ideally a direct index of the status or intent of the giver. Money in that context is more importantly an icon of transcendence, power, and vital efficacy (e.g., in borrowing statist/imperial power and scaling up globally by including exotic European currencies). Yet the vital efficacy of money on altars is still strongly indexical because Tibetan offrants insist on using *real* national or imperial currencies (versus Chinese spirit money).

66. In the valley, this was usually the purview of sngags pa, Nyingma married priests, but Drakpa told me they also consulted the village's well-known deity medium. Geluk monks and lamas will also perform treasure vase rites. See Huber 1999, Da Col 2012a, Jacoby 2014 for more on this.

67. In contrast to widespread practices among Tibetans since at least the tenth century of discovering Buddhist-empowered "treasures" (texts, objects) that emerge from the ground (see Bernstein 2011, Germano 1998, Terrone 2010), in Rebgong Tibetans also put treasures back into the ground to revitalize its and their own fortune. Farming villages in Rebgong had the tradition of annual "placing the treasure" (Tib. *gter rgyag*) rites, in which on an appointed day in spring, men from each household would carry a "treasure bundle" of the kind described here up to regional mountain deity king Shachong's peak, where they would be buried in order to bring fortune for each household that year. Here, the Kharnak men turn that ritual to new, modernist purposes, scaling up from households to the communal unit of the dewa. Evidence suggests such adaptations of treasure rites are spreading in Amdo.

68. See the epilogue for more on the Buddha Drolma.

69. Shawojia told me that he had aspired to raise 2 million yuan in 2008 for county education. I learned that he had charged Gendun with raising 200,000 yuan of that from foreign sources, something he made sure to remind Gendun of whenever he saw him.

70. See Yeh 2013.

4. The Melodious Sound of the Right-Turning Conch

1. Catherine spent about a decade teaching English in Rebgong; indeed her time there coincided with the rise and decline of the Decade of the Foreigner. During that time, she brokered an astonishing number of small grants for Tibetan villagers, bringing in 100,000s of yuan and garnering multiple appreciation awards from the county and prefecture governments. She was also one of the two or three English teachers working among Tibetans, among dozens I have met over the years, who actually worked hard to learn to speak Tibetan. But in 2005 she was still in the early stages of that process.

2. Again, those numbers of inhabitants are only estimates, and do not reflect the actual number of people living there (see below).

3. As it turned out, Catherine too did not leave our 2005 summer visit uncaptured. During the following year she was able to broker another, larger NGO grant to help rebuild the Tshema Monastery stupas.

4. This of course would break down a simple distinction between "objective," or written, history and "subjective," or oral, history. I have explored this in more detail elsewhere (Makley 2005, 2007, 2013). See also Barnett 2010. Western theorists began to consider the politics of historiography with the advent of postcolonial theory from especially the late 1970s on. See Said 1978, White 1981, Nora 1989, Duara 1995, Hall 1998, Chakrabarty 2000, Kansteiner 2002.

5. See especially Duara 1995, but also Anagnost 1994, Makley 2005, 2007, Mazard 2011 on the importance of so-called "speaking bitterness" narratives (Ch. *suku*) as the crux of revolutionary praxis under the CCP during the Maoist years.

6. Indeed in official local histories, the specific history of land transfers and allocations under the CCP is a major space of silence and ambiguity. Note that in the tenth Panchen Lama's report to central authorities in 1961 (1997), he said that land deeds had been burned during the crackdown of 1958, making contemporary land claims very difficult to prove. In the HNZZ (2001), there is no mention at all of the specific process of land allocation even during the 1980s HRS. Land transfers were not tracked in Qinghai province statistical yearbooks through the early 2000s.

7. Note that in the Netherlands government's 2006 online description of its development goals in foreign countries, countries whose development goals were compatible with capitalist privatization and "global" market integration were deemed "partner countries," and China was not named as such. Instead, the description touted the role of NGO's in nonpartner countries to carry out grassroots reforms more friendly to the government's interests.

8. While plans for widespread sedentarization of Tibetan pastoralists have been part of CCP development goals since the 1950s (Weiner 2012), reviving after 1980 (HNZZ 2001, 219), and receiving new impetus with the Great Open the West campaign in the early 2000's, Ptackova (2013) notes that efforts to widely settle pastoralists in Rebgong began again in earnest in 2007 and expanded into 2008, coinciding with my research there, and not coincidentally, with the unrest and crackdown prior to the Olympics. See also Zukosky 2007, Yeh 2013, Bauer and Huatse Gyal 2015.

9. Intermodal gaps between different kinds of signs are what for example allow for the subtle dynamics of voicing in texts and performances (such as innuendo, irony, and sarcasm) that Bakhtin long ago analyzed. See also Silverstein 2001, Agha 2007.

10. See Escobar 1995 for a seminal discussion of the "discovery" of the category of "poverty" in international development circles post–World War II especially. See also Edelman and Haugerud 2005.

11. Langmo elders told me they had narrated the history-petition to a Tshema Monastery monk, who transcribed and printed it for them. Dorje Gyap may well have been the main narrator.

12. The history-petition went on to claim that, "altogether, the village had 350 head of cattle, 300 sheep, 200 goats, and 30 horses, and controlled over 317 mu of grasslands and farm fields, including hillside and riverside fields."

13. Langmo's school during the late commune years (1970 on) was a "privately established" school (Ch. *minban*), but the local state helped pay for a teacher. Postiglione et al. (2005) talk of this process as a widespread one in China's rural western regions after the 1980s reforms. Since land and livelihood now devolved to individual households, grassroots teachers went home to work and rural children were widely withdrawn from school to help with household labor demands. The 1990s and 2000s "universal primary education" campaign was in part an effort to redress that trend.

14. Recall that Kharnak's new school, built to far grander proportions then Langmo's, was completed that same year in 1996. The faded slogan calling for universal compulsory education on Kharnak school walls also dated from that time. It is most likely that local education officials attended Langmo's school opening at the peak village site in 1996 as a way to claim the school as an achievement under that education campaign. Their support however, did not extend far beyond that hospitality spectacle.

15. Despite repeated petitions to the relevant county bureaus, no funds for a drivable road up to the peak village ever materialized. Villagers told me that they moved down onto the fields previously allocated to them by the township, though as usual households engaged in some bartering and exchanges of lands, depending on their needs.

16. Elders implied that a prefecture Education Bureau head, who gave the school construction contracts to his brother-in-law, had siphoned off most of their promised funds to give to other, more favored villages.

17. Langmo villagers complained about their debt burdens to me in multiple conversations, saying that while many had bank loans for their new houses, in recent years new restrictions on loan guarantees meant that most ordinary Tibetans could not get bank loans. Thus many turned to private lenders who charged high interest (up to 30 percent), and the originally lower interest bank loans on houses (up to 11 percent) were set to go up to 15 percent. For example, Dorje Gyap showed me a receipt from the Agricultural Bank of China and pointed to a figure of more than seven thousand yuan, which he said was what they originally owed for their new home construction, but more than two thousand yuan had been added in interest since they had last paid on it in 2004 (an interest rate of over 7 percent).

18. Deji told me that she had married into Langmo village from an impoverished village far downriver in 1964, when she was twenty years old. That was only a few years after the terrible famine years of 1960–61. Her new husband's first wife, Dorje Gyap's mother, may well have died during those harsh years. From Deji's perspective at that time, marrying a salaried official up in Langmo must have been a chance for upward mobility and some food security.

19. This was in fact an odd statement, given that most Langmo villagers in 2008 had only tiny plots of farm fields on the valley floor and few could afford tractors. This seems more like a formulaic echo of the kinds of persuasive rhetoric privileging agriculture that early Chinese Maoist work teams used in the valley, perhaps triggered for her by the pivotal chronotope of "brain," the usage of which dates from that time.

20. Later in the conversation, Deji admitted that when she and the other official households agreed to move down, they were promised that some of their members would gain urban registration status and a state-funded apartment in town. Thus

those households were able to hedge their bets by maintaining both urban and village residences.

21. The elders' history-petition claimed that Langmo village had had sixty mu of arable fields on the valley floor, now reduced to thirty mu after the late movers relocated. In part, they chose those places because the promised running water system never materialized, and since women were charged with carrying water to households every day, villagers wanted to be near the river.

22. The event was all about counting. Village leaders were charged with keeping accounts of each villager's contributions to their annual prayer quota. Throughout my visit, I got the sense of the absolute necessity and importance of hard prayer work, and the sheer amount of time needed to complete chanting obligations, including a "reading" of the entire Kangyur (Buddhist canon). The day ended with the headman publicly shaming those who had not participated.

23. Many Tibetans I spoke to however claimed that several bystanders were also injured or detained. See Makley 2009a for an analysis of that event and how it was portrayed in a foreign media.

24. The Civil Affairs Department is the provincial bureau responsible for both civil development planning and distribution of social welfare and relief benefits.

25. In a recent spate of scholarship published in and outside of China on the causes and conditions of the massive famine and death tolls that followed Mao's highly touted Great Leap Forward (1959–60), scholars point to the fear of county and township officials to disclose to their superiors the actual state of affairs. Instead, local officials staged spectacles of progress and abundance for inspection tours, even as thousands were dying. See Becker 1996, Yang 2013, Dikötter 2011, Johnson 2012.

26. Recall in chapter 3 that the New Socialist Countryside campaign came to the Upper Narrows only in 2007.

27. See Escobar 1995 for a critical history of the rise of "sustainable development" rhetoric in international development organizations from the 1980s on. In China, Prime Minister Zhu Rongji famously embraced that rhetoric at a 2002 international environment summit, but already in the mid-1980s Chinese economists Wang and Bai (1987) were making such a case for Tibetan regions of Qinghai, claiming that rural Tibetans were hopelessly trapped in a "vicious cycle" of poverty and environmental degradation, such that the only solution was to start fresh and build completely new Chinese cities from the ground up. See also Yeh 2013, Scherz 2014.

28. There is a vast literature on the advent of grassland fencing on the Tibetan plateau by the 1990s. Ptackova (2013) gives a detailed account of the policy history of grassland management in Rebgong. See also Yeh 2003a. Note that many of the dire consequences of fencing the grasslands for pastoralist communities were already presaged by similar policies in Inner Mongolia by the 1980s. See Williams 2002.

29. By 2012, fully 31 percent of Qinghai Province's total landmass had been officially marked as differently zoned "nature preserves," much of it requiring the removal of humans or highly restricted usage. Frustrated international experts noted however that these reserves were being established in a largely ad hoc way, and in some cases arbitrarily redrawn so as to allow for resource extraction like mining. See the Epilogue. As Emily Yeh points out, this kind of "green governmentality" was the major impetus for the widespread pastoralist resettlement projects beginning in 2007. The emphasis on resettling Tibetan pastoralists, she asserts, was not

fundamentally about improving their livelihoods, but about addressing "downstream concerns" to preserve access to vital resources (2009, 23).

30. As noted in chapters 2 and 3, the Rebgong region saw increased immigration and population, as well as increasing development pressures from imperial and business interests by the nineteenth century. Robert Ekvall (1954) says that in the 1930s and 1940s Tibetan pastoralist tribes had clearly demarcated grasslands adjudicated by chiefs that were based on mountain ridges and their watersheds, while semipastoralist Tibetan farming villages would sometimes fence their farm fields around dewawide boundaries, but individual households' holdings were rarely fenced. Yet in the winter, dewa fences were often removed so that livestock could move across winter fields to forage. See also Carrasco 1959, Yeh 2003a, Pirie 2008.

31. Note that Langmo villagers' household land contracts were "readjusted" in 1998, just as the struggle over the move down had reached an impasse. The new contracts, I was told, for the first time stipulated a contract period (thirty years), and included the new provision that state bureaus must provide monetary compensation for appropriated land.

32. Benno Weiner (2012) provides a detailed account of the bloody battles that ensued in the Upper Narrows from the early 1950s all the way through the early 1960s, mostly spearheaded by Tibetan militias from pastoralist communities upriver. I heard various stories from Langmo villagers about 1958 especially, but I do not have any evidence of their direct participation in rebellions. Elders described how their fathers and grandfathers had been gathered to chant protection prayers on the day in 1958 that PLA troops came to the village and arrested village leaders.

33. There were separate offices based in Dethang for the township/commune; prominent Dethang village men, along with several Kharnak men I met, most likely also held positions in the township government.

34. See Zukosky 2007, 120; Ptackova 2013, 46.

35. Note that Langmo villagers' household land contracts, redrawn in 1998, stipulate that the contract-issuing party (in this case the rural collective, Dethang) has the right to supervise land use and "change their behavior" if the land is misused or left idle. See Oi and Walder 1999, Yeh 2004, and Lin 2009 on the nonexistent status of so-called "natural villages" like Langmo in the HRS land contracting system.

36. Indeed Drakpa, acting as school district head, had complained to me about Langmo villagers' troublesome noncompliance that year, narrating their resistance to moving their school to the lower site as their irrational propensity to "twist the truth."

37. See the independent documentary *Petition* (2009) by Zhao Liang, filmed in Beijing over more than a decade among desperate petitioners, some of whom camped there for years, for an eye-opening perspective on this phenomenon in the early 2000s through the Beijing Summer Olympics in 2008.

38. There is a burgeoning literature on the rush of rural Tibetans across the plateau to dig caterpillar fungus and other mountain medicinals favored by increasingly wealthy Chinese consumers in the 2000s. By 2008 however, high rents on access to mountain lands (three thousand to ten thousand yuan) meant many Tibetan diggers were in debt, or worked for bosses. See Craig 2012, also the documentary film *Yartsa Rinpoche* (2014) by Tibetan filmmaker Dorje Tsering Chenaktshang.

39. See Germano 1998, Klima 2002, and especially Bernstein 2013 for interesting analyses of Buddhist place and fortune making in the context of the rise of state-sponsored capitalist markets.

40. See especially Harris 2001, Bernstein 2013.

41. Langmo's video celebrating the temple was in fact a collaborative product nonetheless largely directed by Dorje Gyap. His own monk son wrote the narrative, and elders searched for a monk with an elegant-sounding voice to read it, hiring a second monk narrator when the first was deemed insufficiently authoritative. Elders hired a Chinese photographer to film the main ritual events, and then worked with a Chinese editor in town to put together the final video. Altogether it cost some two thousand yuan to do.

42. See JBGP 2009.

43. Jetsha hermitage was a small Geluk community of twenty or so resident renunciants or "sworn ascetics" (Tib. *ri khrod pa*). Langmo dewa traditionally sent sons to reside there, learning enough Tibetan to conduct propitiation rituals. It was destroyed by PLA troops in 1958. Langmo villagers helped to rebuild it in the early 1980s, with about ten elderly renunciants in residence. In 2008, at least half of Jetsha residents were from Langmo. See Nian and Bai 1993, GDKS 2012, Gendun Palzang 2007, JMTC 1988.

44. GDKS (2012, 53) in his reading of the biography of the second Arol Tshang, says that in founding the hermitage, the lama also retamed and replaced several mountain deities, including Kharnak's Makgol. He also did much tantric ritual work to tame demons and purify the lands of polluting illness.

45. See Nian and Bai 1993, BT and SGTR 2005, Gendun Palzang 2007, GDKS 2012.

46. I heard from several people, including a Langmo elder, the story of the third Arol's tensions with the seventh Shartshang when he came of age, as in part the reason for the founding of Drelzong. Shartshang reportedly told Arol to go establish himself elsewhere so as not to compete for patrons with him. Not coincidentally, the third Arol founded Drelzong Monastery in the meditation site and tantric power place made famous by the great Nyingma lama Shapkar (b. 1781).

47. That included competing lineages of Nyingma communities, as well as one of Rebgong's most powerful non-Buddhist Bon communities. Note that these efforts continued through the 1940s and all the way up to 1958. The third Arol Tshang, whom Nian and Bai refer to as "one of most influential lamas in modern Qinghai Buddhist history," (1993, 167) was perhaps the most proactive in this regard. It was he who spearheaded the rebuilding of Tshema Monastery after it was destroyed by Ma's troops in their 1938 crackdown upriver. And, as CCP work teams stepped up their pressure on Tibetans to collectivize in the 1950s, the third Arol Tshang expanded the assembly hall at Drelzong, and gave multiple mass Kalacakra empowerment teachings in the Upper Narrows.

48. Gendun Palzang lists the birth date of the fourth Arol as 1977, but gives no other information on him (2007, 311). According to Amdo Lekshay Gyatsho (personal communication), the fourth Arol Tshang's decision to leave in 1992 was met with great consternation among regional Tibetan officials, one of the most prominent of whom publicly upbraided Arol's monk teachers at Drelzong for inadequately

training him. As a youth in Beijing, he had a reputation for partying, fighting, and playing music. In 2014 he was living in Xining city and running his own music production company.

49. According to Amdo Lekshay Gyamtsho (personal communication), who was his roommate during their monastic studies in Labrang, Denzin Gyamtsho became known for his excellent Tibetan language poetry and his sharp intellect in monastic debate. He was controversial though at his home monastery in Qinghai, sparking intergenerational factionalism among monks there after a particularly critical essay he wrote, which led him to leave for Xining.

50. Dorje Gyap proudly told me that with the prestige and promised blessing power of Denzin Gyamtso's intervention, Langmo villagers had been able to raise over 100,000 yuan from Tibetan communities up and downriver. Including the 98,000 from the Dutch Embassy, he said, they raised 340,000 for their temple.

51. The recognition of Tibetan incarnate lamas has been highly fraught in post-Mao China. In the Geluk context, it requires elaborate divination rituals, and by 2007 central state religion policy attempted to regulate the process by requiring state approval in the form of an "incarnate lama license" (Ch. *huofo zheng*). In fact, when the fourth Arol Tshang left the monkhood, I was told, prominent Tibetan regional leaders, referring to an old story that the third Arol was so entrepreneurial and on such good terms with Muslim businessmen and that he would be reincarnated as a Muslim merchant, angrily declared that this teenager had never been the real fourth Arol Tshang. Rumors also abounded about whether or not Denzin Gyamtsho was an incarnate lama. According to his former roommate, he himself did think he was an incarnation, and one of his teachers had said as much, but not of Arol Tshang. In Langmo, despite especially Dorje Gyap's conviction, not all elders accepted his status as the fourth Arol Tshang.

52. Right-turning conch shells are considered to be auspicious because they are particularly rare.

53. Denzin Gyamtsho did visit the dewa several times in the ensuing years, Chinese disciples in tow, and Langmo villagers hosted delegations of monks and sworn ascetics for teachings held in the new assembly hall.

54. In 2007, elders proudly showed me the gorgeous Buddha images Langmo households had purchased for thousands of yuan each. Each image was captioned with labels naming the patron household's male head. By 2008, they had raised enough cash to purchase complete sets of the Kangyur and Dangyur Buddhist canon. Yet many villagers could not in fact afford the escalating rents on access to digging lands. Thus many took loans privately to cover them, hoping to come out ahead, but often carrying debt over multiple seasons.

5. Spectacular Compassion

1. Chapter 5 is a revised and expanded version of my article, "Spectacular Compassion: "Natural" Disasters and National Mourning in China's Tibet," *Critical Asian Studies* 46 (3): 2014. Reprinted with permission.

2. Hotels were so full of military personnel that spring that my former host Lobzang complained that when his work unit had to conduct inspections in outlying

counties, they had to go all the way to a non-Tibetan county to find vacancies for their group.

3. That year, Tibetan police from town were dispatched up to highland regions in the county to check aspiring diggers' credentials. They were told to turn away anyone who was not from the county.

4. In many large cities across the PRC, Olympic countdown clocks and charts were displayed in town squares, offices, parks, and housing complexes. Countdown ceremonies were held at increasingly frequent intervals as the games approached. In 2007–8, televised ceremonies were held at the six-month and hundred-day (April 30) marks.

5. China's Olympic torch relay began on March 24, 2008, with the lighting of the torch in Athens, Greece. It arrived in Beijing on March 31, it then was run across six continents and included a relay to the top of Mount Everest, ending on August 8 at the games. Organizers called it "the Journey of Harmony," and it ultimately covered 137,000 kilometers (85,000 miles). See Brownell 2008, Foster 2002.

6. For overviews and coverage of the Tibet unrest and torch relay confrontations see Barnett 2009, Makley 2009a, the media watch blogs China Digital Times, China Beat, and High Peaks Pure Earth, as well as the PRC's official Olympics site. For emblematic clashes abroad see coverage and YouTube videos of the Grace Wang affair at Duke University, or the pro-Tibet activist attacking the torch in Paris. For Chinese blogosphere commentary, see especially the April 2008 YouTube video "2008: Zhongguo, Zhanqilai!" ("2008: China, Stand Up!"), its comments section and related videos (available at http://www.youtube.com/watch?v=MSTYhYkASsA, accessed Sept. 1, 2009).

7. See especially Das 1995, 138; and Agamben 2011. See also Hai Ren 2004, Brownell 2008, Fletcher 2008, Smith 2008, Vance 2008.

8. See Smith 2010.

9. *Colors* is Benetton's showcase graphic arts journal, established in 1991 and headquartered in Rome at the corporation's PR arm, the Fabrica research institute. It is published in three English- and European-language editions and sold in some forty countries. I thank my student Christian Anayas for bringing this issue to my attention. See Giroux 1993, Macdonald 2010.

10. See Macleod 2008.

11. See Malkki 1996, Boltanski 1999, Minn 2007, Bornstein and Redfield 2011, Fassin 2012.

12. Ticktin 2006, 34. See also Das and Poole 2004, 28, Langford 2009.

13. See also Foucault 1990, Butler 2004, Bell 2010.

14. See Fassin 2012, Agamben 2011, Møllgaard 2010.

15. See also Hubbert 2014.

16. Li and Ong 2008, 11. See also Link 2009; Greenhalgh and Winckler 2005; Kleinman et al. 2011; Bin Xu 2012, 2014; Teets 2014.

17. Note that in 2009 a reporter for the overseas Chinese news network Boxun leaked commentary from a Beijing propaganda bureau leader stating explicitly that the central government took the Olympics and Disaster Relief Campaigns of 2008 as templates for eliciting public support for the party in the face of mounting criticisms. The official is quoted as saying, "The anti-China forces inside and outside of

the country are working together, looking for their opportunity. How to find effective ways to launch resolute attacks against them and oppose their negative influence domestically and abroad, that has tested our governing abilities. The past few years' experience has shown us that the most important method is precisely to use these kinds of great events, to solidify popular sentiments, and drum up the great Masses' patriotic spirit and attack every last troublemaker" (translation mine, *Boxun* 2009).

18. See Brownell 2008, Chong 2011, Bin Xu 2012, Hubbert 2014, Schneider and Hwang 2014.

19. Tens of thousands of troops had been sent to Tibetan cities from eastern posts during the 2008 unrest, but the militarization of the region began years earlier. See Lam 2008, Thompson 2008.

20. Cited in Smith 2010, 119.

21. At the one-year anniversary of the Sichuan quake, the PRC State Council attempted to routinize the new role of the disaster relief state by declaring May 12 "Disaster Prevention and Reduction Day," and releasing its first-ever White Paper on Disaster Relief in which China is depicted as the country most vulnerable to natural disasters in the world. The white paper calls for enhanced public security infrastructure in disaster relief and, despite some opposition within high command, explicitly states that the PLA will take a principal role in future disaster relief efforts. See Lam 2008, Thompson 2008, Patel 2009.

22. See Metcalf and Huntington 1979, Bloch and Parry 1982, Wakeman 1990, Whyte 1990, Metcalf and Huntington 1979, Mueggler 2001, Klima 2002, Das 2007.

23. See Verdery 1999; Langford 2009, 693; Rosaldo 2004.

24. I am arguing that the close juxtaposition of these events under the Olympic rubric raised both "natural" disaster relief and the status of Tibetans to unprecedented national-scale importance for state officials and citizens alike. This even though statist compassion had already been widely displayed that year in the response to the February 2008 snowstorm, and state leaders had responded to some previous disasters, such as the 1976 Tangshan earthquake or the 1998 floods, with even larger media campaigns (see Yu 2008). Bin Xu (2014) notes that neither the 1975 quake nor the 1998 floods produced national-scale aid campaigns that drew the participation of ordinary citizens.

25. See also Berger 2003; Makley 2007, 2010; Arjia 2010.

26. See Bloch and Parry 1982, 41; Gal 1991, 442; Maurer 2006.

27. See Wakeman 1990, Cheater 1991.

28. See Wakeman 1990, 260; Whyte 1990, 299; Mueggler 2001, 281; Klima 2002, 282.

29. Yang's book was published and sold out in Hong Kong. In his opening paragraph, he explains the title like this, "It is a tombstone for my father who died of hunger in 1959, for the thirty-six million Chinese who also died of hunger, for the system that caused their death, and perhaps for myself for writing this book." See Link 2009, Johnson 2012, Becker 1996.

30. Very early in the post-Mao reform years, Deng Xiaoping talked of China hosting the Olympics when the PRC rejoined the International Olympic Committee in 1979. State leaders unsuccessfully bid for the 2000 Olympics in 1993. See Brownell 2008, 38.

31. Estimates of the number of schoolchildren killed in collapsed school buildings range from seven to ten thousand. State leaders did not issue an official death

toll until a year later, stating that five thousand schoolchildren had died. See the excellent 2009 HBO documentary, "China's Unnatural Disaster: The Tears of Sichuan Province," for graphic coverage of the activist responses of the mourning parents of deceased schoolchildren, many of whom were rural migrants. Also see the 2009 Amnesty International report, *Justice Denied: Harassment of Sichuan Earthquake Survivors and Activists*. The *China Daily* reported on May 28, 2008, that the vice inspector of the Sichuan province Education Department withdrew as an Olympic torch bearer, and several local education officials reportedly committed suicide in the ensuing months.

32. See Snyder and Hwang 2014, 645. Bin Xu (2013a) describes how central state emergency plans were rudimentary until 2003 with the SARS epidemic. Still, central and provincial level disaster preparedness bureaus were woefully understaffed and underfunded in 2008. Chinese seismologists had been warning of impending earthquakes along the Longmenshan fault for years.

33. See Perry, cited in Wines 2009, Schneider and Hwang 2014. Note that the other mass-scale earthquake in China, the Tangshan earthquake in 1976 that reportedly killed more than 240,000 people, occurred just three months before Mao's death and was widely rumored to indicate his loss of the Mandate of Heaven. See Cheater 1991, 79.

34. See also Brownell 2008, Fletcher 2008, Smith 2008, Vance 2008.

35. See Magnier 2008; cf. Hornby and Cang 2008, Smith 2008, Fletcher 2008, Liang Jing 2008, Wines 2009.

36. That view has since been strongly echoed in recent academic analyses of the Sichuan earthquake and its implications for governance and "civil society" in the PRC. The vast majority of academic analyses of the Sichuan earthquake both in and outside of China ignores Tibet and Tibetans. See especially Bin Xu 2014, 2013a, 2013b; also Hui and Lai Hang 2009; Teets 2009, 2014. Perhaps not coincidentally however, Yu Hua's most recent novel, *The Seventh Day* (2015) is an account of the unquiet ghosts of the deceased poor haunting China's corrupt wealthy.

37. See ICT 2008a, Barnett 2009, Smith 2010, HRW 2010.

38. When some high school students in Chengdu, evacuated after the quake to their sports stadium, clowned around on camera and posted their video, they were hounded by Chinese netizens for their disrespect, until all posted tearful apologies to the nation. And when a teen girl in Liaoning posted a video rant against mandatory national mourning, expressing contempt for poor Sichuan masses demanding easterners' sympathy and cash, she was harassed until her mother posted an abject apology and plea. Finally, for an emblematic demand for compassionate silence from Tibet supporters see the YouTube video and comments, "Please Show Some Respect to China Earthquake Victims," posted May 16, 2008: http://www.youtube.com/watch?v=M9fborEIZs8&feature=related (accessed 1 June 2008).

39. The May 12 earthquake's devastation affected Tibetan regions in northwest Sichuan as well as in southwest Gansu province. Thus while the vast majority of the dead and displaced were identified as Han Chinese, thousands of the dead and tens of thousands of the displaced were Tibetans. See Jamyang Norbu 2008.

40. See Ticktin 2006, Bornstein and Redfield 2010.

41. Bin Xu (2014) describes the initial euphoria of Chinese volunteers' and NGOs' participation in disaster relief giving way to disappointment and resentment as central leaders took control and marginalized them.

42. By the end of May 2008, Premier Wen Jiabao became the first central Chinese leader to have a Facebook account, set up by a fan abroad, with more than 13,000 supporters. By summer 2010, more than 200,000 people had signed on as supporters. See Wong 2008, Yu 2008, Bin Xu 2012.

43. Just four days after the quake, the Civil Affairs Ministry reported an estimated total of $192 million in relief donations from all over the country (see Fan 2008). Observers noted the previous lack of an organized philanthropic movement among the new wealthy in China, remarking that China had the lowest rate of charitable giving among "major economies." In the ensuing months, Chinese celebrities in the PRC and abroad, as well as corporate elites, competed to publicize their large earthquake relief pledges. A year later, a reported $11 billion had been donated to Sichuan earthquake relief within the PRC alone. See Makinen 2009, Mackey 2005, Cha 2009, Chen Yong 2008, Bin Xu 2014.

44. Over the ensuing weeks, Chinese netizens documented instances of fake donations for cameras, and increasingly complained about the lack of transparency in the state-run Red Cross' fund management practices. See also Bin Xu 2014, 2013a.

45. The first moments of silence for earthquake victims at torch relays were held within two days of the quake, after Chinese netizens complained about the impropriety of such celebratory events so soon after the disaster. They were then standardized for all related events especially after the nationally televised mourning rites.

46. Bin Xu (2013a) is concerned to emphasize the voluntary and creative nature of Chinese citizens' participation in the national mourning rites, stating that central and provincial leaders stayed out of central plazas and only "softly enforced" participation. But CCTV's coverage emphasized central leaders' guidance and the military's role in managing the flag and Bin Xu gives examples of citizens' own policing of proper mourning. Further, out west in Tibetan regions provincial leaders *did* take center stage in main plazas, while work units and schools had no choice but to participate (see below).

47. See Watkins 1990, Whyte 1990, Wakeman 1990, Cheater 1991.

48. Martin Whyte noted that cremation never really took hold as the norm in rural regions, even though it became increasingly widespread in the cities. Further, elderly urbanites still traveled to rural homes to die, hoping to ensure proper burial rites. Finally, post-Mao reforms saw a resurgence of elaborate funeral practices, and even when loved ones were cremated, their relatives often placed great, emotional weight on the proper care of their ashes (1990, 302–14).

49. Wakeman 1990, 270. Ironically, as Frederic Wakeman and A. P. Cheater both pointed out, Mao's embattled would-be successors positioned the deceased Mao to transcend death as an icon of the enduring party. In contrast to Mao's earlier orders to all officials requiring them to be cremated upon death, Mao's body was embalmed and displayed in a new "memorial hall" on Tiananmen Square that invoked a synthesis of Chinese folk and nationalist cosmologies of life and death. Cheater argues Mao never intended to be cremated like his peers; he had visited his home region and secured himself a gravesite near his ancestors (1991, 81).

50. See Verdery 1999. Before 2008, the national moment of silence, first used during World War I in Europe, had only ever been mandated in the PRC for the deaths of Mao Zedong (1976) and then Deng Xiaoping (1997) See Prochnik 2010.

51. Note that according to Schneider and Hwang (2014, 652), victims of the 1976 Tangshan earthquake were retroactively reframed in such humanitarian terms. The

city of Tangshan for the first time installed a plaque in summer 2008 "deeply mourning" the 1976 quake dead.

52. Indeed, within days of the quake, some Chinese netizens in the PRC and abroad complained about Wen Jiabao's ubiquitous tears, interpreting them as a sign of weakness under pressure.

53. The sirens that day were the classic dual tone air raid sirens, signaling impending national peril or attack, first widely used in Europe during World War II. In China their use is controlled by the PLA. Perhaps not coincidentally, it was in the fall of 2008 that they were put to use for the first time since World War II in southeastern Chinese cities, as a signal to Taiwan.

54. Thus for example, CCP leaders were also interested in staving off challenges to their sovereignty from postdisaster international relief efforts, in which international organizations and foreign government aid can, as in the case of the 2004 Sri Lanka tsunami or in the 2010 Haiti earthquake, circumvent states' laws and literally set up sovereign "humanitarian zones" in others' territory. See Bankoff 2001, 27; Hewitt 1983; Oliver-Smith 1996, 2002; Schuller 2008; Gamburd and McGilvray 2010.

55. Regarding the epigraph above, CCP work teams had arrived in Amdo Tibetan regions in 1949, but PLA troops arrived in 1958 to put down Tibetan resistance to collectivization.

56. See Yeh 2013; Fischer 2009a, 2012, 2013.

57. In part to avoid Olympic year media coverage, state leaders, unlike the response to the previous spate of Tibetan protests in Lhasa (1987–89), never officially declared martial law during the crackdown on the 2008 Tibetan unrest. See Smith 2010.

58. All outside sources, and testimonies of former detainees who escaped to exile suggest a pattern, used in Tibetan regions since reforms, of routine beatings and torture of detained Tibetans during and after the 2008 unrest. See Smith 2010, ICT 2008a, HRW 2010.

59. Recall that Rebgong, though predominantly Tibetan for centuries, has long been a multiethnic region, and some Chinese and Muslim Chinese families have lived there for more than a hundred years. Many of them, like the Chinese contractor Mr. Zhang we met in chapter 3, speak fluent Tibetan and have many friends and associates among Tibetans. During the crackdown, I learned, non-Tibetans in the valley were also highly anxious and disoriented.

60. Translation mine. See Xinhua 2008b.

61. I was told that most of the more than one hundred monks detained on April 17 had been released in early May, but at least eighteen remained in prison.

62. Within two weeks of the outbreak of Tibetan unrest in March, important monks and lamas at the main monasteries (including Jamyang Shepa of Labrang and Shartshang of Rebgong's Rongbo) were featured on state television reading statements condemning the unrest as a Dalai Lama–led separatist plot and the monk participants as violating the essence of Buddhist compassion. Under such circumstances though, it is doubtful any had much choice (cf. Smith 2010).

63. See Zhi and Chen 2008, China News Web 2008, Qinghai News Web 2008, Xinhua 2008.

64. Translation mine; see Zhi and Chen 2008.

65. See Stone 2005, 59; Tucci 1980; Beyer 1973; Lopez 1997a; Germano 1997.

66. See Halperin 1999. I thank James Benn (personal communication) of Mc-Master University for this insight.

67. See also Mills 2003, 249.

68. Gendun Palzang 2007, 563. Note that 1953 was the same year that Huangnan prefecture was officially established, after the seventh Shartshang had just given at least five mass Kalacakra empowerments in the Upper Narrows (Gendun Rabsal 2013, 57).

69. Lamas' competing claims to have tantrically tamed demons and evil forces, thereby protecting the central Jokhang temple and the Lhasa valley from calamitous flooding, were at the heart of the Buddhist sectarian battles that resulted in the rise of the Geluk monastic state. See Akester 2001, Sørensen 2003, Dalton 2012.

70. As far as I can tell, the artillery explosions were most likely blanks fired from the towed howitzer-type cannons I saw in the town stadium, used in highland regions to shell targets on nearby mountainsides from valley floors. Such PLA guns have an estimated range of around eleven to fifteen kilometers.

71. Floods and avalanches began in the south on May 26, lasting almost the entire month of June and affecting fifteen eastern and southern provinces. More than two hundred people were killed or missing, and more than 1.6 million people were forced to evacuate. See Hornby and Cang 2008, Magnier 2008.

72. Note the fourteenth Dalai Lama himself in his famous autobiography narrates the earthquake that hit Lhasa and elsewhere in Tibet in 1950 as not "just a simple earthquake but an omen from the gods, a portent of terrible things to come." Not coincidentally, he recounts how Premier Zhou Enlai himself flew to Kham Tibetan regions upon the 1956 earthquake there (1990, 50, 102). In 2008, the moral implications of such rumors were actually the subject of much debate among Tibetans both on and offline. The American actress Sharon Stone was vilified among Chinese netizens for publicly implying in 2008 that the earthquake was karmic retribution for Chinese policies in Tibet. She has since been banned from visiting China.

73. As Jacqueline Stone (2005, 63) and Ruth Langford point out, monks' exclusive capacity for merit transfer as the principal medium transforming gifts of the living to forms accessible to the dead was the main way that Buddhist ritualists historically intervened in prior practices of feeding the dead, channeling funeral offerings to monastic communities instead. Tucci remarks that Tibetan monks' and lamas' death rituals in fact glorify their transcendent power because, far from just guiding the deceased through inexorable, karma-driven transmigration, the rites claim to help purify or clear away karmic sins, thereby powerfully intervening in the deceased's fate at the last minute (1980, 194). See also Stone 2005, Tucci 1980, Beyer 1973, Lopez 1997a, Germano 1997.

74. See Ramble 1982, Rinchenrdorje and Stuart 2009.

75. See Huber 1994, Akester 2001, Mills 2003, Arjia 2010, Dalton 2012.

76. Indeed, as Shayne Clarke (personal communication) points out, in ancient Buddhist texts, earthquakes in unpopulated areas were frequently celebrated as auspicious signs of a Buddha or bodhisattva's sovereign power. However, Tibetan lamas more recently have interpreted such events as terribly inauspicious signs and indices of moral degeneration when faced with crises of sovereignty, i.e., the thirteenth Dalai Lama's (1876–1933) famous last testament about the Chinese military threat. See Bell 1946, Ciurtin 2009, Akester 2001, Sørensen 2003.

77. See Stevenson 1999, 15–16; Weiner 2012; HNZZ 2001, 847–48. In his 1962 petition to CCP central leaders about atrocities committed in Tibetan regions during the 1958 "Democratic Reforms," the tenth Panchen Lama tells of thousands of Tibetans who died after being sent to remote prisons, and notes that not all of their corpses could be properly buried. He speaks of the desperate grief of Tibetans he met who had lost relatives to battle, starvation, and prison, who "wailed and cried bitterly" in his presence. "This situation . . . is difficult to describe," he counsels, but "it is quite natural that every member of the nationality, upon seeing and hearing of this situation, had unendurable feelings of bitterness and sadness" (1997, 102–3).

78. The recent memoir (2010) of Arjia Rinpoche, the Mongolian-Tibetan incarnate lama and former abbot of Kumbum Monastery who defected to the United States in 1998, vividly illustrates this. His entire story of coming of age during the Maoist years, and rising in PRC state religion ranks under reforms, is framed in the moral politics of good and bad deaths. In contrast to the terrible, untimely deaths of those who committed Maoist violence, he describes the uncanny living power of the cremated remains of the ninth Panchen Lama, discovered hidden from Maoist desecration, and the perfectly intact corpse of Tsongkhapa, hair and fingernails still growing, unearthed by youthful Red Guards who smashed his stupa at Kumbum. Arjia's proudest moment after reforms, he says, was when he restored Tsongkhapa's stupa to its former glory.

79. Since 2008, state media announced a new offensive against Tibetan popular media to combat such messages. Several prominent and local Tibetan folk singers and poets have been arrested for lyrics and verse invoking the crackdown and the Dalai Lama directly or indirectly. Tashi Dhondup, the author of the song featured in the epigraph above, was detained and beaten for that song, and then arrested again in December 2009 for his album. He was tried and sentenced to fifteen months prison and "re-education through labor" in January 2010 (RFA 2010).

80. See also ICT 2009, Raman 2009.

81. See Xinhua 2008c.

82. See Amnesty 2009, Bin Xu 2014.

83. See Ford 2010.

84. Pace, e.g., Cunningham 2010, Shimatsu 2010. See also the online comments to Willy Lam's critical op-ed on the Yushu earthquake (2010), in which readers lambast him for his criticisms of Chinese state disaster relief: "Tragedies are just tragedies," one tells him, ". . . Don't you have a simple heart just to mourne [sic] for these tragic victims?"

85. The Yushu earthquake brought massive donations from Chinese citizens in and outside the PRC, many of whom used private donation networks and organizations, like those of celebrities Jet Li and Yao Ming, first established during the Sichuan quake relief campaign. Catherine Lewis reports on the blog Shanghaiist that Chinese state efforts to control disaster response extended to multinational corporations as well. See Richburg 2010, Saunders 2010.

86. Experts estimate that more than 85 percent of buildings in and around the county town of Jiegu (Jyekundo) collapsed, with more than 100,000 residents rendered homeless. Local education officials stated that up to 80 percent of primary schools and half the secondary schools in the prefecture were damaged. More than 200 students and teachers were reported dead or missing and almost 700 injured in school building collapses. See Fish 2010, UNICEF 2010.

87. See Topden Tsering 2010, Saunders 2010.

88. For a compilation of these images and footage in an emblematic You-Tube video and comments section, see "The Revelation of TRUE HEROES! 2010 Kyegundo/Jyegundo Yushu Tibet," available at http://www.youtube.com/watch ?v=YM0firEENYM&feature=PlayList&p=C9AA9208AD5A5701&playnext_ from=PL&playnext=5 (accessed 1 June 2010). This video could stand as a counter to the equally emblematic Chinese-made video from 2008, "2008: China Stand Up!"

89. Sienna Craig (2010), who visited the quake zone in June 2010, wrote of the now prominent role of Buddhist monks throughout the region as locals worked to nurture the untimely dead. She describes hillsides dotted with prayer flags mark-ing burial sites, monks and laywomen collecting bones from cremation grounds to purify in the tiny clay *tsa tsa* to be released in rivers, and a registry in one of the only standing shops for monks to perform rituals for the dead.

Epilogue

1. It was said in Rebgong that Li Xuansheng in fact had a Tibetan mother. His official career bios list him as Han Chinese.

2. Between 2008 and 2014, Rebgong emerged alongside Ngaba (Ch. Aba, Sich-uan) and Labrang (Ch. Gannan, Gansu) as one of the most important centers of Tibetan protest across the plateau.

3. The song, entitled "A Heartfelt Return," (Tib. *sems kyi log phebs*) was written as a poem by a Tibetan teacher at the Qinghai Nationalities University in Xining (Abho, personal communication). It was set to music and recorded by four of the most famous and cosmopolitan of Tibetan male singers. The climax of the song is when Yadong, the eldest and brawniest of the four, sings the call to all Tibetans in the style of a Western rock star, "Oh! Tibetans, my brothers!"

4. As both Li and the Tourism Bureau annual report state, this massive jump in tourism visits in 2006 was made possible by the previous years' investment in transportation, hydroelectric, and accommodation infrastructure funded in part by central state investment under the Open the West rubric.

5. Not surprisingly, some prominent Tibetan lamas, including the young Manipatshang at Rongbo who had returned from exile and was very promarket, have in recent years cultivated their Chinese devotees by building Drolma or Guanyin temples and pilgrimage sites.

6. He was not the only Tibetan resident I heard sing the praises of Party Secre-tary Li. Many urban Tibetans I knew at that time praised Li, and perhaps because he was said to be half Tibetan himself, enthused that he really cared for Tibetans and their culture.

7. Meanwhile, the prayer wheels along the back of the monastery remained small and cheaply made. No donor plaques adorned them.

8. Though I could not find definitive corroborating evidence, it is most likely from the sources that Li Xuansheng himself had dominant shareholder status in the Beijing tourism development company he engaged. Indeed, Chuangjing Tianxia lists two subsidiary companies, a Rebgong culture industry company, and a Rebgong tourism company. Those companies are mentioned in other contract signings Li was

involved with throughout his tenure and beyond. For example, in 2007 he signed with officials of Beijing's central Chongwen district in order to sell Rebgong Tibetan art in the run-up to the Olympics (*Regong Wenhua* 2007, 41). And he shows up, along with Rongbo's Shartshang lama, at the contract signings for two "Rebgong Art Galleries" in Beijing and Tianjin in 2015, three years after he was purged from office in Huang-nan prefecture. See http://collection.sina.com.cn/yjjj/20150430/2107186228.shtml (accessed May 10, 2015).

9. That phrase was famously coined by Karl Polanyi in his groundbreaking study of the rise of capitalism in Western Europe (2001, 79).

10. According to Gendun Palzang (2007, 23), a two-story demon-taming stupa was placed on the shelf above the Middle Table, which was called the Upper Table (Tib. *cog tse gong ma*). Such a stupa would have asserted the Shartshang lamas' tran-scendent control over both mundane protectors like Machen Bomra and the mer-chant villagers below. Photos of Rongbo Monastery from before CCP intervention are very rare, though a contemporary painting reconstructing the campus depicts Machen's cairn in front of the main gate.

11. Emphasis in the original. Akhu Tenzin insisted, however, that, in an act of Buddhist compassion, one of the returned incarnate lamas eventually decreed that the former activist-turned-monk would be allowed to return to the assembly, but he was barred from holding any office, and he carried the stigma the rest of his days. He was eighty-one years old in 2008.

12. I avoid the term *suicide*, because it does not necessarily reflect Tibetans' notions of personhood and death in these contexts. "Immolation" denotes any form of self-sacrifice by death, but Western observers tend to recognize only those that are by fire. Note as well that the very first self-immolation by fire protest by a Tibetan monk had occurred in Ngaba, south of Rebgong, just ten days earlier (see Mak-ley 2015). It is unclear how widely known Akhu Sheldrup's death was in Rebgong, though Xinhua news reported it because they saw it as the suicide of a mentally unstable depressive. See http://www.savetibet.org/official-acknowledgement-of-suicide-of-monk-after-protests-due-to-stress/ (accessed May 1, 2015).

13. Education officials I knew told me in 2011 and 2013 that now their budgets were much larger, and their superiors had huge discretionary "project" funds. Mean-while, state TV news featured photo op spectacles of direct giving, with officials handing off consumer items like televisions to Tibetan pastoralists. See Fischer 2009a, 2012, 2013; Yeh 2013.

14. As many observers have pointed out, 2006–7 was when major infrastructure construction under the Open the West slogan was well underway or completed (like the much-touted opening of the unprecedented Qinghai-Tibet railway), which paved the way for a renewed push to find, excavate and transport mineral, oil, and gas reserves across the plateau. See Buckley 2014.

15. Contrast those investments with the paltry 4.7 million yuan county officials claimed for education projects that same year.

16. In an item that an editor crossed out, and thus was perhaps deemed too sensi-tive for even party superiors to see, they complain, "Every project that attracts invest-ment comes out of all kinds of discussions on what each side demands, and when we are at the county town learning about the investment plans, there are always brave

and proud words, and magnificent blueprints. But when actually doing the work, due to subjective reasons, construction progress is slow, and investment shrinks, so that the gap between relevant parties' plans and actual results is extremely wide."

17. This is presumably because Li's plans for the development of the culture industry were packaged with requests for investment in basic infrastructure (roads, hydroelectric), which then attract and benefit resource extraction investors.

18. See Lin 2009.

19. Education officials assured protestors that Tibetan language curricula would remain in Rebgong schools, only with the addition of Chinese language electives. Note also that teachers reportedly initially complained when monks joined the protests, arguing that these student protests were not "political."

20. These included the city-block-sized Rebgong Culture Park shopping complex in the center of town (where the stadium and cinema had been) and the Rebgong Plaza and Culture Museum in the new northern part of town, sponsored in part by the prefecture's new State Council–assigned sister city of Tianjin.

21. Note that in this new plan, in contrast to the expansiveness of the 2006–7 plan, Tibetan Buddhist monasteries are conspicuously absent as exploitable "cultural resources."

22. The company in question was the multibillion yuan Qinghai subsidiary of the Beijing-based China Railway Resources Conglomerate (CREC, or Zhongtie), one of the largest construction companies in the world and responsible for at least two-thirds of the PRC's railway system, including the Qinghai-Tibet railway. In recent years, the corporation touted its diversification into both resource extraction and tourism development services in the PRC and abroad. See http://www.crecg.com/ and http://www.crfeb.com.cn/swsyb/tabid/1030/InfoID/73240/settingmoduleid/ 2424/frtid/1023/Default.aspx (accessed May 15, 2015).

23. In popular and official usage in Rebgong, *rang skyong* or *rang dbang* are most often used to refer to Tibetan forms of autonomous governance within the PRC nation-state, while *rang btsan* refers to Tibetan governance independent of the PRC.

24. This included Li Xuansheng's own home region of Huangzhong, near Kumbum Monastery, where his partner corporation Western Mining (the main donor for Drolma's statue) had been accused by Tibetan residents of running a lead mining and smelting operation that had poisoned hundreds of villagers since 2006, and worsened in 2011 after thousands of farmers had been relocated for the plant's expansion. See ICT 2011, McKown 2011.

25. There is now a substantial international literature analyzing these events. See especially McGranahan and Litzinger 2012, Buffetrille and Robin 2012, Makley 2015, Tsering Woeser 2014, Whalen-Bridge 2015. For online tracking, see http://www. savetibet.org, http://www.rfa.org, and http://tibetdata.

26. Cited on Palden Gyal's blog, November 29, 2012. http://www.paldengyal. com/?p=1994 (accessed March 2015).

27. Trackers abroad, relying on smuggled cell phone data, have counted twenty-eight immolations by fire by Tibetans in November 2012 alone, nine of which took place during the CCP Congress. See Tsering Woeser 2014, Tibet Data 2015.

28. I did not find any record of a protester in Rebgong at that time shouting or holding up signs calling for "independence for Tibet" (*Tib. bod rang btsan*). Messages

we know of included calls for the Dalai Lama's return, equal rights for Tibetans, keeping Tibetan language curricula, protecting the environment, removing military presence, and the release of the Panchen Lama.

29. Of the fifteen immolators in 2012, only two were women, both nuns. There were two monks. All were young, the oldest, Sonam Dargye was forty-four. These were all children of the post-Mao reform era, and the majority were part of the early post-Mao generation who could not attend school.

30. Note that in 2015, after two more immolations by fire in 2014, during what has become the spring protest season in Rebgong, even fiercer-sounding rules were announced ahead of March 10 that widened the culture war to criminalize any collective activity among Tibetans that could be taken to be "Tibet-related" (Ch. *she-zang*). Such regional rules do not necessarily mean Tibetan collective practices do not occur, only that security officials can criminalize them opportunistically when faced with further unrest.

31. Katia Buffetrille, personal communication.

32. Popular dedication prayer and part of traditional Tibetan Buddhist monastic practices on behalf of the deceased. Translation by Lama Zopa Rinpoche, with some editing by myself. I thank Amdo Lekshay Gyamtso for the Tibetan verse.

References

Abrams, Philip. 1988 (1977). "Notes on the Difficulty of Studying the State." *Journal of Historical Sociology* 1(1) (March): 58–89.

Agamben, Giorgio. 1998. *Homo Sacer: Sovereign Power and Bare Life.* Translated by Daniel Heller-Roazen. Stanford, CA: Stanford University Press.

——. 2011. *The Kingdom and the Glory: For a Theological Genealogy of Economy and Government.* Translated by Lorenzo Chiesa and Matteo Mandarini. Stanford, CA: Stanford University Press.

Agha, Asif. 2007. "Recombinant Selves in Mass Mediated Spacetime." *Language and Communication* 27(3): 320–35.

Akester, Matthew. 2001. "The *vajra* Temple of *gter ston zhig po gling pa* and the Politics of Flood Control in 16th Century Lhasa." *Tibet Journal* 26(1): 3–24.

Amnesty International. 2009. *Justice Denied: Harassment of Sichuan Earthquake Survivors and Activists.* London: Amnesty International Publications.

Anagnost, Ann. 1994. "Who Is Speaking Here? Discursive Boundaries and Representation in Post-Mao China." In *Boundaries in China,* edited by John Hay, 257–79. London: Reaktion Books.

——. 1997. *National Pastimes: Narrative, Representation, and Power in Modern China.* Durham, NC: Duke University Press.

——. 2004. "The Corporeal Politics of Quality (Suzhi)." *Public Culture* 16(2): 189–208.

Arjia Rinpoche. 2010. *Surviving the Dragon: A Tibetan Lama's Life under Chinese Rule.* New York: Rodale.

Asad, Talal. 2004. "Where Are the Margins of the State?" In *Anthropology in the Margins of the State,* edited by Veena Das and Deborah Poole, 279–88. Santa Fe: School of American Research Press.

Bakhtin, Mikhail. 1981. *The Dialogic Imagination: Four Essays.* Edited by Michael Holquist. Translated by Caryl Emerson and Michael Holquist. Austin: University of Texas Press.

Bakken, Borge. 2000. "Dreams: Technocracy, Social Engineering, and 'Human Quality.'" In *The Exemplary Society: Human Improvement, Social Control, and the Dangers of Modernity in China,* 50–81. Oxford: Oxford University Press.

Bangoo, Ellen. 2004. *Teaching and Learning in Tibet: A Review of Research and Policy Publications.* Copenhagen: Nordic Institute of Asian Studies Press.

Bankoff, Gregory. 2001. "Rendering the World Unsafe: 'Vulnerability' as Western Discourse." *Disasters* 25(1): 19–35.

Barnett, Robert. 1997. Preface to *A Poisoned Arrow: The Secret Report of the 10th Panchen Lama,* by Panchen Lama, H. H. London: Tibet Information Network.

——. 2006. *Lhasa: Streets with Memories.* New York: Columbia University Press.

——. 2009. "The Tibet Protests of Spring 2008: Conflict between the Nation and the State." *China Perspectives* 3: 6–23.

——. 2010. "Understated Legacies: Uses of Oral History and Tibetan Studies." *Inner Asia* 12(1): 63–93.

Bass, Catriona. 1998. *Education in Tibet: Policy and Practice since 1950*. New York: St. Martin's Press.

Bauer, Kenneth, and Huatse Gyal, eds. 2015. *Resettlement among Tibetan Nomads in China*. Special Issue of *Nomadic Peoples* 19(2).

Bauman, Richard, and Charles L. Briggs. 1990. "Poetics and Performance as Critical Perspectives on Language and Social Life." *Annual Review of Anthropology* 19: 59–88.

Becker, Jaspar. 1996. *Hungry Ghosts: China's Secret Famine*. London: John Murray.

Beer, Robert. 2003. *The Handbook of Tibetan Buddhist Symbols*. Boston: Shambhala.

Bell, Sir Charles. 2003 (1946). "The Political Testament of H. H. the 13th Dalai Lama." Reprinted in *The History of Tibet*. Vol. 3. *The Modern Period 1895–1959 Encounter with Modernity*, edited by Alex Mckay, 509–13. London: Routledge Curzon.

Bell, Christopher. 2007. "Tibetan Deity Cults." *The Tibetan and Himalaya Library*, May. http://www.thlib.org/bibliographies/wiki/tibetan%20deity%20cults%20bibliography.html.

Bell, Vikki. 2010. "New Scenes of Vulnerability, Agency, and Plurality: An Interview with Judith Butler." *Theory, Culture, and Society* 27: 130–52.

Benewick, Robert, Irene Tong, and Jude Howell. 2004. "Self-Governance and Community: A Preliminary Comparison between Villagers' Committees and Urban Community Councils." *China Information* 18(1): 11–28.

Berger, Patricia. 2003. *Empire of Emptiness: Buddhist Art and Political Authority in Qing China*. Honolulu: University of Hawai'i Press.

Bernstein, Anya. 2011. "The Post-Soviet Treasure Hunt: Time, Space, and Necropolitics in Siberian Buddhism." *Comparative Studies in Society and History* 53(3): 623–53.

——. 2013. *Religious Bodies Politic: Rituals of Sovereignty in Buryat Buddhism*. Chicago: University of Chicago Press.

Bessire, Lucas. 2014. *Behold the Black Caiman: A Chronicle of Ayoreo Life*. Chicago: University of Chicago Press.

Bessire, Lucas, and David Bond. 2014. "Ontological Anthropology and the Deferral of Critique." *American Ethnologist* 41: 440–56.

Beyer, Stephan. 1973. *Magic and Ritual in Tibet: The Cult of Tārā*. Berkeley: University of California Press.

Bilu, Yorum. 2015. "Dialogic Anthropology." in *Dialogue as a Trans-disciplinary Concept: Martin Buber's Philosophy of Dialogue and its Contemporary Reception*, edited by Paul Mendes-Flohr, 141–57. Berlin: Walter de Gruyter.

Bin Xu. 2012. "Grandpa Wen: Scene and Political Performance." *Sociological Theory* 30(2): 114–29.

——. 2013a. "Mourning Becomes Democratic." *Contexts* 12(1): 42–46.

——. 2013b. "For Whom the Bell Tolls: State-Society Relations and the Sichuan Earthquake Mourning in China." *Theory and Society* 42(5): 509–42.

——. 2014. "Consensus Crisis and Civil Society: The Sichuan Earthquake Response and State-Society Relations." *China Journal* 71: 91–108.

Bloch, Maurice, and Jonathan Parry, eds. 1982. *Death and the Regeneration of Life*. Cambridge: Cambridge University Press.

Blommaert, Jan. 2015. "Chronotopes, Scales, and Complexity in the Study of Language in Society." *Annual Review of Anthropology* 44: 105–16.

Blondeau, A. M., ed. 1995. *Tibetan Mountain Deities, Their Cults and Representations: Papers Presented at a Panel of the 7th Seminar of the International Association for Tibetan Studies, Graz 1995*. Vol. 6. Vienna: Verlag der Österreichischen Akademie der Wissenschaften.

Boddy, J. 1994. "Spirit Possession Revisited: Beyond Instrumentality." *Annual Review of Anthropology* 23: 407–34.

Boltanski, Luc. 1999. *Distant Suffering: Morality, Media, and Politics*. New York: Cambridge University Press.

Bornstein, Erica, and Peter Redfield. 2011. "An Introduction to the Anthropology of Humanitarianism." In *Forces of Compassion: Humanitarianism Between Ethics and Politics* (School for Advanced Research Advanced Seminar Series), edited by Erica Bornstein and Peter Redfield, 3–30. Santa Fe: SAR Press.

Boxun News. 2009. "An Official in Beijing Revealed, 'Choose a Patriotic Theme Each Year to Unite the People and Attack Dissidents.'" October 2, accessed November 1, 2010, news.boxun.com/news/gb/china/2009/10/200910022302.shtml.

——. 2010. "Qingqiu Dalai Lama lai Zaiqu. Yushu Zaiqu Renmin zhi Hu Zhuxi he Wen Zongli de Yifengxin" (Request that the Dalai Lama Come to the Disaster Zone, a Letter from the People of the Yushu Disaster Zone to President Hu Jintao and Premier Wen). April 16, accessed May 1, news.boxun.com/news/gb/china/2010/04/201004160551.shtml.

Bray, David. 2006. "Building 'Community': New Strategies of Governance in Urban China." *Economy and Society* 35(4): 530–49.

Briggs, Charles. 1986. *Learning How to Ask: A Sociolinguistic Appraisal of the Role of the Interview in Social Science Research*. Cambridge: Cambridge University Press.

Briggs, Charles L., and Richard Bauman. 1992. "Genre, Intertextuality, and Social Power." *Journal of Linguistic Anthropology* 2(2): 131–72.

Brownell, Susan. 2008. *Beijing's Games: What the Olympics Mean to China*. Lanham, MD: Rowman and Littlefield.

——. 2009. "China's Olympic Road." In *China in 2008: A Year of Great Significance*, edited by Kate Merkel-Hess, Kenneth L. Pommeranz, and Jeffrey Wasserstrom, 147–61. London: Routledge.

BT and SGTR ('brug thar and sangs rgyas tshe ring). 2005. *mdo smad rma khug tsha 'gram yul gru'i lo rgyus deb ther chen mo* (Great Historical Annals of the Region along the Banks of the Yellow River in Amdo). Beijing: Minzu Chubanshe.

Buckley, Michael. 2014. *Meltdown in Tibet: China's Reckless Destruction of Ecosystems from the Highlands of Tibet to the Deltas of Asia*. New York: Palgrave Macmillan.

Buffetrille, Katia. 2008. "Some Remarks on Mediums: The Case of the lha pa of the Musical Festival (glurol) of Sogru (A mdo)." In "Mongolo-TibeticaPragensia, edited by J. Vacek and A. Oberfalzerová, Special Issue, *Mediums and Shamans in Central Asia* 1(2): 13–66.

——. 2014. "The Pilgrimage to Mount Kha ba dkar po: A Metaphor for Bardo?" In *Searching for the Dharma, Finding Salvation—Buddhist Pilgrimage in Time and Space. Proceedings of the Workshop "Buddhist Pilgrimage in History and Present Times,"* edited by Christoph Cueppers and Max Deeg, 197–220. Lumbini: Lumbini International Research Institute.

Buffetrille, Katia, and Françoise Robin, eds. 2012. "Tibet Is Burning: Self-Immolation, Ritual or Political Protest?" Special Issue, *Revue d'Etudes Tibétaines* 25: v–x.

Butler, Judith. 2004. *Precarious life: The Powers of Mourning and Violence.* London: Verso.

Cai Yongshun. 2003. "Collective Ownership or Cadres' Ownership? The Non-agricultural Use of Farmland in China." *China Quarterly* 175: 662–80.

Candea, Matei, and Giovanni da Col. 2012. "The Return to Hospitality." In "The Return to Hospitality: Strangers, Guests, and Ambiguous Encounters," edited by Matei Candea and Giovanni da Col, Special Issue, *Journal of the Royal Anthropological Institute*, n.s., 18, s1: s1–s19.

Caple, Jane Eluned. 2011. "Seeing Beyond the State? The Negotiation of Moral Boundaries in the Revival and Development of Tibetan Buddhist Monasticism in Contemporary China." Ph.D. diss., University of Leeds.

Carrasco, Pedro. 1959. *Land and Polity in Tibet.* Seattle: University of Washington Press.

Carsten, Janet. 2000. *Cultures of Relatedness: New Approaches to the Study of Kinship.* Cambridge: Cambridge University Press.

——. 2003. *After Kinship.* Cambridge: Cambridge University Press.

Cartier, Carolyn. 2005. "City-Space: Scale Relations and China's Spatial Administrative Hierarchy." In *Restructuring the Chinese City: Changing Society, Economy and Space,* edited by Laurence J.C. Ma and Fulong Wu, 21–39. London: Routledge.

De Castro, Eduardo Viveiros. 1998. "Cosmological Deixis and Amerindian Perspectivism." *Journal of the Royal Anthropological Institute* 4(3): 469–88.

CGDJTR (chab 'gag rdo rje tshe ring). 2006. "kha btags." *yul srol.* TBRC W2DB25434. lan kru'u: kan su'u mi rigs dpe skrun khang: 53–55.

Cha, Ariana Eunjung. 2009. "China's Pusher of Philanthropy." *Washington Post,* January 31, http://www.washingtonpost.com/wp-dyn/content/article/2009/01/30/AR2009013003594.html.

Chakrabarty, Dipesh. 2000. *Provincializing Europe: Postcolonial Thought and Historical Difference.* Princeton, NJ: Princeton University Press.

Chau, Adam. 2005. "Politics of Legitimation and the Revival of Popular Religion in Shaanbei, China." *Modern China* 31(2): 236–78.

Cheater, A. P. 1991. "Death Ritual as Political Trickster in the People's Republic of China." *Australian Journal of Chinese Affairs* 26: 85–94.

Chen Yong. 2008. "Giving Long-Term Relief." *China Beat* (blog). May 23, accessed October 1, thechinabeat.blogspot.com/2008/05/giving-long-term-relief.html.

Chenaktsang, Wuqi. 2010. "Traditional Tibetan Pilgrimage and the Eight Holy Sites of Rebgong." In *Pilgrims and Travellers in Search of the Holy,* edited by René Gothóni, 183–204. Oxford: Peter Lang.

China News Web. 2008. "Labrang Monks Fundraise (Gannan Labolengsi Zangchuan Fojiao Siyuan Sengren Juankuan)." May 15, accessed August 1. news.qq.com/a/20080515/003922.htm.

Chong, Gladys Pak Lei. 2011. "Volunteers as the 'New' Model Citizens: Governing Citizens through Soft Power." *China Information* 25(1): 33–59.

Chong Thargyal (khyung thar rgyal). 1994. "kun gzigs pan chen sku phreng bcu ba mchog rtse khog mdzong du phebs pa'i gnas tshul mdo tsam mrjod pa" (Brief Report on the All-Seeing Tenth Panchen Lama's Visit to rtse khog). *rtse khog rdzong gi rig gnas lo rgyus dpyad yig bdams bsgrigs (deb dang po).* Zeku xian Wenshi Ziliao (Historical Information on Zeku County). Vol. 1.

Chu, Julie Y. 2014. "When Infrastructures Attack: The Workings of Disrepair in China." *American Ethnologist* 14(2): 351–67.

Ciurtin, E. 2009. "The Buddha's Earthquakes on Water: Earthquakes and Seaquakes in Buddhist Cosmology and Meditation, with an Appendix on Buddhist Art." *STVDIA ASIATICA: Revue Internationale d'Etudes Asiatiques* 10(1–2): 59–123.

Comaroff, Jean. 2007. "Beyond Bare Life: AIDS, (bio)politics, and the Neoliberal Order." *Public Culture* 19(1): 197–219.

Comaroff, Jean, and John L. Comaroff. 1999. "Occult Economies and the Violence of Abstraction: Notes from the South African Postcolony." *American Ethnologist* 26(2): 279–303.

Cooper, Frederick, and Randall Packard, eds. 1997. *International Development and the Social Sciences.* Berkeley: University of California Press.

Coronil, Fernando. 1997. *The Magical State: Nature, Money, and Modernity in Venezuela.* Chicago: University of Chicago Press.

Coronil, Fernando, and Julie Skurski, eds. 2006. *States of Violence.* Ann Arbor: University of Michigan Press.

Course, Magnus. 2010. "Of Words and Fog: Linguistic Relativity and Amerindian Ontology." *Anthropological Theory* 10(3): 247–63. doi:10.1177/1463499610372177.

Craig, Sienna. 2010. "Rubble and Resilience: A Dispatch from Yushu." Unpublished report.

——. 2012. *Healing Elements: Efficacy and the Social Ecologies of Tibetan Medicine.* Berkeley: University of California Press.

Cuevas, Bryan J. 2008. *Travels in the Netherworld: Buddhist Popular Narratives of Death and the Afterlife in Tibet.* Oxford: Oxford University Press.

Cunningham, Philip J. 2010. "Qinghai Quake Spared Media Circus." *China Daily,* April 20, http://www.chinadaily.com.cn/opinion/2010–04/20/content_9750218.htm.

Da Col, Giovanni. 2007. "The View from Somewhen: Events, Bodies, and the Perspective of Fortune around Mount Karpo, a Tibetan Sacred Mountain in Yunnan Province." *Inner Asia* 9: 215–35.

——. 2012a. "The Elementary Economies of Dechenwa Life: Fortune, Vitality, and the Mountain in Sino-Tibetan Borderlands." *Social Analysis* 56(1): 74–98.

——. 2012b. "The Poisoner and the Parasite: Cosmoeconomics, Fear, and Hospitality among Dechen Tibetans." In *The Return to Hospitality: Strangers, Guests, and Ambiguous Encounters,* edited by Matei Candea and Giovanni da Col, special issue, supplement, *Journal of the Royal Anthropological Institute,* n.s., 18 s1: s210–s217.

Dalai Lama of Tibet, the Fourteenth. 1990. *Freedom in Exile. The Autobiography of the Dalai Lama: Tenzin Gyatso, the Fourteenth Dalai Lama of Tibet.* New York: Harper Collins.

Dalton, Jacob P. 2012. *The Taming of the Demons: Violence and Liberation in Tibetan Buddhism.* New Haven, CT: Yale University Press.

Das, Veena. 1995. *Critical Events: An Anthropological Perspective on Contemporary India*. Oxford: Oxford University Press.

——. 2007. *Life and Words: Violence and the Descent into the Ordinary*. Berkeley: University of California Press.

Das, Veena, and Arthur Kleinman. 2000. "Introduction." In *Violence and Subjectivity*, edited by Veena Das, Arthur Kleinman, Mamphela Ramphele, and Pamela Reynolds. Berkeley: University of California Press.

Das, Veena, and Deborah Poole. 2004. "State and its Margins: Comparative Ethnographies." In *Anthropology in the Margins of the State*, edited by Veena Das and Deborah Poole, 3–34. Santa Fe: School of American Research Press.

Daub, Travis. 2010. "China's War on Illegal Buildings." *PBS Newshour*. August 17, accessed October 1, 2013, http://www.pbs.org/newshour/rundown/chinas-war-on-illegal-buildings/.

Day, Alexander, and Matthew A. Hale. 2007. Guest Editors' Introduction to *Chinese Sociology and Anthropology* 39(4): 3–9.

Dehaene, Michiel, and Lieven de Cauter. 2008. "Heterotopia in a Postcivil Society." In *Heterotopia and the City: Public Space in a Postcivil Society*, edited by Michiel Dehaene and Lieven de Cauter, 3–11. London: Routledge.

Deleuze, Gilles, and Félix Guattari. 1987. *A Thousand Plateaus: Capitalism and Schizophrenia*. Minneapolis: University of Minnesota Press.

Derrida, Jacques. 1992. *Given Time: i. Counterfeit Money*. Translated by Peggy Kamuf. Chicago: University of Chicago Press.

Diemberger, Hildegard. 2005. "Female Oracles in Modern Tibet." In *Women in Tibet*, edited by Janet Gyatso and Hanna Havnevik, 113–69. London: Hurst.

——. 2007. "Festivals and Their Leaders: the Management of Tradition in the Mongolian/Tibetan Borderlands." In *The Mongolia-Tibet Interface: Opening New Research Terrains in Inner Asia*, edited by Uradyn E. Bulag and Hildegard Diemberger, 109–34. Leiden: Brill.

Dikötter, Frank. 2011. *Mao's Great Famine: The History of China's Most Devastating Catastrophe, 1958–1962*. New York: Walker.

Dorje Tsering Chenaktshang. 2014. *Yartsa Rinpoche: Precious Caterpillar* (documentary). 101 min., DVD.

Dreyer, June. 2006. "Economic Development in Tibet under the People's Republic of China." In *Contemporary Tibet: Politics, Development, and Society in a Disputed Region*, edited by Barry Sautman and June Dreyer, 129–152. Armonk, NY: M. E. Sharpe.

Duara, Prasenjit. 1995. *Rescuing History from the Nation: Questioning Narratives of Modern China*. Chicago: University of Chicago Press.

Durkheim, Émile. 1915 (1912). *The Elementary Forms of the Religious Life: A Study in Religious Sociology*. Translated by Joseph Ward Swain. London: George Allen and Unwin.

Dwyer, Kevin. 1979. "The Dialogic of Ethnology." *Dialectical Anthropology* 4(3): 205–24.

Edelman, Marc, and Angelique Haugerud, eds. 2005. *The Anthropology of Development and Globalization: From Classical Political Economy to Contemporary Neoliberalism*. Malden, MA: Wiley.

Ekvall, Robert. 1939. *Cultural Relations on the Kansu-Tibetan Border*. Chicago: University of Chicago Press.

———. 1954. "Some Differences in Tibetan Land Tenure and Utilization." *Sinologica* 4: 39–48.

Empson, Rebecca M. 2011. *Harnessing Fortune: Personhood, Memory, and Place in Mongolia.* Oxford: Oxford University Press.

Engelke, Matthew. 2007. *A Problem of Presence: Beyond Scripture in an African Church.* Chicago: University of Chicago Press.

Epstein, Lawrence, and Peng Wenbin. 1998. "Ritual, Ethnicity, and Generational Identity." In *Buddhism in Contemporary Tibet: Religious Revival and Cultural Identity*, edited by Melvyn C. Goldstein and Matthew T. Kapstein, 120–39. Berkeley: University of California Press.

Escobar, Arturo. 1995. *Encountering Development: The Making and Unmaking of the Third World.* Princeton, NJ: Princeton University Press.

Fabian, Johannes. 1983. *Time and the Other: How Anthropology Makes Its Object.* New York: Columbia University Press.

Fan, Maureen. 2008. "Chinese Open Wallets for Quake Aid." *Washington Post*, May 16, http://www.washingtonpost.com/wp-dyn/content/article/2008/05/16/AR20 08051600181.html.

Fassin, Didier. 2012. *Humanitarian Reason: A Moral History of the Present.* Berkeley: University of California Press.

Faubion, James. 2008. "Heterotopia: An Ecology." In *Heterotopia and the City: Public Space in a Postcivil Society*, edited by Michiel Dehaene and Lieven de Cauter, 31–40. London: Routledge.

Fehervary, Krisztina. 2013. *Politics in Color and Concrete: Socialist Materialities and the Middle Class in Hungary.* Bloomington: Indiana University Press.

Feuchtwang, Stephen, ed. 2004. *Making Place: State Projects, Globalisation, and Local Responses in China.* London: University College London Press.

Feuchtwang, Stephen, and Mingming Wang. 2001. *Grassroots Charisma in China: Four Local Leaders in China.* Routledge Studies in China in Transition, Vol. 10. London: Routledge.

Fischer, Andrew Martin. 2005. *State Growth and Social Exclusion in Tibet: Challenges of Recent Economic Growth.* Copenhagen: Nordic Institute of Asian Studies Press.

———. 2008. "'Population Invasion' versus Urban Exclusion in the Tibetan Areas of Western China." *Population and Development Review* 34(4): 631–62.

———. 2009a. "The Political Economy of Boomerang Aid in China's Tibet." *China Perspectives* 3, accessed November 13, 2012. http://chinaperspectives.revues. org/4842.

———. 2009b. Educating for Exclusion in Western China: Structural and Institutional Dimensions of Conflict in the Tibetan Areas of Qinghai and Tibet. Crise Working Paper No. 69 (July), Center for Research on Inequality, Human Security and Ethnicity, University of Oxford.

———. 2012. "The Revenge of Fiscal Maoism in China's Tibet." International Institute of Social Studies of Erasmus University, Working Paper Series 547, 1–32.

———. 2013. *The Disempowered Development of Tibet in China: A Study in the Economics of Marginalization.* Lanham, MD: Lexington Books.

Fish, Isaac. 2010. "A Sympathetic Hearing." *Newsweek Online*. April 15, accessed June 10, http://www.newsweek.com/id/236452/output/print.

Fletcher, Hannah. 2008. "China Bloggers Cook Up Quake Conspiracies." *Times Online.* May 13, accessed June 1, http://www.timesonline.co.uk/tol/news/world/asia/article3925096.ece.

Ford, Peter. 2010. "China Mudslides Were Predicted Thirteen Years Ago." *Christian Science Monitor,* August 12, http://www.csmonitor.com/World/Asia-Pacific/2010/0812/China-mudslides-were-predicted-13-years-ago.

Foster, Robert. 2002. "News of the World: Millenarian Christianity and the Olympic Torch Relay." In *Materializing the Nation: Commodities, Consumption, and Media in Papua New Guinea,* 131–51. Bloomington: Indiana University Press.

Foucault, Michel. 1986 (1967). "Of Other Spaces." Translated by Jay Miskowiec. *Diacritics* 16(1): 22–27.

——. 1990 (1978). "Right of Death and Power over Life." In *The History of Sexuality.* Vol. 1. *An Introduction,* translated by Robert Hurley, 133–61. New York: Vintage Books.

Gal, Susan. 1991. "Bartok's Funeral: Representations of Europe in Hungarian Political Rhetoric." *American Ethnologist* 18(3): 440–58.

Gamburd, Michele, and Dennis McGilvray. 2010a. Introduction to *Tsunami Recovery in Sri Lanka: Ethnic and Regional Dimensions,* edited by Michele Gamburd and Dennis McGilvray, 1–16. London: Routledge.

——, eds. 2010b. *Tsunami Recovery in Sri Lanka: Ethnic and Regional Dimensions.* London: Routledge.

GDKS (akhu rgya mtsho). 2012. *Rebgong mkhar nag gi lo rgyus shel dkar me long* (A Clear Mirror: the History of Rebgong Kharnak). Lanzhou: Gansu Minzu Chubanshe.

GDLT (dge 'dun legs tshogs). 2002. *re skong rong bo dgon chen gyi lo rgyus mdor bsdus* (An Abridged History of Rebgong's Great Rongbo Monastery). Rebgong: rongbo dgon chen do dam khang.

Gell, Alfred. 1998. *Art and Agency: An Anthropological Theory.* Oxford: Clarendon Press.

Gendun Palzang (dge 'dun dpal bzang). 2007. *Rebgong yul skor zin tho* (Notes on the Rebgong Region). Lanzhou: Gansu Minzu Chubanshe.

Gendun Rabsal. 2013. "reb kong gyi nyi ma nub pa: shar skal ldan rgya mtsho sku phreng bdun pa'i sku tshe: 1916–1978" (The Sun Disappears in Rebkong: The Life of the Seventh Shar skal ldan rgya mtsho: 1916–1978). In *Monastic and Lay Traditions in North-east Tibet,* edited by Yangdon Dhondup, Ulrich Pagel, and Geoffrey Samuels, 49–67. Leiden: Brill.

Germano, David. 1997. "Death, Dying, and Other Opportunities." In *Religions of Tibet in Practice,* edited by Donald S. Lopez Jr., 458–93. Princeton, NJ: Princeton University Press.

——. 1998. "Re-membering the Dismembered Body of Tibet: Contemporary Tibetan Visionary Movements in the People's Republic of China." In *Buddhism in Contemporary Tibet: Religious Revival and Cultural Identity,* edited by Melvyn C. Goldstein and Matthew T. Kapstein, 53–95. Berkeley: University of California Press.

GGLMTR (Gling rgya bla ma tshe ring). 2002. *reb gong gser mo ljong kyi chos srid byung ba brjod pa 'dod 'byung gter gyi bum bzang* (An Excellent Wish-Fulfilling Vase: Documents on the Origins of Buddhist Governance in the Golden Realm of Rebgong). Xining: Tianma.

Giroux, Henry. 1993. "Consuming Social Change: The 'United Colors of Benetton.'" *Cultural Critique* 26: 5–32.

Goffman, Erving. 1981. "Footing." In *Forms of Talk,* 124–59. Philadelphia: University of Pennsylvania Press.

——. 1983. "Felicity's Condition." *American Journal of Sociology* 89(1): 1–53.

Goodman, David S. G. 2004a. "The Campaign to 'Open up the West': National, Provincial Level, and Local Perspectives." *China Quarterly* 178: 317–34.

——. 2004b. "Qinghai and the Emergence of the West: Nationalities, Communal Interaction, and National Integration." *China Quarterly* 178: 379–99.

Goldstein, Melvyn C. 1997. *The Snow Lion and the Dragon: China, Tibet, and the Dalai Lama.* Berkeley: University of California Press.

——. 2009. *A History of Modern Tibet.* Vol. 2. *The Calm before the Storm, 1951–1955.* Berkeley: University of California Press.

——. 2013. *A History of Modern Tibet.* Vol. 3. *The Storm Clouds Descend, 1955–1957.* Berkeley: University of California Press.

Goldstein, Melvyn C., Ben Jiao, and Tanzen Lhundrup. 2009. *On the Cultural Revolution in Tibet: The Nyemo Incident of 1969.* Berkeley: University of California Press.

Graeber, David. 2001. *Toward an Anthropological Theory of Value: The False Coin of Our Own Dreams.* New York: Palgrave Macmillan.

Greenhalgh, Susan, and Edwin A. Winckler. 2005. *Governing China's Population: From Leninist to Neoliberal Biopolitics.* Stanford, CA: Stanford University Press.

Guide to the Development of Western China: Qinghai Province (Xibu diqu Kaifa zhinan). 1988. Beijing: China Science and Technology Press.

Gunewardena, Nandini, and Mark Schuller, eds. 2008. *Capitalizing on Catastrophe: Neoliberal Strategies in Disaster Reconstruction.* Lanham, MD: AltaMira Press.

Guo Xiaolin. 2001. "Land Expropriation and Rural Conflicts in China." *China Quarterly* 166: 422–39.

Guyer, Jane. 2007. "Prophecy and the Near Future: Thoughts on Macroeconomic, Evangelical, and Punctuated Time." *American Ethnologist* 34(3): 409–21.

Hai Ren. 2004. "The Countdown of Time and the Practice of Everyday Life." *Rhizomes: Cultural Studies in Emerging Knowledge* 8 (spring). http://www.rhizomes.net/issue8/ren.htm.

——. 2010. *Neoliberalism and the Cultural in China and Hong Kong: The Countdown of Time.* London: Routledge.

Hall, Jacquelyn Dowd. 1998. "You Must Remember This: Autobiography as Social Critique." *Journal of American History* 85(2): 439–65.

Halperin, Mark. 1999. "Buddhist Temples, the War Dead, and the Song Imperial Cult." *Asia Major,* 3rd ser. 12(2): 71–99.

Handman, Courtney. 2014. "Mediating Denominational Disputes: Land Claims and the Sound of Christian Critique." In *Critical Christianity: Translation and Denominational Conflict in Papua New Guinea,* chapter 7. Berkeley: University of California Press.

Hanks, William. 1996. "Exorcism and the Description of Participant Roles." In *Natural Histories of Discourse,* edited by Michael Silverstein and Greg Urban, 160–220. Chicago: University of Chicago Press.

Hansen, Thomas, and Finn Stepputat. 2006. "Sovereignty Revisited." *Annual Review of Anthropology* 35: 295–315.

Harding, Susan F. 1986. "Convicted by the Holy Spirit: The Rhetoric of Fundamental Baptist Conversion." *American Ethnologist* 14(1): 167–81.

Harrell, Stevan. 1995. "Introduction: Civilizing Projects and the Reaction to Them." In *Cultural Encounters on China's Ethnic Frontiers*, edited by Stevan Harrell, 3–37. Seattle: University of Washington Press.

Harrell-Bond, Barbara, Mark Leopold, and Eftihia Voutira. 1992. "Counting the Refugees: Gifts, Givers, Patrons, and Clients." *Journal of Refugee Studies* 5(3/4): 205–25.

Harris, Clare. 2001. "The Politics and Personhood of Tibetan Buddhist Icons." in *Beyond Aesthetics: Art and the Technologies of Enchantment*, edited by Christopher Pinney and Nicolas Thomas, 181–99. Oxford: Berg.

Hart, Laurie Kain. 2004. "Space and Place." In *Making Place: State Projects, Globalisation, and Local Responses in China*, edited by Stephan Feuchtwang, 183–96. London: University College London Press.

Hartley, Lauran R. and Patricia Schiaffini-Vedani. 2008. "Introduction." In *Modern Tibetan Literature and Social Change*, edited by Lauran R. Hartley and Patricia Schiaffini-Vedani, xiii–xxxviii. Durham, NC: Duke University Press.

Henare, Amiria, Martin Holbraad, and Sari Wastell. 2006. *Thinking through Things: Theorising Artefacts Ethnographically*. London: Routledge.

Herzfeld, Michael. 2012. "Afterword: Reciprocating the Hospitality of These Pages." In "The Return to Hospitality: Strangers, Guests, and Ambiguous Encounters," edited by Matei Candea and Giovanni da Col, special issue, *Journal of the Royal Anthropological Institute*, n.s., 18, s1: s210–2s217.

Hevia, James. 1995. *Cherishing Men from Afar: Qing Guest Ritual and the Macartney Embassy of 1793*. Durham, NC: Duke University Press.

Hewitt, Kenneth, ed. 1983. *Interpretation of Calamity: From the Viewpoint of Human Ecology*. Crows Nest, New South Wales, Australia: Allen and Unwin.

Hill, Jane H. 1986. "The Refiguration of the Anthropology of Language." *Cultural Anthropology* 1(1): 89–102.

———. 1995. "The Voices of Don Gabriel: Responsibility and Self in a Modern Mexicano Narrative." In *The Dialogic Emergence of Culture*, edited by Dennis Tedlock and Bruce Mannheim, 97–147. Urbana: University of Illinois Press.

Hill, Jane H., and Judith T. Irvine. 1993. Introduction to *Responsibility and Evidence in Oral Discourse*, edited by Jane H. Hill and Judith T. Irvine, 1–23. Cambridge: Cambridge University Press.

HNGK. 1985. *Huangnan Zangzu Zizhizhou Gaikuang* (Introduction to Huangnan Tibetan Autonomous Prefecture). Xining: Qinghai Renmin Chubanshe.

HNWSZL 1. 1992. *rma lho'i rig gnas lo rgyus kyi dpyad yig* (Ma Bufang's Activities in Rebgong). Vol. 1 Huangnan Wenshi Ziliao (Huangnan Prefecture Party Committee).

HNWSZL 3. 1996. *Huangnan Wenshi Ziliao*. Vol. 3. Huangnan Prefecture Party Committee.

HNWSZL 4. 1997. *Shi shi Panchen Dashi Guancha Huangnan Zhuanqi* (*kun gzigs pan chen rin po che blo bzang chos rgyan zhabs nas reb gong gser mo ljongs la gzigs zhib mdzad pa'i sdi*) *Huangnan Wenshi Ziliao*. Vol. 4. Huangnan Prefecture Party Committee.

HNZZ. 2001. *Huangnan Zhou Zhi* (Huangnan Prefecture Gazeteer). Lanzhou: Gansu Minzu Chubanshe.

Ho, Peter. 2001. "Who Owns China's Land? Policies, Property Rights, and Deliberate Institutional Ambiguity." *China Quarterly* 166: 394–421.

Hoffmann, Susanna M., and Anthony Oliver-Smith, eds. 2002. *Culture and Catastrophe: The Anthropology of Disaster.* Santa Fe, NM: School of American Research Press.

Holbig, Heike. 2004. "The Emergence of the Campaign to Open Up the West: Ideological Formation, Central Decision-Making and the Role of the Provinces." *China Quarterly* 178: 335–57.

Holston, James. 1989. *The Modernist City: An Anthropological Critique of Brasilia.* Chicago: University Of Chicago Press.

Hornby, Lucy, and Alfred Cang. 2008. "Curse of the Fuwa Fulfilled by Floods." *Reuters.* June 19, accessed November 1, http://www.reuters.com/article/2008/06/19/us-curse-idUSPEK15196420080619.

Hubbert, Jennifer. 2014. "The Darfur Olympics: Global Citizenship and the 2008 Beijing Olympic Games." *Positions: East Asia Cultures Critique* 22(1): 203–36. doi:10.1215/10679847-2383894.

Huber, Toni. 1994. "Putting the Gnas Back into Gnas-Skor: Rethinking Tibetan Buddhist Pilgrimage Practice." *Tibet Journal* 19(2): 23–60.

——. 1999. *The Cult of Pure Crystal Mountain: Popular Pilgrimage and Visionary Landscape in Southeast Tibet.* New York: Oxford University Press.

Hui, Dennis, and Lai Hang. 2009. "Research Note: Politics of Sichuan Earthquake, 2008." *Journal of Contingencies and Crisis Management* 17(2): 137–40.

Human Rights Watch (HRW). 2010. "'I Saw It with My Own Eyes': Abuses by Chinese Security Forces in Tibet, 2008–2010." July 21. Accessed August 1. http://www.hrw.org/en/reports/2010/07/22/i-saw-it-my-own-eyes.

Humphrey, Caroline. 2002. *The Unmaking of Soviet Life: Everyday Economies after Socialism.* Ithaca, NY: Cornell University Press.

Hymes, Dell. 1972 (1969). "The Use of Anthropology: Critical, Political, Personal." In *Reinventing Anthropology*, edited by Dell Hymes, 3–83. New York: Random House.

ICT (International Campaign for Tibet). 2008a. "Tibet at a Turning Point: The Spring Uprising and China's New Crackdown: A Report." August, http://www.savetibet.org/wp-content/uploads/2013/03/Tibet_at_a_Turning_Point.pdf.

——. 2008b. "Tibetans in Monasteries under Crackdown Hold Prayer Ceremonies for Earthquake Victims: Message of Reconciliation from Monastery." May 21, accessed October 1, http://www.savetibet.org/media-center/ict-news-reports/tibetans-monasteries-under-crackdown-hold-prayer-ceremonies-earthquake-victims-message-rec.

——. 2009. "Tibetans in Mourning as Chinese New Year Begins." January 29, accessed February 10, http://www.indigenousportal.com/Culture/Tibetans-in-mourning-as-Chinese-New-Year-begins.html.

——. 2011a. "Bold Online Appeals Address Persistent Lead Poisoning in Qinghai Water Supply." July 29, accessed May 1, 2015, http://www.savetibet.org/bold-online-appeals-address-persistent-lead-poisoning-in-qinghai-water-supply/.

——. 2011b. "Tibetans in Amdo Suffer Lead Exposure from Chinese Factories." August 3, http://www.thetibetpost.com/en/news/tibet/1910-tibetans-in-amdo-suffer-lead-exposure-from-chinese-factories.

IOSCPRC (Information Office of the State Council of the People's Republic of China). 2005. "China's Peaceful Development Road." December 12, accessed November 1, 2009, http://www.china.org.cn/english/features/book/152684.htm.

Irvine, Judith T. 1979. "Formality and Informality in Communicative Events." *American Anthropologist* 16: 248–67.

——. 1982. "The Creation of Identification in Spirit Mediumship and Possession." In *Semantic Anthropology,* edited by David J. Parkin, 241–57. London: Academic Press.

Jacoby, Sarah. 2014. *Love and Liberation: Autobiographical Writings of the Tibetan Buddhist Visionary Sera Khandro.* New York, Columbia University Press.

James, Wendy, and N. J. Allen, eds. 1998. *Marcel Mauss: A Centenary Tribute.* New York: Berghahn Books.

Jamyang Norbu. 2005. "Body Snatchers," and "Back to the Future: Enduring Phobias and Superstitions in Tibetan Society (Part Two)." http://jnorbu.blogspot.com/2005/03/back-to-future-enduring-phobias-and.html.

——. 2008. "The Karmapa and the Cranes." *Phayul.com.* May 28, accessed October 10, http://www.phayul.com/news/tools/print.aspx?id=21401&t=1.

JBGP ('jam dbyangs grags pa). 2009. *reb kong rus mdzod lta ba mkha' khyab phyogs bral* (An Impartial and All-Pervasive View: Geneologies and Histories of Rebgong Clans). Beijing: Minzu Chubanshe.

JMTC ('jigs med theg mchog). 1988. *rong bo dgon chen gyi gdan rabs rdzogs ldan gtam gyi rang sgra zhes bya ba bzhugs so* (The Golden Age of Spontaneous Speech: History of the Great Monastery of Rongbo). Xining: mtsho sngon mi rigs dpe skrun khang.

Johnson, Ian. 2012. "China: Worse Than You Ever Imagined." *New York Review of Books.* November 22, accessed December 10, http://www.nybooks.com/articles/archives/2012/nov/22/china-worse-you-ever-imagined/.

Kansteiner, Wulf. 2002. "Finding Meaning in Memory: A Methodological Critique of Collective Memory Studies." *History and Theory* 41(2): 179–97.

Karmay, Samten Gyaltsen. 1994. "Mountain Cults and National Identity in Tibet." In *Resistance and Reform in Tibet,* edited by Robert Barnett and Shirin Akiner, 112–20. Bloomington: Indiana University Press.

——. 1998. "Myths and Rituals." In *The Arrow and the Spindle: Studies in History, Myths, Rituals and Beliefs in Tibet,* 3–25. Kathmandu: Mandala Book Point.

Keane, Webb. 1997a. *Signs of Recognition: Powers and Hazards of Representation in an Indonesian Society.* Berkeley: University of California Press.

——. 1997b. "Religious Language." *Annual Review of Anthropology* 26: 47–71.

——. 2001. "Voice." In *Key Terms in Language and Culture,* edited by Alessandro Duranti, 268–72. Malden, MA: Blackwell.

——. 2003. "Semiotics and the Social Analysis of Material Things." *Language and Communication* 23: 409–25.

——. 2008a. "The Evidence of the Senses and the Materiality of Religion." *Journal of the Royal Anthropological Institute* 14(1): 110–27.

——. 2008b. "Market, Materiality, and Moral Metalanguage." *Anthropological Theory* 8(1): 27–42.

——. 2009. "On Multiple Ontologies and the Temporality of Things." In *Material World: A Global Hub for Thinking About Things From the Occasional Paper*

Series: N 4—*Properties & Social Imagination: Explorations & Experiments with Ethnography Collections.* http://www.materialworldblog.com/2009/07/on-multiple-ontologies-and-the-temporality-of-things/.

———. 2013. "Ontologies, Anthropologists, and Ethical Life." *Hau: Journal of Ethnographic Theory* 8(1): 186–91.

———. 2014. "Affordances and Reflexivity in Ethical Life: An Ethnographic Stance." *Anthropological Theory* 14(1): 3–26.

Kipnis, Andrew. 2007. "Neoliberalism Reified: Suzhi Discourse and Tropes of Neoliberalism in the People's Republic of China." *Journal of the Royal Anthropological Institute* 13(2): 383–400.

Kleinman, Arthur, Yunxiang Yan, Jing Jun, Sing Lee, Everett Zhang, Pan Tianshu, Wu Fei, and Jinhua Guo. 2011. *Deep China: The Moral Life of the Person.* Berkeley: University of California Press.

Klima, Alan. 2002. *The Funeral Casino: Meditation, Massacre, and Exchange with the Dead in Thailand.* Princeton, NJ: Princeton University Press.

Kohn, Eduardo. 2015. "Anthropology of Ontologies." *Annual Review of Anthropology* 44: 311–27.

Kojima, Kazuko, and Ryosei Kokubun. 2002. "The 'Shequ Construction' Programme and the Chinese Communist Party." *Copenhagen Journal of Asian Studies* 16: 86–105.

Kolås, Åshild, and Monika P. Thowsen. 2005. *On the Margins of Tibet: Cultural Survival on the Sino-Tibetan Frontier.* Seattle: University of Washington Press.

Korf, Benedikt, Shahul Habullah, Pia Hollenbach, and Bart Klem. 2010. "The Gift of Disaster: The Commodification of Good Intentions in Post-Tsunami Sri Lanka." supplement, *Disasters* 34, s1: S60–S77. doi:10.1111/j.1467-7717.2009. 01099.x.

Kristoff, Nicolas. 2008. "The Terrified Monks." *New York Times*, May 15.

KTG (mkhar rtse rgyal). 2005. Radio interview on Qinghai Tibetan radio station.

———. 2006. "mdo smad reb gong drug pa'i klu rol gyi cho ga bstar mkhan lha pa'i skor la dpyad pa (An Analysis of the lha pa, the Ones Who Carry Out the Rituals of Amdo Rebgong's 6th Month klu rol Festival)." *Zhongguo Zangxue* 2: 122–43.

———. 2009. 'jig rten mchod bstod: mdo smad reb gong yul gyi drug pa'i lha zla chen mo'i mchod pa dang 'brel ba'i dmangs srol rig gnas lo rgyus skor gyi zhib 'jug (Worldly Deities of Offering and Praise: Research on the History and Folk Culture of the Great Month of the Gods Offering Festival in the Amdo Rebgong Region). Beijing: Zhongguo Minzu Chubanshen.

Lafitte, Gabriel. 2010. "Set Aside Your Grudges." Paper presented at International Association of Tibetan Studies Meetings, Vancouver, BC, August.

Lai, Hongyi Harry. 2002. "China's Western Development Program: Its Rationale, Implementation, and Prospects." *Modern China* 28(4): 432–66.

Laidlaw, James. 2012. "Ontologically Challenged." *Anthropology of the Century* 4. http:// aotcpress.com/articles/ontologically-challenged/.

Langford, Jean. 2009. "Gifts Intercepted: Biopolitics and Spirit Debt." *Cultural Anthropology* 24(4): 681–711.

Lam, Willy. 2008. "Sichuan Quake Reveals Gross Failings in the System." *China Brief* 8(12). http://www.jamestown.org/single/?tx_ttnews%5Btt_news%5D=4965& no_cache=1#.VYCQcildUrw.

——. 2010. "Questions over Quake Toll in Tibet." *Asian Sentinel.* April 21, accessed May 1, asiasentinel.com/index.php?option=com_content&task=view&id=2411&Itemid=164.

Lassiter, Luke Eric. 2005. "Collaborative Ethnography and Public Anthropology." *Current Anthropology* 46(1): 83–106.

Latour, Bruno. 2005. *Reassembling the Social: An Introduction to Actor Network Theory.* Oxford: Oxford University Press.

Lawrence, Denise, and Setha Low. 1990. "The Built Environment and Spatial Form." *Annual Review of Anthropology* 19: 453–505.

Lawrence, Patricia. 2000. "Violence, Suffering, Amman: The Work of Oracles in Sri Lanka's Eastern War Zone." In *Violence and Subjectivity,* edited by Veena Das, Arthur Kleinman, Mamphela Ramphele, and Pamela Reynolds, 171–204. Berkeley: University of California Press.

Lempert, Michael. 2012. *Discipline and Debate: The Language of Violence in a Tibetan Buddhist Monastery.* Berkeley: University of California Press.

Lewis, I. M. 1971. *Ecstatic Religion: An Anthropological Study of Spirit Possession and Shamanism.* Hammondsworth, UK: Penguin.

Li Xuansheng. 2007. "Fazhan Regong Wenhua Chanye, Jianshe Hexie 'Wenhua Huangnan'" (Develop the Rebgong Culture Industry, Construct a Harmonious 'Cultural Huangnan'). *Regong Wenhua (Rebgong Culture)* 1(1): 10–15.

Li Zhang. 2006. "Contesting Spatial Modernity in Late-Socialist China." *Current Anthropology* 47(3): 461–84.

Li Zhang and Aihwa Ong, eds. 2008. *Privatizing China: Socialism from Afar.* Ithaca, NY: Cornell University Press.

Liang Jing. 2008. "2008 and China's 'National Destiny.'" Translated by David Kelly. *China Digital Times.* Accessed October 10, chinadigitaltimes.net/2008/12/liang-jing-2008-and-chinas-national-destiny/.

Lichter, David, and Lawrence Epstein. 1983. "Irony in Tibetan Notions of the Good Life." In *Karma: An Anthropological Inquiry,* edited by Charles F. Keyes and E. Valentine Daniel, 223–60. Berkeley: University of California Press.

Lin, George C. S. 2009. *Developing China: Land, Politics and Social Conditions.* London: Routledge.

Lin Yi. 2005. "Choosing between Ethnic and Chinese Citizenships: The Educational Trajectories of Tibetan Minority Children in Northwestern China." In *Chinese Citizenship: Views from the Margins,* edited by Vanessa L. Fong and Rachel Murphy, 41–67. London and New York: Routledge.

Link, Perry, trans. 2009. "China's Charter 08." *New York Review of Books.* January 15, accessed February 1, http://www.nybooks.com/articles/archives/2009/jan/15/chinas-charter-08/.

Lopez, Donald S. Jr. 1997a. "Mindfulness of Death." In *Religions of Tibet in Practice,* edited by Donald S. Lopez Jr., 421–41. Princeton, NJ: Princeton University Press.

——, ed. 1997b. *Religions of Tibet in Practice.* Princeton, NJ: Princeton University Press.

——. 1998. *Prisoners of Shangri-La: Tibetan Buddhism and the West.* Chicago: University of Chicago Press.

——, ed. 2005. *Critical Terms for the Study of Buddhism.* Chicago: University of Chicago Press.

LZDD (blo bzang don ldan). 1997. *Bod lugs rten rdzas kha btags kyi gleṅ ba*. Dharamsala: bod kyi dpe mdzod khang.

LZKR (blo bzang mkhyen rab). 2005. *mdo smad re skong rig pa 'byung ba'i grong khyer le lag dang bcas pa'i lugs gnyis gtam gyi bang mdzod las bsdus pa'i chos 'byung sa yi lha mo zhes bya ba bzhugs so* (Goddess of the Earth: A Buddhist History Compiled from the Storehouse of Documents on Buddhism and Governance in Amdo Rebgong, the Town which is the Source of Knowledge). Delhi: Self-published manuscript.

MacClancy, Jeremy, ed. 2002. *Exotic No More: Anthropology on the Front Lines*. Chicago: University of Chicago Press.

Macdonald, Alexander W., ed. 1997. *Mandala and Landscape*. New Delhi: D. K. Printworld.

Macdonald, Skye. 2010. "Tibet/China United through Benetton: An Analysis of Benetton's Advertising Strategy and Its Engagement in the 2008 Tibet–China Dialogue." Unpublished manuscript.

Macinnis, Laura. 2009. "Natural Disasters Cost China $110 Billion in 2008." *Reuters*. January 22, accessed February 1, http://www.reuters.com/article/2009/01/22/us-disasters-un-idUSTRE50L50020090122.

Mackey, Michael. 2005. "The New China Philanthropy." *Asia Times*, May 14, http://www.atimes.com/atimes/China/GE14Ad06.html.

Macleod, Duncan. 2008. "Colors of Benetton Prayers for China." *The Inspiration Room*. August 13, accessed April 18, 2014, theinspirationroom.com/daily/2008/colors-of-benetton-prayers-for-china/.

Magnier, Mark. 2008. "China Swats at Latest Threat to Perfect Games." *LA Times*, July 3, http://articles.latimes.com/2008/jul/03/world/fg-locust3.

Mahmood, Saba. 2005. *Politics of Piety: The Islamic Revival and the Feminist Subject*. Princeton, NJ: Princeton University Press.

Makinen, Julie. 2009. "In China, Philanthropy as a New Measuring Stick." *New York Times*, September 22, http://www.nytimes.com/2009/09/23/business/global/23donate.html?_r=0.

Makley, Charlene. 2005. "Speaking Bitterness: Autobiography, History, and Mnemonic Politics on the Sino-Tibetan Frontier." *Comparative Studies in Society and History* 47(1): 40–78.

——. 2007. *The Violence of Liberation: Gender and Tibetan Buddhist Revival in Post-Mao China*. Berkeley: University of California Press.

——. 2009a. "Ballooning Unrest: Tibet, State Violence, and the Incredible Lightness of Knowledge." In *China in 2008: a Year of Great Significance*, edited by Kate Merkel-Hess, Kenneth L. Pommeranz, and Jeffrey Wasserstrom, 44–55. Lanham, MD: Rowman and Littlefield.

——. 2009b. Review of *On the Cultural Revolution in Tibet: The Nyemo Incident of 1969*, by Melvyn C. Goldstein, Ben Jiao, and Tanzen Lhundrup. *China Journal* 62: 127–30.

——. 2010a. "Minzu, Market, and the Mandala: National Exhibitionism and Tibetan Buddhist Revival in Post-Mao China." In *Faiths on Display: Religion, Tourism, and the Chinese State*, edited by Timothy Oakes and Donald Sutton, 127–56. Lanham, MD: Rowman and Littlefield.

——. 2010b. "The Politics of Presence: Rethinking Deity Possession." Paper presented at International Association of Tibetan Studies, Vancouver, BC, August.

——. 2013. "The Amoral Other: State-Led Development and Mountain Deity Cults among Tibetans in Amdo Rebgong." In *Mapping Shangrila: Nature, Personhood, and Polity in the Sino-Tibetan Borderlands,* edited by Emily Yeh and Chris Coggins, 229–54. Seattle: University of Washington Press.

——. 2015. "The Sociopolitical Lives of Dead Bodies: Tibetan Self-Immolation as Mass Media." *Cultural Anthropology* 30(3): 448–76.

Malkki, Liisa. 1996. "Speechless Emissaries: Refugees, Humanitarianism, and Dehistoricization." *Cultural Anthropology* 11(3): 377–404.

Martin, Emily. 2007. "Review Essay: Violence, Language and Everyday Life." *American Ethnologist* 34(4): 741–45.

Martinson, Joel. 2008. "Scholarship and Education. Boom and Bust for 'Hope Schools.'" *Danwei,* December 1, http://www.danwei.org/scholarship_and_education/boom_and_bust_for_hope_schools.php#comments.

Maurer, Bill. 2006. "The Anthropology of Money." *Annual Review of Anthropology* 35: 15–36.

Mauss, Marcel. 1954 (1925). *The Gift: Forms and Functions of Exchange in Archaic Societies.* Translated by Ian Cunnison. Glencoe, IL: Free Press.

Mazard, Mireille. 2011. "Powerful Speech: Remembering the Long Cultural Revolution in Yunnan." *Inner Asia* 13(1): 161–82.

McGranahan, Carole, and Ralph Litzinger. 2012. "Self-Immolation as Protest in Tibet." *Fieldsights-Hot Spots, Cultural Anthropology Online.* April 08, http://www.culanth.org/fieldsights/93-self-immolation-as-protest-in-tibet.

Mckay, Alex, ed. 2003. *The History of Tibet.* Vol. 3. *The Modern Period 1895–1959: Encounter with Modernity.* London: Routledge Curzon.

McKown, Colleen. 2011. "Tibetans in Amdo Suffer Lead Exposure from Chinese Factories." *Tibet Post.* August 3, accessed May 1, 2015, http://www.thetibetpost.com/en/news/tibet/1910-tibetans-in-amdo-suffer-lead-exposure-from-chinese-factories.

Melhuish, Clare. 2005. "Towards a Phenomenology of the Concrete Megastructure." *Journal of Material Culture* 10(1): 5–29.

——. 2007. "Concrete as Conduit of Experience at the Brunswick, London." In *Material Matters: Architecture and Material Practice,* edited by Katie Lloyd Thomas, 199–209. London: Routledge.

Merkel-Hess, Kate, Kenneth Pomeranz, and Jeffrey N. Wasserstrom, eds. 2009. *China in 2008: A Year of Great Significance.* Lanham, MD: Rowman and Littlefield.

Metcalf, Peter, and Richard Huntington. 1979. *Celebrations of Death: The Anthropology of Mortuary Ritual.* New York: Cambridge University Press.

Mi Shih. 2013. "Making Rural China Urban." *China Story Journal.* June 18, accessed October 1, http://www.thechinastory.org/2013/06/making-rural-china-urban/.

Mills, Martin A. 2003. *Identity, Ritual, and State in Tibetan Buddhism.* London: Routledge.

——. 2007. "Re-Assessing the Supine Demoness: Royal Buddhist Geomancy in the Srongbtsansgampo Mythology." *The Journal of the International Association of Tibetan Studies* 3. http://www.thlib.org/collections/texts/jiats/#!jiats=/03/mills/.

——. 2008. "Small Shoes and Painted Faces: Possession States and Embodiment in Buddhist Ladakh." In *Modern Ladakh: Anthropological Perspectives on Continuity and Change,* edited by Martijn Van Beek and Fernanda Pirie, 139–52. Leiden: Brill.

Minn, Pierre. 2007. "Toward an Anthropology of Humanitarianism." *Journal of Humanitarian Assistance.* August 6, http://jha.ac/2007/08/06/toward-an-anthropology-of-humanitarianism.

Møllgaard, Eske. 2010. "Confucianism as Anthropological Machine." *Asian Philosophy* 20(2): 127–40.

Moore, Malcolm. 2008. "2008: A Testing Year for China." *Telegraph*, December 16, http://www.telegraph.co.uk/news/worldnews/asia/china/3797002/2008-Chinas-character-test-in-messy-year.html.

Mueggler, Erik. 2001. *The Age of Wild Ghosts: Memory, Violence, and Place in Southwest China.* Berkeley: University of California Press.

Mumford, Stan Royal. 1989. *Himalayan Dialogue: Tibetan Lamas and Gurung Shamans in Nepal.* Madison: University of Wisconsin Press.

Nagano, Sadako. 2000. "Sacrifice and lha pa in the glu rol Festival of Reb-skong." In *New Horizons in Bon Studies*, edited by Samten Karmay and Yasuhiko Nagano, 567–649. Delhi: Saujanya Publications.

Naughton, Barry. 1988. The Third Front: Defence Industrialization in the Chinese Interior. *China Quarterly* 115 (September): 351–86.

——. 2002. "China's Economic Think Tanks: Their Changing Roles in the 1990s." *China Quarterly* 171: 625–35.

de Nebeskey-Wojkowitz, Rene. 1956. *Oracles and Demons of Tibet: The Cult and Iconography of the Tibetan Protective Deities.* London: Oxford University Press.

Nevins, Eleanor. 2015. "'Grow with That, Walk with That': Hymes, Dialogicality, and Text Collections." in *The Legacy of Dell Hymes: Ethnopoetics, Narrative Inequality, and Voice*, edited by Paul V. Kroskrity and Anthony K. Webster, 71–107. Indianapolis: Indiana University Press.

Nian Zhihai, and Bai Gengdeng, eds. 1993. *Qinghai Zangchuan Fojiao Siyuan Mingjian* (Bright Mirror of Qinghai Tibetan Buddhist Monasteries). Lanzhou: Gansu Minzu Chubanshe.

Nietupski, Paul. 1999. *Labrang: A Tibetan Buddhist Monastery at the Crossroads of Four Civilizations.* New York: Snow Lion.

Nora, Pierre. 1989. "Between History and Memory: Les Lieux de Memoire." *Representations* 26: 7–24.

NTNDLZ (nags tshang nus ldan blo bzang). 2007. *Nags tshang zhi lu'i skyid sdug* (The Happiness and Suffering of the Boy from Naktshang). Xining: Qinghai Xining Yinshua chang.

Oakes, Tim. 2004. "Building a Southern Dynamo: Guizhou and State Power." *China Quarterly* 178: 467–87.

Oakes, Tim, and Louisa Schein, eds. 2006. *Translocal China: Linkages, Identities and the Reimagining of Space.* London: Routledge.

Oakes, Tim, and Donald Sutton, eds. 2010. *Faiths on Display: Religion, Tourism, and the Chinese State.* New York: Routledge.

Ohnuma, Reiko. 2005. "Gift." In *Critical Terms for the Study of Buddhism*, edited by Donald S. Lopez, Jr., 103–23. Chicago: University of Chicago Press.

Oi, Jean, and Andrew G. Walder, eds. 1999. *Property Rights and Economic Reform in China.* Stanford, CA: Stanford University Press.

Oliver-Smith, Anthony. 1996. "Anthropological Research on Hazards and Disaster." *Annual Review of Anthropology* 25: 303–28.

————. 2002. "Theorizing Disasters: Nature, Power and Culture." In *Culture and Catastrophe: The Anthropology of Disaster,* edited by Susannah M. Hoffmann and Anthony Oliver-Smith, 23–48. Santa Fe, NM: School of American Research Press.

O'Neill, Matthew, Jon Alpert, and Matt O'Neill, directors. 2009. *China's Unnatural Disaster: The Tears of Sichuan Province.* HBO short film/documentary, 38 min. http://www.hbo.com/documentaries/chinas-unnatural-disaster-tears-of-sichuan-province/.

Ong, Aihwa. 1987. *Spirits of Resistance and Capitalist Discipline: Factory Women in Malaysia.* Albany: State University of New York Press.

————. 1999. *Flexible Citizenship: The Cultural Logics of Transnationality.* Durham, NC: Duke University Press.

Ortner, Sherry B. 1978. *Sherpas through Their Rituals.* Cambridge: Cambridge University Press.

Panchen Lama, H.H. 1997 (1962). *A Poisoned Arrow: The Secret Report of the 10th Panchen Lama.* London: Tibet Information Network.

Patel, Nirav. 2009. "Chinese Disaster Relief Operations: Identifying Critical Capability Gaps." *Joint Force Quarterly* 52, 1st quarter: 111.

Pedersen, Morten Axel. 2013. *Not Quite Shamans: Spirit Worlds and Political Lives in Northern Mongolia.* Ithaca, NY: Cornell University Press.

Pedersen, Morten Axel, Rebecca Empson, and Caroline Humphrey. 2007. "Editorial Introduction: Inner Asian Perspectivisms." In "Perspectivism," special issue, *Inner Asia* 9(2): 141–52.

Pema Bhum. 2008 (1999). "'Heartbeat of a New Generation': A Discussion of the New Poetry." In *Modern Tibetan Literature and Social Change,* edited by Lauran R. Hartley and Patricia Schiaffini-Vedani, 112–34. Durham, NC: Duke University Press.

Perdue, Peter. 2005. *China Marches West: The Qing Conquest of Central Eurasia* Cambridge: Harvard University Press.

Perry, Elizabeth J. 2011. "From Mass Campaigns to Managed Campaigns: 'Constructing a New Socialist Countyside.'" In *Mao's Invisible Hand: The Political Foundations of Adaptive Governance in China,* edited by Sebastian Heilmann and Elizabeth J. Perry, chapter 2. Harvard Contemporary China Series 17. Cambridge, MA: Harvard University Press.

Philips, Matthew. 2007. "China Regulates Buddhist Reincarnation." *Newsweek,* August 15, http://www.newsweek.com/china-regulates-buddhist-reincarnation-99067.

Pieke, Frank N. 1995. "Witnessing the 1989 Chinese People's Movement." In *Fieldwork under Fire: Contemporary Studies of Violence and Survival,* edited by Carolyn Nordstrom and Antonius C. G. M. Robben, 62–80. Berkeley: University of California Press.

Pirie, Fernanda. 2008. "Violence and Opposition among the Nomads of Amdo: Expectations of Leadership and Religious Authority." In *Conflict, Religion and Social Order in Tibet and Inner Asia,* edited by Fernanda Pirie and Toni Huber, 217–40. Leiden: Brill.

Polanyi, Karl. 2001. *Great Transformation: The Political and Economic Origins of Our Times.* Boston: Beacon Press.

Postiglione, Gerard, Ben Jiao, and Sonam Gyatso. 2005. "Education in Rural Tibet: Development, Problems and Adaptations." *China: An International Journal* 3(1): 1–23.

Power, Marcus. 2003. *Rethinking Development Geographies*. London: Routledge.

Prochnik, George. 2010. *In Pursuit of Silence: Listening for Meaning in a World of Noise*. New York: Knopf.

Ptackova, Jarmila. 2013. "The *Great Opening of the West* Development Strategy and Its Impact on the Life and Livelihood of Tibetan Pastoralists: Sedentarisation of Tibetan Pastoralists in Zeku County as a Result of Implementation of Socioeconomic and Environmental Development Projects in Qinghai Province, P.R. China." Ph.D. diss., Humboldt-Universität zu Berlin. http://edoc.hu-berlin.de/dissertationen/ptackova-jarmila-2013-06-19/PDF/ptackova.pdf.

Pu Wencheng, ed. 1990. *Gan Qing ZangchuanFojiaoSiyuan* (Tibetan Buddhist Monasteries of Gansu and Qinghai). Xining: Qinghai Renmin Chubanshe.

Qin Shao. 2013. *Shanghai Gone: Domicide and Defiance in a Chinese Megacity*. London: Rowman and Littlefield.

Qinghai News Web. 2008. "Kumbum Monks Fundraise." May 30, accessed October 10. http://www.china2551.org/Article/fjdt/q/200805/6330.html.

Radio Free Asia (RFA). 2010. "Tibetan Singer Gets Prison." March 5. http://www.rfa.org/english/news/tibet/court-03052010115917.html.

Raman, B. 2009. "Tibetan Mourning Period Starts." *South Asian Analysis Group*. February 28, accessed March 1, http://www.southasiaanalysis.org/%5Cpapers31%5Cpaper3073.html.

Ramble, Charles. 1982. "Status and Death: Mortuary Rites and Attitudes to the Body in a Tibetan Village." *Kailash* 9: 333–59.

——. 2014. "The Complexity of Tibet Pilgrimage." In *Searching for the Dharma, Finding Salvation—Buddhist Pilgrimage in Time and Space*. Proceedings of the Workshop "Buddhist Pilgrimage in History and Present Times," Lumbini International Research Institute (LIRI), edited by Christoph Cueppers and Max Deeg, 179–96. Lumbini: Lumbini International Research Institute.

Regong Wenhua (Rebgong Culture). 2007. Inaugural Issue 1(1).

RG et al. (rang sgra, tshe ring 'bum, and dbang drag rdo rje). 2005. "kha btags." *bod kyi dgon sde'i rig gnas spyi bshad me tog phreng ba*. TBRC W00KG01063. zi ling: mtsho sngon mi rigs dpe skrun khang: 143–44.

ri gdengs. 1994. mdo smad du dar ba'i drug pa'i glu rol (The Sixth-Month Lurol Festival of Amdo). In *rma lho'i rtsom bsdus padma dkar po'i tshom bu* (The White Lotus: Collected Essays from Huangnan). Lanzhou: Gansu Minzu Chubanshe.

Richburg, Keith B. 2010. "China's Crackdown on Nonprofit Groups Prompts New Fears among Activists." *Washington Post*, May 11, http://www.washingtonpost.com/wp-dyn/content/article/2010/05/10/AR2010051004801.html.

Rinchenrdorje, and Charles Kevin Stuart. 2009. "Seating, Money and Food at an Amdo Village Funeral." *Asian Highland Perspectives* 1: 237–94.

Robben, Antonius C. G. M., and Carolyn Nordstrom, eds. 1995. *Fieldwork under Fire: Contemporary Studies of Violence and Survival*. Berkeley: University of California Press.

de Roerich, Georges. 1958. *Le parler de l'Amdo: étude dialecte archaïque du Tibet*. Serie Orientale Roma, 18. Roma: Istituto Italiano per il Medio ed Estremo Oriente.

Rohlf, Gregory. 2003. "Dreams of Oil and Fertile Fields: The Rush to Qinghai in the 1950s." *Modern China* 29(4): 455–89.

——. 2016. *Building New China, Colonizing Kokonor: Resettlement in Qinghai in the 1950s*. Lanham, MD: Lexington Books.

Rosaldo, Renato. 2004. "Grief and a Headhunter's Rage." In *Violence in War and Peace: An Anthology*, edited by Nancy Scheper-Hughes and Philippe Bourgois, 150–56. Malden, MA: Blackwell.

Sahlins, Marshall. 2000. "The Sadness of Sweetness, or, the Native Anthropology of Western Cosmology." In *Culture in Practice: Selected Essays*, 527–84. New York: Zone Books.

Said, Edward W. 1978. *Orientalism*. New York: Pantheon Books.

Samuel, Geoffrey. 1993. *Civilized Shamans: Buddhism in Tibetan Societies*. Washington DC: Smithsonian Institution Press.

Saunders, Kate. 2010. "Beyond the Headlines: The Earthquake in Tibet." *Huffington Post*, June 26, http://www.huffingtonpost.com/kate-saunders/http/www.huffingtonpost.com/kate-saunders/beyond-the-headlines-the_b_550281.html.

SBPG (sha bo padma rgyal). 2007. *bod spyi'i lo rgyus dang dus rabs gcig gi ring du byung ba'i lo rgyus gnad chen 'ga' phyogs gcig tu gsal bor bkod pa shel dkar me long zhes bya ba gzhugs* (A Crystal Mirror: A Clearly Arranged and Simplified History of Outer Tibet and Several Important Events During a Single Century). Rebgong: Rongbo Monastery Printing House.

Schein, Louisa. 2000. *Minority Rules: The Miao and the Feminine in China's Cultural Politics*. Durham, NC: Duke University Press.

Scheper-Hughes, Nancy, and Philippe Bourgois, eds. 2004. *Violence in War and Peace: An Anthology*. Malden, MA: Blackwell.

Scherz, China. 2014. "Performance Philanthropy: Sustainable Development and the Ethics of Audit." *Having People, Having Heart: Charity, Sustainable Development, and Problems of Dependence in Central Uganda*, chapter 5. Chicago: University of Chicago Press.

Schneider, Florian, and Yih-Jye Hwang. 2014. "The Sichuan Earthquake and the Heavenly Mandate: Legitimizing Chinese Rule through Disaster Discourse." *Journal of Contemporary China* 23(88): 636–56. doi:10.1080/10670564.2013.861145.

Schuller, Mark. 2008. "Deconstructing the Disaster after the Disaster: Conceptualizing Disaster Capitalism." In *Capitalizing on Catastrophe: Neoliberal Strategies in Disaster Reconstruction*, edited by Nandini Gunewardena and Mark Schuller, 17–27. Lanham, MD: Alta Mira Press.

Schwartz, Ronald. 1994. *Circle of Protest: Political Ritual in the Tibetan Uprising, 1987–1992*. New York: Columbia University Press.

Shimatsu, Yoichi. 2010. "After Earthquake, Tibet Needs More Engineers, Fewer Monks." *New America Media*. April 23, accessed March 10, 2011, news.newamericamedia.org/news/view_article.html?article_id=3e97809ec61c1cecc6841a105d6fe5a3.

Shryock, Andrew. 2012. "Breaking Hospitality Apart: Bad Hosts, Bad Guests, and the Problem of Sovereignty." In *The Return to Hospitality: Strangers, Guests, and Ambiguous Encounters*, edited by Matei Candea and Giovanni da Col, special issue, *Journal of the Royal Anthropological Institute*, n.s., 18, s1: s20–s33.

Sihlé, Nicolas. 2013. "Money, Butter, and Religion: Remarks on Participation in the Large-Scale Collective Rituals of the Rep kong Tantrists." In *Monastic and Lay Traditions in North-Eastern Tibet*, edited by Yangdon Dhondup, Ulrich Pagel, and Geoffrey Samuels, 165–86. Leiden: Brill.

Silber, Ilana. 1998. "Modern Philanthropy: Reassessing the Viability of a Maussian Perspective." In *Marcel Mauss: a Centenary Tribute,* edited by Wendy James and N. J. Allen, 134–46. New York: Berghahn.

Silk, John. 2004. "Caring at a Distance: Gift Theory, Aid Chains, and Social Movements." *Social and Cultural Geography* 5(2): 229–51.

Silverstein, Michael. 2001 (1976). "The Limits of Awareness." In *Linguistic Anthropology: A Reader,* edited by A. Duranti, 382–401. Malden, MA: Blackwell.

——. 2003. "Translation, Transduction, Transformation: Skating Glossando on Thin Semiotic Ice." In *Translating Cultures: Perspectives on Translation and Anthropology,* edited by P. Rubel and A. Rosman, 75–105. Oxford: Berg.

——. 2004. "'Cultural' Concepts and the Language-Culture Nexus." *Current Anthropology* 45(5): 621–52.

Silverstein, Michael, and Greg Urban, eds. 1996. *Natural Histories of Discourse.* Chicago: University of Chicago Press.

Skurski, Julie, and Fernando Coronil. 2006. "Introduction: States of Violence and the Violence of States." *States of Violence.* Ann Arbor: University of Michigan Press.

Smith, Steve. 2008. "Rumor and the Sichuan Earthquake." *China Beat* (blog). May, accessed October 10, thechinabeat.blogspot.com/2008_05_01_archive.html.

Smith, Warren W. 2010. *Tibet's Last Stand? The Tibetan Uprising of 2008 and China's Response.* Lanham, MD: Rowman and Littlefield.

Smyer-Yu, Dan. 2013. *The Spread of Tibetan Buddhism in China: Charisma, Money, Enlightenment.* New York: Routledge.

snying bo rgyal, and R. Solomon Rino. 2009. "Deity Men: Reb Gong Tibetan Trance Mediums in Transition." *Asian Highlands Perspectives* 3. http://plateauculture.org/sites/plateauculture.org/files/deity-men-reb-gong-tibetan-trance-mediums-transition.pdf.

Sørensen, Per K. 2003. "Lhasa Diluvium, Sacred Environment at Stake: The Birth of Flood Control Politics, the Question of Natural Disaster Management, and Their Importance for the Hegemony over a National Monument in Tibet." special issue, *Cosmogony and the Origins: Lungta* 16: 85–134.

Stasch, Rupert. 2009. *Society of Others: Kinship and Mourning in a West Papuan Place.* Berkeley: University of California Press.

——. 2012. "Linguistic Anthropology and Sociocultural Anthropology." In *The Cambridge Handbook of Linguistic Anthropology,* edited by N. J. Enfield, Paul Kockelman, and Jack Sidnell, 626–43. Cambridge: Cambridge University Press.

Stevenson, Mark Jeffrey. 1999. "Wheel of Time, Wheel of History: Cultural Change and Cultural Production in an Amdo Tibetan Community." Ph.D. diss., University of Melbourne.

——. 2005. *Many Paths: Searching for Old Tibet in New China.* South Melbourne, Victoria, Australia: Lothian Books.

Stoddard, Heather. 2013. "A Short Life of Rigzin Palden Tashi (1688–1743) Founder of the '1900 Dagger-Wielding, White-Robed, Long-Haired Yogins of Rebkong' (phur-thog gos-dkar lcang-lo-can) Also Known as the 'Community of the Many Yogins' (sngags mang)." In *Monastic and Lay Traditions in Northeast Tibet,* edited by Yangdon Dhondup, Ulrich Pagel, and Geoffrey Samuel, 89–116. Leiden: Brill.

Stone, Jacqueline. 2005. "Death." In *Critical Terms for the Study of Buddhism*, edited by Donald S. Lopez Jr., 56–76. Chicago: University of Chicago Press.

Strathern, Marilyn. 1988. *The Gender of the Gift: Problems with Women and Problems with Society in Melanesia*. Berkeley: University of California Press.

———, ed. 2000. *Audit Cultures: Anthropological Studies in Accountability, Ethics, and the Academy*. London: Routledge.

Stuart, Kevin, Banmadorji, and Huangchojia. 1995. "Mountain Gods and Trance Mediums: A Qinghai Tibetan Summer Festival." *Asian Folklore Studies* 54: 219–37.

Sun Baohua. 2001. "Zongjiaoyu Xiejiao de Falu Jieding" (The Legal Distinction Between Religion and Evil Cults). *Qinghai Minzu Yanjiu* 4: 1–4.

Sun Yat-sen. 1922. *The International Development of China*. New York: Putnam.

Sundar, Nandini. 2004. "Toward an Anthropology of Culpability." *American Ethnologist* 31(2): 145–63.

Taussig, Michael T. 1993. *Mimesis and Alterity: A Particular History of the Senses*. New York: Routledge.

Tedlock, Dennis, and Bruce Mannheim, eds. 1995. *The Dialogic Emergence of Culture*. Urbana: University of Illinois Press.

Teets, Jessica C. 2009. "Post-Earthquake Relief and Reconstruction Efforts: The Emergence of Civil Society in China?" *China Quarterly* 198: 330–47.

———. 2014. *Civil Society under Authoritarianism: The China Model*. New York: Cambridge University Press.

Tenzin Jinba. 2014. *In the Land of the Eastern Queendom: The Politics of Gender and Ethnicity on the Sino-Tibetan Border*. Seattle: University of Washington Press.

Terrone, Antonio. 2010. "Bya rog prog zhu, The Raven Crest: The Life and Teachings of bDe chen 'od gsal rdo rje Treasure Revealer of Contemporary Tibet." Ph.D. diss., Leiden University. https://openaccess.leidenuniv.nl/handle/1887/14644.

TEW (Tibet Environmental Watch). 2005. "Zone of Peace." Accessed November 1, 2009, http://www.tew.org/zop/index.html.

Thomas, Katie Lloyd, ed. 2006. *Material Matters: Architecture and Material Practice*. New York: Routledge.

Thomas, Nicholas, and Caroline Humphrey, eds. 1996. *Shamanism, History, and the State*. Ann Arbor: University of Michigan Press.

Thompson, Drew. 2008. "International Disaster Relief and Humanitarian Assistance: A Future Role for the PLA?" *China Brief* 8(11). Accessed June 10, http://www.jamestown.org/programs/chinabrief/single/?tx_ttnews[tt_news]=4941&tx_ttnews[backPid]=168&no_cache=1#.U13YpMdR1Do.

THF (Tibet Heritage Fund). 2010. "Tibetan Communities in China." Accessed October 1, 2010, http://www.tibetheritagefund.org/pages/projects/rural-tibet-projects.php.

Tibet Data. 2015. "Self-Immolations in Tibet." Accessed May 15, 2015, http://tibetdata.github.io/projects/selfimmolationData/index.html.

Ticktin, Miriam. 2006. "Where Ethics and Politics Meet: The Violence of Humanitarianism in France." *American Ethnologist* 33(1): 33–49.

Tomba, Luigi. 2006. Comments in "Contesting Spatial Modernity in Late-Socialist China," by Li Zhang, *Current Anthropology* 47(3): 461–84.

Topden Tsering. 2010. "Tibet Earthquake: The Deepening Divide of Identities." *Berkeley Daily Planet.* April 20, accessed May 1, http://www.berkeleydailyplanet.com/issue/2010-04-20/article/35063?headline=NEWS-ANALYSIS-Tibet-Earthquake-The-Deepening-Divide-of-Identities-.

Tournadre, Nicolas, and Peter Brown. 2003. "The Dynamics of Tibetan-Chinese Bilingualism: The Current Situation and Future Prospects." *China Perspectives* 45: 30–36.

Trouillot, Michel-Rolph. 2003. *Global Transformations: Anthropology and the Modern World.* New York: Palgrave Macmillan.

TRXZ. 2001. *Tongren Xian Zhi* (Gazetteer of Tongren County).

Tsering Shakya. 1994. "Politicisation and the Tibetan Language." In *Resistance and Reform in Tibet,* edited by Robert Barnett and Shirin Akiner, 157–65. Bloomington: Indiana University Press.

——. 1999. *The Dragon in the Land of the Snows.* NY: Columbia University Press.

Tsering Woeser. 2014. "Self-Immolation in Tibet: The Shame of the World." Translated by Kevin Carrico. Unpublished manuscript.

Tsing, Anna. 1993. *In the Realm of the Diamond Queen: Marginality in an Out-of-the-Way Place.* Princeton, NJ: Princeton University Press.

——. 2000. "Inside the Economy of Appearances." *Public Culture* 12(1): 115–44.

——. 2005. *Friction: An Ethnography of Global Connection.* Princeton, NJ: Princeton University Press.

Tucci, Guiseppe. 1980 (1970). *The Religions of Tibet.* Translated from the German and Italian by Geoffrey Samuel. London: Routledge and K. Paul.

Turner, Terence. 2002. "Representation, Politics, and Cultural Imagination in Indigenous Video: General Points and Kayapo Examples." In *Media Worlds: Anthropology on New Terrain,* edited by Faye D. Ginsburg, Lila Abu-Lughod, and Brian Larkin, 75–89. Berkeley: University of California Press.

Tuttle, Gray. 2005. *Tibetan Buddhists in the Making of Modern China.* New York: Columbia University Press.

UNICEF. 2010. "News Note: Children Seriously Affected by Qinghai Earthquake." April 19, accessed June 10, http://www.unicef.org/media/media_53357.html.

Upton, Janet L. 1999. "Schooling Shar-khog: Time, Space and the Place of Pedagogy in the Making of the Tibetan Modern." Ph.D. diss., University of Washington.

Van der Hoorn, Melanie. 2009. *Indispensable Eyesores: An Anthropology of Undesired Buildings.* New York: Berghahn.

Vance, Robert. 2008. "Superstitions about China Earthquake Worry Some." May 16, accessed August 1, 2013, http://www.teachabroadchina.com/china-earthquake-superstitions-worry-some/.

Verdery, Katherine. 1996. *What Was Socialism, and What Comes Next?* Princeton, NJ: Princeton University Press.

——. 1999. *The Political Lives of Dead Bodies: Reburial and Postsocialist Change.* New York: Columbia University Press.

Visweswaran, Kamala. 1997. "Histories of Feminist Ethnography." *Annual Review of Anthropology* 26: 591–621.

Wagner, Roy. 1977. "Analogic Kinship: A Daribi Example." *American Ethnologist* 4(4): 623–42.

Wakeman, Frederic Jr. 1990. "Mao's Remains." In *Death Ritual in Late Imperial and Modern China*, edited by James L. Watson and Evelyn S. Rawski, 254–88. Berkeley: University of California Press.

Wang, Hui. 2004. "The Year 1989 and the Historical Roots of Neoliberalism in China." Translated by Rebecca E. Karl. *positions: east asia cultures critique* 12(1) (spring): 7–70.

Wang Xiaoqiang and Bai Nanfeng. 1991 (1987). *The Poverty of Plenty (Furao de Pinkun)*. Translated by Angela Knox. New York: St. Martin's Press.

Watson, James L., and Evelyn S. Rawski, eds. 1990. *Death Ritual in Late Imperial and Modern China*. Berkeley: University of California Press.

Weiner, Benno Ryan. 2012. "The Chinese Revolution on the Tibetan Frontier: State Building, National Integration and Socialist Transformation, Zeku (Tsékhok) County, 1953–1958." Ph.D. diss., Columbia University. http://hdl.handle.net/10022/AC:P:14943.

Whalen-Bridge, John. 2015. *Tibet on Fire: Buddhism, Protest, and the Rhetoric of Self-Immolation*. London: Palgrave Macmillan.

White, Hayden. 1981. "The Value of Narrativity in the Representation of Reality." In *On Narrative*, edited by W. J. T. Mitchel, 1–20. Chicago: University of Chicago Press.

Whyte, Martin. 1990. "Death in the People's Republic of China." In *Death Ritual in Late Imperial and Modern China*, edited by James L. Watson and Evelyn S. Rawski, 289–316. Berkeley: University of California Press.

Williams, Dee Mack. 2002. *Beyond Great Walls: Environment, Identity, and Development on the Chinese Grasslands of Inner Mongolia*. Stanford, CA: Stanford University Press.

Wines, Michael. 2009. "China's Leaders See a Calendar Full of Trouble." *The New York Times*, March 9, http://www.nytimes.com/2009/03/10/world/asia/10china.html.

Wong, Edward. 2008. "China Leader Makes Debut in Great Wall of Facebook." *The New York Times*, May 28, http://www.nytimes.com/2008/05/28/world/asia/28wen.html.

World Bank. 2007. "Cost of Pollution in China: Economic Estimates of Physical Damages." Accessed October 1, 2013. http://documents.worldbank.org/curated/en/2007/02/7503894/cost-pollution-china-economic-estimates-physical-damages).

Wu Hung. 1997. "The Hong Kong Clock—Public Time-Telling and Political Time/Space." *Public Culture* 9(3): 329–54.

Xinhua News Online. 2007. Huangnan Zhou Zhaokai Xin Nongcun Xin Muqu Jianshe Gongzuo Huibao Hui (Huangnan Prefecture Holds a Report Meeting on the Work of Constructing New Farming Villages and New Pastoralist Districts), July 4. http://www.qh.xinhuanet.com/misc/2007-07/04/content_10482210.htm.

——. 2008a. "Qinghai Zangchuan Fojiao Zongkang, Sha'erzang Huofo Gaoseng wei juankuan aifu" (Qinghai Tibetan Lamas Zongkang and Shartshang Fundraise and Pray for Blessings). May 15, accessed October 1. politics.people.com.cn/GB/14562/7246992.html.

——. 2008b. "Qinghai Gezu Minzu Shenqie Aidao Sichuan Dizhen Yunanzhe" (All Nationalities of Qinghai Deeply Mourn the Victims of the Sichuan Earthquake).

May 19, accessed October 1. http://www.qh.xinhuanet.com/wenchuan/2008-05/19/content_13308016.htm.

——. 2008c. "Tibetan Lamas in Qinghai Pray for Quake Victims." May 19, accessed August 1. http://www.china.org.cn/china/wenchuan_earthquake/2008-05/19/content_15343935.htm.

Xirejiancuo. 2008. "Klu-rol (lu-rol) Ritual: a Symbolic Communication between Mountain Deities and Human Agency." B.A. Thesis, Reed College.

Yan Hairong. 2003a. "Spectralization of the Rural: Reinterpreting the Labor Mobility of Rural Young Women in Post-Mao China." *American Ethnologist* 30(4): 578–96.

——. 2003b. "Neoliberal Governmentality and Neohumanism: Organizing Suzhi/Value Flow through Labor Recruitment Networks." *Cultural Anthropology* 18(4): 493–523.

Yang Jisheng. 2013 (2008). *Tombstone: The Great Chinese Famine, 1958–1962*. Translated by Stacy Mosher and Guo Jian. New York: Farrar, Straus and Giroux.

Yang Yang and Wang Yanchun. 2007. "Xuexiao Chebing Houyizheng Yinqi Zhengxie weiyuan Guanzhu" (The After-Effects of School Consolidation Attract the Scrutiny of the Government Consultative Committee). *Jingji Guanchabao* (Economic Observer Magazine), March 4, http://finance.sina.com.cn/g/2007 0304/13353374557.shtml.

Yangdon Dhondup. 2011. "Rebkong: Religion, History and Identity of a Sino-Tibetan Borderland Town." *Revue d'Etudes Tibétaines* 20: 33–59.

——. 2013. "Rebkong's Tantric Practitioners: Origin, History and Development." In *Monastic and Lay Traditions in North-east Tibet*, edited by Yangdon Dhondup, Ulrich Pagel and Geoffrey Samuel, 117–141. Leiden: Brill.

Yeh, Emily T. 2003a. "Tibetan Range Wars: Spatial Politics and Authority on the Grasslands of Amdo." *Development and Change* 34(3): 499–523.

——. 2003b. "Modernity, Memory and Agricultural Modernisation in Central Tibet, 1950–1980." In *Proceedings of the Tenth Seminar of the IATS, 2003*. Vol. 11. *Tibetan Modernities: Notes from the Field on Cultural and Social Change*, edited by Robert Barnett and Ronald Schwartz, 37–72. Leiden: Brill.

——. 2004. "Property Relations in Tibet Since Decollectivization and the Question of Fuzziness." *Conservation and Society* 2(1): 163–88.

——. 2009. "Greening Western China: A Critical View." *Geoforum: Journal of Physical, Human and Regional Geosciences* 40: 884–94.

——. 2013. *Taming Tibet: Landscape Transformation and the Gift of Chinese Development*. Ithaca, NY: Cornell University Press.

Yeh, Emily and Mark Henderson 2008. "Interpreting Urbanization in Tibet: Administrative Scales and Discourses in Modernization." *Journal of the International Association of Tibetan Studies* 4: 1–44. http://www.thlib.org/collections/texts/jiats/#!jiats=/04/yeh.

Yu Maochun. 2008. "From Tiananmen to the Sichuan Quake: A Profile of Wen Jiabao." *China Brief* 8(12). http://www.jamestown.org/programs/chinabrief/single/?tx_ttnews%5Btt_news%5D=4966&tx_ttnews%5BbackPid%5D=168&no_cache=1#.VYC1AyldUrw.

Yurchak, Alexie. 2005. *Everything Was Forever, Until It Was No More: The Last Soviet Generation*. Princeton: Princeton University Press.

Zhao Liang (director). 2009. *Petition* (documentary). 120 min.

Zhi Zhenpu and Chen Yushan. 2008. "Huangnan Zhou Guangda Sengluwei Dizhen Zaiqu Juankuan Qifu" (The Great Masses of Monks of Huangnan Prefecture Fundraise and Pray for Blessings for the Earthquake Disaster Zone). *Xinhua News Online,* May 15, http://www.86ne.com/News/HTML/122687.html.

Zivkovic, Tanya. 2013. *Death and Reincarnation in Tibetan Buddhism: In-Between Bodies.* London: Routledge.

Zukosky, Michael T. 2007. "Making Pastoral Settlement Visible in China." *Nomadic Peoples* 11(2): 107–33.

INDEX

Studies of the
Weatherhead East Asian Institute
Columbia University

Selected Titles

(Complete list at: http://weai.columbia.edu/publications/studies-weai/)

Resurrecting Nagasaki: Reconstruction and the Formation of Atomic Narratives, by Chad Diehl. Cornell University Press, 2018.

Making Time: Astronomical Time Measurement in Tokugawa Japan, by Yulia Frumer. University of Chicago Press, 2018.

Promiscuous Media: Film and Visual Culture in Imperial Japan, 1926–1945, by Hikari Hori. Cornell University Press, 2018.

The End of Japanese Cinema: Industrial Genres, National Times, and Media Ecologies, by Alexander Zahlten. Duke University Press, 2017.

The Chinese Typewriter: A History, by Thomas S. Mullaney. The MIT Press, 2017.

Forgotten Disease: Illnesses Transformed in Chinese Medicine, by Hilary A. Smith. Stanford University Press, 2017.

Aesthetic Life: Beauty and Art in Modern Japan, by Miya Mizuta Lippit. Harvard University Asia Center, 2017.

Youth For Nation: Culture and Protest in Cold War South Korea, by Charles R. Kim. University of Hawaii Press, 2017.

Socialist Cosmopolitanism: The Chinese Literary Universe, 1945–1965, by Nicolai Volland. Columbia University Press, 2017.

The Social Life of Inkstones: Artisans and Scholars in Early Qing China, by Dorothy Ko. University of Washington Press, 2017.

Darwin, Dharma, and the Divine: Evolutionary Theory and Religion in Modern Japan, by G. Clinton Godart. University of Hawaii Press, 2017.

Dictators and Their Secret Police: Coercive Institutions and State Violence, by Sheena Chestnut Greitens. Cambridge University Press, 2016.

The Cultural Revolution on Trial: Mao and the Gang of Four, by Alexander C. Cook. Cambridge University Press, 2016.

Inheritance of Loss: China, Japan, and the Political Economy of Redemption after Empire, by Yukiko Koga. University of Chicago Press, 2016.

Homecomings: The Belated Return of Japan's Lost Soldiers, by Yoshikuni Igarashi. Columbia University Press, 2016.

Samurai to Soldier: Remaking Military Service in Nineteenth-Century Japan, by D. Colin Jaundrill. Cornell University Press, 2016.

The Red Guard Generation and Political Activism in China, by Guobin Yang. Columbia University Press, 2016.

Accidental Activists: Victim Movements and Government Accountability in Japan and South Korea, by Celeste L. Arrington. Cornell University Press, 2016.

Ming China and Vietnam: Negotiating Borders in Early Modern Asia, by Kathlene Baldanza. Cambridge University Press, 2016.

Ethnic Conflict and Protest in Tibet and Xinjiang: Unrest in China's West, coedited by Ben Hillman and Gray Tuttle. Columbia University Press, 2016.

One Hundred Million Philosophers: Science of Thought and the Culture of Democracy in Postwar Japan, by Adam Bronson. University of Hawaii Press, 2016.

Conflict and Commerce in Maritime East Asia: The Zheng Family and the Shaping of the Modern World, c. 1620–1720, by Xing Hang. Cambridge University Press, 2016.

Chinese Law in Imperial Eyes: Sovereignty, Justice, and Transcultural Politics, by Li Chen. Columbia University Press, 2016.

Imperial Genus: The Formation and Limits of the Human in Modern Korea and Japan, by Travis Workman. University of California Press, 2015.

Yasukuni Shrine: History, Memory, and Japan's Unending Postwar, by Akiko Takenaka. University of Hawaii Press, 2015.

The Age of Irreverence: A New History of Laughter in China, by Christopher Rea. University of California Press, 2015.

The Knowledge of Nature and the Nature of Knowledge in Early Modern Japan, by Federico Marcon. University of Chicago Press, 2015.

The Fascist Effect: Japan and Italy, 1915–1952, by Reto Hofmann. Cornell University Press, 2015.

The International Minimum: Creativity and Contradiction in Japan's Global Engagement, 1933–1964, by Jessamyn R. Abel. University of Hawai'i Press, 2015.

Empires of Coal: Fueling China's Entry into the Modern World Order, 1860–1920, by Shellen Xiao Wu. Stanford University Press, 2015.

CPSIA information can be obtained
at www.ICGtesting.com
Printed in the USA
LVOW03s1830060418
572590LV00002B/121/P